The UK and EMEA Corporate Counsel Handbook

AF770133

The UK and EMEA Corporate Counsel Handbook

Walter J Thomas
BA, JD, LLM (CANTAB)

and

Robert Grimes
B.Comm, Barrister

Bloomsbury Professional

LONDON • DUBLIN • EDINBURGH • NEW YORK • NEW DELHI • SYDNEY

BLOOMSBURY PROFESSIONAL
Bloomsbury Publishing Plc
41–43 Boltro Road, Haywards Heath, RH16 1BJ, UK

BLOOMSBURY and the Diana logo are trademarks of Bloomsbury Publishing Plc

Copyright © Bloomsbury Professional Ltd, 2020

All rights reserved. No part of this publication may be reproduced or transmitted in any form or by any means, electronic or mechanical, including photocopying, recording, or any information storage or retrieval system, without prior permission in writing from the publishers.

While every care has been taken to ensure the accuracy of this work, no responsibility for loss or damage occasioned to any person acting or refraining from action as a result of any statement in it can be accepted by the authors, editors or publishers.

All UK Government legislation and other public sector information used in the work is Crown Copyright ©. All House of Lords and House of Commons information used in the work is Parliamentary Copyright ©. This information is reused under the terms of the Open Government Licence v3.0 (http://www.nationalarchives.gov.uk/doc/open-government-licence/version/3) except where otherwise stated.

All Eur-lex material used in the work is © European Union, http://eur-lex.europa.eu/, 1998-2020.

British Library Cataloguing-in-Publication Data

A catalogue record for this book is available from the British Library.

ISBN:	PB:	978-1-52650-950-5
ISBN:	Epub:	978-1-52650-951-2
ISBN:	Epdf	978-1-52650-952-9

Typeset by Evolution Design & Digital Ltd (Kent)
Printed and bound by CPI Group (UK) Ltd, Croydon, CR0 4TT

To find out more about our authors and books visit www.bloomsburyprofessional.com. Here you will find extracts, author information, details of forthcoming events and the option to sign up for our newsletters

Foreword

The view from North America

As the General Counsel of a US publicly-traded company with international operations and a keen appetite to expand its global footprint through acquisitions, I have experienced first-hand the challenge of educating myself, my US legal team and our business partners about the legal and regulatory implications of doing business in new countries with different, diverse and often unfamiliar laws and regulations. These challenges are magnified as you come to appreciate that understanding the differences in history and culture between the US and the other country is an integral part of being able to effectively counsel and advise US-based executives as they plan and execute strategic and operational objectives and integrate the acquired company. Now consider EMEA which is comprised of numerous sovereign nations, made up of citizens from diverse ethnic and racial backgrounds who speak many different languages, with legal systems that developed from fundamentally different historical principles. Navigating these waters efficiently and cost effectively can seem a daunting task.

With their EMEA Legal Handbook, Walter Thomas and Robert Grimes, two experienced in-house UK lawyers, have created a comprehensive and practical roadmap designed to educate US in-house legal counsel about the legal and regulatory frameworks that govern the general business operations of companies in EMEA. Most importantly, their advice and counsel is provided within the context of the cultural norms across the region which differ markedly from one another and from the US as well as the natural tensions that inevitably arise when integrating two companies with different histories, operating models and cultures. With these intertwined perspectives, US in-house legal counsel will be well prepared to tackle the previously mentioned challenges as their companies grow and expand in EMEA.

Pamela R Schneider

Ms Schneider is the General Counsel of ACCO Brands Corporation, one of the world's largest designers, marketers and manufacturers of branded academic, consumer and business products. ACCO Brands products are sold in more than 100 countries around the world. During her more than 20 years as an in-house lawyer, Ms Schneider has worked as the senior legal officer for small entrepreneurial businesses as well as large multinational corporations in manufacturing, retail, financial services and technology and outsourced services. Ms Schneider is a graduate of the University of Chicago Law School and obtained her BA from the University of Pennsylvania.

The view from EMEA

Walter and Rob, two experienced and commercially astute legal counsel with EMEA responsibilities have put together a legal handbook, a seemingly unique resource, from which to learn about the many and varied laws and practices in EMEA. I believe this Handbook would be beneficial to all foreign in-house counsel and business executives with responsibility for operations in EMEA – especially those involved in mergers & acquisitions.

This legal handbook covers many critical and diverse legal issues which can contribute to either the success of, or be a leading cause of, serious difficulties in EMEA operations, especially in the thorny area of planning or executing cross border (or trans-Atlantic) mergers and acquisitions. 'Employees are company's greatest asset' is a mantra credited to and certainly expounded by Anne Mulkahy (CEO OF Xerox). It is also something in which I passionately believe and expound. 'Happy Employees Make Happy Customers' – a triptych expounded by a former fellow HP board member (and a point with which I unequivocally agree) runs through the very DNA of this handbook. Happy employees will in turn provide shareholder value.

Anne Mulkahy's mantra and my colleague's triptych, both, take on new meaning and complexity for expatriates working in EMEA, and Europe more specifically. Persons from outside of Europe are often, unsurprisingly, ignorant of the laws, customs and practices of the many, many nations that make up Europe, the middle East and Africa. It is not uncommon that these individuals also seriously underestimate how costly (even seemingly minor) transgressions of these laws and customs are financially and in terms of employee morale.

These transgressions are, to the locals, demonstrations of a lack respect for local law and custom which can negatively impact employee engagement. For the unaware the different employment laws (Napoleonic laws generally in Europe, Common Law in the UK all overplayed by supra national EU regulations) and a natural cultural bias can combine with a minor transgression of local practice to form an explosively dangerous mixture for an acquiring non-European based business.

Implementation of data protection, whistle blowing policies, the retrenchment of staff, implementation of corporate policy, EHS at work, negotiations with EU works councils (and unions) are programmes that, in EMEA, can last months, or even years, if not implemented sensitively and in accordance with local custom and practice. Clunky due diligence that only focuses on savings and synergies that do not involve Legal and HR early enough, can lead to a poor integration, a clash of cultures and a failure of the acquired workforce to be willing to embrace a new practice, cultural change or assimilation into the acquiring organisation. During my years at HP it was our practice, during large acquisitions, to appoint firms such as Freshfields and Lee Hetch Harrison to provide legal briefings to those of our US colleagues involved. These briefings covered the law, practice and the cultural idiosyncrasies, country by country, to these colleagues before they, or the US business, made any decisions which impacted employees.

I would like to commend and congratulate the two authors, Walter and Rob, for putting pen to paper and giving us a rare and possibly unique glimpse into their combined decades of in-house experience in Europe, the Middle East and Africa.

Needless to say, this legal Handbook will be of assistance to both senior execs and in-house counsels based or originating outside of the EU. It is an invaluable primer and issue-spotting tool for those faced with the pitfalls, snares and traps that await all who find themselves managing business operations in this exceedingly diverse, vast region of our planet.

Worth reading!

Francois Michel Volpi MBA, PhD

Former HR Vice President Rio Tinto
Former HR Vice President Boots Walgreens
Former HR Vice President Hewlett Packard

Acknowledgements

The authors wish to offer their sincere gratitude to following people, without whose contribution this text would be forever poorer.

Mark Gregory	General Counsel	Rolls Royce plc
Chad Jerdee	General Counsel & Chief Compliance Officer	Accenture
Rob Booth	General Counsel and Company Secretary	Crown Estate
Jonathan Graham	General Counsel and Secretary	Amgen Inc.
Paul Lister	Director of Legal Services and Company Secretary	Associated British Foods plc
Deborah Majoras	Chief Legal Officer and Secretary	Procter and Gamble
Stuart Levey	Chief Legal Officer	HSBC Holdings plc
Richard Price	Group General Counsel and Company Secretary	Anglo American plc
Richard Buchband	Senior Vice President, General Counsel and Secretary	Manpower Group
Rob Chestnut	General Counsel	Airbnb

The authors also wish to express a gracious thank you to our friends, colleagues and all those at ACCO Brands Corporation who collaborated on this project. This text sought to embrace the expertise, creativity and diversity of our global colleagues and network of fellow professionals. In particular, we extend our heartfelt thanks to Boris Elisman (Chief Executive Officer) and Pamela R. Schneider (General Counsel).

Special thanks

I would like to acknowledge and thank my parents, Dr & Mrs Walter Joe Thomas. They devoted themselves without reservation or hesitation to the unenviable task of helping me learn to read, manage dyslexia and obtain an education. To them, I will be forever grateful.

I also wish to thank his Honour Judge David Cleveland; Professor Janet Kerr; Professor Barry Rider OBE PhD LLD; Marie Staunton CBE; Eileen Carroll QC (Hon) and Professor Carla K Potok, Avocat à la Cour. Each of whom generously through example, encouragement and guidance, during my legal education and the early years of my career, showed me a path and how by following the path I could make a difference, build a varied fulfilling career, love the job and have more than a little fun along the way.

To Pamela Schneider, Francois Volpe, Robert Grimes, Kate Prior; I will be forever grateful for your friendship and support, without which, the idea for this book would never have sparked.

Walter J Thomas

I also wish to recognise and thank my colleagues for their support in this endeavour. In particular, my co-author, friend and the very model of a modern corporate counsel, Walter Thomas, who effortlessly occupies the high ground in any battle of wits.

I am most grateful to Gavin Mooney SC for his formative influence, integrity and friendship. I would also like to remember Thomas J Fallon BL – a man for all seasons, a learned mentor and dear uncle.

Love and much gratitude to my indefatigable mum Maura, while fondly remembering my dad, Thomas Grimes – the best and wisest man whom I have ever known. Finally, I remain forever grateful to my wife Doireann for her ever-present love and encouragement and in particular, for gracing us with our delightful daughter, Sophie … sail on silver girl.

Rob Grimes

For those with the courage to speak truth to power.

For the Gina Millers of this world.

Contents

Table of statutes

[All references are to paragraph numbers]

Table of EU legislation

[*All references are to paragraph numbers*]

Table of other legislation

[All references are to paragraph numbers]

Table of cases

[All references are to paragraph numbers]

1 Introduction

'Lawyers love fire-fighting and crises and all that kind of stuff, but you need to move as quickly as you can from crisis mode into having some element of control. You have to have that group of communications, IT, legal, HR, security people all working together. Being organised gives you the best chance of picking up on all the issues and not looking like an idiot in front of the board when something goes wrong. … You want people to get on with their jobs, because it is all-consuming. Once you're out of the crisis days, actually very few of the executive committee need to be involved in it from day to day, and the most important part of their job is to be out there in front of the rest of the employees, being positive. You need people to think about other things without forgetting that the case is ongoing, for two reasons – one, you need to drive cultural change; and two, if they forget about it and then you suddenly start talking about it again because of a disclosure obligation, then people are surprised all over again. It's a difficult balance you've got to strike.'

Mr Mark Gregory

General Counsel, Rolls Royce plc

1.1 All in all, no truer words were ever spoken nor was more valuable advice ever offered, to a business; whether it's in crisis or not. But sadly, experience has led me to believe that the wisdom in Mr Gregory's sage advice is seldom heeded, outside of a period of crisis, by the majority of those who occupy the boardroom.

1.2 It's been an interesting ride through my professional career. First, as UK solicitor and then as a European Union based General Counsel, I've witnessed a great number of changes to the methods employed by and opportunities offered to the profession. In my professional life the use of the ballpoint pen, paper notepad, dictaphone and typewriter have gone (or are quickly going) the way of the inkpot, quill pen and vellum. The fax machine is an anachronism, mobile phones are no longer the size (and weight) of bricks (nor, for that matter, aspiring to be the size of match boxes) and business communication now seldom, if ever, arrives by Royal Mail. In short, it's a different world and it expects instantaneous universal communication, response, gratification and the business of the business, demands it.

1.3 Recent decades have seen a whirlwind of social, commercial and technological change (many say progress) and yet the potholes in the road travelled through that period have continue to throw up the old truths. For instance, even in this fast-paced digital environment, only the most progressive, sophisticated and experienced business leaders view their in-house lawyer as a business partner. It is my experience that many continue to cling to the more traditional view that the lawyer is nothing more than a holstered weapon, there and only there, to be drawn in a crisis.

1.4 Yet, all hope is not lost as I've been hearing something unusual from my in-house colleagues. It has been a long time coming but savvy businesses leaders, those who understand and embrace change, are now inviting their in-house legal counsels to the table as regular participants in their businesses. Not just in times of crisis, not just as a weapons or firefighting appliances, but as strategic business partners. In this context, and arguably as never before, in-house counsels are starting to influence, guide and shape their businesses. They have the ability to proactively contribute to their employer's endeavours and contribute to the success of the business of their business.

1.5 In another time of desperate, radical social, commercial and technological upheaval, in a 1943 radio address to the British people, Winston Churchill set forth a vision for the European continent, ravaged by a ruinous war, a war whose outcome was far from certain and far from over. To those listening by their firesides, it must have seemed an incongruously optimistic idea to turn the nation's mind to the restoration of the economic health of Europe and its peripheries, when victory was not yet assured and European order lay in pieces. Churchill was aware that the complexities associated with re-establishing the necessary legal, political and social structures were such as to almost overwhelm the will of an already war-weary people. Hence, he sought to banish the dark complexity of such aims with the light of optimism and promises of a future of plenty for those willing to embrace the challenge. He distilled this idea, with typical Churchillian eloquence, into one phrase:

> 'Difficulties mastered are opportunities won.'
>
> Winston Churchill[1]

1.6 Three-quarters of a century later, the legal, political and social structures of Europe (and wider region encompassing the Middle-East and Africa, which is so often incongruously grouped together as a commercial operating unit by multinational business) whilst relatively stable, are no less complex, and remain in a state of flux. It is not surprising therefore, that the accumulation of laws and customs from across this region may seem impenetrable or even bewildering to the uninitiated.

1.7 We now live and work in a time of unprecedented social, commercial and technological change; an ever more open and larger European Union (also currently beset by the strife and uncertainly of BREXIT) with its layers of local, national and

1 Charles Eade (ed), *The War Speeches of Winston Churchill, Volume 2* (London, Cassell & Company LTD, 1965) 560, at pp 425–37, 21 March 1943, an address revealing his vision of how post-war Europe should develop.

supranational laws and regulation. Commercial enterprises have unparalleled access to cross-border commercial opportunities in Europe and beyond; yet the change in the legal, regulatory and commercial environment has never been more fast paced and the array of different linguistic, social and cultural characteristics of the market has never been more diverse.

1.8 In a multinational business with all parts of the business active, informed and participating in the prosecution of the *business of the business,* the difficulties do not simply disappear, however with all professional competencies at the table, operating in real time as a team, the difficulties are, however, more readily subject to early identification and commercially palatable proactive navigation of those difficulties is more likely possible than not.

1.9 Proactive navigation through and around difficult issues is as close to difficulties mastered as we are likely to get. Executive teams work in this proactive manner and will allow commercial business leaders to get on with the most important parts of their job … to be out there in front of the rest of the employees, being positive … and in my experience that is a benefit to the business and that is almost always an opportunity won.

1.10 No matter the sophistication of your enterprise, the authors hope and intend this book will prove useful and enlightening. A tool to arm you with the information on EMEA generally and on Europe, the European Union and the European Economic Area more specifically which will enable you to issue spot in a crisis, to be a positive and proactive partner to colleagues and, unlike many other legal tomes, not be a particularly dense or unpleasant read.

The problem facing corporate counsel

1.11 While one may argue about the exact definition of the eponymous region of EMEA, it is beyond doubt that it spans four continents and multiple time zones, is home to in excess of 2 billion people, who hail from more ethnic backgrounds and speak more native languages than in any other comparative region. EMEA accounts for approximately $27trn of combined GDP and contains some of the richest, *and poorest*, on the planet, on a per capita basis.[2] Dozens of countries, each with their own national (and in some cases) supra-national legal systems, can trace their respective genesis to influences as diverse as Napoleonic laws, Breton Law, ancient common law, sharia law and civil codes. Comparatively, there is no more byzantine a region than EMEA in which to do business. One would forgive corporate counsel directed to acquire a business in EMEA or employed into a position with pan-EMEA responsibilities for thinking such challenges to be almost insurmountable, given this fog of diversity, of thought, of custom, language and law.

1.12 To add further complexity, it is almost axiomatic to say that globalisation, the advent of on-line retail and mobile capability have thrust small and medium sized enterprises into the centre of worldwide marketplaces, once the preserve of much larger organisations. As a result, corporate functions are no longer so rigidly organised on the basis of geography, and tend to transcend national boundaries and do not happily obey the strict lines of jurisdictional demarcation lawyers so dearly love to cling on to. While these changes have spurred international trade expansion, the legal resources underpinning these functions have typically struggled to keep pace.

2 The UN National Accounts Main Aggregates Database (https://unstats.un.org/unsd/snaama/dnllist.asp).

1.13 Every aspect of the commercial experience is touched by legal consideration. Once a decision has been taken to establish (or acquire) a commercial presence in the EU or wider EMEA jurisdiction, the most basic questions arise; what are the legal implications of the chosen route to market, in particular, what are the implications of selecting a direct route to market, a third party, an agency or distribution model? In the event of the acquisition of an existing business in EMEA the most basic of these questions become of tantamount importance.

1.14 When it comes to sales and the 'business of the business', the manner in which the legal function utilises and deploys its resources, from both internal and external sources, can and frequently does have a significant impact on both sales revenue and the cost, ease and or difficulty associated with any future changes to the model selected. The creation and addition of value to the business in this regard, is a key concern for the legal function.

1.15 Employees are and will remain the beating heart of any business. How and where the business will want to employ its personnel; how those employees are hired, and or indeed fired; is not solely the preserve of our frequently underappreciated much maligned siblings in Human Resources. These choices can often have serious strategic legal implications for a business in EMEA.

1.16 Good governance of the business demands endless vigilance. One only has to consider recent developments in the sphere of anti-corruption, and anti-money laundering (key areas of compliance concern for every General Counsel) to appreciate that local or regional legislation now has the ability to govern and capture corporate behaviour on an extra-jurisdictional basis. The dramatic growth in the regulatory and compliance burden faced by corporates in recent decades[3] now means that the legal and compliance function increasingly gravitates towards the centre of the organisation rather than the periphery.[4] It has been stated that the General Counsel is now often seen as having importance and stature comparable to the Chief Financial Officer by directors, CEOs and business leaders because the health of the corporation requires that it navigate complex and fast-changing legal, regulation, litigation, public policy, politics, media and interest group pressures across the globe. As a result, the expertise, quality, breadth, and power of the General Counsel and in-house counsel have increased dramatically.[5]

The shifting legal services landscape

1.17 The model is changing.[6] It would appear that two themes are recurrent; the proliferation of the corporate global footprint is making it increasingly unsustainable to engage and retain external counsel in each of the many jurisdictions of operation; and General Counsels are increasingly choosing to deal with an ever-growing number of matters in-house. Accordingly, the relationship dynamic between General Counsel/

3 Deloitte, 'The legal department of the future: How disruptive trends are creating a new business model for in-house legal', 5 January 2018, available at www2.deloitte.com/us/en/pages/advisory/articles/legal-department-of-the-future.html.

4 Benjamin W Heineman Jr, 'The Inside Counsel Revolution' (Harvard Law School and Harvard Kennedy School of Government, Tuesday 29 March 2016).

5 'The rise of the General Counsel | Thomson Reuters', 27 April 2016, available at https://blogs.thomsonreuters.com/answerson/general-counsel-transforming-law-business/.

6 Elaine McArdle, 'In the Driver's Seat: The changing role of the general counsel' (2012) *Harvard Law Bulletin*, available at https://today.law.harvard.edu/feature/in-the-drivers-seat-the-changing-role-of-the-general-counsel/.

in-house counsel and external law firms is realigning. Alternate fee structures are now commonplace, and talented lawyers are opting to follow this shift of influence in-house, to gain multi-jurisdictional experience that is seen as central to future success. This is a sentiment not lost on the Law Society of England and Wales, who have identified the need for all types of lawyers to expand their skills base beyond technical legal knowledge, to encompass business and project management skills and a better understanding of complex risk.[7] The Law Society has also noted the apparent competitive advantage in-house counsel enjoys as they already work with clients and in environments which expects an expanded skill set as the norm.

1.18 The other tectonic plate that has shifted beneath the legal landscape relates to the mix of compliance responsibilities now thrust upon legal departments. Traditionally it may have sufficed to confine one's view to the regulatory burdens on the company. However, the company is increasingly expected to be mindful of a range of environmental, social and governance issues. Mere legislative adherence is increasingly insufficient. The promotion of such policy aims is now a key consideration at the highest echelons of corporate management and can serve as an impactful differentiator to employees, customers, suppliers, shareholders and the wider community.

The imperative to act responsibly

1.19 The legal function is ideally positioned to provide added value to all their stakeholders by transcending the mere traditional, transactional day-to-day provision of narrow advices on strictly legal issues. Instead, it would appear inevitable that corporate counsel will become ever more involved in providing leadership, strategic direction and becoming an agent for change on questions that affect the company's staff and the wider community. This may manifest as less about a corporation adopting a political stance on any given question but, rather, demonstrably advocating on behalf of their staff, fostering a welcoming atmosphere that is conducive to enhanced innovation, inclusivity and creativity.

1.20 It will also be submitted that in the light of the above, legal practitioners in an in-house capacity should perhaps be mindful that it is increasingly insufficient to ask whether a particular standpoint is simply legal in the narrow sense. Rather, it is incumbent upon them to ask and reflect upon whether the course of action is right. 'Right' in this case being framed not in a moralistic sense, but rather what is in the best interests of a large group of corporate stakeholders both inside and outside of the company.

Diversity and inclusion

1.21 Aside from any ethical imperative that may exist, it is uncontroversial to say that within the major powers in Western Europe, diversity of every hue, be it of thought, background, belief, or orientation, leads to an optimal environment through which the business can carry out the business of the business, and that legal advice in this environment must be informed by (and advocated for) ever increasing diversity, inclusion and equality. The business will be all the more robust for it.

1.22 The importance of diversity and gender equality, the challenge in achieving it and how it might be fostered has been eloquently stated as:

---

7 'The Future of Legal Services', January 2016, The Law Society of England and Wales, available at www.lawsociety.org.uk.

> Diversity feeds itself, and in that regard you need to make less of a conscious effort as time goes on. But every geography is different. In some geographies it is more challenging to get diverse talent on the board or in leadership. I believe that whoever is best positioned to win the role should win the role, but there is a lot you can do to drive diversity, and having diverse slates is a key starting position, as is making sure you have a good pipeline. Women may be less inclined to put themselves forward for promotions and more shy to try; therefore you need to make sure you encourage women, particularly in leadership.[8]

Ritva Sotamaa, Chief Legal Officer and Group Secretary,

Unilever plc

1.23 Providing thought leadership on such questions and issues is a role, if not the duty of, the General Counsel, who is particularly well-placed to advocate on behalf of these legal and ethical imperatives. Such leadership is increasingly evident in comments expressed succinctly by General Counsel, such as those in relation to marriage equality in the United States:

> 'We have always supported our employees and fostered a culture of inclusion and respect – this includes the right to marry whomever they choose and to have that union legally recognized.'

Deborah P Majoras, Chief Legal Officer & Secretary

Procter and Gamble Co[9]

1.24 Also, the case for a commercial imperitive for diversity was set out in a recent discussion where the General Counsel for Airbnb made a powerful case:

> 'for why diversity at the table produces diversity of thought, and therefore stronger teams and work.'

Mr Rob Chestnut

General Counsel

Airbnb

1.25 The importance of reflecting diversity in the selection of panels of law firms to provide advice was noted and commented on as follows:

> 'We're trying to be more diverse as an organisation – it helps if we're working alongside diverse law firms,' he says. 'As clients, we can help to drive the agenda and get a better team.'

Mr Richard Price,

Group General Counsel and Company Secretary,

Anglo American plc

8 As told to *GC Magazine* by Ms Sotamaa in 2016: https://www.legal500.com/assets/pages/gc/diversity-and-inclusion-report-uk-2016/ritva-sotamaa#sthash.9Ch5syCi.dpbs.

9 The Procter & Gamble Company is an American multi-national consumer goods corporation headquartered in downtown Cincinnati, Ohio, founded in 1837 by English American William Procter and Irish American James Gamble.

The authors argue that it is the duty of the General Counsel to be the advocate and arbiter of diversity and inclusion in their business. If any group is adversely treated, discriminated against or otherwise harmed by an advised or indeed ill-advised corporate policy then the General Counsel must be the CEO's own personal conscience, his or her Jiminy Cricket.

1.26 The evolving role of the corporate legal function as an advocate for social change was further highlighted by the recent marriage equality debate and subsequent constitutional amendment successfully adopted in Ireland in 2015. What was quite notable during the course of that debate was the willingness of large corporations to explicitly support the introduction of a constitutional guarantee to marriage equality, not on the basis of a political expedient but because it's a matter that affects its staff, their customers and the wider community, whose views where considered and acted upon.

1.27 Corporate policy has the power to alter the very social fabric. The evolution of mass market retail business models, driven by automation, is fundamentally changing the DNA of main street commerce. Blue chip automotive giants are facing disruption to a century old business model as the way in which people choose to transport themselves via a patchwork of online driven services diverges significantly from the historical model of car ownership. All of the above has undoubted societal implications. How corporate actors deal with the legal issues at all levels of the supply chain, will be a continuing challenge in decades to come.

The civil and criminal risks

1.28 The General Counsel is the ethical gatekeeper, the barometer of right and wrong, the gatekeeper of not just what is legal but of that which is right, correct and ethical. Recall the latin, fiat justitia ruat caelum or put another way 'let your conscious be your guide'.[10]

1.29 To operate a business across international borders brings with it an inherent risk, whether the leaders of the business know and understand those risks is immaterial to the reality of their existence.

1.30 It goes without saying that to plead ignorance of the law or a transgression thereof is as poor risk mitigation strategy as it is a defence. In a place as diverse as EMEA it is the sort of wilful mixture of ignorance, hubris and folly that will land a corporate officer in prison and/or cause untold reputational damage to a business.

1.31 Regard must be had to the geopolitical influences on the business. An Officer or Director of a multinational based in North America with a subsidiary or an agent or a distributor in Russia, at the time of this book's development for instance, had better have taken all necessary and prudent steps to make sure that its subsidiary or an agent or a distributor in Russia is not selling to any party in, or selling to any party who will sell to any party in the Crimea, which according to Russia Law is part of Russia. The rub you'll no doubt understand is that Russia forcibly annexed Crimea from the Ukraine. As a result, and in addition to the widespread condemnation of Russia's unilateral action against Ukraine, there are, as a result, international sanctions forbidding certain actions in Russia (by Russian resident citizens, individuals and companies) otherwise legal in Russia under their domestic law and breaching those

10 Jiminy cricket.

could make the unsuspecting, the unwary as well as the criminally minded a guest in a US or EU correctional facility and/or the subject of fines and/or institutional unpleasantness.

1.32 Likewise, the failure to diligently police one's own employment practices in production facilities based in distant lands or the employment practices in one's third-party supplier's production facilities against such reprehensible practices as forced or child labour, could have a rather lasting and negative impact on the reputation of a business:

> 'The point we would make is it didn't need to take three years … they had the evidence, this could have been solved in three weeks,' he said. 'Primark has become the poster boy of child labour in the UK … It is very difficult to know if it harmed sales – Primark has been very successful in the intervening period – in terms of reputation that is why we pursued it,'

Mr Paul Lister

Director of Legal Services and Company Secretary,

Associated British Foods

Mr Lister succinctly illustrates the impact that adverse allegations may have and the time and effort that can be required in undoing the consequences.

The first place to look

1.33 While the above trends are relatively well established and oft commented on,[11] ink has been disproportionately spared in providing the necessary practical assistance to this burgeoning group of corporate counsel who are increasingly responsible for guiding senior business leaders on complex multi-jurisdictional issues.

1.34 Frequently, it is for corporate counsel to assess legal implications generally, frame the issues and guide the business direction towards a solution and away from exposure, rather than to advise on and execute specific local legal actions.

1.35 This book is designed specifically with these responsibilities in mind, though it also provides a grounding in key legal principles, it is less a legal textbook in the classic sense and more a legally informed reference tool and barometer. On any given issue it is designed to be the first port of call, though perhaps not necessarily, the last word. It does not purport to have the comprehensive answer to every local question posed by or to internal counsel but, rather, seeks to provide the reader with a framework for identifying pertinent issues and guiding counsel and executive leadership towards the right questions. It would be disingenuous to suggest that the need for externally sourced legal advice will be entirely obviated, however, it is hoped that this text will serve to narrow issues sufficiently to allow corporate counsel to add value by way of cost rationalisation. The intent of the work is to complement the existing body of literature in each of the subject areas, not to directly compete with it, but to provide a unifying thought process for corporate counsel, together with a sense of personal wisdom that, it is hoped, will help enhance prudential instincts.

---

11 'Through the looking glass: How corporate Leaders view the General Counsel of today and tomorrow', KPMG International, September 2016. Available at kpmg.com/generalcounsel.

Innovative features

1.36 Early and accurate issue identification is of paramount importance to internal counsel in conveying advice to executive leadership, particularly in acute situations. To aid and expedite this process, each chapter contains innovative graphics which should not only assist with issue resolution but also balance the information asymmetry between different functional areas allowing counsel to provide background and context to colleagues unfamiliar with legal considerations. It will also allow counsel to assimilate general thematic information with greater rapidity.

1.37 The primary goal is to provide a resource that allows the reader to quickly and accurately assess a particular problem and provide sufficient understanding to senior leaders to enable them to understand the scope of the problem before them.

1.38 The authors have given particular consideration to the layout of the text, and have adopted an innovative approach in mapping the legal discussion to the typical corporate functional areas. This will provide for expedient accessibility and, it is hoped, will assist counsel establish an ever closer union with the leaders of the 'business of the business'.

Difficulties and opportunities

1.39 It is the hope of the authors to bring a degree of order to the perceived chaos. This text is written by experienced corporate counsel who wish to assist, not only legal professionals, but all those who are required to brief or advise senior leadership on legal implications that may arise from time to time within their business irrespective of the industry they may operate in.

1.40 Ultimately, the purpose of this book is to assist all those tasked with giving pragmatic advice whilst reducing external counsel spend. The authors hope to assist the reader to master the myriad difficulties and gain the benefit of the opportunities afforded.

PART 1

REGARDING THE 'BUSINESS OF THE BUSINESS'

2 Selling in EMEA

'The effort you put in is very much correlated to the result you get out. It's incumbent on in-house teams to put in that effort if, as a function, you want to deliver value and a competitive advantage for your business. If you use any element of outsourcing, your ability to pick the best lawyer to provide the best service for the best value forms a big part of how successful you are. It's worth putting that extra effort in.'

Rob Booth

General Counsel and Company Secretary, Crown Estate

Introduction

2.1 Human beings are the beating heart of the business and are key to the sales function. The above point from Mr Booth is well made. The manner in which the legal function utilises and deploys its resources, from both internal and external sources, can and frequently does have a significant impact on sales revenue. The creation and addition of value to the business is a key concern for all in-house legal teams.

2.2 The concept of 'free movement of goods' is one of the central ideological pillars at the heart of the EU. At its most basic level, it means that business trading in Europe benefits from all that comes from access to the EU 'single market' and also from certain trade arrangements with other European countries. In essence it means that goods can move freely within the EU territory without any extra costs or significant restrictions.

2.3 The single or internal market has permitted the creation of what is referred to as an internal market from which EU citizens (amounting to nearly half a billion in number!) and business derive significant benefits. Central to its aim, the internal market seeks to make it as easy as possible to buy and sell goods in the member states of the European Union, in an open diverse and competitive environment. Harmonised legislation in many areas now frames the essence of what the internal market is, backed up by a range of institutions and processes designed to protect and preserve a functioning internal market. This chapter is largely concerned with how access to this internal market is obtained from a legal perspective, though it is very definitely not a full exposition on the central ideology of the European Project!

The composition of the EU

2.4 It may be beneficial to commence by simply recalling that the EU countries are: Austria, Belgium, Bulgaria, Croatia, Republic of Cyprus, Czech Republic, Denmark, Estonia, Finland, France, Germany, Greece, Hungary, Ireland, Italy, Latvia, Lithuania, Luxembourg, Malta, Netherlands, Poland, Portugal, Romania, Slovakia, Slovenia, Spain, Sweden and (for the moment at least) the United Kingdom.

European Economic Area (EEA)

2.5 The European Economic Area (EEA) deserves to be distinguished as it includes EU countries and also Iceland, Liechtenstein and Norway. It allows them to be part of the EU's single market.

Switzerland

2.6 Special note should be taken of Switzerland as it is neither an EU nor EEA member but is part of the single market – this means Swiss nationals have the same rights to live and work in other EU member states as other EEA nationals.

2.7 When goods are imported or exported between the EU and any non-EU country (including the European Economic Area, Switzerland, Turkey, Andorra and San Marino) customs formalities must be completed. This most fundamental of requirements has been a most vexed and debated element of the negotiations on the withdrawal of the UK from the EU and deserves constant vigilance.

Product rules and regulations

2.8 In order to bring goods into the EU market, certain (at times onerous) product requirements must be met to protect human and animal health, the environment and consumers rights. In certain circumstances such requirements will be governed by harmonised legislation and in other cases local (national) laws which are recognised by the EU will take precedence (this concept is referred to as mutual recognition.)

Undifferentiated access to goods

2.9 A core idea underpinning the internal market as it relates to corporate counsel's typical responsibilities concerns general terms and conditions of sale. Whilst a company might retain liberty to style their general terms and conditions of sale in many respects, as they wish, they nevertheless face the obligation to ensure that all customers based in the EU have the same access to goods, no matter where they are located, as their local customers enjoy. Where special prices, promotions or sales conditions are offered in one location, these should be accessible to all customers irrespective of which EU country they are located in, their nationality, place of residence or business location.

Guidance for traders on product requirements

2.10 The EU estimate that around 85% of the product rules are harmonised in the EU meaning that the same rules apply in all EU countries.[1] The EU helpfully provide significant and voluminous guidance on a product by product basis on what it calls its trade helpdesk for EU product requirements.[2] The trade helpdesk database is essential reading for entrants to the single market and offers information on a state by state basis, on the:

- rules and regulations for individual products;
- competent authorities that may be contacted for specific product requirements;
- VAT and excise duty rates applied to your product in the EU country of sale;

Non-discriminatory sales across the Union

Geo-blocking

2.11 The European Union and its internal market, by its nature, require the abolition of obstacles to anything inconsistent with the free movement of goods within the Union. The proliferation of online retailing has created the potential for the creation of a new species of obstacle to occur where traders operating in one member state block or limit access to their online interfaces, such as websites and apps, by customers from other member states wishing to engage in cross-border transactions (known as 'geo-blocking').[3] Such obstacles can also occur when certain traders apply different general conditions of access to their goods and services with respect to such customers from other member states, both online and offline. Although such different treatment might, in some cases, be objectively justified, in other cases, it may not.[4] To address these concerns the European Union implemented a Regulation of 28 February 2018 on addressing unjustified geo-blocking and other forms of discrimination based on customers' nationality, place of residence or place of establishment within the internal market.[5] This instrument is an EU Regulation, so much like the General Data Protection Regulation (GDPR), it is directly effective in member states.

Trader obligations – access to online interfaces

2.12 A trader shall not, through the use of technological measures or otherwise, block or limit a customer's access to the trader's online interface for reasons related to the customer's nationality, place of residence or place of establishment.[6]

2.13 Nor may a trader, for reasons related to a customer's nationality, place of residence or place of establishment, redirect that customer to a version of the trader's online interface that is different from the online interface to which the customer

---

1 YourEU – www.europa.eu.
2 https://trade.ec.europa.eu/tradehelp/eu-product-rules-and-member-states-taxes.
3 Recital 1 of Regulation (EU) 2018/302 of the European Parliament and of the Council of 28 February 2018 on addressing unjustified geo-blocking and other forms of discrimination based on customers' nationality, place of residence or place of establishment within the internal market and amending Regulations (EC) No 2006/2004 and (EU) 2017/2394 and Directive 2009/22/EC.
4 ibid.
5 Regulation (EU) 2018/302 of the European Parliament and of the Council of 28 February 2018 on addressing unjustified geo-blocking and other forms of discrimination based on customers' nationality, place of residence or place of establishment within the internal market and amending Regulations (EC) No 2006/2004 and (EU) 2017/2394 and Directive 2009/22/EC.
6 ibid, Art 3(1).

initially sought access, by virtue of its layout, use of language or other characteristics that make it specific to customers with a particular nationality, place of residence or place of establishment, unless the customer has explicitly consented to such redirection.[7]

2.14 In the event of redirection with the customer's explicit consent, the version of the trader's online interface to which the customer initially sought access shall remain easily accessible to that customer.[8]

Trader obligations – access to goods or services

2.15 A trader shall not apply different general conditions of access to goods or services, for reasons related to a customer's nationality, place of residence or place of establishment, where the customer seeks to:[9]

- buy goods from a trader and either those goods are delivered to a location in a member state to which the trader offers delivery in the general conditions of access or those goods are collected at a location agreed upon between the trader and the customer in a member state in which the trader offers such an option in the general conditions of access;
- receive electronically supplied services from the trader, other than services the main feature of which is the provision of access to and use of copyright protected works or other protected subject matter, including the selling of copyright protected works or protected subject matter in an intangible form;
- receive services from a trader, other than electronically supplied services, in a physical location within the territory of a member state where the trader operates.

The above does not prevent traders from offering general conditions of access, including net sale prices, which differ between member states or within a member state and which are offered to customers on a non-discriminatory basis.[10]

What is meant by a consumer?

2.16 A consumer is broadly defined and means any natural person who is acting for purposes which are outside his or her trade, business, craft or profession.[11]

What is meant by a customer?

2.17 A customer means a consumer who is a national of, or has his or her place of residence in, a member state, or an undertaking which has its place of establishment in a member state, and receives a service or purchases a good, or seeks to do so, within the Union, for the sole purpose of end use.[12]

What is meant by trader?

2.18 A trader means any natural person or any legal person, irrespective of whether privately or publicly owned, who is acting, including through any other person acting

7 ibid, Art 3(2).
8 ibid, Art 3(2).
9 ibid, Art 4(1).
10 ibid, Art 4(2).
11 ibid, Art 2.
12 ibid, Art 2.

in the name or on behalf of the trader, for purposes relating to the trade, business, craft or profession of the trader.[13]

What is meant by general conditions of access?

2.19 General conditions of access means all terms, conditions and other information, including net sale prices, regulating the access of customers to goods or services offered for sale by a trader, which are set, applied and made available to the public at large by or on behalf of the trader and which apply in the absence of an individually negotiated agreement between the trader and the customer.[14]

Practical implications

2.20 It is clear that giving effect to the above requirements of EU law may represent a significant challenge to IT functions within organisations that have substantial trading across borders in the EU. Corporate counsel should be aware that the Regulation came into force on 22 March 2018.

Brexit implications

2.21 If the UK exits the European Union without a substantive agreement (ie, a 'no deal Brexit') it has been recognised by the UK government that the Geo-blocking Regulation would lose elements of reciprocity necessary for it to function. The rational was set out as follows:

> 'Regulators in other EU states would be very unlikely to enforce the Regulation on behalf of UK customers as the framework for cross border cooperation will be repealed in a "no deal" exit from the EU … Therefore, if we did not revoke the Geo-Blocking Regulation, UK traders would continue to have obligations to EU customers under the Regulation while UK customers are unlikely to receive any of its benefits. To avoid this asymmetry of enforcement obligations in the EU's favour, we are revoking the Geo-Blocking Regulation in the UK.'

Thus it is clear that in the event of a 'no deal Brexit' the above provisions of the Geo-blocking Regulation will cease to be effective as regards the United Kingdom.[15] Counsel should maintain a high surveillance index in respect of geo-political developments in this regard.

Delivery and collection issues

2.22 Generally, delivery and collection issues must not act as a potential discriminator. So where a collection service is offered, a company must ensure that customers based in EU countries where delivery service is not offered have the right to order products for example from the company website, and arrange delivery or collection by a third party.

---

13 ibid, Art 2.
14 ibid, Art 2.
15 The Geo-Blocking Regulation (Revocation) (EU Exit) Regulations 2019, Section 2.

Reporting obligations

2.23 Companies are required to fulfil certain reporting obligations pursuant to EU Regulation (EC) No 638/2004 of the European Parliament and of the Council of 31 March 2004 on Community statistics relating to the trading of goods between Member States and repealing Council Regulation (EEC) No 3330/91.

What obligations are there

2.24 Where a company exports and/or imports within the EU and does so in excess of a certain value, a statistical report (sometimes referred to as an intrastate declaration) must be made to record intra-EU trade flows.[16] The threshold values above which reports are required are established every year by each of the EU countries (usually in the last quarter) and they apply for the whole of the following calendar year. Usually these returns can be made electronically and typically must be retained for a period of years.[17]

Country	2019 Arrivals (EUR)	2019 Dispatches (EUR)
Austria	750,000	750,000
Belgium	1,500,000	1,000,000
Bulgaria	235,194	143,163
Cyprus	160,000	55,000
Czech Republic	480,000	480,000
Germany	800,000	500,000
Denmark	897,000	500,000
Estonia	230,000	130,000
Greece	150,000	90,000
Spain	400,000	400,000
Finland	600,000	600,000
France	460,000	460,000
Croatia	297,000	162,000
Hungary	515,152	303,030
Ireland	500,000	635,000
Italy	800,000	400,000
Lithuania	250,000	150,000
Luxembourg	200,000	150,000
Latvia	200,000	100,000
Malta	700	700
Netherlands	800,000	1,000,000
Poland	939,500	469,000
Portugal	350,000	250,000

16 For guidance in respect of the UK please see www.gov.uk/intrastat.
17 Source Intrastat 2019.

Country	2019 Arrivals (EUR)	2019 Dispatches (EUR)
Romania	193,690	193,690
Sweden	872,000	436,000
Slovenia	140,000	220,000
Slovakia	200,000	400,000
United Kingdom	1,690,650	281,775

What data to report?

2.25 Typically, a monthly Intrastat report should include the following information:

- your VAT ID number;
- the period (month) being reported on;
- the direction of the trade flow: dispatch or arrival;
- the 8-digit product code of the Combined Nomenclature (CN) (the CN is published each year in the Official Journal of the EU);
- the code of the EU country of dispatch/destination;
- the value of the goods – excluding VAT and excise duties;
- the quantity of goods in net mass (gross weight minus the weight of the packaging);
- the unit of measurement according to CN (eg, litre, number of items. square metres);
- the code for the nature of transaction (which identifies the buying, selling or processing activity).

Additional information may be required, such as delivery terms as specified in your contractual arrangement (eg, EXW, CIF, FOB) or the mode of transport (eg, sea/road/rail transport).

3 Agency and distribution agreements

'Hic sunt Dracones!'[1]

Introduction

3.1 Wisdom is better than silver and gold and a late 1960s early 1970s childhood in rural Texas taught me more than a few home truths. Like, for instance, that farm animals are not pets. Unless treated with care and respect the most unassuming of farm animals can be dangerous. I also learned that even when treated with care and respect many animals are just damn well dangerous anyway; especially humans. Now as an inhouse counsel, operating for 20 years plus in the EU (and EMEA) I can say, hand on heart, that agents and distributors are analogous to the latter of these two truths.

3.2 To the uninitiated (or overconfident) business executive tasked with selling into a region as vast and diverse as EMEA, the idea of appointing agents for various regions is a seductive panacea. No need for a local presence, local employees or local investment *et cetera, et cetera.*

3.3 Time and again I've received an urgent instruction from an enthusiastic CEO, President, SVP, RVP or VP: 'draw up the paperwork the business is appointing an Agent or Distributor in …'. At that point they see only unbridled opportunity, their decision as nothing short of genius. They are indefatigable in their self-belief; of the correctness of their decision and in their resolve that even in the face of legal advice it is an opportunity worthy of the nature of the risk and it is ultimately their prerogative to accept the risk and to override the advice of their lawyer. Now, point of order, for those of you who are new to the inhouse game put your advice on this point, to your budding genius, in writing and keep it. You are going to need it later.

1 Hunt–Lenox Globe (circa 1503–07); author unknown.

3.4 How a business gets to market is without doubt an existential matter for all. It is worth recalling the nature and scope of the diversity in the EMEA region that informs this decision.

3.5 While one may argue about the exact definition of the eponymous region of EMEA, it is beyond doubt that it spans four continents and multiple time zones and is home to in excess of 2 billion people, who hail from more ethnic backgrounds and speak more native languages than in any other comparative region. EMEA accounts for approximately $27trn of combined GDP and contains some of the richest, *and poorest*, on the planet, on a per capita basis.[2] Dozens of countries, each with their own national (and in some cases) supra-national legal systems, can trace their respective genesis to influences as diverse as Napoleonic laws, Breton Law, ancient common law, sharia law and civil codes. Comparatively, there is no more byzantine a region than EMEA in which to do business. One would forgive corporate counsel with pan-EMEA responsibilities for thinking such challenges to be almost insurmountable, given this fog of diversity, of thought, of custom, language and law.

3.6 Every aspect of the commercial experience is touched by legal consideration. Once a decision has been taken to establish a commercial presence in an EMEA jurisdiction, the most basic question arises; what are the legal implications of the chosen route to market, in particular, what are the implications of selecting an agency or distribution model.

Agency

3.7

> 'Abandon all hope, ye who enter here.'
>
> Dante Alighieri; The Devine Comedy

It's not at the beginning, it's at the close of the agency relationship when all Hades usually ensues.

3.8 Generally, it really does not matter how the end of the relationship comes about; your fault, their fault nobody's fault; your client is almost certainly going to be liable to pay the agent anywhere from one to three years' worth of commission, calculated as a multiple of the average of the previous five years' commission, and perhaps other additional compensation, depending on the jurisdiction, for good measure. The sole reason being the termination.

3.9 It's usually at this point when your in-house client suffers an intense bout of debilitating, yet predictable, selective amnesia. Your client will likely bring you a single random sheet of paper; explain the sheet is a page from the agency agreement; point to a clause on that page that reads something like; 'Either party may terminate this Agreement by giving the other X months written notice' and then will say; 'All we have to do to terminate this (insert derogatory term) agent is to give them X months' written notice, correct? The (insert derogatory term) has underperformed for the past X years so we don't have to pay them anything, correct?' It's at this point you'll be wanting the advice that I previously advised you to retain. Whether you do or do not

2 See the UN National Accounts Main Aggregates Database, available at https://unstats.un.org/unsd/snaama/ dnllist.asp.

have said advice handy, if your client is perhaps prone to bouts of excitement, I advise that you don a tin hat and laboratory technician's face shield.

3.10 It's not that all hope is lost; it's not the 'one ring' you're faced with destroying; it's just managing the quantum due at the termination of agency relationship. That said, never, ever have I encountered a business owner or budget holder that when faced with this news did not gnash its teeth, foam at the mouth, and then in one memorable instance proceed to carry on like a man whose wife and mistress had just appeared simultaneously in his office reception.

3.11 The choice of law in the agency agreement may assist; as may the jurisdiction in which the agent resides; but don't leave it to chance or dare to leave it to hope. Do a bit of early research, make sure the business is (if at all possible demonstrably) aware of the risk and practice prophylactic damage limitation, where possible, crafting said prophylactics into the agency agreement.

3.12 The legal status of commercial agents in the European Union is regulated by Council Directive 86/653/EEC of 18 December 1986 on the coordination of the laws of the member states relating to self-employed commercial agents. It is a minimum directive, which sets the lower limits for protecting commercial agents in the EU.[3] Member states are entitled to implement the directive with a degree of variation.

Definition of 'agent'

3.13 Commercial agent means a self-employed intermediary who has continuing authority to negotiate the sale or the purchase of goods on behalf of another person, hereinafter called the 'principal', or to negotiate and conclude such transactions on behalf of and in the name of that principal.[4] Specifically excluded from this definition are:[5]

- a person who, in his capacity as an officer, is empowered to enter into commitments binding on a company or association;
- a partner who is lawfully authorised to enter into commitments binding on his partners;
- a receiver, a manager, a liquidator or a trustee in bankruptcy.

Rights and obligations

3.14 A commercial agent must look after his principal's interests and act dutifully and in good faith and must make proper efforts to negotiate and, where appropriate, conclude the transactions he is instructed to take care of. Additionally, the agent must communicate to his principal all the necessary information available to him and comply with reasonable instructions given by his principal.[6]

3.15 A principal is under a reciprocal duty to act dutifully and in good faith.[7] The principal must provide the documentation relating to the goods concerned and for

3 Council Directive of 18 December 1986 on the coordination of the laws of the member states relating to self-employed commercial agents (86/653/EEC).
4 ibid, Art 1.
5 ibid, Art 1.3.
6 ibid, Art 3.
7 ibid, Art 4.1.

his commercial agent the information necessary for the performance of the agency contract, and in particular notify the commercial agent within a reasonable period once he anticipates that the volume of commercial transactions will be significantly lower than that which the commercial agent could normally have expected.[8] Neither principal nor agent can contract out of the provisions set out above.[9]

Remuneration

3.16 In the absence of any agreement on this matter between the parties, and without prejudice to the application of the compulsory provisions of the member states concerning the level of remuneration, a commercial agent shall be entitled to the remuneration that commercial agents appointed for the goods forming the subject of his agency contract are customarily allowed in the place where he carries on his activities. If there is no such customary practice a commercial agent shall be entitled to reasonable remuneration taking into account all the aspects of the transaction.[10]

3.17 The directive creates certain guiding principles in relation to commissions that are beyond the scope of this work.[11]

Conclusion and termination

3.18 An issue of central importance to corporate counsel concerns what happens on the termination of the agency agreement. Given the potential implications it is most necessary to consider these implications prior to entering into such an agreement. Hence the majority of the directive concerns itself with this issue.

Formalities

3.19 Each party shall be entitled to receive from the other on request a signed written document setting out the terms of the agency contract including any terms subsequently agreed. Waiver of this right shall not be permitted.[12] However, national law may provide that an agency contract shall not be valid unless evidenced in writing.[13] Such deviations in respect of formality shall be considered below.

Duration and termination

3.20 An agency contract for a fixed period which continues to be performed by both parties after that period has expired shall be deemed to be converted into an agency contract for an indefinite period.[14] Where an agency contract is concluded for an indefinite period either party may terminate it by notice.[15] The period of notice shall be one month for the first year of the contract, two months for the second year commenced, and three months for the third year commenced and subsequent years. The parties may not agree on shorter periods of notice.[16]

---

8 ibid, Art 4.2.
9 ibid, Art 5.
10 ibid, Art 6.
11 ibid, Arts 6–12.
12 ibid, Art 13.
13 ibid, Art 13.2.
14 ibid, Art 14.
15 ibid, Art 15.
16 ibid, Art 15.2.

Indemnification

3.21 National provisions are required to take the measures necessary to ensure that the commercial agent is, after termination of the agency contract, indemnified or compensated for damage in accordance with the below. The commercial agent shall be entitled to an indemnity if and to the extent that:[17]

- he has brought the principal new customers or has significantly increased the volume of business with existing customers and the principal continues to derive substantial benefits from the business with such customers; and
- the payment of this indemnity is equitable having regard to all the circumstances and, in particular, the commission lost by the commercial agent on the business transacted with such customers.

The amount of the indemnity may not exceed a figure equivalent to an indemnity for one year calculated from the commercial agent's average annual remuneration over the preceding five years and if the contract goes back less than five years the indemnity shall be calculated on the average for the period in question.[18] It is important to note that the grant of such an indemnity shall not prevent the commercial agent from seeking damages.[19]

Compensation for damage

3.22 As a basic principle, the commercial agent shall be entitled to compensation for the damage he suffers as a result of the termination of his relations with the principal. In particular, this shall be the case where termination occurs in circumstances that are depriving the commercial agent of the commission (which proper performance of the agency contract would have procured him) whilst providing the principal with substantial benefits linked to the commercial agent's activities, and/or which have not enabled the commercial agent to amortise the costs and expenses that he had incurred for the performance of the agency contract on the principal's advice.[20]

Survival of claims upon death of the agent

3.23 Any entitlement to an indemnification or to compensation for damage shall also arise where the agency contract is terminated as a result of the commercial agent's death.[21] This may be of particular relevant when dealing with agents who operate as sole traders.

Limitations

3.24 The commercial agent shall lose his entitlement to the indemnity or to compensation for damage in the instances provided for in paragraph 3, if the agent, within one year following termination of the contract has not notified the principal that he intends pursuing his entitlement.[22]

---

17 ibid, Art 17.
18 ibid, Art 17.2.
19 ibid, Art 17.2.c.
20 ibid, Art 17.3.
21 ibid, Art 17.4.
22 ibid, Art 17.5.

Exclusions

3.25 The indemnity or compensation referred to above shall not be payable:

- where the principal has terminated the agency contract because of default attributable to the commercial agent which would justify immediate termination of the agency contract under national law;
- where the commercial agent has terminated the agency contract, unless such termination is justified by circumstances attributable to the principal or on grounds of age, infirmity or illness of the commercial agent in consequence of which he cannot reasonably be required to continue his activities;
- where, with the agreement of the principal, the commercial agent assigns his rights and duties under the agency contract to another person.

It is also important to note that the terms of the Agency Directive are not necessarily determinative in all circumstances. It is important to consider national legislative measures as the directive itself states that it shall affect the application of the law of the member states where the latter provides for the immediate termination of the agency contract because of the failure of one party to carry out all or part of his obligations or where exceptional circumstances arise.[23]

Restraint of trade clauses

3.26 An agreement restricting the business activities of a commercial agent following termination of the agency contract is referred to by the directive as a restraint of trade clause. Such clauses are valid only if and to the extent that it is concluded in writing; and it relates to the geographical area or the group of customers and the geographical area entrusted to the commercial agent and to the kind of goods covered by his agency under the contract.[24] Further, such clauses shall be valid for not more than two years after termination of the agency contract.[25] These restrictions will not affect or supersede provisions of national law which impose other restrictions on the validity or enforceability of restraint of trade clauses or which enable the courts to reduce the obligations resulting from such an agreement.[26]

National laws

3.27

Country	National law – agents	National law – distributors
Austria	Austrian Commercial Agents Act (Handelsvertretergesetz)	No specific legal provisions – analogous application may apply
Belgium	Act of 13 April 1995 (the 'Agency Act'), Economic Law Code – Book 10	Act of July 27, 1961, a specific law on the 'Unilateral Termination of Exclusive Distributorship Agreements granted for an indefinite duration'. Economic Law Code – Book 10

23 ibid, Art 16.
24 ibid, Art 20.2.
25 ibid, Art 20.3.
26 ibid, Art 20.4.

Country	**National law – agents**	**National law – distributors**
Bulgaria	Section II, Chapter VI, Part I of the Bulgarian Commercial Act	No specific legal provisions – analogous application may apply
Cyprus	Articles 142–198 of the Contract Law	Articles 142–198 of the Contract Law
	The Commercial Agents Law 1986 as amended by Laws 21(I) of 1994 and 148(I) of 2000	
	The Commercial Agents (Formation and Functioning of the Board, Registration of Members and Charges) (Amending) Regulations of 2003	
Czech Republic	Sections 2483 to 2520 of Act No 89/2012 Coll, Civil Code	No specific legal provisions – analogous application may apply
Denmark	Act on Commercial Agents Act No 272 of 2 May 1990	No specific legal provisions – analogous application may apply
Egypt	Commercial Code No 17 of 1999	No specific legal provisions
	Egyptian Civil Code	
	Commercial Agency Law No 120 of 1982	
Estonia	Sections 670–691 of the Law of Obligations Act	No specific legal provisions
Finland	Act on Commercial Representatives and Salesmen (417/1992)	No specific legal provisions
France	Articles L.134-1 to L.134-17 of the French Commercial Code	No specific legal provisions
Germany	Sections 84–92 c of the German Commercial Code	No specific legal provisions – analogous application may apply
Greece	Presidential Decree No 219/1991	Supreme Court Decision 139/2006 – analogous application may apply
Hungary	Act No V of 2013 of the Civil Code	No specific legal provisions – analogous application may apply
	Decree No 65 of 2014 on Commission of Agents Acting in Long-Term Agency Relationship	
	Act No CXVII of 2000 on Independent Commercial Agent	

Country	National law – agents	National law – distributors
Ireland	European Communities (Commercial Agents) Regulations 1994, SI 33/1994	No specific legal provisions
	European Communities (Commercial Agents) Regulations 1997, SI 31/1997	
Italy	Collective Agreement for Agents of Commercial Principals, 10 March 2010	Article 1470 of the Italian Civil Code
	Collective Agreement for Agents of Industrial Principals, renewed on 30 July 2014	Article 1559 of the Italian Civil Code.
	Civil Code	
Kazakhstan	Special Part of the Civil Code Law of the Republic of Kazakhstan dated 1 July 1999	No specific legal provisions
Latvia	Commercial Law ('Komerclikums' 2000)	No specific legal provisions – analogous application may apply
Lithuania	Articles 2.152–2.175 of the Civil Code of the Republic of Lithuania	Articles 6.796–6.806 of the Civil Code on Distribution
Luxembourg	Article 1 of the law of 3 June 1994 organising relations between independent commercial agents and their principals	No specific legal provisions
Malta	Commercial Code – Chapter 13 of the Laws of Malta and the Civil Code – Chapter 16 of the Laws of Malta	No specific legal provisions
	Act IX of 2003 and subsequent amendments through Act XIII of 2008	
Morocco	A commercial agency contract is defined under Articles 393–404 of the Commercial Code	Law 06-99 relating to freedom of pricing and competition
		Moroccan Obligations and Contracts Code
Netherlands	Book 7, Title 7, Chapter 4 of the Dutch Civil Code	No specific legal provisions
Norway	Act No 56 of 19 June 1992 relating to Commercial Agents and Commercial Travellers	No specific legal provisions – analogous application may apply
Poland	Polish Civil Code	No specific legal provisions – analogous application may apply

Country	National law – agents	National law – distributors
Portugal	Decree Law 178/86, dated 3 July (as amended by Decree Law 118/93 dated 13 April) on Agency Law	No specific legal provisions – analogous application may apply
Romania	Articles 2072 et seq of the Romanian Civil Code	No specific legal provisions – analogous application may apply
Russian Federation	Chapter 49-52 Part I of the Civil Code 1 January 1995; Part II of the Civil Code 1 March 1996	No specific legal provisions – analogous application may apply
Saudi Arabia	Commercial Agency Regulations issued under Royal Decree M/11 dated to 22/07/1962G)	Commercial Agency Regulations issued under Royal Decree M/11 dated to 22/07/1962G)
Slovakia	Sections 652–672a of Act No. 513/1991 Coll, Commercial Code	No specific legal provisions
Slovenia	Slovenian Obligations Code – Official Gazette of the Republic of Slovenia, No 83/2001	No specific legal provisions – analogous application may apply
South Africa	Consumer Protection Act, 2008	No specific legal provisions – analogous application may apply
Spain	Law 12/1992, dated May 27, on Agency Agreements	No specific legal provisions – analogous application may apply
Sweden	Swedish Commercial Agents Act (SFS 1991:351)	No specific legal provisions – analogous application may apply
Switzerland	Articles 418a–418v et seq. of the Swiss Code of Obligations	No specific legal provisions – analogous application may apply
Turkey	Articles 102–123 of the Turkish Commercial Code	No specific legal provisions – analogous application may apply
UAE	Federal Law No 18 of 1981	Federal Law No 18 of 1981
	Federal Law No 18 of 1993	Federal Law No 18 of 1993
	Federal Law No 5 of 1985 on Civil Transactions	Federal Law No 5 of 1985 on Civil Transactions
UK	Commercial Agents (Council Directive) Regulations 1993, SI 1993/3053 and SI 1998/2868	No specific legal provisions – analogous application may apply

Determining the nature of the relationship notwithstanding the label – indicative questions to consider

3.28

- For how many years has there been a relationship between the parties?
- Does either party sell only the supplier's products in the territory? If they do sell another company's products, how much (what percentage) of their business relates to non-supplier products?
- On average, how much (by value) would each party purchase from the supplier annually?

- Has either party, to their knowledge, always bought products directly from the supplier and then resold them after first purchasing them from the supplier?
- What is: (i) each party's size relative to the market it operates in? (ii) each party's supplier base (ie, is the supplier one of many suppliers or the sole supplier of products to the other party)?
- Has either party, to their knowledge, ever made sales on behalf of the supplier or represented the supplier's interests in the territory?
- Has either party, at any time during the relationship, been empowered or authorised by the supplier (orally or in writing) to negotiate or enter into any deal, agreement or other arrangement in the supplier's name or to their benefit? If so, has that party ever been paid or otherwise remunerated for such activity?
- Are there any features of the agreement/oral understanding with either party that are consistent with an annual review or approval of the contract/oral understanding between the parties?
- Has either party ever breached any terms of the contract/oral understanding (or terms as the supplier understood them to be) that is, late payment or failure to purchase an agreed minimum amount?
- Has a party introduced new customers to the supplier and if so how many by number and by value of business transacted.
- What targets, if any, have been set with each party, and have they achieved them historically? What is the aggregate amount of sales achieved each year for the past five years?

Distributors

3.29 Generally, distribution relationships are not provided for prescriptively in law in EMEA. It can be said however, by way of generalisation, that counsel can safely make the assumption that much of what has been stated in relation to agency agreements applies *mutatis mutandis* to distribution arrangements. Typically, this is how national courts in EMEA (with some exceptions) tend to approach questions relating to distribution agreements and is a good rule of thumb for corporate counsel. Hence reiteration of the above features would be repetitive and redundant.

4 Advertising and promotion

'For fools rush in where angels fear to tread'

Alexander Pope

Introduction

4.1 Is it really the case that the idea that publicity can do no harm is a statement that is clearly open to question? Only a select few, those who seek notoriety, arguably, for notoriety's sake crave the celebrity status that, sporadically, delivers fame and wealth but only to those who risk a life or personal brand and are forever associated with scandal. The late great Marie Lloyd, the now fabulously remembered Mae West or more recently the tragic Anna Nicole Smith and currently Kim Kardashian may come to one's mind. For they seem at home and at one with Oscar Wilde in that within their world *the only thing worse than being talked about is not being talked about.*

4.2 I dare say, however, that your board of directors and shareholders would be somewhat less happy to risk their company's hard-won brand reputation (not to mention their share price) on a similar strategy. Yet even in the largest of corporations, with the strongest of household brands to protect, there still reside the ill-advised, the untutored who are blissfully unaware of both the world around them and that PT Barnum's methods along with his famously attributed mantra 'there's no such thing as bad publicity' are not gospel in all circumstances. Either that or they are just idiots; but that's for you to judge, in your own time, when this peculiar situation arises (and it will).

4.3 In all my years in-house I can honestly say that I've never met a marketing person who didn't think their new campaign was anything other than pure unadulterated genius. Every time I'm asked to review one of these piques of inspiration my mind always fixates on a warning most often attributed to Oscar Wilde that, 'all great ideas are dangerous'.

4.4 If you harbour any doubt of the truth in Wilde's warning let us quickly review some recent and very public history. In January of 2018 the clothing giant H&M ran an advertisement on its website with photos of two male adolescents, one Caucasian and one of African lineage. Each child was wearing a near identical screen printed hooded sweatshirt from H&M's children's range. Well what's wrong with that?

4.5 Looking more closely at the screen printing the Caucasian boy's shirt read 'Mangrove Jungle Official Survival Expert Junior Tour Guide' and that shirt was further emblazoned with the likeness of a majestic Tiger. The second boy's shirt read 'COOLEST MONKEY IN THE JUNGLE'. H&M, given the extreme media and social media reaction, issued the following statement: 'We have got this wrong and we agree that, even if unintentional, passive or casual racism needs to be eradicated wherever it exists.' Shortly thereafter, the company appointed its first ever global leader for diversity and inclusiveness.

4.6 Now if you harbour any doubt about my assertion that in the marketing departments of the greatest of corporations, those with the most famous of household brands to safeguard, reside individuals who are ill-advised, untutored and who are apparently astoundingly unaware (whether or not they are knowing supporters of PT Barnham), dial back the clock to 2017 when the very same H&M were first heavily criticised for advertising, you guessed it, a similar hooded sweatshirt, worn by another youthful male model (who was not Caucasian), emblazoned with the word 'Unemployed'. If further proof is needed then leap forward in time to February 2019 when Gucci had to apologise for advertising, and discontinue selling, an $850 US dollar sweater that came with the peculiar ability to transform its wearer into a blackface minstrel. Yes, a la Mr Al Jolson, through an intended design feature included in the garment's turtle neck collar.

4.7 My points here are twofold. First, advertising and promotional activities are by definition very public ergo a surprisingly easy way, say in a fit of genius, to garner that very type of publicity that can severely damage a brand or kill it altogether. If the above examples are not persuasive, Google Gerald Ratner. Secondly, advertising and promotional activities in Europe attract some of the most onerous regulation which in turn carries the risk of significant and at times disproportionate financial penalties and the naturally associated reputational risk for unwary companies.

4.8 Now to give credit where credit is due (given I've had a little fun here at another profession's expense). Whether it's the celebrated mad men of Madison Avenue or your inhouse PR department, the advertising, promotions and the brand awareness they create are central to the success of business today. Some of their genius is just that; it's genius, and we as in-house lawyers would do well to remember that and the Pope quote 'For fools rush in where angels fear to tread'. Meaning we must be mindful in the execution of our duty not to overstep the mark, or otherwise stop, stifle or hinder their good work or the business of the business.

4.9 As a General Counsel or a business leader I believe it's our absolute duty to just keep our company's advertising (and promotions) within the law. But I also believe it is good practice for a business to have someone; whether it's a leader for diversity and inclusiveness or just another level headed, astute and commercially aware adult (a type of corporate conscience) who is not ego invested or a part of the creative team that developed the campaigns reviewing those campaigns. Someone who is not easily intimidated, who is not afraid to plainly point out a risk, if not an error, in the genius so graciously and sometimes condescendingly served up by the little emperors of advertising. And should they refuse to pay heed to the advice of your corporate *Jiminy Cricket* make sure to have a clear mechanism to enable the matter to be escalated to you for further consideration.

4.10 Whilst an essential element for almost every corporate entity, advertising and promotional activities attract some of the most onerous regulation and carry with them the risk of significant and at times disproportionate, financial and/or reputational penalties for companies. The authors have sought to give corporate counsel a sense of the minutiae by examination of relevant provisions in the UK, whilst also providing directional advice as regards the legal frameworks in a variety of nations.

Advertising

4.11 The governance of advertising and other such measures associated with enhancing the public perception of a brand or product, be it digital or otherwise, is relatively sophisticated in terms of its regulation across Europe. Frequently, the risk for corporate counsel is in the significant financial and reputational implications that await those who breach national laws, codes or guidelines.

Recurring themes

4.12 A wide array of national regulatory and oversight approaches have historically been adopted, nonetheless, certain themes emerge consistently across jurisdictions.

National legal frameworks

4.13 Sources of such regulatory frameworks are often diffuse at a national level. While a full exposition on this topic is beyond the ambition of this text, it is considered useful to set out the key legislative instruments, on a national level, for the purposes of allowing corporate counsel to commence examination of discreet issues.

Country	Key legislation and sources of rules
Belgium	Belgian Code of Economic Law
	Book VI (Fair trade practices and Consumer Protection)
	Book VII (Payment and credit services)
	Book XI (IP rights)
	Book XII (E-Commerce)
	Belgian Privacy Act 2018
Denmark	Marketing Practices Act 2017
	Consumer Agreement Act 2014
	The E-Commerce Act
	Gambling Act 2016

Country	Key legislation and sources of rules
Finland	The Information Society Code 2014
	Unfair Business Practices Act 2002
	Consumer Protection Act
	Act on the Exercise of Freedom of Expression in Mass Media
France	French Advertising Authority Guidelines
	Consumer Rights Act 2004
	French Consumer Code
	French Language Act 1994
Germany	Unfair Competition Act
	German Civil Code
Italy	Consumer Code (Decree No 206/2005)
	Decree on misleading and unlawful advertising No 146/2007
	Italian Civil Code Article 2598 on unlawful advertising
Netherlands	Dutch Civil Code – Book 6, Article 194 et seq
	Dutch Advertising Code
	Games of Chance Act
	Unfair Commercial Practices Act
Poland	Act on Competition and Consumer Protection
	Act on Counteracting Unfair Trade Practices
	Act on Combatting Unfair Competition
Spain	The Law on Unfair Competition 1991
	The General Law on Advertising 1998
	The Consumer Act 2007
Sweden	Marketing Practices Act 2008
	Act on Names and Pictures in Advertising 1978
	E-Commerce Act 2002
United Kingdom	Consumer Protection from Unfair Trading Regulations 2008
	Business Protection from Misleading Marketing Regulations 2008
	Committee of Advertising Practice Code as enforced by the Advertising Standards Authority

Advertising in the UK

4.14 The governance of advertising, and specifically the content of advertising, in the UK is perhaps worthy of separate and special attention, given the relative size of the market and its position as one of a small number of countries with English as its primary language within the EU (subject of course to Brexit negotiations). In the context of selecting a useful analogue by which to determine a useful 'high water mark' which corporate actors may wish to use to guide their compliance policies relating to advertising in EMEA, it would be submitted that the UK regime in this regard is a good place to start.

4.15 There are a number of core pieces of governing legislation and guidance that should be considered by corporate counsel and will be illuminated in greater detail below. They are: (i) the Consumer Protection from Unfair Trading Regulations 2008, SI 2008/1277; (ii) the Business Protection from Misleading Marketing Regulations 2008, SI 2008/1276; (iii) UK Code of Non-broadcast Advertising, Sales Promotion and Direct Marketing;[1] and (iv) the UK Code of Broadcast Advertising.[2] In addition, there are a broad range of sector specific guidance and regulation of advertising which are too numerous to elucidate hereafter, however, special consideration will be given to matters relating to consumer credit advertising given the onerous compliance requirement in this regard in the UK.

Consumer protection from unfair trading[3]

4.16 These Regulations are perhaps best understood from the starting point of understanding the negative prohibitions they contain.[4]

General prohibition on unfair commercial practices

4.17 Unfair commercial practices are prohibited.[5] A particular practice is deemed unfair if it contravenes the requirements of professional diligence; and it materially distorts or is likely to materially distort the economic behaviour of the average consumer with regard to the product.[6] Additionally, a commercial practice will be deemed unfair if it is misleading in nature, contains or amounts to a misleading omission, is considered aggressive, or is a practice that is listed in Schedule 1 of the Regulations which are set out below.

Key definitions

4.18 It should be noted that 'commercial practice' means any act, omission, course of conduct, representation or commercial communication (including advertising and marketing) by a trader, which is directly connected with the promotion, sale or supply of a product to or from consumers, whether occurring before, during or after a commercial transaction (if any) in relation to a product.[7]

---

1 Also referred to as the CAP Code. See www.asa.org.uk/codes-and-rulings/advertising-codes/non-broadcast-code.html.
2 Also referred to as the BCAP Code. See www.asa.org.uk/codes-and-rulings/advertising-codes/broadcast-code.html.
3 As governed by the Consumer Protection from Unfair Trading Regulations 2008.
4 It should also be noted that the Regulations establish specific offences which give rise to an array of sanctions. For further detail on offences and sanctions please see Parts 3 and 4 of the Regulations.
5 The Consumer Protection from Unfair Trading Regulations 2008, reg 3(1).
6 ibid, reg 3(a)–(b).
7 ibid, reg (2)(1).

4.19 It should be further noted that the term 'consumer' is broadly defined as meaning any individual who in relation to a commercial practice is acting for purposes which are outside his business.[8]

Misleading actions

4.20 A commercial practice is a misleading action (and therefore prohibited) if:

(a) it concerns any marketing of a product (including comparative advertising) which creates confusion with any products, trademarks, trade names or other distinguishing marks of a competitor; or[9]

(b) it concerns any failure by a trader to comply with a commitment contained in a code of conduct which the trader has undertaken to comply with, if:[10]

 (i) the trader indicates in a commercial practice that he or she is bound by that code of conduct; and

 (ii) the commitment is firm and capable of being verified and is not aspirational,

(c) it causes or is likely to cause the average consumer to take a transactional decision they would not have taken otherwise, taking account of its factual context and of all its features and circumstances;[11]

(d) it causes or is likely to cause the average consumer to take a transactional decision they would not have taken otherwise;[12]

(e) if it contains false information and is therefore untruthful in relation to any of the matters set out below or if it or its overall presentation in any way deceives or is likely to deceive the average consumer in relation to any of the matters in that paragraph, even if the information is factually correct:[13]

 (i) the existence or nature of the product;

 (ii) the extent of the trader's commitments;

 (iii) the motives for the commercial practice;

 (iv) the nature of the sales process;

 (v) any statement or symbol relating to direct or indirect sponsorship or approval of the trader or the product;

 (vi) the price or the manner in which the price is calculated;

 (vii) the existence of a specific price advantage;

 (viii) the need for a service, part, replacement or repair;

 (ix) the nature, attributes and rights of the trader (eg, in relation to the trader's qualifications, affiliations etc);[14]

 (x) the consumer's rights or the risks they may face; and

 (xi) the main characteristics of the product (as defined below).

---

8 ibid, reg (2)(1).
9 ibid, reg 5(3)(a).
10 ibid, reg 5(3)(b).
11 ibid, reg (5)(2)(b).
12 ibid, reg (5)(3).
13 ibid, reg (5)(2)(a).
14 Which are set out in further detail at reg 5(6).

The main characteristics of the product referred to above at point (xi) include the following: availability of the product; benefits of the product; risks of the product; execution of the product; composition of the product; accessories of the product; after-sale customer assistance concerning the product; the handling of complaints about the product; the method and date of manufacture of the product; the method and date of provision of the product; delivery of the product; fitness for purpose of the product; usage of the product; quantity of the product; specification of the product; geographical or commercial origin of the product; results to be expected from use of the product; and results and material features of tests or checks carried out on the product.

Misleading omissions

4.21 Generally, the legislative aim involved here is to prevent an average consumer from taking a transactional decision they would not otherwise have taken but for the misleading omission. To that end a commercial practice, in its factual context, and taking account of all the features and circumstances of the commercial practice and the limitations of the medium used to communicate the commercial practice (including limitations of space or time), is a misleading omission if:[15]

(a) the commercial practice omits material information;

(b) the commercial practice hides material information;

(c) the commercial practice provides material information in a manner which is unclear, unintelligible, ambiguous or untimely; or

(d) the commercial practice fails to identify its commercial intent, unless this is already apparent from the context, and as a result it causes or is likely to cause the average consumer to take a transactional decision they would not have taken otherwise.

Aggressive commercial practices

4.22 A commercial practice is aggressive if, it significantly impairs or is likely significantly to impair the average consumer's freedom of choice or conduct in relation to the product concerned through the use of harassment, coercion or undue influence; and it thereby causes or is likely to cause them to take a transactional decision they would not have taken otherwise.[16]

4.23 In determining whether a commercial practice uses harassment, coercion[17] or undue influence,[18] the legislation will take into account a range of issues, including:

- its timing, location, nature or persistence;
- the use of threatening or abusive language or behaviour;
- the exploitation by the trader of any specific misfortune or circumstance of such gravity as to impair the consumer's judgment, of which the trader is aware, to influence the consumer's decision with regard to the product;

15 ibid, reg 6(2).
16 ibid, reg 7(1).
17 The regulation defines 'coercion' as including the use of physical force.
18 The regulation defines 'undue influence' as meaning the exploitation of a position of power in relation to the consumer so as to apply pressure, even without using or threatening to use physical force, in a way which significantly limits the consumer's ability to make an informed decision.

- any onerous or disproportionate non-contractual barrier imposed by the trader where a consumer wishes to exercise rights under the contract, including rights to terminate a contract or to switch to another product or another trader; and
- any threat to take any action which cannot legally be taken.

Other commercial practices which are in all circumstances considered unfair

4.24 The commercial practices set out below are, where they are found to have occurred, considered to be unfair in nature and would attract the general prohibition as set out in Regulation 3. They are as follows:[19]

(1) Claiming to be a signatory to a code of conduct when the trader is not.

(2) Displaying a trust mark, quality mark or equivalent without having obtained the necessary authorisation.

(3) Claiming that a code of conduct has an endorsement from a public or other body which it does not have.

(4) Claiming that a trader (including their commercial practices) or a product has been approved, endorsed or authorised by a public or private body when the trader, the commercial practices or the product have not or making such a claim without complying with the terms of the approval, endorsement or authorisation.

(5) Making an invitation to purchase products at a specified price without disclosing the existence of any reasonable grounds the trader may have for believing that they will not be able to offer for supply, or to procure another trader to supply, those products or equivalent products at that price for a period that is, and in quantities that are, reasonable having regard to the product, the scale of advertising of the product and the price offered (bait advertising).

(6) Making an invitation to purchase products at a specified price and then:

   (a) refusing to show the advertised item to consumers;

   (b) refusing to take orders for it or deliver it within a reasonable time; or

   (c) demonstrating a defective sample of it, with the intention of promoting a different product (bait and switch).

(7) Falsely stating that a product will only be available for a very limited time, or that it will only be available on particular terms for a very limited time, in order to elicit an immediate decision and deprive consumers of sufficient opportunity or time to make an informed choice.

(8) Undertaking to provide after-sales service to consumers with whom the trader has communicated prior to a transaction in a language which is not an official language of the EEA state where the trader is located and then making such service available only in another language without clearly disclosing this to the consumer before the consumer is committed to the transaction.

(9) Stating or otherwise creating the impression that a product can legally be sold when it cannot.

(10) Presenting rights given to consumers in law as a distinctive feature of the trader's offer.

---

19 These practices are specifically listed in the first Schedule to the Regulations.

(11) Using editorial content in the media to promote a product where a trader has paid for the promotion without making that clear in the content or by images or sounds clearly identifiable by the consumer (advertorial).

(12) Making a materially inaccurate claim concerning the nature and extent of the risk to the personal security of the consumer or their family if the consumer does not purchase the product.

(13) Promoting a product similar to a product made by a particular manufacturer in such a manner as deliberately to mislead the consumer into believing that the product is made by that same manufacturer when it is not.

(14) Establishing, operating or promoting a pyramid promotional scheme where a consumer gives consideration for the opportunity to receive compensation that is derived primarily from the introduction of other consumers into the scheme rather than from the sale or consumption of products.

(15) Claiming that the trader is about to cease trading or move premises when they are not.

(16) Claiming that products are able to facilitate winning in games of chance.

(17) Falsely claiming that a product is able to cure illnesses, dysfunction or malformations.

(18) Passing on materially inaccurate information on market conditions or on the possibility of finding the product with the intention of inducing the consumer to acquire the product at conditions less favourable than normal market conditions.

(19) Claiming in a commercial practice to offer a competition or prize promotion without awarding the prizes described or a reasonable equivalent.

(20) Describing a product as 'gratis', 'free', 'without charge' or similar if the consumer has to pay anything other than the unavoidable cost of responding to the commercial practice and collecting or paying for delivery of the item.

(21) Including in marketing material an invoice or similar document seeking payment which gives the consumer the impression that they have already ordered the marketed product when they have not.

(22) Falsely claiming or creating the impression that the trader is not acting for purposes relating to their trade, business, craft or profession, or falsely representing oneself as a consumer.

(23) Creating the false impression that after-sales service in relation to a product is available in an EEA state other than the one in which the product is sold.

(24) Creating the impression that the consumer cannot leave the premises until a contract is formed.

(25) Conducting personal visits to the consumer's home ignoring the consumer's request to leave or not to return, except in circumstances and to the extent justified to enforce a contractual obligation.

(26) Making persistent and unwanted solicitations by telephone, fax, email or other remote media except in circumstances and to the extent justified to enforce a contractual obligation.

(27) Requiring a consumer who wishes to claim on an insurance policy to produce documents which could not reasonably be considered relevant as to whether the

claim was valid, or failing systematically to respond to pertinent correspondence, in order to dissuade a consumer from exercising their contractual rights.

(28) Including in an advertisement a direct exhortation to children to buy advertised products or persuade their parents or other adults to buy advertised products for them.

(29) Demanding immediate or deferred payment for or the return or safekeeping of products supplied by the trader, but not solicited by the consumer, except where the product is a substitute supplied in accordance with regulation 19(7) of the Consumer Protection (Distance Selling) Regulations 2000 (inertia selling).

(30) Explicitly informing a consumer that if he or she does not buy the product or service, the trader's job or livelihood will be in jeopardy.

(31) Creating the false impression that the consumer has already won, will win, or will on doing a particular act win, a prize or other equivalent benefit, when in fact either:

(a) there is no prize or other equivalent benefit; or

(b) taking any action in relation to claiming the prize or other equivalent benefit is subject to the consumer paying money or incurring a cost.

Business protection from misleading marketing[20]

4.25 Similar to the consumer regulations, these Regulations are perhaps also best understood from the starting point of understanding the negative prohibitions they contain.[21] It should also be noted that the Regulations establish specific offences which give rise to an array of sanctions. For further detail on offences and sanctions please see Parts 2 and 3 of the Regulations.

General prohibition

4.26 Advertising which is misleading is prohibited.[22] Advertising is deemed misleading which in any way, including its presentation, deceives or is likely to deceive the traders to whom it reaches; and by reason of its deceptive nature, is likely to affect their economic behaviour, or injures a competitor.[23]

Key definitions

4.27 As regards these Regulations the legislation opts once again for broad definitions Importantly, it should be noted that 'advertising' means any form of representation which is made in connection with a trade, business, craft or profession in order to promote the supply or transfer of a product.[24] Additionally, it should be noted that 'comparative advertising' means advertising which in any way, either explicitly or by implication, identifies a competitor or a product offered by a competitor.[25]

---

20 As governed by the Business Protection from Misleading Marketing Regulations 2008, SI 2008/1276.

21 It should also be noted that the Regulations establish specific offences which give rise to an array of sanctions. For further detail on offences and sanctions please see Parts 3 and 4 of the Regulations.

22 The Business Protection from Misleading Marketing Regulations 2008, reg 3(1).

23 ibid, reg 3(2).

24 ibid, reg 2(1).

25 ibid, reg 2(1).

Misleading advertising

4.28 In determining whether advertising is misleading, the legislation requires consideration of, inter alia, any information it contains concerning:

(a) the price or manner in which the price is calculated;

(b) the conditions on which the product is supplied or provided;

(c) the nature, attributes and rights of the advertiser (including their qualifications, awards, ownership of IP rights etc); and[26]

(d) the characteristics of the product (as defined below).[27]

The main characteristics of the product referred to above at point (d) include the following: the availability of the product; nature of the product; execution of the product; composition of the product; method and date of manufacture of the product; method and date of provision of the product; fitness for purpose of the product; uses of the product; quantity of the product; specification of the product; geographical or commercial origin of the product; results to be expected from use of the product; or results and material features of tests or checks carried out on the product.

Comparative advertising

4.29 A common pitfall for corporate counsel relates to how, and under what circumstances, comparative advertising may be deployed. The Regulations are largely prescriptive in that they require that comparative advertising shall, as far as the comparison is concerned, be permitted only when the following baseline conditions are met:[28]

- it is not misleading (as defined in the above section);[29]
- it is not a misleading action or a misleading omission.[30]

Further, the comparative advertising must:[31]

- compare products meeting the same needs or intended for the same purpose;
- objectively compare one or more material, relevant, verifiable and representative features of those products, which may include price;
- not create confusion among traders as between the advertiser and a competitor, nor as between the trademarks, trade names, other distinguishing marks or products of the advertiser and those of a competitor;
- not discredit or denigrate the trademarks, trade names, other distinguishing marks, products, activities, or circumstances of a competitor.

The CAP Code

4.30 The UK Code of Non-broadcast Advertising and Direct & Promotional Marketing (CAP Code) is the rule book for non-broadcast advertisements, dealing

26 As set out in reg 3(5).
27 And as set out in reg 3(4).
28 ibid, reg 4.
29 As set out in reg 3.
30 As defined by regs 5 and 6 respectively of the Consumer Protection from Unfair Trading Regulations 2008 which are set out above.
31 ibid, reg 4 contains further mandatory criteria.

with such issues as sales promotions and direct marketing communications (marketing communications).[32]

What kind of advertising does the code apply to?

4.31 The code applies to a range of non-broadcast marketing communications, some of which are set out below:[33]

> *Print advertisements*
>
> Advertisements in newspapers, magazines, brochures, leaflets, circulars, mailings, emails, text transmissions (including SMS and MMS), fax transmissions, catalogues, follow-up literature and other electronic or printed material are all subject to the CAP code.
>
> *Public Space Advertising*
>
> Posters and other promotional media in public places, including moving images, except where they appear unlawfully will similarly be subject to the CAP code.
>
> *Screen advertisements*
>
> Such as those as may appear in cinema, video, DVD and Blu-ray media are subject to the CAP code.
>
> *Advertisements in non-broadcast electronic media*
>
> The CAP code covers online advertisements in paid-for space (including banner or pop-up advertisements and online video advertisements and a range of other web platform related media.

The CAP code also applies to marketing databases containing consumers' personal information.[34]

General themes of the CAP Code

4.32 Marketing communications should be legal, decent, honest and truthful[35] and must reflect the spirit, not merely the letter, of the Code.[36] Additionally, marketing communications must be prepared with a sense of responsibility to consumers and to society[37] and must comply with all general rules and with relevant sector-specific rules[38] while not bringing advertising into disrepute.[39]

4.33 Marketing communications must be obviously identifiable as such[40] and all unsolicited email marketing communications must be obviously identifiable as marketing communications without the need to open them.[41] Marketers and publishers must also make clear that advertorials are marketing communications; for example, by heading them 'advertisement feature'.[42]

32 See www.asa.org.uk.
33 And are set out in detail in the Cap Code Introduction.
34 ibid, as per introductory comments.
35 CAP Code, r 1.1.
36 CAP Code, r 1.2.
37 CAP Code, r 1.3.
38 CAP Code, r 1.4.
39 CAP Code, r 1.5.
40 CAP Code, r 2.1.
41 CAP Code, r 2.2.
42 CAP Code, r 2.4.

Misleading advertising

4.34 The Advertising Standards Authority considers the Consumer Protection from Unfair Trading Regulations 2008 and the CAP Code builds on those fundamental provisions to create a significant body of guidance for advertisers. The code provides substantive advice on the following issues in determining whether an advertisement is misleading:

Generally[43]

The advertisement must not mislead in a material way. Neither can it contain obvious exaggerations, or omit material information or obfuscate information by means of presenting it in an unclear or unintelligible way. The marketer must be readily identifiable.

Substantiation[44]

Prior to issuing communications, marketers must hold documentary evidence to prove claims that consumers are likely to regard as objective, ie their claims must be capable of substantiation on an objective basis.

Qualification[45]

It must be stated clearly as to whether there are any significant limitations and/ or qualification to the claims that are being proffered which should not be contradictory in nature.

Exaggeration[46]

The capability or performance of a product must not be exaggerated and marketers must not present legal rights as distinctive features of a product.

Prohibited claims[47]

Products must not explicitly claim that the advertiser's job or livelihood is in jeopardy if the consumer does not buy the advertised product. Particular attention is given to pyramid schemes as the code requires that no marketing communication may promote a pyramid promotional scheme. Pyramid promotional schemes are defined by the code as being schemes in which consumers pay for the opportunity to receive payments derived primarily from the introduction of other consumers into the scheme, not from the sale or consumption of products.

Prices[48]

Price statements must not mislead by omission, undue emphasis or distortion. Quoted prices must include non-optional taxes, duties, fees and charges that apply to all or most buyers. However, VAT-exclusive prices may be given if all those to whom the price claim is clearly addressed pay no VAT or can recover VAT. Such VAT-exclusive prices must be accompanied by a prominent statement of the amount or rate of VAT payable. Marketing communications that state prices must also state applicable delivery, freight or postal charges or, if those cannot reasonably be calculated in advance, state that such charges are payable. Price

43 CAP Code, rr 3.1–3.6.
44 CAP Code, rr 3.7–3.8.
45 CAP Code, rr 3.9–3.10.
46 CAP Code, rr 3.11–3.13.
47 CAP Code, rr 3.14–3.16.
48 CAP Code, rr 3.17–3.22.

claims such as 'up to' and 'from' must not exaggerate the availability or amount of benefits likely to be obtained by the consumer.

Free of Charge[49]

Marketing communications must make clear the extent of the commitment the consumer must make to take advantage of a 'free' offer. An item is not 'free' if handling or administration charges apply, the quality of the product has reduced, or the cost of response has increased.

Availability[50]

Marketers must make a reasonable estimate of demand for advertised products and where estimated demand exceeds supply, marketing communications must make clear that stock is limited.

Comparisons[51]

Marketing communications that include a comparison with an identifiable competitor must not mislead, or be likely to mislead, the consumer about either the advertised product or the competing product.

Imitation and Denigration[52]

The consumer must not be misled as to the manufacturer of the product and must not discredit another product or trademark nor take advantage of a competitor's reputation.

Endorsements and Testimonials[53]

Marketers must hold documentary evidence that a testimonial or endorsement used in a marketing communication is genuine and hold contact details for the person who, or organisation that, gives it. A testimonial must not in itself mislead and must be obtained with permission. A product must not falsely purport to display a trust mark or be subject to a code of conduct.

Guarantees and After Sales Service[54]

Marketing communications must not use the word 'guarantee' in a way that could cause confusion about a consumer's rights. Marketers must promptly refund consumers who make valid claims under an advertised money-back guarantee.

The BCAP Code

4.35 The UK Code of Broadcast Advertising and Direct & Promotional Marketing (BCAP Code) is the rule book for broadcast advertisements, dealing with such issues as teleshopping, content on self-promotional television channels, television text and interactive television ads.[55]

4.36 Many of the features of the BCAP Code are similar in nature to those contained in the CAP Code (though not without divergence in certain respects) and seeking to avoid repetition, the authors would direct corporate counsel to the

49 CAP Code, rr 3.23–3.26.
50 CAP Code, rr 3.27–3.32.
51 CAP Code, rr 3.33–3.37.
52 CAP Code, rr 3.41–3.44.
53 CAP Code, rr 3.45–3.52.
54 CAP Code, rr 3.53–3.57.
55 See www.asa.org.uk.

comments on the CAP code above by way of analogy and the BCAP code itself which can be found in its entirety on the ASA website at www.asa.org.uk.

Consumer credit advertising in the UK

4.37 Consumer credit is a heavily regulated sphere of interest in the UK with a vast array of governing provision that can trace their genesis to a patchwork of legislation going back almost 50 years. The corpus of law in this regard is so enormous as to be prohibitively difficult to deal with in the context of this text. However, for the purposes of basic compliance considerations, it is useful to set out some key pieces of information relating to consumer credit hereafter. The authors would firmly counsel toward the retention of specialist advice if embarking upon a detailed examination of issues arising in relation to consumer credit, not least as the sanctions that await wrongdoers are draconian in some cases.

Regulation

4.38 The Financial Conduct Authority is the conduct regulator for 58,000 financial services firms and financial markets in the UK and the prudential regulator for over 18,000 of those firms. They are responsible for protecting consumers and have stewardship of a vast array of consumer protection provisions relating to the provision of consumer credit.

FCA Handbook

4.39 The FCA Handbook[56] contains the complete record of FCA Legal Instruments. Whilst voluminous in nature, the key provisions as pertaining to consumer credit are contained in the Consumer Credit Sourcebook held in the Specialist Sourcebooks section sometimes referred to in the shorthand CONC. CONC 3 contains the rules governing financial promotions and communications with customers and is highly prescriptive in nature. A full exposition of these provisions is beyond the scope of this work but by way of summary they deal with advertising issues arising in relation to:

- Application.
- The clear, fair and not misleading rule.
- Risk warning for high-cost short-term credit.
- Financial promotions about credit agreements not secured on land.
- Financial promotions about credit agreements secured on land.
- Financial promotions and communications: credit brokers.
- Financial promotions and communications: P2P agreements.
- Financial promotions and communications: lenders.
- Financial promotions and communications: debt counsellors and debt adjusters.
- Financial promotions not in writing.
- Not approving certain financial promotions.

56 See www.handbook.fca.org.uk/.

Promotion

4.40 The governance of promotional contests, prize draws, competitions, 'sweepstakes' and other such games of skill and chance associated with commercial marketing, be it digital or otherwise, is relatively sophisticated in terms of its regulation across Europe.

Recurring themes

4.41 Whilst there is a broad spectrum of approaches adopted, certain themes emerge consistently across jurisdictions. Such promotional activities tend to fall into three categories, which are worthy of close examination by Counsel as frequently a promotional activity that presents as benign initially may, on closer inspection, unintentionally meet the criteria for a lottery.

Competitions

4.42 A competition by its nature tends to involve a promotion where successful entrants are determined by means of some challenge involving the use of skill or judgement or intellect. Generally, there is no payment or other consideration required from the entrant in order to participate.

Prize draws

4.43 Prize draws tend to involve a promotion where those who are successful are determined by random chance but importantly, no payment or other kind of consideration is required in order to take part. They are typically deployed free of any charge on a commercial basis to incentivise purchase of goods. Typically there is no opportunity for the entrant to influence the draw.

Lotteries

4.44 A lottery is typically a species of promotion that involves entrants making a payment or providing other consideration in order to enter. Prizes tend to be distributed to those successful entrants in a random fashion and typically there is no opportunity for the entrant to influence the game. Usually, active participation by the entrant is not a feature of the game. Critically, lotteries are usually heavily regulated by national authorities and require some element of official approval either by licence or certification. There tends to be significant financial sanctions (if not criminal sanctions) attached to offences related to operating an illegal lottery. As stated, Counsel should be alive to any perceived risk that a given promotional activity would unintentionally stray into the territory of being deemed a lottery.

National legal frameworks

4.45 Sources of such regulatory frameworks are often diffuse at a national level in relation to promotional activities. While a full exposition on this topic is beyond the ambition of this text, it is considered useful to set out the key legislative instruments and guidance, on a national level, for the purposes of allowing corporate counsel to commence examination of discreet issues.

Country	**Key legislation and sources of rules**
Belgium	Belgian Code of Economic Law – Book VI
	International Chamber of Commerce Conduct Code
	Belgian Direct Marketing Association Conduct Code
Denmark	The Gambling Act 2016
Finland	Consumer Protection Act 1978
	Lotteries Act 2001
France	French Consumer Code
Germany	German Unfair Competition Act
	Inter-State Treaty on Gambling
Italy	Decree 430/2001 on Prize Promotion
Netherlands	Advertising Code for Games of Chance
Poland	The Act on Combatting Unfair Competition
	Civil Code
	The Act on Gambling Games
Spain	Spanish Gambling Law 2011
Sweden	Lotteries Act 1994
	Marketing Practices Act 2008
	The Advertising Guidelines from the Ethical Council of the Gaming Industry
United Kingdom	The Gambling Act 2005

PART 2

REGARDING HUMANS: THE HEARTBEAT OF THE BUSINESS

5 Human resources

'While I do believe we need to focus on inclusion for people with disabilities, I also think we need to look beyond labels. What is a disability? Truly, every person faces adversity at some point in their lives. The idea that some receive a full package of "abilities" and that the world is divided neatly between the "abled" and "disabled" is misdirected.'

Chad Jerdee

General Counsel & Chief Compliance Officer,

Accenture

Introduction

5.1 Contained at the very heart of the business, the most profound difference between North American and European based businesses, is the way in which these vastly different societies, their respective legal systems and their respective business cultures, regard the human condition that is employment. I have seen it time and again and I advise that a misunderstanding of this difference is a clear and present danger to transatlantic senior management relations; a danger to the effective management of the business; as well as a danger to European employee morale (at all levels) and the continued smooth, efficient operation of a EU based business.

5.2 I have often heard it glibly said that 'Europeans work to live, and Americans live to work'. Granted it's a gross oversimplification of a rather more complex cultural dichotomy but if you're the leader of a business which is about to buy or you have just become the leader or General Counsel of a business with a presence, in Europe, you'd better come to understand the factors that perpetuate the basic truth contained in that oversimplification, or hire someone who does, and *toot sweet*!

5.3 At the risk of coining another gross oversimplification I would offer this suggestion to executives or General Counsels; the only similarity between employment ethos in the EU and in the USA is no person who is *employed* works without an agreed level of renumeration. There the similarities in employment practice and culture pretty much end.

5.4 Practices that seem simple and quite commonplace in North America such as: (1) the unilateral rollout and implementation of corporate policies, such as a code of conduct policy, a bring your own device policy; anticorruption and bribery policy, IT/email system policy (access, use, storage and monitoring etc); or (2) a short notice quick corporate restructure; (3) the accelerated integration of an acquisition target; (4) the two week notice to terminate employment agreements; and (5) alterations to compensation and benefits, to name but a few, are simply not acceptable in Europe without adaptation to the various jurisdictions.

5.5 There have been many instances during my years in-house that I've been called in, after the fact, to clean up on the occasions when on orders from (take your pick Atlanta, San Francisco, San Jose, Omaha, New York, Tampa, etc) to implement restructure or headcount reduction was carried out to a normal North American plan and timetable without regard to the law or rights of their EU employees in (take your pick Germany, Italy, France, the United Kingdom, the Netherlands, etc). I now have a stock reply I use on these occasions and it goes something like this:

> 'You should have come to see me first, but as you didn't, you must now look into the eyes of the dragon and despair, you've consigned your assumed budgetary savings for this year and possibly next to oblivion.'

Yes, it's a little theatrical (and partially appropriated from the film *Excalibur*) but as it's often said, all lawyers are just failed thespians, so why should I be anything less and thereby disappoint.

The case of the intimidated Fortune 100 multinational

5.6 I was once made aware of a retrenchment programme then underway in a very large US based multinational, a household name, with operations globally. This cost cutting and headcount reduction exercise was, I was informed, being implemented globally by the business but, curiously, not in Europe. One of the business' executives, who was one of the owners of this mammoth corporate exercise, is a lifelong friend.

5.7 As I listened to the detail of the then nearly completed exercise I enquired why there were no similar activities taking place in Europe. My first thought was the European business must have been healthier than the rest and therefore not ripe for restructure. To my astonishment I learned their European business was actually in the same and perhaps worse shape than the rest of their business. I was then informed that it had not been targeted by this (or the last such) exercise because the European based management had convinced their CEO and Board that the employment laws in Europe would not allow them to undertake the exercise.

5.8 I was amazed to say the least. This is one of the largest businesses of its type in the United States, if not the world, and it was intimidated into inaction by, for all intents and purposes, the formidable reputation of European employment law and, I was to learn, all due to a distant corporate memory of a previous, botched, European restructure from the 1980s.

5.9 I queried whether legal advice had been sought and I then learned that no such advice had been obtained. It would seem that because of the mere memory of a long distant European calamity (and no doubt the sackings that resulted from it) no one in the business would rise to the challenge and question the word of the European executives on the subject.

5.10 The simple truth was (and is) that their programme could certainly have been adapted for implementation in Europe. True, in its then accelerated, slash and burn incarnation, it was unthinkable for European implementation. However, over a three, six or perhaps even nine-month period it would have been, and is, perfectly possible to achieve their goal with a proper localised HR authored plan, a good project manager, patience and a certain amount of fortitude.

How not to change a global corporate policy

5.11 Late one Friday night, while I was out to dinner in London, my mobile phone went into a sort of meltdown. It was dinging, pinging, ringing and vibrating like seldom before or since. I was quite sure someone in my immediate family had been injured or, God forbid, had died. I made my excuses, apologies and departed the dinner table for what I hoped would be a brief sojourn into Berkeley Square to discover the cause behind my phone's then slowing but continued cacophony.

5.12 My first glance at the phone indicated that no one died, at least not in my immediate family, but the worrying possibility of a corporate officer kidnapping, serious industrial accident; a major IT system failure or huge security breach were now the main possibilities whirring in my head given the EMEA President, the EMEA COO, the EMEA CIO, the EMEA CFO and the European HR Officer were among the people ringing, texting and emailing me frantically at 21.30 on a Friday night. Most of the messages, helpfully, just said 'Call me, urgently!' or some such similarly ineloquent gibberish.

5.13 I called the EMEA President. His first words to me were, 'Have you seen the email that arrived this evening?!' I explained that it was now after 21.30 on a Friday evening, I was out to dinner in London, and no I'd not been monitoring emails. He then blabbered on, in an angry and yet strikingly panicky voice, to explain that a global email had been circulated (at the close of business in the United States) by a global headquarters based Executive Vice President stating that all corporate issued Blackberries, mobile phones and other mobile wireless technology devices issued to employees were being withdrawn, were to be returned to the company and their service provider contracts were being terminated immediately. The employees who had seen it that evening were rather upset and were ringing their bosses to protest (some in the strongest terms possible) and then he said to me and I quote 'How the hell did you let this happen!' My reply was: 'I had no advance knowledge of this policy change and that I was not consulted about it prior to the change.' I had had a glass or two of wine that evening but I did just mange to filter out a profanity laden suffix to my reply.

5.14 The offending email stated that the company was instituting a Bring Your Own Device (BYOD) policy. It was a cost saving measure. The key elements of the policy were:

- the company would no longer provide Blackberries, mobile phones or other wireless devices for their employees to use in the course of their employment and employees with company provided devices would be required to return them;

- employees who required wireless devices in order to undertake their work for the company must use their own personal devices;
- the company would not be reimbursing the full cost of acquiring, maintaining or operating the devices to any employee. Rather, the company would stratify the various employees subjectively, and offer varying degrees of reimbursement depending on the person's role, through the expense system. All expenses in excess of the subjective and arbitrarily assigned USD cap, regardless of whether business related or not, would be the employee's sole responsibility;
- that upon an employee leaving the company the employee's device would be confiscated by the company and wiped or if the employee did not surrender the device it would be remotely wiped by a security programme that was required to be loaded on the device before it could be linked to the company's IT systems and email network; and
- post-termination of employment any finance agreement or other related cost of the device would be the employee's sole responsibility.

5.15 Needless to say, the North American headquarters' based centralised functions of HR, IT and Legal departments had all signed off on the policy and, when asked why they didn't consult or even merely out of courtesy give us a heads up, they explained every company is doing it, it is accepted practice (in the US) and 'we didn't think there was any need to consult with you on the matter'.

5.16 Keep in mind this email went to circa 2,000 individual employees in 28 European countries. With that, and brevity, in mind I'm going to break down the consequences in the UK only, as its law and legal system is arguably the most employer-friendly of the lot.

5.17 On the facts above, our external counsel at the start of the next week, found in their UK analysis that every UK employee (200 of them with company issued devices) through the past custom and practice of the company had acquired a contractual entitlement: (i) to be provided with a mobile device by the company; (ii) to use that device for personal as well as business purposes; and (iii) had no obligation to pay anything towards the line rental or other usage costs of the company provided devices.

5.18 Therefore, such a unilateral action by the company:

- was itself, in all probability, a breach of contract; and
- amounted to a probable breach of contract in requiring its employees to then bear the costs of using personal devices for work purposes, even partially.

5.19 The basis for these breaches (likely successfully) could be argued either as breaches of terms implied by the business' actual former custom and practice or alternatively a breach of the term of trust and confidence implied by law into every employment agreement. In addition, the company's course of action was also highly likely to be a breach of its implied duty to indemnify certain employees in respect of costs, claims and expenses correctly and necessarily incurred by the employee in the carrying out of their duties. Finally, all such breaches may be committed on an 'anticipatory basis'. The mere communication of a settled intention to introduce the new policy would constitute a breach.

5.20 In a nutshell; three seemingly well educated, experienced teams of professionals working together (but without reference to their global colleagues), all stationed in the company's US Global Corporate Headquarters, approved a global policy change rollout that with one email policy fundamentally breached the employment agreements of almost 200 UK employees, each of whom was then immediately, perfectly entitled to down tools, leave work and treat themselves as constructively dismissed. In such circumstances each employee could have then claimed damages for pay and benefits they would have received in their notice period (contractual or statutory, whichever was longer) and those with more than one year of service could make a further claim for unfair dismissal for an amount then capped at £72,000. Do the math! That's a (likely reportable) legal contingent liability of £14,400,000 without the notice and other costs for just the UK sales operation, from just one email!

5.21 In addition, believe it or not, as if to add insult to injury the company could have also been pushed into a potential collective redundancy situation with a duty to inform the government, and consult with appropriately elected UK employee representatives. I won't elaborate any further because just reliving it as a mere memory still makes my head hurt.

5.22 In the end we retracted the notice in writing across EMEA and held our collective breath. No one in the UK left or sued but employee trust in the business was shattered, the esteem in which the employees previously held the European Executive leadership team was seriously undermined and the business relationship between the European Executive leadership and their American masters was very, very badly (I'd say irreparably) damaged.

5.23 Ultimately, I'd like to point out that the intended change was to create a global annual saving of less than $1M for a company with a multi-billion annual turnover.

5.24 Every time I think of this episode of my career the following quote comes to mind:

> 'There are three kinds of men. The one that learns by reading. The few who learn by observation. The rest of them have to pee on the electric fence for themselves.'
>
> Will Rogers

Employment terms and conditions

5.25 Under the terms of the European Union Written Statement Directive all employees must be given a written statement setting out their terms and conditions within 28 days of starting employment. This right does not give rise or amount to a general legal requirement for all businesses to have written employments of contract with each and every one of its employees. Indeed, whether or not there is a legal requirement for written contractual employment agreements is a matter for legislation in each of the member states.

5.26 It goes without saying that best practice dictates written contractual employment agreements for medium and large businesses with Human Resource functions.

5.27 It is axiomatic to say that contracts of employment are legally binding agreements between employer and employee. In the UK they consist of express written or oral terms, together with implied terms which are usually not expressly stated but incorporated in some other way, usually by law. Although employment contracts are governed by contract law, there are many statutory rules which affect employment contracts too.

5.28 A full exposition on the species of employment contracts, their comparative benefits and risks and their suitability is a matter for a full text in and of itself. However, it is useful to consider some topics in this context as it represents a common pitfall for corporate counsel.

Basic terms of employment

5.29 Certain basic terms should be included in an employment contract:[1]

(1) parties to the employment contract (employer and employee);

(2) place of work – if there is no fixed place of work, you should highlight that the employee will work in various locations and say where your business is registered;

(3) title, grade, category of work or a job description/brief specification of tasks;

(4) start date;

(5) expected duration of the job if the contract is temporary;

(6) number of days of paid annual holidays;

(7) length of notice periods for you and the employee if one of you terminates the contract;

(8) initial basic salary, frequency of payment, any other components of remuneration;

(9) length of the normal working day or working week (working hours);

(10) rules of any collective agreements governing the employee's conditions of work, if appropriate.

Working Time Directive

5.30 The European Union's Working Time Directive (2003/88/EC) was implemented in the United Kingdom in 1998. It introduced a maximum 48-hour work week; a daily rest period of at least 11 consecutive hours; a weekly rest period of 24 consecutive hours and rest breaks during the working day.

5.31 The directive also provides, amongst other things, employees a statutory right to paid annual leave and this right was further extended through the ECJ's interpretation, to give employees who fall ill during a period of scheduled leave the right to reschedule that leave.

5.32 An employer, in the UK for instance, found to be in breach of the Working Time Regulations, may be liable to sanction. This may range from the service of an improvement notice, which if left unaddressed or where subsequent breaches are found, may lead to unlimited fines and/or imprisonment. Alternatively, breaches may

1 Guidance provided by the European Union at https://europa.eu/youreurope/business/human-resources/ employment-contracts/employment-terms/index_en.htm.

be referred by an employee to an Employment Tribunal which can order payment of compensation to the employee.

Maternity rights

5.33 The European Union's Pregnant Workers Directive (92/85/EEC) provided pregnant employees with an array of statutory rights, including but not limited to 14 weeks maternity leave (two of which must occur before birth); paid time off for ante-natal appointments; a duty for employers to undertake risk assessments and to adjust working conditions (for instance the transfer of a pregnant or breastfeeding employee to alternative work and in certain circumstances to suspend the employee on paid leave).

5.34 More importantly the directive makes it clear that treating a woman unfavourably because of pregnancy or maternity leave amounts to direct sex discrimination and that it is not necessary to identify a non-pregnant comparator, in circumstances similar, to prove discrimination.

5.35 Through the judicial interpretation the ECJ has also extended the directive's protections against dismissal, on grounds of pregnancy or maternity leave, to fixed-term workers as well as full employees.

5.36 In the UK as an example, since 2008, women on additional maternity leave have had access to the same contractual rights as women on ordinary maternity leave as a result of ECJ case law. This means, for example, that employers are obliged to make contributions into occupational pension schemes for longer than the first 26 weeks of their ordinary leave.

Parental leave

5.37 Under the European Union's Parental Leave Directive (2010/18/EU) working parents have the right to take unpaid leave from work to look after a child. In addition, under the auspices of the Parental Leave Directive, employees are also afforded the right to time off work for urgent family reasons, for example, if they have a sick child (or possibly other dependant) who they need to take to the doctor or for who's care the employee needs time to arrange.

5.38 Regardless of their type of contract (part-time, full-time, etc), given the disparity between national provisions on this topic it is necessary to obtain local advice, but the following points might be made generally:

- Employees must not be treated detrimentally simply because they requested parental leave, nor treated relatively less favourably than other staff.
- Both parents are entitled to at least four months leave each, typically non-transferable, though this varies.
- Under EU rules, staff can take parental leave at any time until the child is eight years old. However, this age limit may be lower in some countries, under national law.
- On return from parental leave, an employee is entitled to return to the same job. If that is not possible, a similar job in line with their employment contract must be offered.

- If returning employees request temporary changes to their working hours/patterns, you are obliged to give this request due consideration and make a sound business case for any refusal.
- In the UK by way of example, the amount of leave any parent is legally entitled to take is 18 weeks per child and the upper age limit of the child or dependant, determining the right, is now 18 years of age.

Discrimination

5.39 Employees in the UK and the EU benefit from a wide range of protections against discrimination on the basis of their sex, race, age, religion or belief, sexual orientation, disability and gender reassignment.

5.40 It is also noteworthy that:

- the EU Burden of Proof Directive (97/80/EC) provides for a reversal of the burden of proof in sex discrimination cases. Thus, where a plaintiff shows an arguable case of discrimination, the burden of proof shifts to the defendant, who has to demonstrate that there has been no discrimination (this directive does not apply to criminal cases); and
- under EU law member states are not permitted to enact legislation that would cap or place an upper limit on the quantum of compensation that may be awarded in discrimination cases.

A comparative analysis of discriminatory protections is beyond the scope of this work, the authors felt it useful to set out the provisions of UK national law with regard to employment issues to serve as an example and analogue of how such protections are practically applied at a local level. Corporate counsel should consider the appropriateness of local legal advice in every case.

Whistleblowing and protected disclosures

5.41 This topic is of particular relevance to corporate counsel, especially in a human resources context, as unlawful activities and abuse of law may occur in any organisation, whether private or public, big or small. In this regard, the treatment by the organisation of a person seeking to make or who has made a protected disclosure is a sensitive and danger ridden path for corporate counsel.

Background

5.42 Whistleblowers, that is, persons who report (within the organisation concerned or to an outside authority) or disclose (to the public) information on a wrongdoing obtained in a work-related context, may help prevent damage and detect threat or harm to the public interest that may otherwise remain hidden. However, they are often discouraged from reporting their concerns for fear of retaliation. For these reasons, the importance of providing effective whistleblower protection for safeguarding the public interest is increasingly acknowledged both at European and international level. The whistleblower protection currently available across the EU is fragmented, hence the EU has drafted a proposal for a new directive on the protection of persons reporting on breaches of Union law which sets out a range of protections. Of significant relevance to corporate counsel is the proposed requirement that workers and their trade unions should be fully consulted on envisaged internal procedures for facilitating whistleblowing.[2] Counsel should maintain a watching brief on this topic.

National example

5.43 Fragmented protections are available at a national level around Europe. In particular, a good example is that of the UK and its Public Interest Disclosure Act of 1998[3] which seeks to protect individuals who make certain disclosures of information in the public interest; to allow such individuals to bring action in respect of victimisation. Such disclosures may be defined as

> '... any disclosure of information which, in the reasonable belief of the worker making the disclosure, tends to show one or more of the following:[4]
>
> (a) that a criminal offence has been committed, is being committed or is likely to be committed,
>
> (b) that a person has failed, is failing or is likely to fail to comply with any legal obligation to which he is subject,
>
> (c) that a miscarriage of justice has occurred, is occurring or is likely to occur,
>
> (d) that the health or safety of any individual has been, is being or is likely to be endangered,
>
> (e) that the environment has been, is being or is likely to be damaged, or
>
> (f) that information tending to show any matter falling within any one of the preceding paragraphs has been, is being or is likely to be deliberately concealed.'
>
> 'A worker has the right not to be subjected to any detriment by any act, or any deliberate failure to act, by his employer done on the ground that the worker has made a protected disclosure.'[5]

Health and Safety at Work

5.44 The welfare of people whilst at work has undergone a revolution in the EMEA region over many decades. While patchy and piecemeal attempts at safeguarding those at work typically occurred in conjunction with the ebb and flow of workers' rights on a political level, the EU sought, since its creation, to create a framework to harmonise and encourage efforts in this regard.

Legislative aims

5.45 A battery of legislation has been developed committed to the adoption of minimum requirements for encouraging improvements, especially in the working environment, to guarantee a better level of protection of the safety and health of

2 See Proposal for a Directive of the European Parliament and of the Council on the protection of persons reporting on breaches of Union law – Brussels, 23.4.2018 COM (2018) 218.

3 Which amends the Employment Rights Act 1996.

4 Public Interest Disclosure Act 1998, s 1.

5 Public Interest Disclosure Act 1998, s 2.

workers,[6] encouraging improvements in conditions in this area and harmonising conditions while maintaining the improvements made.

5.46 Member states have a basic responsibility to encourage improvements in the safety and health of workers on their territory,[7] whereas taking measures to protect the health and safety of workers at work also helps, in certain cases, to preserve the health and possibly the safety of persons residing in those territories.

5.47 It was recognised that member states' legislative systems covering safety and health at the workplace differed widely and needed to be improved. Further, national provisions on the subject, which often include technical specifications and/or self-regulatory standards, typically result in different levels of safety and health protection and allow competition at the expense of safety and health.[8]

5.48 It has been historically considered axiomatic at an institutional level, that the incidence of accidents at work and occupational diseases were too high and that preventive measures must be introduced or improved without delay in order to safeguard the safety and health of workers and ensure a higher degree of protection.

5.49 The Council Directive of 1989 sought to ensure an improved degree of protection, it was noted therein that as a basic requirement, workers and/or their representatives must be informed of the risks to their safety and health and of the measures required to reduce or eliminate these risks. Similarly, workers must also be in a position to contribute, by means of balanced participation in accordance with national laws and/or practices, to seeing that the necessary protective measures are taken.

Relevant legislative instruments

5.50 A full treatise on health and safety legislation in the EMEA region is most certainly beyond the scope of this work. However, it is considered by the authors beneficial to set out some preliminary information, relevant to corporate counsel at a European level, to allow for a wider discussion on the matter and to allow for issue identification. The implementation of such policy at a national level should, in specific cases, be referred to local counsel.

Framework Directive

5.51 Council Directive 89/391/EEC deals with the introduction of measures to encourage improvements in the safety and health of workers at work (Framework Directive).

Pregnant and breastfeeding workers

5.52 Council Directive 92/85/EEC sets out the minimum requirements to ensure the safety of pregnant workers and workers who have recently given birth or are breastfeeding. The directive also includes provisions for physical movements and postures, mental and physical fatigue and other types of physical and mental stress.

6 Council Directive 89/391/EEC of 12 June 1989 on the introduction of measures to encourage improvements in the safety and health of workers at work.
7 See preamble to Council Directive 89/391/EEC of 12 June 1989 on the introduction of measures to encourage improvements in the safety and health of workers at work.
8 ibid, as per directive recitals.

Such workers may not be exposed to agents that might harm their health or that of their child.[9]

Protections for young people at work

5.53 Council Directive 94/33/EC provides for the protection of young people at work. Member states are required to take the necessary measures to prohibit work by children. The minimum working or employment age must not be lower than the minimum age at which compulsory full-time schooling, as imposed by national law, ends or 15 years in any event.[10] This directive shall apply to any person under 18 years of age having an employment contract or an employment relationship defined by the law in force. Exceptions can be adopted by member states for occasional work or short-term work, involving domestic service in a private household or work regarded as not being harmful, damaging or dangerous to young people in a family undertaking. The legislation defines 'young people' as people under the age of 18 and 'children' as young people under the age of 15 or who are still in full-time compulsory education in accordance with national legislation. Adolescents are young people between the ages of 15 and 18 who are no longer in full-time compulsory education in accordance with national legislation.

Manual handling of loads

5.54 Council Directive 90/269/EEC sets outs employers' obligations in respect of manual handling of loads where there is a risk of injury. Employers shall take appropriate organisational measures, or shall use the appropriate means, in particular mechanical equipment, in order to avoid the need for the manual handling of loads by workers. Where the need for the manual handling of loads by workers cannot be avoided, the employer shall take the appropriate organisational measures, use the appropriate means or provide workers with such means in order to reduce the risk involved in the manual handling of such loads.[11] In particular, the guidance notes that wherever the need for manual handling of loads by workers cannot be avoided, the employer shall organise workstations in such a way as to make such handling as safe and healthy as possible and assess, in advance if possible, the health and safety conditions of the type of work involved, and in particular examine the characteristics of loads.

The use of work equipment by workers at work

5.55 Directive 2009/104/EC, now inter alia governs this area. In particular, the employer is required under the directive to take every measure to ensure the safety of the work equipment made available to workers. During the selection of the work equipment the employer shall pay attention to the specific working conditions which exist at the workplace, especially in relation to safety and health of the workers. If risks cannot be fully eliminated during the operation of the work equipment, the employer shall take appropriate measures to minimise them. Furthermore it is a requirement that throughout its working life, the employer must keep the work equipment compliant by means of adequate maintenance. The employer shall ensure that the work equipment is installed correctly and is operating properly by inspection/testing of the

---

9 'Pregnant and breastfeeding workers may under no circumstances be obliged to perform duties for which the assessment has revealed a risk of exposure to agents, which would jeopardize their safety or health', European Agency for Safety and Health at Work.

10 See guidance provided by the European Agency for Safety and Health at Work.

11 See guidance provided by the European Agency for Safety and Health at Work and Annex 1 thereto

work equipment (initial, after assembly, periodic and special) by competent persons. The results of inspections shall be recorded and kept.[12]

The use of personal protective equipment at the workplace

5.56 Council Directive 89/656/EEC sets out the employers' obligations as regards the provision and use of personal protective equipment. Personal protective equipment must be used when the risks cannot be avoided or sufficiently limited by technical means of collective protection or procedures of work organisation. All personal protective equipment must:[13]

- be appropriate for the risks involved, without itself leading to any increased risk;
- correspond to existing conditions at the workplace;
- take account of ergonomic requirements and the worker's state of health;
- fit the wearer correctly after any necessary adjustment.

Work with display screen equipment

5.57 Council Directive 90/270/EEC requires that employers are obliged to perform an analysis of workstations in order to evaluate the safety and health conditions to which they give rise for their workers, particularly as regards possible risks to eyesight, physical problems and problems of mental stress. They shall take appropriate measures to remedy the risks found taking account of the additional and/or combined effects of the risks so found. Workers shall also receive information on all aspects of safety and health relating to their workstation. Workers or their representatives shall be informed of any health and safety measure taken by the employer. Every worker must also receive training in use of the workstation before commencing this type of work and whenever the organisation of the workstation is substantially modified.

Requirements at temporary or mobile construction sites

5.58 Council Directive 92/57/EEC sets out that the project supervisor must nominate person(s) responsible for the coordination of health and safety at sites where several firms are present. Where a person responsible for coordination is appointed, the project supervisor or client remains responsible for safety and health. The person(s) responsible for coordination on the site shall ensure that employers and self-employed persons apply the general prevention principles, particularly in respect of the situations described, and that the health and safety plan is taken into account when necessary. They shall also organise cooperation between employers in matters of health and safety and check that the working procedures are being implemented correctly as well as ensure that no unauthorised persons enter the site.[14] The employers' obligations are, inter alia:

- to adhere to the minimum safety and health requirements applicable to work sites set out in Annex IV to the directive. The aspects covered include energy distribution systems, emergency routes and exits, ventilation, temperature, traffic routes and danger areas, sanitary installations, etc;
- to act on the comments of the health and safety coordinator.

---

12 See guidance provided by the European Agency for Safety and Health at Work.

13 See Annexes to legislation and guidance from the European Agency for Safety and Health at Work for specific advice relating to requirements in this regard.

14 See guidance provided by the European Agency for Safety and Health at Work.

Workers in surface and underground mineral-extracting industries

5.59 Council Directive 92/104/EEC requires that employers must take the following measures to safeguard the health and safety of workers by ensuring that:

- workplaces are designed, constructed, equipped, commissioned, operated and maintained to allow workers to perform the work assigned to them without endangering their own and others' health or safety;
- operation of workplaces takes place under the supervision of a person in charge;
- work involving a special risk is only carried out by competent staff in accordance with employers' instructions;
- all safety instructions are comprehensible to workers;
- appropriate first aid facilities are available; and
- any relevant safety drills are performed regularly.

Requirements for work on board fishing vessels

5.60 Council Directive 93/103/EC requires that workers and their representatives must be informed of all measures to be taken regarding safety and health on board vessels and this information must be comprehensible to the workers concerned. Workers must be given suitable training on safety and health on board vessels and on accident prevention. The training must cover fire-fighting, the use of life-saving and survival equipment, the use of fishing gear and hauling equipment as well as the use of signs and hand signals. Moreover, any person likely to command a vessel must be given detailed training.[15]

Requirements for improved medical treatment on board vessels

5.61 The objective of Council Directive 92/29/EEC is to improve medical assistance at sea since a vessel represents a workplace involving a wide range of risks. Specific advice and guidance is available via the European Agency for Safety and Health at Work as to the medical equipment and supplies that must be provided on board vessels.

Protection of the health and safety of workers from the risks related to chemical agents

5.62 Council Directive 98/24/EC governs the protection of workers from the risks related to chemical agents at work. The employer must determine whether any hazardous chemical agents are present at the workplace and assess any risk to safety and health arising from their presence. The employer must be in possession of an assessment of the risk and this assessment shall be kept up-to-date, particularly if there have been significant changes or if the results of health surveillance show it to be necessary. In the case of activities involving exposure to several hazardous chemical agents, the risks must be assessed on the basis of the risk presented by all such chemical agents in combination.

15 See guidance provided by the European Agency for Safety and Health at Work.

Protection of workers from the risks related to exposure to asbestos

5.63 A common fear for corporate counsel arises in this regard. Council Directive 2009/148/EC sets out the protection requirements of workers from the risks related to exposure to asbestos. This directive applies to activities in which workers are or may be exposed to dust arising from asbestos or materials containing asbestos in the course of their work. If any activity is likely to involve such risk of exposure, a risk assessment must be carried out including consultation with the workers. The risk assessment has to determine the nature and degree of the workers' exposure to dust arising from asbestos or materials containing asbestos and it must be revised if circumstances change significantly. If the exposure of the worker is sporadic and of low intensity with the exposure limit not exceeded, the activity need not be notified, health assessment of workers and clinical surveillance are not obligatory and workers need not be registered.[16]

Protection from carcinogens or mutagens

5.64 Council Directive 2004/37/EC relates to the protection of workers from the risks related to exposure to carcinogens or mutagens. The employer must assess and manage the risk of exposure to carcinogens or mutagens. This process shall be renewed regularly and data shall be supplied to the authorities upon request. Special attention should be paid to investigate and take account of all possible ways of exposure (including all skin-related possibilities), and to persons at particular risk. The directive requires that workers' exposure must be prevented. If replacement is not possible, the employer shall use a closed technological system. The employer shall reduce the use of carcinogens or mutagens by replacing them with a substance that is not dangerous or is less dangerous. Where a closed system is not technically possible, the employer shall reduce exposure to the minimum.

Exposure of workers to noise

5.65 Noise induced hearing loss claims are a frequent occurrence, though the frequency with which these cases arise may be said to be waning and they typically arise on a historical basis given the broad adoption of improved practices. Council Directive 2003/10/EC sets out the requirements regarding the exposure of workers to the risks from noise at work. The employer shall assess and, if necessary, measure the levels of exposure to noise to which workers are exposed. This has to be done in accordance with the obligations laid down by the Framework Directive. Results of the risk assessment have to be recorded on a suitable medium and kept up to date on a regular basis. The risk assessment shall be updated on a regular basis, particularly if there have been significant changes which could render it out of date, or if the results of health surveillance show it to be necessary. When carrying out the risk assessment, the employer must give particular attention to level, type and duration of exposure, exposure limit/action values, health effects spreading from particular sensitivity of the worker, interactions with other risks (ototoxic substances, vibrations), the exposure to noise beyond normal working hours under his responsibility, and noise caused by warning signals at work. The risks arising from exposure to noise must be eliminated or reduced to a minimum

16 This directive was adopted and the previous Directive 83/477/EEC and its amendments have been repealed.

Protection of workers from exposure to biological agents

5.66 Council Directive 2000/54/EC sets out the protections for workers from risks related to exposure to biological agents at work. Employers should avoid using a harmful biological agent by replacing it with one which is not dangerous or is less dangerous to workers' health, if possible. Workers' risk of exposure to biological agents should be reduced where possible to protect their health and safety. Where the results of the risk assessment reveal a risk to workers' health or safety, employers shall, when requested, make available to the competent authority appropriate information. Employers must ensure hygiene and individual protection by prohibiting eating or drinking in working areas, providing protective clothing, providing appropriate toilet and washing facilities and maintaining protective equipment properly. Further, workers and their representatives must receive appropriate training involving working with biological agents and be provided with written instructions and display notices of the procedure to be followed in case of a serious accident.

Protection for temporary employees

5.67 Council Directive 91/383/EEC on the safety of temporary workers (Temporary Workers Directive) provides that a temporary worker must be informed beforehand of any risks he/she faces in any activity he takes up. They must be informed of any special occupational qualifications or skills or special medical surveillance required, and if there are increased specific risks involved in the activity.[17]

Staff handbooks

5.68 Whilst not a strict requirement under UK law or European law, the provision of comprehensive staff handbooks to employees of all manner has represented an effective way for organisations to communicate essential policy aims and objectives to employees. Frequently the contents of staff handbooks form key evidences in any employment law claims and actions brought. Below is a sample table of contents that might inform corporate counsel of key aspects of what is typically included. However, a full exposition on the exact contents of each, relevant to each EMEA jurisdiction, is beyond the scope of this work.

1. Welcome
2. Introduction to Company

Part One – Contractual Rules and Policies and Procedures

3. Conflicts of Interest
4. Discoveries and Inventions

Part Two – Non Contractual Policies

5. Equal Opportunities Policy
6. Code of Business Conduct and Ethics
7. Agency Workers
8. Bullying and Harassment
9. Disciplinary Procedure
10. Annual Performance

17 See guidance provided by the European Agency for Safety and Health at Work.

11. Performance Management Policy
12. Grievance Procedure

Absence and Leave Policies

13. Holidays and Time Off
14. Sickness Absence Policy
15. Whistleblowing Policy
16. Maternity Policy
17. Paternity Leave
18. Adoption Policy
19. Shared Parental Leave Policy
20. Leave for dependants
21. Parental Leave
22. Flexible Working
23. Data Protection Policy
24. Social Media Policy
25. Company Car Policy
26. Pensions and Life Insurance
27. Security
28. Company Property
29. Personal and Lost Property
30. Right of Search
31. Overtime Policy
32. Smoking
33. Staff Purchases
34. Long Service Awards

Miscellaneous

35. Health and Safety Policy
36. Drugs and alcohol
37. Environmental Policy
38. Group Quality Policy
39. Policy Guidelines on employing family members and significant others
40. Training and Development
41. Electronic communications Policy
42. Travelling and Expenses Policy
43. Leaving ACCO UK Limited
44. Life assurance cover for those working beyond age 65
45. Pension options for those working beyond age 65

46. Relocation Policy
47. Company Sick Pay for production Workers
48. Overtime and Shifts
49. Accidents
50. Canteen
51. Change of address
52. Fire Procedure
53. First Aid
54. Notice Boards
55. Protective Clothing, footwear and other PPE
56. Personal Electronic Equipment
57. Speed Limits on Company property
58. Pregnant Workers Procedure
59. Health & safety
60. Work related Upper Limb Disorder Procedure
61. Young Persons Protection Policy

Whistleblowing and protected disclosures

5.69 This topic is of particular relevance to corporate counsel, especially in a human resources context, as unlawful activities and abuse of law may occur in any organisation, whether private or public, big or small. In this regard, the treatment by the organisation of a person seeking to make or who has made a protected disclosure is a sensitive and danger ridden path for corporate counsel.

Background

5.70 Whistleblowers, that is, persons who report (within the organisation concerned or to an outside authority) or disclose (to the public) information on a wrongdoing obtained in a work-related context, help prevent damage and detect threat or harm to the public interest that may otherwise remain hidden. However, they are often discouraged from reporting their concerns for fear of retaliation. For these reasons, the importance of providing effective whistleblower protection for safeguarding the public interest is increasingly acknowledged both at European and international level. The whistleblower protection currently available across the EU is fragmented, hence the EU has drafted a proposal for a new directive on the protection of persons reporting on breaches of Union law which sets out a range of protections. Of significant relevance to corporate counsel is the proposed requirement that workers and their trade unions should be fully consulted on envisaged internal procedures for facilitating whistleblowing.[18]

18 See Proposal for a Directive of the European Parliament and of the Council on the protection of persons reporting on breaches of Union law – Brussels, 23.4.2018 COM (2018) 218.

National example

5.71 Fragmented protections are available at a national level around Europe. In particular, a good example is that of the UK and its Public Interest Disclosure Act of 1998[19] which seeks to protect individuals who make certain disclosures of information in the public interest; to allow such individuals to bring action in respect of victimisation. Such disclosures may be defined as

> '... any disclosure of information which, in the reasonable belief of the worker making the disclosure, tends to show one or more of the following:[20]
>
> (a) that a criminal offence has been committed, is being committed or is likely to be committed,
>
> (b) that a person has failed, is failing or is likely to fail to comply with any legal obligation to which he is subject,
>
> (c) that a miscarriage of justice has occurred, is occurring or is likely to occur,
>
> (d) that the health or safety of any individual has been, is being or is likely to be endangered,
>
> (e) that the environment has been, is being or is likely to be damaged, or
>
> (f) that information tending to show any matter falling within any one of the preceding paragraphs has been, is being or is likely to be deliberately concealed.'
>
> 'A worker has the right not to be subjected to any detriment by any act, or any deliberate failure to act, by his employer done on the ground that the worker has made a protected disclosure.'[21]

Recruitment issues

Discrimination

5.72 The Charter on Fundamental Human Rights is the foundation stone for much of the anti-discriminatory provisions of national law as they pertain to recruitment. It is worth restating some fundamental ideas contained therein on the subject of equality.

European background

5.73 Everyone is equal before the law.[22] Any discrimination based on any ground such as sex, race, colour, ethnic or social origin, genetic features, language, religion or belief, political or any other opinion, membership of a national minority, property, birth, disability, age or sexual orientation is prohibited.[23] It should also be recalled that within the scope of application of the Treaties and without prejudice to any of their specific provisions, any discrimination on grounds of nationality is also prohibited.[24]

---

19 Which amends the Employment Rights Act 1996.
20 Public Interest Disclosure Act 1998, s 1.
21 Public Interest Disclosure Act 1998, s 2.
22 The Charter on Fundamental Human Rights, Art 20.
23 ibid, Art 21.
24 ibid, Art 21(3).

5.74 Equality between women and men must also be ensured in all areas, including employment, work and pay[25] though the principle of equality shall not prevent the maintenance or adoption of measures providing for specific advantages in favour of the under-represented sex.[26]

5.75 Whilst the Charter Rights on this topic create a series of policy aims, national legislatures are left with a significant degree of autonomy as to how such aims are met. A comparative analysis of discriminatory protections is beyond the scope of this work; however it is useful to set out the provisions of UK national law with regard to employment issues, to serve as an example and analogue of how such protections are practically applied at a local level. Corporate counsel should consider the necessity for and appropriateness of local legal advice in every case.

Equality Act 2010 (UK)

5.76 The general statement of the law is that an employer (A) must not discriminate against a person (B) in the arrangements A makes for deciding to whom to offer employment and/or as to the terms on which A offers B employment and/or by not offering B employment.[27]

5.77 Legislative guidance on this section is worthy of consideration:[28]

> 'This section makes it unlawful for an employer to discriminate against or victimise employees and people seeking work. It applies where the employer is making arrangements to fill a job, and in respect of anything done in the course of a person's employment. In respect of discrimination because of sex or pregnancy and maternity, a term of an offer of employment which relates to pay is treated as discriminatory where, if accepted, it would give rise to an equality clause or if an equality clause does not apply, where the offer of the term constitutes direct or dual discrimination.'

5.78 The guidance goes on to helpfully provide examples of such behaviour which is similarly worthy of consideration:[29]

- 'An employer decides not to shortlist for interview a disabled job applicant because of her epilepsy. This would be direct discrimination.
- An employer offers a woman a job on lower pay than the set rate because she is pregnant when she applies. She cannot bring an equality clause case as there is no comparator. However, she will be able to claim direct discrimination.
- An employer refuses to interview a man applying for promotion, because he previously supported a discrimination case against the employer brought by another employee. This would be victimisation.
- An employer enforces a "no beards" policy by asking staff to shave. This could be indirect discrimination, because it would have a particular impact on Muslims or Orthodox Jews.'

---

25 ibid, Art 23.
26 ibid, Art 23.
27 Equality Act 2010, s 39(1).
28 Para 143 et seq of the explanatory notes to the Equality Act 2010.
29 ibid.

5.79 When enquiring about disability and health matters, a person (A) to whom an application for work is made must not ask about the health of the applicant (B) before offering work to B, or where A is not in a position to offer work to B, before including B in a pool of applicants from whom A intends (when in a position to do so) to select a person to whom to offer work.[30] Legislative guidance on this section is also illuminating:[31]

> 'Except in the situations specified in this section, an employer must not ask about a job applicant's health until that person has been either offered a job (on a conditional or unconditional basis) or been included in a pool of successful candidates to be offered a job when a suitable position arises. The specified situations where health-related enquiries can be made are for the purposes of:
>
> - finding out whether a job applicant would be able to participate in an assessment to test his or her suitability for the work;
> - making reasonable adjustments to enable the disabled person to participate in the recruitment process;
> - finding out whether a job applicant would be able to undertake a function that is intrinsic to the job, with reasonable adjustments in place as required;
> - monitoring diversity in applications for jobs;
> - supporting positive action in employment for disabled people; and
> - enabling an employer to identify suitable candidates for a job where there is an occupational requirement for the person to be disabled.'
>
> The section also allows questions to be asked where they are needed in the context of national security vetting.
>
> Where an employer makes a health or disability-related enquiry which falls outside the specified situations, he or she would be acting unlawfully under the Equality Act 2006. Together with Schedule 26, this section gives the Equality and Human Rights Commission (EHRC) an enforcement role. (Section 120(8) ensures that only the EHRC can enforce a breach of this provision.) This means, for example, that the EHRC would be able to conduct an investigation if there was evidence that a large employer might be routinely asking prohibited questions when recruiting.
>
> Where the employer asks a question not allowed by this section and rejects the applicant, if the applicant then makes a claim to the employment tribunal for direct disability discrimination, it will be for the employer to show that it had not discriminated against the candidate.
>
> As well as applying to recruitment to employment, the section also applies to the other areas covered by Part 5 of the Act, such as contract work, business partnerships, office-holders, barristers and advocates.'

30 Equality Act 2010, s 60.
31 Para 197 et seq of the explanatory notes to the Equality Act 2010.

5.80 The guidance goes on to helpfully provide examples of such behaviour which is similarly worthy of consideration:[32]

> 'Applicants are asked on an application form whether they have a disability that requires the employer to make a reasonable adjustment to the recruitment process. This is to allow, for example, people with a speech impairment more time for interview. This enquiry would be permitted.
>
> An applicant applies for a job in a warehouse, which requires the manual lifting and handling of heavy items. As manual handling is a function which is intrinsic to the job, the employer is permitted to ask the applicant questions about his health to establish whether he is able to do the job (with reasonable adjustments for a disabled applicant, if required). The employer would not be permitted to ask the applicant other health questions until he or she offered the candidate a job.'

Immigration

5.81 Matters of immigration are subject to such a degree of divergence across the EMEA region that local advice should be sought in all circumstances and a synopsis of immigration issues would not be helpful to this discussion in the absence of specifics.

Holiday entitlement, working time and pay

Holiday entitlement

Annual leave

5.82 Over and above daily and weekly rest periods, employees are entitled to, at minimum, four weeks of paid holidays per year. Payment in lieu will not suffice for holidays unless the employment contract has ended before the employee has used up all their annual leave.

Parental leave

5.83 Employees (male and female) are entitled to parental leave on the birth or adoption of a child – regardless of their type of contract (part-time, full-time, etc). Given the disparity between national provisions on this topic it is necessary to obtain local advice but the following points might be made generally:[33]

- Employees must not be treated detrimentally simply because they requested parental leave, nor treated relatively less favourably than other staff.
- Both parents are entitled to at least four months leave each, typically non-transferable, though this varies.
- Under EU rules, staff can take parental leave at any time until the child is eight years old. However, this age limit may be lower in some countries, under national law.

---

32 ibid.

33 See Your Europe, European Union Information Portal, available at https://europa.eu/youreurope/business/human-resources/working-hours-holiday-leave/parental-leave/index_en.htm.

- On return from parental leave, an employee is entitled to return to the same job. If that's not possible, a similar job in line with their employment contract must be offered.
- If returning employees request temporary changes to their working hours/ patterns, you are obliged to give this request due consideration and make a sound business case for any refusal.

Working time

5.84 Council Directive 2003/88/EC, referred to as the 'Working Time' Directive is of particular practical importance to corporate counsel. It is a wide-ranging directive designed to ensure that every worker is entitled to a minimum daily rest period of 11 consecutive hours per 24-hour period. Moreover, they shall take the measures necessary to ensure that, per each seven-day period, every worker is entitled to a minimum uninterrupted rest period of 24 hours (plus the 11 hours' daily rest if possible). In addition the directive requires that every worker is entitled to a rest break if the working day is longer than six hours. Details including duration and the terms on which it is granted, shall be laid down in collective agreements, agreements between the two sides of industry or by national legislation. Further, the average weekly working time must not exceed 48 hours and every worker is entitled to paid annual leave of at least four weeks. This minimum period of paid annual leave cannot be replaced by an allowance except where the employment relationship is terminated.[34]

5.85 The minimum European requirements in relation to a number of aspects of working time are set out below in greater detail,[35] however in order to establish exact working time practices and rights on a jurisdictional basis, local legal advice should be obtained.

Rest

5.86 As a minimum protection, staff must not work more than 48 hours per week on average (including overtime), over a reference period of up to four months. All employees must be given at least 11 consecutive hours of daily rest and at least 24 hours of uninterrupted weekly rest every seven days, over a reference period of two weeks.

Breaks

5.87 Adequate breaks must be provided to employees who work more than six hours a day and the duration of said break is typically specified in collective agreements or by national law.

Night work

5.88 Where an employee works at least three hours of their daily shift or a certain proportion of their yearly working time in a period of seven hours defined by national law and including the time from midnight to 05:00, they will qualify as night workers.

34 Significant guidance is available from the European Agency for Safety and Health at Work.

35 Drawn from the Working Time Directive 2003/88/EC.

5.89 Night workers may not work more than an average of eight hours per 24 hours. If their work involves special hazards or heavy physical or mental strain, such employees must not exceed the daily limit of eight hours in any 24-hour period.

5.90 Additionally, the directive requires that night workers should also be guaranteed free health assessments respecting medical confidentiality before they start carrying out night work and at regular intervals afterwards. Where health problems occur related to the fact that the employee works nights, they must transfer to day work whenever possible.

Different working time obligations

5.91 Derogations from some of the working time obligations are possible if allowed by national law. Local legal advice should be taken in advance of concluding contracts of employment to ensure compliance.

Opting out of the 48-hour week

5.92 Once over 18 years of age, it is possible for an employee to opt out of the 48-hour working week. The employee may be requested to opt out but cannot be compelled to do so (unless they are part of specific industries) and may not be sacked or treated unfairly for refusing to do so. Opt outs may be of indefinite or fixed periods and must adhere to the usual requirement that the person has the appropriate capacity to enter into the opt out and does so voluntarily and it is done in writing.[36]

5.93 Example of opt-out agreement:

I [worker's name] agree that I may work for more than an average of 48 hours a week. If I change my mind, I will give my employer [amount of time – up to 3 months'] notice in writing to end this agreement.

Signed...

Dated..

Social security

5.94 A full consideration of social security provision of individual countries is a task beyond the scope of this work as each EU country has its own social security laws. The obligations and rights under these laws are the same for all workers in that country, whether local or from abroad. However, EU rules coordinate national systems to make sure people moving to another EU country do not lose their social security cover (eg, pension rights and healthcare) and always know which national laws apply to them. Under EU rules, someone can be subject to only one country's social security laws at a time, so they must pay their social security contributions in that country only.

Minimum wage

5.95 As of 1 January 2019, 22 out of the 28 member states of the European Union (EU) have national minimum wages: only Denmark, Italy, Cyprus, Austria, Finland

36 See UK government guidance on maximum working week and opting out at www.gov.uk.

and Sweden do not have any.[37] The 22 EU member states that have national minimum wages are as follows:

Country	Minimum wage (per month) in EUR
Latvia	430
Romania	446
Hungary	464
Croatia	506
Czech Republic	519
Slovakia	520
Poland	523
Estonia	540
Lithuania	555
Greece	684
Portugal	700
Malta	762
Slovenia	887
Spain	1050
United Kingdom	1453
France	1521
Germany	1557
Belgium	1594
Netherlands	1616
Ireland	1656
Luxembourg	2071

By way of comparison, as of January 2019, the US federal minimum wage was $1,098.[38]

Staff handbooks

5.96 Whilst not a strict requirement under UK law or European law, the provision of comprehensive staff handbooks to employees of all manner has represented an effective way for organisations to communicate essential policy aims and objectives to employees. Frequently the contents of staff handbooks form key evidences in any employment law claims and actions brought. Below is a sample table of contents that might inform corporate counsel of key aspects of what is typically included. However, a full exposition on the exact contents of each, relevant to each EMEA jurisdiction, is beyond the scope of this work.

1. Welcome
2. Introduction to Company

Part One – Contractual Rules and Policies and Procedures

3. Conflicts of Interest

37 Eurostat report 1/1/19.
38 As per Eurostat.

4. Discoveries and Inventions

Part Two – Non Contractual Policies

5. Equal Opportunities Policy
6. Code of Business Conduct and Ethics
7. Agency Workers
8. Bullying and Harassment
9. Disciplinary Procedure
10. Annual Performance
11. Performance Management Policy
12. Grievance Procedure

Absence and Leave Policies

13. Holidays and Time Off
14. Sickness Absence Policy
15. Whistleblowing Policy
16. Maternity Policy
17. Paternity Leave
18. Adoption Policy
19. Shared Parental Leave Policy
20. Leave for dependants
21. Parental Leave
22. Flexible Working
23. Data Protection Policy
24. Social Media Policy
25. Company Car Policy
26. Pensions and Life Insurance
27. Security
28. Company Property
29. Personal and Lost Property
30. Right of Search
31. Overtime Policy
32. Smoking
33. Staff Purchases
34. Long Service Awards

Miscellaneous

35. Health and Safety Policy
36. Drugs and alcohol

37. Environmental Policy
38. Group Quality Policy
39. Policy Guidelines on employing family members and significant others
40. Training and Development
41. Electronic communications Policy
42. Travelling and Expenses Policy
43. Leaving ACCO UK Limited
44. Life assurance cover for those working beyond age 65
45. Pension options for those working beyond age 65
46. Relocation Policy
47. Company Sick Pay for production Workers
48. Overtime and Shifts
49. Accidents
50. Canteen
51. Change of address
52. Fire Procedure
53. First Aid
54. Notice Boards
55. Protective Clothing, footwear and other PPE
56. Personal Electronic Equipment
57. Speed Limits on Company property
58. Pregnant Workers Procedure
59. Health & safety
60. Work related Upper Limb Disorder Procedure
61. Young Persons Protection Policy

Acquisitions, mergers and corporate restructure

> 'Employees are a company's greatest asset – they're your competitive advantage. You want to attract and retain the best; provide them with encouragement, stimulus, and make them feel that they are an integral part of the company's mission.'

Anne M Mulcahy
former CEO of Xerox

> 'Boards have seen the damage a small group of disengaged workers can do.'

Laura Inman MAICD
Non Executive Director
Super Retail Group and Precinct Properties New Zealand

5.97 Acquisitions and mergers, in the realm of international business, are a risky undertaking. Getting it wrong can have serious negative consequences; HP & Compaq, AOL & Time Warner, and Daimler & Chrysler are examples that spring readily to mind. But getting it right can return huge rewards; Disney Pixar, Disney Marvel, eBay & PayPal, and Berkshire Hathaway's acquisition of See's Candy, all need no further explanation, as they speak for themselves.

5.98 Given the risks and potential rewards it is not surprising, when acquisitions and mergers (as well as the restructuring of said businesses) are the order of the day, that the minds of most business leaders (at least the ones I've worked with over the past 20 plus years) turn to many, many different subjects simultaneously. Concurrently these business leaders are also besieged by hordes of professional advisers all with varying interests; each proffering advice on a myriad of different subjects; all of which compete for the time and attention of those leaders negotiating and planning for the proposed transaction. It's difficult, if not impossible, for those in charge to retain and process the avalanche of information they receive, progress negotiations and complete the transaction. Having experienced it I'd liken it to what I believe it would be like to try to take a sip from a firehose.

5.99 Under these circumstances it's no small wonder that certain subjects are 'parked' and the detail and planning related to those issues left to days less fraught and crowded with data, competing opinions and time sensitive priorities. Cultural fit and cultural integration concerns (and other HR considerations) of mergers and acquisitions and/or restructures are often a casualty, are easily parked, and usually not given proper consideration during both diligence and the period up to the closing. That day those issues were parked for, in the context of these transactions, never actually arrives and potential disaster awaits in those issues unwarily parked.

5.100 It is estimated that over 30% of mergers fail because businesses have failed to adequately deal either with culture incompatibility and/or and the organisational trauma resulting from an acquisition. No matter how your look at this, in my opinion, this inaction is a false economy at best and a serious derogation of duty at worst:[39]

> 'As I said, it was beyond certainly my abilities to figure out how to blend the old media and the new media culture. They were like different species, and in fact, they were species that were inherently at war.'
>
> Richard Parsons, President Time Warner.
>
> Taken from the *New York Times* Article
>
> 'How the AOL-Time Warner Merger Went So Wrong' by Tim Arango
>
> 11 January 2010

5.101 As a General Counsel or business leader involved in the planning of any European Acquisition I would urge you to strongly suggest the involvement of experienced HR professionals, from the very beginning of the diligence and negotiations. There will likely be many considerations and obstacles that the negotiation of an iron clad share purchase agreement won't overcome and which could delay or worst case, in a time sensitive transaction, kill an acquisition or merger not to mention add cost. For instance:

39 'Big Mergers that Were Killed by Culture (And how to Stop it from Killing Yours)' workhuman.com, Darcy Jacobsen 26 September 2012. Also see 'Protecting Employees from Organisational Trauma' workhuman.com, Darcy Jacobsen 18 November 2012.

- The existence of Local Works Councils and/or a European Works Council will likely necessitate their being informed if not properly consulted. A failure to properly consult can lead to lengthy delays.
- Unions: consider their authority and your messaging and deal confidentiality as, in Sweden for instance, there may be union members on the boards of the Target's various EU subsidiaries.
- Collective Bargaining Agreements.
- Labour code/local collective consultation obligations.
- ARD (AKA the EU Directive on Transfers of Undertakings).

The now famous quote above by Ann Mulcahy, in my opinion, takes on even greater importance in the context of the acquisition or associated restructure of an EU or EMEA organisation by a non-European corporation.

5.102 Missteps with Works Councils, Unions during an acquisition and ignorance of local labour law and practice carry a procedural, time and sometimes statutory penalty. However, worse in my opinion, these mistakes imply and are locally understood by employees to be rooted in wilful ignorance, arrogance (a casual disregard for local custom) and a lack of competence to lead or operate a business in their country. Like Jane Austin's Mr Darcy, once their good favour is lost it is likely lost forever – and as the 1966 Madison Avenue advertising slogan for Botany Suits read, 'there are no second chances to make first impressions'.

5.103 When it comes to corporate messaging and especially so in messaging to a multi-cultural, multi-jurisdictional employee bases, the language of business, is most effective when the timing is good, and the message is honest, culturally correct and brief.

5.104 A lack of planning, tripping over the law and local custom will harm employee engagement and damage morale. As a General Counsel you are the legal custodian, a guardian, who works to keep the business operating within the law, a custodian of the corporate assets and therefore of the shareholder's equity. In my assessment that includes the good will, morale and willing engagement of the business' employees.

EU Directive on Transfers of Undertakings

5.105 Of the multitude of quirks, complexities and nuances that interconnect the law with the practice of human resource management in Europe the one likely to be the most multi-faceted and legally complex, in my experience, is the application of the EU Directive on Transfers of Undertakings (the 'ARD') by the 28 member states of the European Union.

5.106 The purpose of the directive is to impose obligations on employers and to protect certain employee rights that might be otherwise adversely affected by certain types of corporate transactions.

5.107 The existence and application of ARD will be a bit of an alien concept for most non-Europeans and it certainly was for me as a naive Texas/California educated lawyer back in the very late 1990s when my then firm sent me on a course to come to terms with this EU legislation. Then I did not yet fully understand the full meaning of 'Europeans work to live, and Americans live to work' nor the degree of protection, if not affection, the labour law offered the employed citizens of the UK not to mention the greater rights and protections offered in the EU.

5.108 If there is one thing to keep in the back of your mind when planning an acquisition in Europe it is the ARD. Examine the acquisition target, establish the locations of their subsidiaries and the acquirers'. If your businesses' footprint overlaps the targets and, in any after acquisition integration, intends to transfer employees (or jobs) across borders, or between companies, or to merge legal entities (with employees) in Europe, the ARD will likely apply. Your business will likely need specialist local legal advice to accomplish this within the law. An in-house generalist will probably never understand the ARD as enacted by the local laws of the 28 countries. After nearly 20 years I neither pretend to, nor need to. I know enough to spot the probable existence of an ARD issue and I have excellent local counsel to help with the rest. I hope the rest of this chapter will arm you with the same knowledge.

5.109 As previously indicated the purpose of the ARD is the safeguarding of employees' rights in the event of transfers of undertakings, businesses or parts of undertakings or businesses. It represents a large body of complex law across Europe. What happens to employees and how their rights are affected and protected during company sale and purchase is of relevance to corporate counsel not simply in the context of mergers and acquisitions but also features in terms of internal corporate reorganisation. Employee rights in such circumstances should be to the forefront of counsels' planning in such circumstances.

5.110 The EU Directive on the matter[40] has sought to harmonise and approximate national provisions and update previous European-centric attempts at providing for such protections. Consideration will be given to this directive in this chapter in addition to the commensurate UK national law, which typically attracts much attention.

5.111 This directive was drafted mindful of economic trends which have brought, at both national and community level, changes in the structure of undertakings, through transfers of undertakings, businesses or parts of undertakings or businesses to other employers as a result of legal transfers or mergers.[41] The EU were most keen to provide for the protection of employees in the event of a change of employer, in particular, to ensure that their rights are safeguarded as it was perceived that significant differences existed in the member states as regards the extent of the protection of employees in this respect.

To whom does the directive apply?

5.112 The directive applies broadly. Any transfer of an undertaking, business, or part of an undertaking or business to another employer as a result of a legal transfer or

40 Council Directive 2001/23/EC of 12 March 2001 on the approximation of the laws of the Member States relating to the safeguarding of employees' rights in the event of transfers of undertakings, businesses or parts of undertakings or businesses.

41 See preamble to Council Directive 2001/23/EC of 12 March 2001 on the approximation of the laws of the Member States relating to the safeguarding of employees' rights in the event of transfers of undertakings, businesses or parts of undertakings or businesses.

merger attracts the attention of the directive.[42] The directive even applies to public and private undertakings engaged in economic activities whether or not they are operating for gain.[43] In terms of geographic application, the directive applies where and insofar as the undertaking, business or part of the undertaking or business to be transferred is situated within the territorial scope of the Treaty.[44]

What are the key definitions?[45]

What is a 'transferor?'

5.113 'Transferor' means any natural or legal person who, by reason of a transfer within the meaning of the directive, ceases to be the employer in respect of the undertaking, business or part of the undertaking or business.

What is a 'transferee?'

5.114 'Transferee' means any natural or legal person who, by reason of a transfer within the meaning of the directive, becomes the employer in respect of the undertaking, business or part of the undertaking or business.

What are 'representatives of employees?'

5.115 'Representatives of employees' and all such related expressions shall mean the representatives of the employees provided for by the laws or practices of the member states.

What is an 'employee?'

5.116 Employee means any person who, in the member state concerned, is protected as an employee under national employment law.

Safeguarding employee rights

5.117 The basic tenet underpinning the legislation is that the transferor's rights and obligations arising from a contract of employment or from an employment relationship existing on the date of a transfer shall, by reason of such transfer, be transferred to the transferee.[46]

Joint and several liability

5.118 Some member states of the European Union may provide in their national laws that the transferor and the transferee shall be jointly and severally liable in respect of obligations which arose before the date of transfer from a contract of employment

42 Council Directive 2001/23/EC of 12 March 2001 on the approximation of the laws of the Member States relating to the safeguarding of employees' rights in the event of transfers of undertakings, businesses or parts of undertakings or businesses, Art 1.

43 ibid, Art 1(1)(c).

44 ibid, Art 1(2). Note that the directive does not apply to seagoing vessels.

45 Art 2 of the Directive requires that the directive shall be without prejudice to national law as regards the definition of contract of employment or employment relationship.

46 Council Directive 2001/23/EC of 12 March 2001 on the approximation of the laws of the Member States relating to the safeguarding of employees' rights in the event of transfers of undertakings, businesses or parts of undertakings or businesses, Art 3.

or an employment relationship existing on the date of the transfer.[47] Corporate counsel should be mindful of such deviations.

State of knowledge

5.119 It should be noted that ignorance of one's obligations shall not amount to a defence. A failure by the transferor to notify the transferee of any such right or obligation shall not affect the transfer of that right or obligation and the rights of any employees against the transferee and/or transferor in respect of that right or obligation.[48]

Survival of existing collective agreements

5.120 Following the transfer, the transferee shall continue to observe the terms and conditions agreed in any collective agreement on the same terms applicable to the transferor under that agreement, until the date of termination or expiry of the collective agreement or the entry into force or application of another collective agreement.[49] However, this obligation to observe existing agreements may be limited by national law and consultation should be taken locally as national law may limit the period for observing such terms and conditions with the proviso that it shall not be less than one year.[50]

Old-age, invalidity or survivors' benefits

5.121 Special provision is made in relation to employees' rights to old-age, invalidity or survivors' benefits under supplementary company or intercompany pension schemes outside the statutory social security schemes. Counsel should take advice on these matters locally as national laws may take steps necessary to protect the interests of employees and of persons no longer employed in the transferor's business at the time of the transfer in respect of rights conferring on them immediate or prospective entitlement to old age benefits, including survivors' benefits, under supplementary schemes.[51]

Dismissal of employees

5.122 It is a central distinction to make that the transfer of the undertaking or business or part of the undertaking or business shall not in itself constitute grounds for dismissal by the transferor or the transferee. This provision shall not stand in the way of dismissals that may take place for economic, technical or organisational reasons entailing changes in the workforce.[52]

5.123 If the contract of employment or the employment relationship is terminated because the transfer involves a substantial change in working conditions to the detriment of the employee, the employer shall be regarded as having been responsible for termination of the contract of employment or of the employment relationship.

---

47 ibid, Art 3(1).
48 ibid, Art 3(2).
49 ibid, Art 3(3).
50 ibid, Art 3(3).
51 ibid, Art 3(4).
52 ibid, Art 4.

Where a transferor is insolvent?

5.124 The above protections will typically not apply to any transfer of an undertaking, business or part of an undertaking or business where the transferor is the subject of bankruptcy proceedings or any analogous insolvency proceedings which have been instituted with a view to the liquidation of the assets of the transferor and are under the supervision of a competent public authority.[53] Though it should be noted that national law may provide for certain exceptions to this general rule.[54] Typically, national laws provide for appropriate measures with a view to preventing misuse of insolvency proceedings in such a way as to deprive employees of the rights provided for in the directive so that insolvency proceedings should not be deployed tactically.[55]

Preservation of protections for employee representatives

5.125 If the undertaking, business or part of an undertaking or business preserves its autonomy, the status and function of the representatives or of the representation of the employees affected by the transfer shall be preserved on the same terms and subject to the same conditions as existed before the date of the transfer by virtue of law, regulation, administrative provision or agreement, provided that the conditions necessary for the constitution of the employee's representation are fulfilled.[56]

5.126 These protections for employee representatives may be preserved throughout any insolvency proceedings where national law so provides. Specifically, where the transferor is the subject of bankruptcy proceedings or any analogous insolvency proceedings which have been instituted with a view to the liquidation of the assets of the transferor and are under the supervision of a competent public authority (which may be an insolvency practitioner authorised by a competent public authority), necessary measures may be instituted to ensure that the transferred employees are properly represented until the new election or designation of representatives of the employees.[57] Further, these protections for representatives shall endure in certain circumstances. If the term of office of the representatives of the employees affected by the transfer expires as a result of the transfer, the representatives shall continue to enjoy

53 ibid, Art 5.

54 Art 2 of the Directive is relevant here. 'Where Articles 3 and 4 apply to a transfer during insolvency proceedings which have been opened in relation to a transferor (whether or not those proceedings have been instituted with a view to the liquidation of the assets of the transferor) and provided that such proceedings are under the supervision of a competent public authority (which may be an insolvency practitioner determined by national law) a Member State may provide that: (a) notwithstanding Article 3(1), the transferor's debts arising from any contracts of employment or employment relationships and payable before the transfer or before the opening of the insolvency proceedings shall not be transferred to the transferee, provided that such proceedings give rise, under the law of that Member State, to protection at least equivalent to that provided for in situations covered by Council Directive 80/987/EEC of 20 October 1980 on the approximation of the laws of the Member States relating to the protection of employees in the event of the insolvency of their employer(7), and, or alternatively, that, (b) the transferee, transferor or person or persons exercising the transferor's functions, on the one hand, and the representatives of the employees on the other hand may agree alterations, in so far as current law or practice permits, to the employees' terms and conditions of employment designed to safeguard employment opportunities by ensuring the survival of the undertaking, business or part of the undertaking or business.'

55 Council Directive 2001/23/EC of 12 March 2001 on the approximation of the laws of the Member States relating to the safeguarding of employees' rights in the event of transfers of undertakings, businesses or parts of undertakings or businesses, Art 5.

56 ibid, Art 6.

57 ibid, Art 6.

the protection provided by the laws, regulations, administrative provisions or practice of the member states.[58]

What information and consultation with employees is required?

5.127 The transferor and transferee shall be required to inform the representatives of their respective employees affected by the transfer of the following:[59]

- the date or proposed date of the transfer;
- the reasons for the transfer;
- the legal, economic and social implications of the transfer for the employees; and
- any measures envisaged in relation to the employees.

What are the time constraints?

5.128 Furthermore, the transferor must give such information to the representatives of his employees in good time, before the transfer is carried out.[60] Additionally, the transferee must give such information to the representatives of his employees in good time, and in any event before his employees are directly affected by the transfer as regards their conditions of work and employment.

5.129 Where the transferor or the transferee envisages measures in relation to his employees, consultations with the representatives of these employees shall also be had in good time on such measures with a view to reaching an agreement.[61]

5.130 The obligations laid down in terms of information and consultation apply irrespective of whether the decision resulting in the transfer is taken by the employer or an undertaking controlling the employer.[62]

In the case that there are no employee representatives

5.131 Where there are no representatives of the employees in an undertaking or business through no fault of their own, the employees concerned must nonetheless be informed in advance of:[63]

- the date or proposed date of the transfer;
- the reason for the transfer;
- the legal, economic and social implications of the transfer for the employees;
- any measures envisaged in relation to the employees.

Minimum protection levels

5.132 It should be noted that the above protections represent a base line. It remains open to national law to provide for or introduce laws, regulations or administrative

58 ibid, Art 6.
59 ibid, Art 7(1).
60 ibid, Art 7(1).
61 ibid, Art 7(2).
62 ibid, Art 7(4).
63 ibid, Art 7(6).

provisions which are more favourable to employees or to promote or permit collective agreements or agreements between social partners more favourable to employees.[64]

Right of recourse

5.133 It almost goes without saying that aggrieved employees have a right to challenge any wrongdoing to them or infringement of their rights. Nonetheless, the directive goes on to require that member states must introduce into their national legal systems such measures as are necessary to enable all employees and representatives of employees who consider themselves wronged by failure to comply with the obligations arising from this directive to pursue their claims by judicial process after possible recourse to other competent authorities.[65]

Transfer of undertakings – UK

Background

5.134 Whilst the EU legislation on this topic creates a series of policy aims, national legislatures are left with a significant degree of autonomy as to how such aims are met. A comparative analysis of transfer of undertakings protections is beyond the scope of this work, the authors felt it useful to set out the provisions of UK national law[66] in this regard to serve as an example and analogue of how such protections are practically applied at a local level. Given the level of divergence on this topic across the EMEA region, corporate counsel should consider the appropriateness of local legal advice in every case.

What amounts to a transfer?

5.135 For the purposes of UK law, a 'relevant transfer' means a transfer or a service provision change to which the Transfer of Undertakings Regulations[67] apply in accordance with regulation 3 of the 2006 Regulations and 'transferor' and 'transferee' shall be construed accordingly and in the case of a service provision change,[68] 'the transferor' means the person who carried out the activities prior to the service provision change and 'the transferee' means the person who carries out the activities as a result of the service provision change.[69]

To whom do the Regulations apply?

5.136 These Regulations apply to:

(a) a transfer of an undertaking, business or part of an undertaking or business situated immediately before the transfer in the United Kingdom to another person where there is a transfer of an economic entity which retains its identity;

---

64 ibid, Art 8.

65 ibid, Art 9.

66 The Transfer of Undertakings (Protection of Employment) Regulations 2006 (UK) as amended by The Collective Redundancies and Transfer of Undertakings (Protection of Employment) (Amendment) Regulations 2014.

67 Both The Transfer of Undertakings (Protection of Employment) Regulations 2006 (UK) and The Collective Redundancies and Transfer of Undertakings (Protection of Employment) (Amendment) Regulations 2014

68 Falling within reg 3(1)(b) of the 2006 Regulations.

69 The Transfer of Undertakings (Protection of Employment) Regulations 2006, reg 2.

(b) a service provision change, that is a situation in which:

  (i) activities cease to be carried out by a person ('a client') on his own behalf and are carried out instead by another person on the client's behalf ('a contractor');

  (ii) activities cease to be carried out by a contractor on a client's behalf (whether or not those activities had previously been carried out by the client on his own behalf) and are carried out instead by another person ('a subsequent contractor') on the client's behalf; or

  (iii) activities cease to be carried out by a contractor or a subsequent contractor on a client's behalf (whether or not those activities had previously been carried out by the client on his own behalf) and are carried out instead by the client on his own behalf, and in which the conditions set out in paragraph (3) are satisfied.

5.137 It should be further noted that these Regulations apply to:

(a) public and private undertakings engaged in economic activities whether or not they are operating for gain;

(b) a transfer or service provision change howsoever effected notwithstanding:

  (i) that the transfer of an undertaking, business or part of an undertaking or business is governed or effected by the law of a country or territory outside the United Kingdom or that the service provision change is governed or effected by the law of a country or territory outside Great Britain;

  (ii) that the employment of persons employed in the undertaking, business or part transferred or, in the case of a service provision change, persons employed in the organised grouping of employees, is governed by any such law;

  (iii) a transfer of an undertaking, business or part of an undertaking or business (which may also be a service provision change) where persons employed in the undertaking, business or part transferred ordinarily work outside the United Kingdom.

Safeguarding employee rights

Essential protection

5.138 Generally, a relevant transfer shall not operate so as to terminate the contract of employment of any person employed by the transferor and assigned to the organised grouping of resources or employees that is subject to the relevant transfer, which would otherwise be terminated by the transfer, but any such contract shall have effect after the transfer as if originally made between the person so employed and the transferee.[70]

5.139 For the avoidance of doubt, the Regulations set out that on the completion of a relevant transfer, all the transferor's rights, powers, duties and liabilities under or in connection with any such contract shall be transferred by virtue of the Regulations to the transferee.[71]

70 ibid, reg 4(1).
71 ibid, reg 4(2).

5.140 Similarly, the Regulations provide clarity in relation to acts or omissions pre-transfer. The Regulations require that any act or omission before the transfer is completed, of or in relation to the transferor in respect of that contract, shall be deemed to have been an act or omission of or in relation to the transferee.[72]

Variation of contracts[73]

5.141 The regulations will render any purported variation of a contract of employment void where the sole or principal reason for the variation is the transfer.[74] Though contractual variation is permitted where the sole or principal reason for the variation is an economic, technical, or organisational reason entailing changes in the workforce, provided that the employer and employee agree that variation or the terms of that contract permit the employer to make such a variation.[75]

Collective agreement implications?

5.142 Where there exists a collective agreement at the time of a relevant transfer made by or on behalf of the transferor with a trade union recognised by the transferor in respect of any employee whose contract of employment is preserved then that agreement, will, after the transfer, have effect as if made by or on behalf of the transferee with that trade union. It should be noted that anything done under that agreement, by the transferor before the transfer, shall, after the transfer, be deemed to have been done by the transferee.[76]

Continuity of trade union recognition

5.143 UK law preserves the continuity of trade union recognition as the regulation applies where after a relevant transfer the transferred organised grouping of resources or employees maintains an identity distinct from the remainder of the transferee's undertaking.[77] Where an independent trade union was recognised to any extent by the transferor in respect of employees of any description before a transfer who in consequence of the transfer become employees of the transferee, then, after the transfer, the trade union shall be deemed to have been recognised by the transferee to the same extent in respect of employees.[78]

Dismissal of employees

5.144 Specific protection exists in this regard in the UK. Where either before or after a relevant transfer, any employee of the transferor or transferee is dismissed, that employee is to be treated as unfairly dismissed if the sole or principal reason for the dismissal is the transfer.[79]

---

72 ibid, reg 4(2).
73 Where the variation has been agreed post 31 January 2014.
74 The Transfer of Undertakings (Protection of Employment) Regulations 2006 (UK) as amended by The Collective Redundancies and Transfer of Undertakings (Protection of Employment) (Amendment) Regulations 2014, reg 4, para 4.
75 ibid, reg 4, para 5.
76 ibid, reg 5.
77 ibid, reg 6, para 1.
78 ibid, reg 6, para 2.
79 ibid, reg 7.

What is the effect of insolvency?

5.145 Specific guidance is available where if at the time of a relevant transfer the transferor is subject to relevant insolvency proceedings.[80] Counsel should consider specific legal advice in relation to this matter and in particular where contractual variation is contemplated,[81] from an insolvency practitioner given the level of complexity.

Information and consultation

Transferor to transferee

5.146 Generally, the transferor shall notify to the transferee the employee liability information of any person employed by him and subject of a relevant transfer and should do so in writing; or by making it available in a readily accessible form.[82]

5.147 Employee liability information has been defined as:[83]

(a) the identity and age of the employee;

(b) those particulars of employment that an employer is obliged to give to an employee under UK law;

(c) information in relation to any disciplinary procedure taken against an employee and/or grievance procedure taken by an employee within the previous two years;

(d) information of any court or tribunal case, claim or action brought by an employee against the transferor, within the previous two years. Additionally, information of any court or tribunal case, claim or action that the transferor has reasonable grounds to believe that an employee may bring against the transferee, arising out of the employee's employment with the transferor; and

(e) information of any collective agreement which will have effect after the transfer, in its application in relation to the employee.

All such employee liability information must be accurate as of a specified date not more than 14 days before the date on which the information is notified to the transferee.[84]

5.148 Counsel should also be mindful that on or after a relevant transfer, the transferee may present a complaint to an employment tribunal that the transferor has failed to comply with any of the information provision requirements.[85]

Employer to employee

5.149 Without specifying an explicit timeframe, the Regulations provide that the employer must inform employees of certain matters 'Long enough before a relevant transfer to enable the employer of any affected employees to consult the appropriate representatives of any affected employees'.[86]

80 ibid, reg 8, para 1 et seq.
81 ibid, reg 9.
82 ibid, reg 11, para 1.
83 ibid, reg 11, para 2.
84 ibid, reg 11, para 3.
85 ibid, reg 12.
86 ibid, reg 13, para 2.

5.150 The following information must be provided:[87]

- the fact that the transfer is to take place, the date or proposed date of the transfer and the reasons for it;
- the legal, economic and social implications of the transfer for any affected employees;
- the measures which he envisages he will, in connection with the transfer, take in relation to any affected employees or, if he envisages that no measures will be so taken, that fact; and
- if the employer is the transferor, the measures, in connection with the transfer, which he envisages the transferee will take in relation to any affected employees who will become employees of the transferee after the transfer or, if he envisages that no measures will be so taken, that fact.

The transferee is required to cooperate with the transferor in order to meet the above commitments.[88] Complaints in relation to failures in this regard are actionable before employment tribunals and as to further particulars of what information is to be provided and the means and mode of such consultation, together with consequences for failures, please consult Regulation 13 et seq and local legal advice.

Misuse of non-disclosure agreements

Recent developments

5.151 Following on from a number of high-profile cases, there has been an increased level of legislative scrutiny, particularly in the UK, regarding the use of confidentiality clauses, typically deployed in non-disclosure type agreements. In 2019, the UK government issued a proposal to alter how such clauses are deployed and used and set upon a course of consultation with stakeholders as to how to shape a legislative response to the misuse of confidentiality clauses. The intention of the government was set out in a paper of March 2019:[89]

> 'The Government is committed to upholding and upgrading workers' rights, having placed good work and good jobs at the centre of the modern Industrial Strategy. As part of our commitment to this upgrade, we are now consulting to ensure that harassment or discrimination of any sort cannot be tolerated in the workplace. The purpose of this consultation is to seek evidence and views of the use of confidentiality clauses in the employment context, and to propose further regulation to tackle their misuse.'

5.152 Noting the legitimate deployment of confidentiality clauses in a corporate context as:

> '… having a right and proper place in the employment context. They can be used primarily in two ways: as part of employment contracts, to protect trade secrets for example, and as part of settlement agreements, for example to allow both sides of an employment dispute to move on with a clean break.'

87 ibid, reg 13, para 2.
88 ibid, reg 13, para 5.
89 Confidentiality Clauses – Consultation on measures to prevent misuse in situations of workplace harassment or discrimination. See gov.uk.

It went on to comment however, that:

> '... there is evidence that despite these protections some employers have used confidentiality clauses to suggest victims of harassment cannot make any disclosures and intimidate them into silence when they have faced harassment or discrimination. For example, a confidentiality clause might be all encompassing, to make a worker believe that they cannot discuss anything that occurs in the workplace with anybody, despite case law establishing that this is not necessarily the case. A confidentiality clause might suggest to the worker that they do not have rights, such as whistleblowing or taking a matter to a tribunal that in fact cannot be abrogated. Or they could be unreasonably expansive and insist that a worker not discuss the issue under consideration with people such as the police, a doctor, or a therapist.'

5.153 Hence, the UK government is now exploring whether there should be more limitations on confidentiality clauses in the employment context, to make it easier for workers and their advisers to understand when they are permitted in law to make a disclosure to the police or other people despite the existence of a confidentiality clause. Similarly it will explore how to ensure workers are clear about the rights they maintain when they sign a confidentiality clause or start work for a new employer and also how to enforce any new regulations on confidentiality clauses.[90]

Conclusion

5.154 Whilst concrete legislative measures are, perhaps, some distance off, it would be submitted that corporate counsel be mindful of how such UK measures (which may adopt a broad extra-jurisdictional reach) may impact their utilisation of non-disclosure agreements in the future.

5.155 However it could be predicted that where improper use of NDAs has historically occurred in organisations, the possibility (if not probability) of civil or criminal proceedings for historical transgressions by corporate officers being resolved by use of NDAs is no longer remote. The confidentiality protection traditionally assumed by those NDAs could evaporate along with any purported enforceability to keep individuals silent thereafter. Corporate Counsel may, in due course, require a review of NDA deployment in the context of inappropriate corporate behaviour of officers on a historical basis.

The EU member states were given some flexibility in how to implement the directive on Transfers of Undertakings. As a result, there are differences in implementation from member state to member state with some of the differences being significant. These differences naturally give rise to legal uncertainty in the case of cross border transfers as the directive does not provide for solutions in the event of a conflict of laws.

90 See Confidentiality Clauses – Consultation on measures to prevent misuse in situations of workplace harassment or discrimination. See gov.uk.

PART 3

REGARDING THE GOVERNANCE OF THE BUSINESS

6 Accounting and the law

Introduction

6.1 In the close relationship and mutual reliance (as well as the occasional enmity) that typically exists in many companies between corporate legal departments and the accounting and/or finance functions, it is necessary to set out some of the legal implications and matters of mutual interest. This is particularly so where a corporate counsel also acts as company secretary or other officer who can exercise statutory authority relating to filing accounts or binding the company or has wider additional responsibilities in relation to the management and oversite of a group's corporate secretariat or the corporate governance of a group of companies.

6.2 Generally, there is a requirement under EU law that limited liability companies have to prepare financial statements to monitor the health of their business and provide a true and fair view of their state of the company. The EU has introduced rules to promote the convergence of accounting standards at a global level and to ensure consistent and comparable financial reporting across the EU. Under EU rules, listed companies (those whose securities are traded on a regulated market) must prepare their consolidated financial statements in accordance with a single set of international standards called IFRS (international financial reporting standards). Other requirements apply to non-listed companies and small businesses[1] and to carry on business in the EU, they must prepare annual financial statements and submit them to their respective national authority.

6.3 Alternatively, where companies are limited liability in nature and carry on business in the EU, they must prepare annual financial statements and submit them to their respective national authority. Groups of companies must prepare consolidated financial statements.[2] Financial statements must include:

1 European Commission Guidance – Financial Reporting and EU rules on financial information disclosed by companies. https://ec.europa.eu/info.

2 ibid.

- the balance sheet;
- the profit and loss account;
- a certain number of notes to the financial statements;
- large and medium-sized companies also have to publish management reports.

6.4 Directive 2013/34/EU sets out the rules that must be followed, concerning in particular the:

- presentation and content of annual or consolidated financial statements;
- presentation and content of management reports;
- measurement basis companies use to prepare their financial statements;
- audit of financial statements;
- publication of financial statements;
- the responsibility of management with regards to all of the above.

6.5 This directive also aims at reducing the administrative burden for small companies. It allows a simplified reporting regime for small and medium-sized enterprises and a very light regime for micro-companies (those with less than 10 employees).

6.6 Critically, the directive includes a definition of micro, small, medium and large companies based on thresholds concerning turnover, total assets and number of employees.[3]

6.7 It must be recalled that as a directive, this instrument is transposed into national law by means of implementing legislation that provides member states with discretion as to how to achieve the goals and aims of the directive in a legislative sense. As such, there may be significant divergence at a national level and the following discussions in this chapter are designed to give corporate counsel a flavour of the *typical* requirements a company of a particular size may face.

6.8 As stated by the EU Commission:[4]

> 'Regulation (EC) No 1606/2002 requires all listed companies to prepare their consolidated financial statements in accordance with a single set of international standards. These are the IFRS (international financial reporting standards), previously known as IAS (international accounting standards).'

It is not proposed to cover these regulations in any significant detail as they are deemed beyond the scope of this work. A general awareness, together with a healthy relationship with colleagues in the Finance/Accounting department should suffice.

3 These thresholds are periodically updated to keep pace with inflation and tend to be widely deployed across a range of regulatory matters, see European Commission Guidance – Financial Reporting and EU rules on financial information disclosed by companies, available at https://ec.europa.eu/info.

4 European Commission Guidance – Financial Reporting and EU rules on financial information disclosed by companies, available at https://ec.europa.eu/info.

The accounting directive

6.9 Directive 2013/34/EU, referred to as the accounting directive, contains a myriad of information that is of significance to corporate counsel.

Who does the accounting directive apply to?

6.10 The types of undertakings (meaning the form of the corporate entity) that are captured by this directive are set out in detail in the annexes to the directive which are reproduced in the appendices to this text but typically, the directive applies to undertakings that enjoy some form of limited liability, specifically, public companies limited by shares or by guarantee, private companies limited by shares or by guarantee and, in many cases, to partnerships, limited partnerships and unlimited companies.[5]

What are the various categories of companies?

Micro-undertakings

6.11 Micro-undertakings are defined as undertakings which on their balance sheet dates do not exceed the limits of at least two of the three following criteria:[6]

(a) balance sheet total: EUR 350,000;

(b) net turnover: EUR 700,000;

(c) average number of employees during the financial year: 10.

Small undertakings

6.12 Small undertakings are defined as undertakings which on their balance sheet dates do not exceed the limits of at least two of the three following criteria:[7]

(a) balance sheet total: EUR 4,000,000;

(b) net turnover: EUR 8,000,000;

(c) average number of employees during the financial year: 50.

Medium-sized undertakings

6.13 Medium-sized undertakings are defined as undertakings which are not micro-undertakings or small undertakings and which on their balance sheet dates do not exceed the limits of at least two of the three following criteria:[8]

(a) balance sheet total: EUR 20,000,000;

(b) net turnover: EUR 40,000,000;

---

5 Art 1 of Directive 2013/34/EU of the European Parliament and of the Council of 26 June 2013 on the annual financial statements, consolidated financial statements and related reports of certain types of undertakings, amending Directive 2006/43/EC of the European Parliament and of the Council and repealing Council Directives 78/660/EEC and 83/349/EEC.

6 ibid, Art 3.1.

7 ibid, Art 3.2. Note that in relation to balance sheet total and turnover member states may define thresholds exceeding the thresholds in points (a) and (b). However, the thresholds shall not exceed EUR 6,000,000 for the balance sheet total and EUR 12,000,000 for the net turnover.

8 ibid, Art 3.3.

(c) average number of employees during the financial year: 250

Large undertakings

6.14 Large undertakings are defined as undertakings which on their balance sheet dates exceed at least two of the three following criteria:[9]

(a) balance sheet total: EUR 20,000,000;

(b) net turnover: EUR 40,000,000;

(c) average number of employees during the financial year: 250.

Small groups

6.15 Small groups are defined as groups consisting of parent and subsidiary undertakings to be included in a consolidation and which, on a consolidated basis, do not exceed the limits of at least two of the three following criteria on the balance sheet date of the parent undertaking:[10]

(a) balance sheet total: EUR 4,000,000;

(b) net turnover: EUR 8,000,000;

(c) average number of employees during the financial year: 50.

Medium-sized groups

6.16 Medium-sized groups are defined as groups which are not small groups, which consist of parent and subsidiary undertakings to be included in a consolidation and which, on a consolidated basis, do not exceed the limits of at least two of the three following criteria on the balance sheet date of the parent undertaking:[11]

(a) balance sheet total: EUR 20,000,000;

(b) net turnover: EUR 40,000,000;

(c) average number of employees during the financial year: 250.

Large groups

6.17 Large groups are defined as groups consisting of parent and subsidiary undertakings to be included in a consolidation and which, on a consolidated basis, exceed the limits of at least two of the three following criteria on the balance sheet date of the parent undertaking:[12]

(a) balance sheet total: EUR 20,000,000;

(b) net turnover: EUR 40,000,000;

(c) average number of employees during the financial year: 250.

---

9 ibid, Art 3.4.

10 ibid, Art 3.5. Please note member states may define thresholds exceeding the thresholds in points (a) and (b. However, the thresholds shall not exceed EUR 6,000,000 for the balance sheet total and EUR 12,000,000 for the net turnover.

11 ibid, Art 3.6.

12 ibid, Art 3.7.

What general principles apply?

6.18 At a basic level, the annual financial statements must be drawn up clearly and give a true and fair view of the undertaking's assets, liabilities, financial position and profit or loss, together with additional notes to the financial statements where appropriate.[13] Member states may require undertakings other than small undertakings to disclose information in their annual financial statements which is additional to that required pursuant to this directive.[14] The document containing the financial statements must state the name of the undertaking and the legal form of the company, the location of its registered office and, where appropriate, the fact that the company is being wound up.[15]

What general financial reporting principles apply?

6.19 The amounts entered in the financial statements must be measured in accordance with the following reporting principles (though member states have a number of potential derogations from the below so the following list is indicative in nature):

(a) the undertaking shall be presumed to be carrying on its business as a going concern;

(b) accounting policies and measurement bases shall be applied consistently from one financial year to the next;

(c) recognition and measurement shall be on a prudent basis, and in particular:

  (i) only profits made at the balance sheet date may be recognised;

  (ii) all liabilities arising in the course of the financial year concerned or in the course of a previous financial year shall be recognised, even if such liabilities become apparent only between the balance sheet date and the date on which the balance sheet is drawn up; and

  (iii) all negative value adjustments shall be recognised, whether the result of the financial year is a profit or a loss;

(d) amounts recognised in the balance sheet and profit and loss account shall be computed on the accrual basis;

(e) the opening balance sheet for each financial year shall correspond to the closing balance sheet for the preceding financial year;

(f) the components of asset and liability items shall be valued separately;

(g) any set-off between asset and liability items, or between income and expenditure items, shall be prohibited;

(h) items in the profit and loss account and balance sheet shall be accounted for and presented having regard to the substance of the transaction or arrangement concerned;

(i) items recognised in the financial statements shall be measured in accordance with the principle of purchase price or production cost; and

---

13 ibid, Art 4.3.

14 ibid, Art 4.5.

15 ibid, Art 5.

(j) the requirements set out in this directive regarding recognition, measurement, presentation, disclosure and consolidation need not be complied with when the effect of complying with them is immaterial.

What matters of form and format apply?

6.20 The directive contains a range of requirements that are noteworthy but do not perhaps demand a full exposition here given the highly technical nature of the information. In summary the directive contains requirements relating to:

- General provisions concerning the balance sheet and the profit and loss account.
- Presentation of the balance sheet.
- Special provisions relating to certain balance sheet items.
- Presentation of the profit and loss account.
- Simplifications for small and medium-sized undertakings.
- General provisions concerning the notes to the financial statements.
- Content of the notes to the financial statements relating to all undertakings.
- Additional disclosures for medium-sized and large undertakings and public-interest entities.
- Additional disclosures for large undertakings and public-interest entities.

Management reports

6.21 A management report is required pursuant to the directive and its content is of note to corporate counsel who also share managerial and/or director responsibilities as is often the case. The management report is required to include a fair review of the development and performance of the undertaking's business and of its position, together with a description of the principal risks and uncertainties that it faces.[16] The report must present a balanced and comprehensive analysis of the development and performance of the undertaking's business and of its position, consistent with the size and complexity of the business.

Contents

6.22 It should include both financial and, where appropriate, non-financial key performance indicators relevant to the particular business, including information relating to environmental and employee matters. In providing the analysis, the management report shall, where appropriate, include references to, and additional explanations of, amounts reported in the annual financial statements.[17]

6.23 In addition to the above, the report should also give an indication of:[18]

(a) the undertaking's likely future development;

(b) activities in the field of research and development;

(c) the information concerning acquisitions of its own shares;

---

16 ibid, Art 19.1.
17 ibid, Art 19.1.
18 ibid, Art 19.2.

(d) the existence of branches of the undertaking; and

(e) in relation to the undertaking's use of financial instruments and where material for the assessment of its assets, liabilities, financial position and profit or loss:

  (i) the undertaking's financial risk management objectives and policies, including its policy for hedging each major type of forecasted transaction for which hedge accounting is used; and

  (ii) the undertaking's exposure to price risk, credit risk, liquidity risk and cash flow risk.

Certain categories of undertakings may receive exemptions under national law in relation to the above reporting requirements.

Corporate governance statement

6.24 In addition to the above management report, many cases will require the making of a corporate governance statement which must contain at least a reference to the following, where applicable:[19]

- the corporate governance code to which the undertaking is subject;
- the corporate governance code which the undertaking may have voluntarily decided to apply;
- all relevant information about the corporate governance practices applied over and above the requirements of national law;
- a description of the main features of the undertaking's internal control and risk management systems in relation to the financial reporting process;
- the composition and operation of the administrative, management and supervisory bodies and their committees.

Where reference is made to a corporate governance code direction must be provided to the relevant texts and where they are publicly available. Undertakings must make details of their corporate governance practices publicly available[20]

Revenue recognition

6.25 A new accounting standard in relation to how revenue is recognised for the purposes of reporting in financial statements was published in 2014.[21] It is of particular relevance to corporate counsel as the standard describes the principles an entity must apply to measure and recognise revenue and the related cash flows emanating from a contract. The key point of note is that an entity must recognise revenue at an amount that reflects the consideration to which the entity expects to be entitled in exchange for transferring goods or services to a customer. To do so a number of steps are required to be taken:

- Identify the contract(s) with a customer.
- Identify the performance obligations in the contract.

19 All of which may be subject to elements of national derogation so local advice should be taken prior to formal submission of any reports.

20 ibid, Art 20(a).

21 Accounting Standards Codification (ASC) 606, Revenue from Contracts with Customers, (created by Accounting Standards Update (ASU) 2014-09) and IFRS 15 Revenue from Contracts with Customers

- Determine the transaction price.
- Allocate the transaction price to the performance obligations in the contract.
- Recognise revenue when (or as) the entity satisfies a performance obligation.

6.26 Difficulty may arise in relation to the above where for example contracts for leases are embarked upon. Close collaboration, between legal and accounting functions of a business, is necessary in relation to the development of contracts (especially for leases, or mission critical say for a business which licenses proprietary software and provides related installation, configuration, customisation and maintenance services) to ensure accurate and robust reporting is maintained with regard to how revenue is recognised.

7 Anti-corruption

'Many multinationals with overseas operations are subject to the UK Bribery Act… so rather than having different policies for different jurisdictions they are just adopting the highest common denominator. A lot of companies don't want to have to explain to employees and third parties what payments can and can't be made… it's clearer and there is less risk to have a zero tolerance approach.'

Caroline Cox,

Group General Counsel and Group Company Secretary, BHP Group plc[1]

Introduction

7.1 These most profound words from Caroline Cox above resonate through much of the subtext of this work. Most North American in-house counsel will be familiar with The Foreign Corrupt Practices Act, prior to which bribery was an accepted business practice in many places worldwide.[2] Prior to 1977 it was so commonplace it was often tax deductible in many jurisdictions.[3] In 1977 the United States of America moved to outlaw this practice by US firms and individuals, with the aforementioned Foreign Corrupt Practices Act.

1 BHP, formerly known as BHP Billiton is an Anglo-Australian multinational mining, metals and petroleum dual-listed public company headquartered in Melbourne, Victoria, Australia. Founded in 1885 in New South Wales, by 2017 BHP ranked as the world's largest mining company, based on market capitalisation and as Melbourne's third-largest company by revenue.

2 See Sharifa G Hunter, 'A Comparative Analysis of the Foreign Corrupt Practices Act and the UK Bribery Act, and the Practical Implications of both on International Business' (2011) 18(1) *NSU ISLA Journal of International & Comparative Law.*

3 ibid.

7.2 Those lawyers initially trained outside of the United Kingdom may be forgiven for not having studied the UK Bribery Act of 2010. The UK Bribery Act has a wider breadth (it creates four anti-bribery offences) than the Foreign Corrupt Practices Act and also enjoys the same extra-territorial reach where a challenged act or omission took place physically outside of the United Kingdom.[4]

7.3 Therefore, as a General Counsel or executive, undertaking business in the UK or internationally you should become familiar with its terms.

7.4 Corruption can be thought of quite simply as the abuse of power for private gain.[5] It has been variously referred to as a 'scourge' and as 'blighting lives'.[6] The European Commission view corruption as being multi-faceted as to form, encompassing bribery, trading in influence, abuse of functions, but also nepotism, conflicts of interest, or revolving doors between the public and the private sectors noting the effects are serious and widespread.[7] The Commission have long viewed corruption as 'a threat to security, as an enabler for crime and terrorism. It acts as a drag on economic growth, by creating business uncertainty, slowing processes, and imposing additional costs … lowering investment levels, hampering the fair operation of … markets and reducing public finances'.[8]

7.5 This chapter will endeavour to provide a clear understanding of the key concerns for corporate counsel when operating in EMEA jurisdictions. Anti-corruption legislation is a somewhat rare creature as on a global basis it is dominated by a small number of pieces of national legislation that transcend borders and exert a significant effect extra-jurisdictionally. The Foreign Corrupt Practices Act in the US and the Bribery Act in the UK serve as the de facto anti-corruption legislative framework globally given the predominance of commercial interests that can trace a connection to either the US or the UK. The latter of these, the Bribery Act, will be expounded upon hereafter because, as referred to in the quote opening this chapter, the UK Bribery Act is increasingly being adopted by many multinationals as the de facto governing policy in this area given its extraterritorial reach. In addition, European attempts to curb corruption have focused on anti-money laundering measures that shall be considered elsewhere in this text. However, this chapter will consider the anti-corruption efforts of many of the EMEA nations in summary form.

The Bribery Act 2010

7.6 The Bribery Act 2010 received Royal Assent on 8 April 2010 and creates various new offences, one of which can be committed by commercial organisations which fail to prevent persons associated with them from committing bribery on their behalf. It is a full defence for an organisation to prove that despite a particular case of bribery it nevertheless had adequate procedures in place to prevent persons associated with it from bribing.[9]

4 ibid.
5 As defined by European Commission – Migration and Home Affairs.
6 Guidance on the Bribery Act 2010 as published by the UK government.
7 https://ec.europa.eu/home-affairs/what-we-do/policies/organized-crime-and-human-trafficking/corruption_en
8 ibid.
9 Bribery Act 2010, s 7.

Jurisdiction

7.7 Perhaps the key feature of the Act that gives the provision the transcendent relevance is that UK courts will have jurisdiction not only over offences that occur in the UK but also over offences outside the UK where the person committing them has a close connection with the UK by virtue of being a British national or ordinarily resident in the UK, a body incorporated in the UK or a Scottish partnership.[10] What amounts to a close connection is provided for by the Act and corporate counsel should take careful note of the potential for application of these provisions in all scenarios involving bribery.

A close connection with the UK

7.8 A person has a close connection with the UK if, and only if, the person was one of the following at the time the acts or omissions concerned were done or made:[11]

- a British citizen;
- a British overseas territories citizen;
- a British national (overseas);
- a British overseas citizen;
- a person who under the British Nationality Act 1981 was a British subject;
- a British protected person within the meaning of that Act;
- an individual ordinarily resident in the UK;
- a body incorporated under the law of any part of the UK;
- a Scottish partnership.

Irrelevance of locus of the offence

7.9 An offence is committed irrespective of whether the acts or omissions which form part of the offence take place in the UK or elsewhere.[12]

Offence of bribing another person

7.10 In relation to cases of bribing another person, a person ('P') is guilty of an offence if either of the following cases applies.[13]

- Case 1 is where:[14]
  - (a) P offers, promises or gives a financial or other advantage to another person; and
  - (b) P intends the advantage:
    - (i) to induce a person to perform improperly a relevant function or activity; or
    - (ii) to reward a person for the improper performance of such a function or activity.

---

10 ibid, s 12.
11 ibid, s 12(4).
12 Being an offence under s 7 of the Act. Bribery Act 2010, s 12(5).
13 Bribery Act 2010, s 1(1).
14 ibid, s 1(2).

- Case 2 is where:[15]
  - (a) P offers, promises or gives a financial or other advantage to another person; and
  - (b) P knows or believes that the acceptance of the advantage would itself constitute the improper performance of a relevant function or activity.

In case 1 it does not matter whether the person to whom the advantage is offered, promised or given is the same person as the person who is to perform, or has performed, the function or activity concerned.[16] In cases 1 and 2 it does not matter whether the advantage is offered, promised or given by P directly or through a third party.[17]

Offences relating to being bribed

7.11 A person ('R') is guilty of an offence if any of the following cases applies:[18]

- Case 3 is where R requests, agrees to receive or accepts a financial or other advantage intending that, in consequence, a relevant function or activity should be performed improperly (whether by R or another person).[19]
- Case 4 is where:[20]
  - (a) R requests, agrees to receive or accepts a financial or other advantage; and
  - (b) the request, agreement or acceptance itself constitutes the improper performance by R of a relevant function or activity.
- Case 5 is where R requests, agrees to receive or accepts a financial or other advantage as a reward for the improper performance (whether by R or another person) of a relevant function or activity.[21]
- Case 6 is where, in anticipation of or in consequence of R requesting, agreeing to receive or accepting a financial or other advantage, a relevant function or activity is performed improperly:[22]
  - (a) by R; or
  - (b) by another person at R's request or with R's assent or acquiescence.

In cases 3 to 6 it does not matter:[23]

(a) whether R requests, agrees to receive or accepts (or is to request, agree to receive or accept) the advantage directly or through a third party;

(b) whether the advantage is (or is to be) for the benefit of R or another person.

In cases 4 to 6 it does not matter whether R knows or believes that the performance of the function or activity is improper.[24] In case 6, where a person other than R is

15 ibid, s 1(3).
16 ibid, s 1(4).
17 ibid, s 1(5).
18 ibid, s 2(1).
19 ibid, s 2(2).
20 ibid, s 2(3).
21 ibid, s 2(4).
22 ibid, s 2(5).
23 ibid, s 2(6).
24 ibid, s 2(7).

performing the function or activity, it also does not matter whether that person knows or believes that the performance of the function or activity is improper.[25]

Function or activity to which bribe relates

7.12 The following functions and activities fall within the scope of the Act if it is any function of a public nature, or any activity connected with a business, or any activity performed in the course of a person's employment, or any activity performed by or on behalf of a body of persons (whether corporate or unincorporate).[26]

7.13 Additionally one or more of the following conditions must be met:

- That a person performing the function or activity is expected to perform it in good faith.[27]
- That a person performing the function or activity is expected to perform it impartially.[28]
- That a person performing the function or activity is in a position of trust by virtue of performing it.[29]

A function or activity is a relevant function or activity even if it has no connection with the UK, and is performed in a country or territory outside the UK.[30] For the avoidance of doubt the Act confirms that for the purpose of this offence 'business' will be interpreted widely as including a trade or profession.[31]

Standard of performance

7.14 A function or activity is to be treated as being performed improperly if there is a failure to perform the function or activity and that failure is itself a breach of a relevant expectation.[32] In assessing if a relevant expectation has been breached the test is set out by the Act as being 'a test of what a reasonable person in the United Kingdom would expect in relation to the performance of the type of function or activity concerned'.[33]

Disregard of custom or practice

7.15 In deciding what such a person would expect in relation to the performance of a function or activity where the performance is not subject to the law of any part of the UK, any local custom or practice is to be disregarded unless it is permitted or required by the written law applicable to the country or territory concerned.[34]

---

25 ibid, s 2(8).
26 ibid, s 3(1)–(2).
27 ibid, s 3(3).
28 ibid, s 3(4).
29 ibid, s 3(5).
30 ibid, s 3(6).
31 ibid, s 3(7).
32 ibid, s 4.
33 ibid, s 5(1).
34 ibid, s 5(2).

Bribery of foreign public officials[35]

7.16 A person ('P') who bribes a foreign public official ('F') is guilty of an offence if P's intention is to influence F in F's capacity as a foreign public official.[36] P must also intend to obtain or retain business, or retain an advantage in the conduct of business.[37]

7.17 Additionally, P bribes F if, and only if, directly or through a third party, P offers, promises or gives any financial or other advantage to F, or to another person at F's request or with F's assent or acquiescence, and F is neither permitted nor required by the written law applicable to F to be influenced in F's capacity as a foreign public official by the offer, promise or gift.[38]

7.18 Bona fide hospitality and promotional, or other business expenditure which seeks to improve the image of a commercial organisation, better to present products and services, or establish cordial relations, is recognised as an established and important part of doing business and it is not the intention of the Act to criminalise such behaviour.[39]

Failure of commercial organisations to prevent bribery

The offence

7.19 The offence that will be of key consideration to corporate counsel is where there has been a failure to prevent bribery on the part of a company or corporate entity. The components of this offence, and indeed the associated defence, are set out at section 7 of the Act and it is in relation to section 7 that the extra-jurisdictional aspects of section 1 (set out above) are of key importance. The section speaks for itself and is worthy of reproduction here:[40]

'(1) A relevant commercial organisation ("C") is guilty of an offence under this section if a person ("A") associated with C bribes another person intending—

(a) to obtain or retain business for C, or

(b) to obtain or retain an advantage in the conduct of business for C.

(2) But it is a defence for C to prove that C had in place adequate procedures designed to prevent persons associated with C from undertaking such conduct.

(3) For the purposes of this section, A bribes another person if, and only if, A—

(a) is, or would be, guilty of an offence under section 1 or 6 (whether or not A has been prosecuted for such an offence), or

(b) would be guilty of such an offence if section 12(2)(c) and (4) were omitted.

35 'Foreign public official' means an individual who: (a) holds a legislative, administrative or judicial position of any kind, whether appointed or elected, of a country or territory outside the United Kingdom (or any subdivision of such a country or territory, (b) exercises a public function: (i) for or on behalf of a country or territory outside the United Kingdom (or any subdivision of such a country or territory), or (ii) for any public agency or public enterprise of that country or territory (or subdivision), or (c) is an official or agent of a public international organisation.

36 Bribery Act 2010, s 6(1).

37 ibid, s 6(2).

38 ibid, s 6(3).

39 Guidance on the Bribery Act 2010 as published by the UK government.

40 Bribery Act 2010, s 7.

(4) See section 8 for the meaning of a person associated with C and see section 9 for a duty on the Secretary of State to publish guidance.

(5) In this section—

"partnership" means—

(a) a partnership within the Partnership Act 1890, or

(b) a limited partnership registered under the Limited Partnerships Act 1907, or a firm or entity of a similar character formed under the law of a country or territory outside the United Kingdom,

"relevant commercial organisation" means—

(a) a body which is incorporated under the law of any part of the United Kingdom and which carries on a business (whether there or elsewhere),

(b) any other body corporate (wherever incorporated) which carries on a business, or part of a business, in any part of the United Kingdom,

(c) a partnership which is formed under the law of any part of the United Kingdom and which carries on a business (whether there or elsewhere), or

(d) any other partnership (wherever formed) which carries on a business, or part of a business, in any part of the United Kingdom,

and for the purposes of this section, a trade or profession is a business.'

7.20 For the purposes of the section it is important to be clear as to the definition of what is meant in subsection 1 by the phrase 'associated person'. Section 8 of the Act goes on to elucidate the following points in relation to associated persons which amounts to a rather broad definition:

- A person ('A') is associated with C if (disregarding any bribe under consideration) A is a person who performs services for or on behalf of C.
- The capacity in which A performs services for or on behalf of C does not matter.
- Accordingly A may (for example) be C's employee, agent or subsidiary.
- Whether or not A is a person who performs services for or on behalf of C is to be determined by reference to all the relevant circumstances and not merely by reference to the nature of the relationship between A and C.
- But if A is an employee of C, it is to be presumed unless the contrary is shown that A is a person who performs services for or on behalf of C.

The defence

7.21 Section 7(2) of the Act provides for a defence in that it is a defence for C to prove that C had in place adequate procedures designed to prevent persons associated with C from undertaking such conduct.

7.22 Guidance issued by the UK Government considers that procedures put in place by commercial organisations wishing to prevent bribery from being committed on their behalf should be informed by six principles. They are intended to be flexible and outcome focussed, allowing for the huge variety of circumstances that commercial organisations find themselves in.[41]

41 Guidance on the Bribery Act 2010 as published by the UK government, at p 20.

1. *Proportionate procedures*

   A commercial organisation's procedures to prevent bribery by persons associated with it are proportionate to the bribery risks it faces and to the nature, scale and complexity of the commercial organisation's activities. They must also be clear, practical, accessible, effectively implemented and enforced.[42]

2. *Top-level commitment*

   The top-level management of a commercial organisation (be it a board of directors, the owners or any other equivalent body or person) must be committed to preventing bribery by persons associated with it. They must foster a culture within the organisation in which bribery is never acceptable.[43]

3. *Risk assessment*

   The commercial organisation assesses the nature and extent of its exposure to potential external and internal risks of bribery on its behalf by persons associated with it. The assessment should be periodic, informed and documented.

4. *Due diligence*

   The commercial organisation applies due diligence procedures, taking a proportionate and risk-based approach, in respect of persons who perform or will perform services for or on behalf of the organisation, in order to mitigate identified bribery risks.

5. *Communication (including training)*

   The commercial organisation should seek to ensure that its bribery prevention policies and procedures are embedded and understood throughout the organisation through internal and external communication, including training that is proportionate to the risks it faces.

6. *Monitoring and review*

   The commercial organisation monitors and reviews procedures designed to prevent bribery by persons associated with it and makes improvements where necessary.

UN Convention against corruption

7.23 The United Nations Convention against corruption has been described as the '… only legally binding universal anti-corruption instrument. The Convention's far-reaching approach and the mandatory character of many of its provisions make it a unique tool for developing a comprehensive response to a global problem. The vast majority of United Nations Member States are parties to the Convention.'[44]

7.24 The Convention covers five main areas:[45]

- preventive measures;
- criminalisation and law enforcement;
- international cooperation;

42 ibid, at p 21.
43 ibid, at p 23.
44 See www.unodc.org/unodc/en/corruption/uncac.html.
45 The full text of the convention is available at UN Office on Drugs and Crime website, see www.unodc.org.

- asset recovery; and
- technical assistance and information exchange.

The Convention takes a broad definition on corruption, including behaviours such as bribery, trading in influence, abuse of functions, and various acts of corruption in the private sector.[46]

Country	**Signature date**	**Ratification date**
Afghanistan	20 Feb 2004	25 Aug 2008
Albania	18 Dec 2003	25 May 2006
Algeria	9 Dec 2003	25 Aug 2004
Angola	10 Dec 2003	29 Aug 2006
Armenia	19 May 2005	8 Mar 2007
Austria	10 Dec 2003	11 Jan 2006
Azerbaijan	27 Feb 2004	1 Nov 2005
Bahrain	8 Feb 2005	5 Oct 2010
Belarus	28 Apr 2004	17 Feb 2005
Belgium	10 Dec 2003	25 Sep 2008
Benin	10 Dec 2003	14 Oct 2004
Bosnia and Herzegovina	16 Sep 2005	26 Oct 2006
Botswana		27 Jun 2011 a
Brunei Darussalam	11 Dec 2003	2 Dec 2008
Bulgaria	10 Dec 2003	20 Sep 2006
Burkina Faso	10 Dec 2003	10 Oct 2006
Burundi		10 Mar 2006 a
Cabo Verde	9 Dec 2003	23 Apr 2008
Cameroon	10 Dec 2003	6 Feb 2006
Central African Republic	11 Feb 2004	6 Oct 2006
Chad		26 June 2018 a
Congo		13 Jul 2006 a
Côte d'Ivoire	10 Dec 2003	25 Oct 2012
Croatia	10 Dec 2003	24 Apr 2005
Cyprus	9 Dec 2003	23 Feb 2009
Czechia	22 Apr 2005	29 Nov 2013
Democratic Republic of the Congo		23 Sep 2010 a
Denmark	10 Dec 2003	26 Dec 2006
Djibouti	17 Jun 2004	20 Apr 2005
Egypt	9 Dec 2003	25 Feb 2005
Estonia		12 Apr 2010 a
Ethiopia	10 Dec 2003	26 Nov 2007
European Union	15 Sep 2005	12 Nov 2008 AA

46 See www.unodc.org/unodc/en/corruption/uncac.html.

Country	Signature date	Ratification date
Finland	9 Dec 2003	20 Jun 2006 A
France	9 Dec 2003	11 Jul 2005
Gabon	10 Dec 2003	1 Oct 2007
Gambia		8 Jul 2015 a
Georgia		4 Nov 2008 a
Germany	9 Dec 2003	12 Nov 2014
Ghana	9 Dec 2004	27 Jun 2007
Greece	10 Dec 2003	17 Sep 2008
Holy See		19 Sep 2016 a
Hungary	10 Dec 2003	19 Apr 2005
Iceland		1 Mar 2011 a
Iran (Islamic Republic of)	9 Dec 2003	20 Apr 2009
Iraq		17 Mar 2008 a
Ireland	9 Dec 2003	09 Nov 2011
Israel	29 Nov 2005	4 Feb 2009
Italy	9 Dec 2003	5 Oct 2009
Jordan	9 Dec 2003	24 Feb 2005
Kazakhstan		18 Jun 2008 a
Kenya	9 Dec 2003	9 Dec 2003
Kuwait	9 Dec 2003	16 Feb 2007
Kyrgyzstan	10 Dec 2003	16 Sep 2005
Latvia	19 May 2005	4 Jan 2006
Lebanon		22 Apr 2009 a
Lesotho	16 Sep 2005	16 Sep 2005
Liberia		16 Sep 2005 a
Libya	23 Dec 2003	7 Jun 2005
Liechtenstein	10 Dec 2003	8 Jul 2010
Lithuania	10 Dec 2003	21 Dec 2006
Luxembourg	10 Dec 2003	6 Nov 2007
Madagascar	10 Dec 2003	22 Sep 2004
Malawi	21 Sep 2004	4 Dec 2007
Mali	9 Dec 2003	18 Apr 2008
Malta	12 May 2005	11 Apr 2008
Moldova	28 Sep 2004	1 Oct 2007
Mongolia	29 Apr 2005	11 Jan 2006
Montenegro		23 Oct 2006 d
Morocco	9 Dec 2003	9 May 2007
Mozambique	25 May 2004	9 Apr 2008
Namibia	9 Dec 2003	3 Aug 2004
Netherlands	10 Dec 2003	31 Oct 2006 A

Country	Signature date	Ratification date
Niger		11 Aug 2008 a
Nigeria	9 Dec 2003	14 Dec 2004
North Macedonia	18 Aug 2005	13 Apr 2007
Norway	9 Dec 2003	29 Jun 2006
Oman		9 Jan 2014
Poland	10 Dec 2003	15 Sep 2006
Portugal	11 Dec 2003	28 Sep 2007
Qatar	1 Dec 2005	30 Jan 2007
Romania	9 Dec 2003	2 Nov 2004
Russian Federation	9 Dec 2003	9 May 2006
Rwanda	30 Nov 2004	4 Oct 2006
Saudi Arabia	9 Jan 2004	29 April 2013
Senegal	9 Dec 2003	16 Nov 2005
Serbia	11 Dec 2003	20 Dec 2005
Sierra Leone	9 Dec 2003	30 Sep 2004
Slovakia	9 Dec 2003	1 Jun 2006
Slovenia		1 Apr 2008 a
South Africa	9 Dec 2003	22 Nov 2004
South Sudan		23 Jan 2015 a
Spain	16 Sep 2005	19 Jun 2006
Sri Lanka	15 Mar 2004	31 Mar 2004
State of Palestine		2 Apr 2014 a
Sudan	14 Jan 2005	5 Sep 2014
Sweden	9 Dec 2003	25 Sep 2007
Switzerland	10 Dec 2003	24 Sep 2009
Syrian Arab Republic	9 Dec 2003	
Tajikistan		25 Sep 2006 a
Tunisia	30 Mar 2004	23 Sep 2008
Turkey	10 Dec 2003	9 Nov 2006
Turkmenistan		28 Mar 2005 a
Uganda	9 Dec 2003	9 Sep 2004
Ukraine	11 Dec 2003	02 Dec 2009
United Arab Emirates	10 Aug 2005	22 Feb 2006
United Kingdom of Great Britain and Northern Ireland	9 Dec 2003	9 Feb 2006
United Republic of Tanzania	9 Dec 2003	25 May 2005
Uzbekistan		29 Jul 2008 a
Yemen	11 Dec 2003	7 Nov 2005
Zambia	11 Dec 2003	7 Dec 2007
Zimbabwe	20 Feb 2004	8 Mar 2007

National anti-corruption measures

7.25 The EU Anti-Corruption Report, published in 2014, demonstrated that the nature and scope of corruption varies from one EU country to another and that the effectiveness of anti-corruption policies is quite different.[47]

7.26 The EU Commission noted that 'corruption continues to be a challenge for Europe – a phenomenon that costs the European economy around 120 billion euros per year. EU member countries have taken many initiatives in recent years, but the results are uneven and more should be done to prevent and punish corruption'.

7.27 Findings from a Eurobarometer survey indicated that Europeans are 'deeply worried about corruption – three quarters (76%) of Europeans think that corruption is widespread and more than half (56%) think that the level of corruption in their country has increased over the past three years.'[48]

7.28 Some of the key legislative measures aimed at combatting corruption in various EMEA regions are set out below:

Country	Focus	Provisions
Austria	• Within Jurisdiction	Section 304 to Section 308 of the Austrian Criminal Law Code (Strafgesetzbuch or StGB)
	• Extra-jurisdiction	Sections 309 and 153a of the StGB
		No additional regulations to the above apply
Azerbaijan	• Within Jurisdiction • Extra-jurisdiction	The Law of the Republic of Azerbaijan, On Combatting Corruption, dated 13 January 2004
		Section 1.1 above, the Criminal Code
		Section 1.1 above, the Criminal Code
Belgium	• Within Jurisdiction	Articles 246 to 252 of the Belgian Criminal Code (the 'Public Bribery Statute')
	• Extra-jurisdiction	Article 504 bis and 504 ter of the Private Bribery Statute.
		Article 250 of the Public Bribery Statute, which refers to Articles 246 to 249 of the same statute
Czech Republic	• Within Jurisdiction	Article 331 of the Czech Criminal Code, as well as the Czech Civil Code
	• Extra-jurisdiction	Section 331 of the Czech Criminal Code
Egypt	• Within Jurisdiction	Articles 103 to 111 of the Penal Code
	• Extra-jurisdiction	Articles 103 to 111 of the Penal Code

47 See https://www.ec.europa.eu.
48 ibid, EU Anti-Corruption Report, published in 2014.

Country	**Focus**	**Provisions**
France	• Within Jurisdiction	Articles 433-1, 432-11, of the French Criminal Code
	• Extra-jurisdiction	Articles 445-1 to 445-2 of the French Criminal Code
		Articles 435-1 to 435-3 of the French Criminal Code
		Article 435-6-2 of the French Criminal Code
Germany	• Within Jurisdiction	Sections 331 to 338 of the German Criminal Code
		Sections 299 to 301of the German Criminal Code
	• Extra-jurisdiction	Section 335a German Criminal Code
Hungary	• Within Jurisdiction	Hungarian Criminal Code, Articles 293 to 294 and 298 to 300 of Act C of 2012
	• Extra-jurisdiction	Hungarian Criminal Code, Articles 290 to 291, 295 to 296, 298 to 300 of Act C of 2012
		Hungarian Criminal Code, Articles 293(3) and 294(4) of Act C of 2012
Italy	• Within Jurisdiction	Sections 317, 318, 319, 319-quarter, 320, 321 and 322 of the Italian Criminal Code
	• Extra-jurisdiction	Section 2635 of the Italian Civil Code
		Section 322 of the ICC
Kazakhstan	• Within Jurisdiction	Articles 366 to 368 of the Kazakhstani Criminal Code
	• Extra-jurisdiction	Articles 676 to 681 of the Code of Administrative Offences
		Law on State Service of the Republic of Kazakhstan
		Law on Countering Corruption
		Article 253 of the Criminal Code.
		Articles 366 and 367 of the Criminal Code
Luxembourg	• Within Jurisdiction	Articles 240 and 310 of the Luxembourg Criminal Code
	• Extra-jurisdiction	Article 252 of the Luxembourg Criminal Code
Morocco	• Within Jurisdiction	Articles 248 to 256 and Article 249 of the Moroccan Criminal Code
	• Extra-jurisdiction	No additional regulations to the above apply

Country	Focus	Provisions
Netherlands	• Within Jurisdiction	Articles 177 and 363 of the Dutch Criminal Code
	• Extra-jurisdiction	Article 328ter of the Dutch Criminal Code
		No additional regulations to the above apply
Poland	• Within Jurisdiction	Articles 228 to 230a and Article 296a of the Polish Penal Code (PC)
	• Extra-jurisdiction	No additional regulations to the above apply
Saudi Arabia	• Within Jurisdiction	Royal Decree M/36 dated 29/12/1412H, corresponding to 27/6/1992G
	• Extra-jurisdiction	No additional regulations to the above apply
South Africa	• Within Jurisdiction	Prevention and Combating of Corrupt Activities Act 2004 (PCCAA)
	• Extra-jurisdiction	No additional regulations to the above apply
Switzerland	• Within Jurisdiction	Swiss Criminal Code, Articles 322ter to 322quater
	• Extra-jurisdiction	Swiss Criminal Code, Articles 322octies to 322novies.
		Swiss Criminal Code, Article 322septies
Turkey	• Within Jurisdiction	Turkish Criminal Code No. 5237, Article 252
	• Extra-jurisdiction	Turkish Criminal Code No. 5237, Article 252
Ukraine	• Within Jurisdiction	Criminal Code of Ukraine (Chapter XVII)
	• Extra-jurisdiction	Criminal Code of Ukraine (Chapter XVII)

Final word

7.29 It is no longer, under any circumstances, an acceptable option in anyone's legitimate business play book to tolerate corruption and this included having a corporate policy that pays lip service to the law and at the same time for the business, in practice to look the other way. Active and appropriate steps in education, prevention, detection and action are the final watchwords in relations to this subject.

8 Anti-money laundering

'Put simply, the way we do financial crime compliance is outdated...It is neither as efficient nor effective as it could be at protecting the financial system from abuse and preventing financial crime ... If we do not collaborate better, we risk being one step behind in our efforts to keep illicit actors out of the system while also exacerbating the problem of financial exclusion.'

Stuart Levey

Chief Legal Officer, HSBC Holdings plc[1]

Introduction

8.1 Two words to strike fear into the heart of all corporate counsel – money laundering. For the uninitiated:

> 'Money laundering is a process by which illegally acquired money, or "dirty money", is made to appear legal, or "clean", so that criminals can freely spend it. Examples of dirty money might include proceeds from financial crimes, drug trafficking or other illicit activities.'[2]

---

1 HSBC is one of the largest banking and financial services organisations in the world, with operations in 66 countries and territories. Mr Levey was the first Under Secretary for Terrorism and Financial Intelligence in the US Department of the Treasury, serving from July 2004 to February 2011 under Presidents Bush and Obama. After leaving the Treasury Department, Mr Levey was a Senior Fellow for National Security and Financial Integrity at the Council on Foreign Relations. Prior to his Treasury appointment, Mr Levey served as the Principal Associate Deputy Attorney General at the US Department of Justice, having previously served as an Associate Deputy Attorney General and as the Chief of Staff of the Deputy Attorney General. He joined the Justice Department in 2001 after 11 years in private practice at the Washington law firm Miller, Cassidy, Larroca & Lewin LLP (which merged into Baker Botts LLP), where he had a litigation practice. Mr Levey graduated from Harvard College summa cum laude in 1986 and from Harvard Law School magna cum laude in 1989 (www.hsbc.com/who-we-are/leadership/stuart-levey).

2 Alina Laumann, 'The History of Anti-Money Laundering – Events, Regulations, and Adaptations in the United States' (Kroll, a division of Duff & Phelps) https://www.kroll.com/en/insights/publications/history-anti-money-laundering-united-states.

In the United States of America, the recognition of and the criminalisation of money laundering stems from various efforts to combat criminal activities in the early 20th century. Particularly those of organised crime leaders like Al Capone, who laundered proceeds from illegal liquor sales and prostitution through his chain of literal laundromats. Hence the birth of the term 'money laundering'.[3]

8.2 While the history of the fight against money laundering may trace its roots, arguably, to the wildly romanticised days of Prohibition in the United States of America, the fight against modern money laundering, however, is a comparatively much more recent initiative. Its beginnings are attributed to the US Bank Secrecy Act 1970. This legislation forced financial institutions to record and report large cash transactions, and generally inform the government about any suspicious fiscal activity that might indicate money laundering, tax evasion, or criminal activity.[4]

8.3 Money laundering was first criminalised in the United Kingdom (in respect of the proceeds of drug trafficking) by means of an offence set out in the Drug Trafficking Offences Act 1986.

8.4 Not unlike the revelation in the previous chapter concerning anti-corruption, so too the fight against money laundering is a fairly new international legal construct. As stated above it only really began to take shape in early 1970s, in the USA, and until comparatively recently, by any standard, the participation in the laundering of assets (even those that were known to have stemmed from a criminal enterprise) was not, other than under certain rare circumstances, subject to criminal sanctions in even the more advanced countries in Europe, such as Switzerland.[5] I can even remember one of my English Law professors, during a lecture, likening the Swiss legal view of money laundering (and particularly in the contest of tax avoidance) as being more akin to a sport than anything like criminality.

8.5 Those of you who are now wrestling with the seemingly never-ending process of ultra-intrusive vetting so closely associated with and undertaken by your company's lawyers and bankers would be entirely forgiven for doubting the truth in the preceding paragraph.

8.6 Thanks however to the multibillion-dollar drug cartels and the funding source of the terror group responsible for the 11 September 2001 attacks in the United States, the government of the United States along with the governments of its allies (and states not so closely allied) have greatly accelerated their efforts to combat modern money laundering and other financial crime.

The European Union's Fourth Directive

8.7 The Directive of the European Parliament and of the Council of 20 May 2015 on the prevention of the use of the financial system for the purposes of money

---

3 ibid.

4 'A Brief History of Money Laundering' (*EverCompliant*, 30 September 2017) https://evercompliant.com/brief-history-money-laundering/.

5 Rebecca G Peters, 'Money Laundering and Its Current Status In Switzerland: New Disincentives For Financial Tourism' (1990) 11(1) *Northwestern Journal of International Law & Business*.

laundering or terrorist financing[6] is the key legislative instrument for corporate council purposes. It has been amended in recent years but remains the key source for understanding the obligations faced by corporate actors in the European landscape.

What is money laundering?

8.8 The directive regards the following conduct, 'when committed intentionally' as amounting to money laundering:

(a) the conversion or transfer of property, knowing that such property is derived from criminal activity or from an act of participation in such activity, for the purpose of concealing or disguising the illicit origin of the property or of assisting any person who is involved in the commission of such an activity to evade the legal consequences of that person's action;

(b) the concealment or disguise of the true nature, source, location, disposition, movement, rights with respect to, or ownership of, property, knowing that such property is derived from criminal activity or from an act of participation in such an activity;

(c) the acquisition, possession or use of property, knowing, at the time of receipt, that such property was derived from criminal activity or from an act of participation in such an activity;

(d) participation in, association to commit, attempts to commit and aiding, abetting, facilitating and counselling the commission of any of the actions referred to in points (a), (b) and (c).

Am I obliged to act?

8.9 The first question to address is the obvious one – what are the legal obligations facing the corporation, if any? The following entities, referred to as obliged entities, have obligations under the directive:[7]

- auditors, external accountants and tax advisers;
- notaries and other independent legal professionals, where they participate, whether by acting on behalf of and for their client in any financial or real estate transaction, or by assisting in the planning or carrying out of transactions for their client concerning the:
  - buying and selling of real property or business entities;
  - managing of client money, securities or other assets;
  - opening or management of bank, savings or securities accounts;
  - organisation of contributions necessary for the creation, operation or management of companies;
  - creation, operation or management of trusts, companies, foundations, or similar structures;

---

6 Directive (EU) 2015/849 of the European Parliament and of the Council of 20 May 2015 on the prevention of the use of the financial system for the purposes of money laundering or terrorist financing, amending Regulation (EU) No 648/2012 of the European Parliament and of the Council, and repealing Directive 2005/60/EC of the European Parliament and of the Council and Commission Directive 2006/70/EC.

7 ibid, Art 2(1).

- trust or company service providers not already covered under point (a) or (b);
- estate agents;
- other persons trading in goods to the extent that payments are made or received in cash in an amount of EUR 10,000 or more, whether the transaction is carried out in a single operation or in several operations which appear to be linked;
- providers of gambling services.

What are the key definitions?

8.10 Key to the appreciation of the directive is an understanding of the often technical terms contained within and which will litter the following pages. Hence it is useful to set out a selection of some of the more useful definitions here at the outset.

8.11 Certain definitions are of such central importance, in particular, those relating to beneficial ownership and trusts that a full exposition is required here. Others, while comprising no lesser importance are prohibitively technical and are better served by specific citation, set out below.[8]

Property[9]

8.12 Assets of any kind, whether corporeal or incorporeal, movable or immovable, tangible or intangible, and legal documents or instruments in any form including electronic or digital, evidencing title to or an interest in such assets.

Self-regulatory body[10]

8.13 A body that represents members of a profession and has a role in regulating them, in performing certain supervisory or monitoring type functions and in ensuring the enforcement of the rules relating to them.

Beneficial owner[11]

8.14 Any natural person(s) who ultimately owns or controls the customer and/or the natural person(s) on whose behalf a transaction or activity is being conducted and includes at least:

(a) in the case of corporate entities:

(i) the natural person(s) who ultimately owns or controls a legal entity through direct or indirect ownership of a sufficient percentage of the shares or voting rights or ownership interest in that entity, including through bearer shareholdings, or through control via other means, other than a company listed on a regulated market that is subject to disclosure requirements consistent with Union law or subject to equivalent international standards which ensure adequate transparency of ownership information.

A shareholding of 25% plus one share or an ownership interest of more than 25% in the customer held by a natural person shall be an indication of direct

8 Financial Institution (Art 3.2); Criminal Activity (Art 3.4); Correspondent relationship (Art 3.8).
9 ibid, Art 3.3.
10 ibid, Art 3.5.
11 ibid, Art 3.6.

ownership. A shareholding of 25% plus one share or an ownership interest of more than 25% in the customer held by a corporate entity, which is under the control of a natural person(s), or by multiple corporate entities, which are under the control of the same natural person(s), shall be an indication of indirect ownership. This applies without prejudice to the right of member states to decide that a lower percentage may be an indication of ownership or control. Control through other means may be determined, *inter alia*, in accordance with the criteria in Article 22(1) to (5) of Directive 2013/34/EU of the European Parliament and of the Council (29);

(ii) if, after having exhausted all possible means and provided there are no grounds for suspicion, no person under point (i) is identified, or if there is any doubt that the person(s) identified are the beneficial owner(s), the natural person(s) who hold the position of senior managing official(s), the obliged entities shall keep records of the actions taken in order to identify the beneficial ownership under point (i) and this point;

(b) in the case of trusts:

(i) the settlor;

(ii) the trustee(s);

(iii) the protector, if any;

(iv) the beneficiaries, or where the individuals benefiting from the legal arrangement or entity have yet to be determined, the class of persons in whose main interest the legal arrangement or entity is set up or operates;

(v) any other natural person exercising ultimate control over the trust by means of direct or indirect ownership or by other means;

(c) in the case of legal entities such as foundations, and legal arrangements similar to trusts, the natural person(s) holding equivalent or similar positions to those referred to in point (b).

Trust or company service provider[12]

8.15 Any person that, by way of its business, provides any of the following services to third parties:

(a) the formation of companies or other legal persons;

(b) acting as, or arranging for another person to act as, a director or secretary of a company, a partner of a partnership, or a similar position in relation to other legal persons;

(c) providing a registered office, business address, correspondence or administrative address and other related services for a company, a partnership or any other legal person or arrangement;

(d) acting as, or arranging for another person to act as, a trustee of an express trust or a similar legal arrangement;

(e) acting as, or arranging for another person to act as, a nominee shareholder for another person other than a company listed on a regulated market that is subject to disclosure requirements in accordance with Union law or subject to equivalent international standards.

12 ibid, Art 3.7.

Politically exposed person[13]

8.16 Means a natural person who is or who has been entrusted with prominent public functions and includes the following:

(a) heads of state, heads of government, ministers and deputy or assistant ministers;

(b) members of parliament or of similar legislative bodies;

(c) members of the governing bodies of political parties;

(d) members of supreme courts, of constitutional courts or of other high-level judicial bodies, the decisions of which are not subject to further appeal, except in exceptional circumstances;

(e) members of courts of auditors or of the boards of central banks;

(f) ambassadors, chargés d'affaires and high-ranking officers in the armed forces;

(g) members of the administrative, management or supervisory bodies of state-owned enterprises;

(h) directors, deputy directors and members of the board or equivalent function of an international organisation.

No public function referred to in points (a) to (h) shall be understood as covering middle-ranking or more junior officials.

Family members[14]

8.17 Includes the spouse, or a person considered to be equivalent to a spouse, of a politically exposed person; the children and their spouses, or persons considered to be equivalent to a spouse, of a politically exposed person and/or the parents of a politically exposed person.

Persons known to be close associates[15]

8.18 Natural persons who are known to have joint beneficial ownership of legal entities or legal arrangements, or any other close business relations, with a politically exposed person; natural persons who have sole beneficial ownership of a legal entity or legal arrangement which is known to have been set up for the de facto benefit of a politically exposed person.

Senior management[16]

8.19 An officer or employee with sufficient knowledge of the institution's money laundering and terrorist financing risk exposure and sufficient seniority to take decisions affecting its risk exposure, and need not, in all cases, be a member of the board of directors.

13 ibid, Art 3.9.
14 ibid, Art 3.10.
15 ibid, Art 3.11.
16 ibid, Art 3.12.

Business relationship[17]

8.20 A business, professional or commercial relationship which is connected with the professional activities of an obliged entity and which is expected, at the time when the contact is established, to have an element of duration.

Gambling services[18]

8.21 A service which involves wagering a stake with monetary value in games of chance, including those with an element of skill such as lotteries, casino games, poker games and betting transactions that are provided at a physical location, or by any means at a distance, by electronic means or any other technology for facilitating communication, and at the individual request of a recipient of services.

Shell bank[19]

8.22 A credit institution or financial institution, or an institution that carries out activities equivalent to those carried out by credit institutions and financial institutions, incorporated in a jurisdiction in which it has no physical presence, involving meaningful mind and management, and which is unaffiliated with a regulated financial group.

Customer due diligence

8.23 As a general proposition under the directive, credit institutions and financial institutions are prohibited from keeping anonymous accounts or anonymous passbooks. It is further required that the owners and beneficiaries of existing anonymous accounts or anonymous passbooks be subject to customer due diligence measures as soon as is possible and in any event before such accounts or passbooks are used in any way.[20] Other, previously ubiquitous assets come under the directive's spotlight, in that member states are required to prevent misuse of bearer shares and bearer share warrants, in particular.[21]

When to apply due diligence measures

8.24 As regards when obliged entities, as described above, are required to apply customer due diligence measures, they must do so:

(a) when establishing a business relationship;

(b) when carrying out an occasional transaction that:

    (i) amounts to EUR 15,000 or more, whether that transaction is carried out in a single operation or in several operations which appear to be linked; or

    (ii)) constitutes a transfer of funds exceeding EUR 1,000;

(c) in the case of persons trading in goods, when carrying out occasional transactions in cash amounting to EUR 10,000 or more, whether the transaction is carried out in a single operation or in several operations which appear to be linked;

17 ibid, Art 3.13.
18 ibid, Art 3.14.
19 ibid, Art 3.17.
20 ibid, Art 10.
21 ibid, Art 10.2.

(d) for providers of gambling services, upon the collection of winnings, the wagering of a stake, or both, when carrying out transactions amounting to EUR 2,000 or more, whether the transaction is carried out in a single operation or in several operations which appear to be linked;

(e) when there is a suspicion of money laundering or terrorist financing, regardless of any derogation, exemption or threshold;

(f) when there are doubts about the veracity or adequacy of previously obtained customer identification data.

What measures should be applied

8.25 Where required, obliged entities are required to adopt the following measures:[22]

(a) identifying the customer and verifying the customer's identity on the basis of documents, data or information obtained from a reliable and independent source;

(b) identifying the beneficial owner and taking reasonable measures to verify that person's identity so that the obliged entity is satisfied that it knows who the beneficial owner is, including, as regards legal persons, trusts, companies, foundations and similar legal arrangements, taking reasonable measures to understand the ownership and control structure of the customer;

(c) assessing and, as appropriate, obtaining information on the purpose and intended nature of the business relationship;

(d) conducting ongoing monitoring of the business relationship including scrutiny of transactions undertaken throughout the course of that relationship to ensure that the transactions being conducted are consistent with the obliged entity's knowledge of the customer, the business and risk profile, including where necessary the source of funds and ensuring that the documents, data or information held are kept up-to-date.

When performing the measures referred to in points (a) and (b) above, obliged entities must also verify that any person purporting to act on behalf of the customer is so authorised and identify and verify the identity of that person.

Risk-based approach

8.26 While obliged entities are required to apply each of the customer due diligence requirements laid down above, they may, however, determine the extent of such measures on a risk-sensitive basis.[23] Further, obliged entities are able to demonstrate to competent authorities or self-regulatory bodies that the measures are appropriate in view of the risks of money laundering and terrorist financing that have been identified.[24]

What about the beneficiaries of trusts?

8.27 In the case of beneficiaries of trusts or of similar legal arrangements that are designated by particular characteristics or class, an obliged entity shall obtain sufficient information concerning the beneficiary to satisfy the obliged entity that it will be able

22 ibid, Art 13.1.
23 ibid, Art 13.2.
24 ibid, Art 13.2.

to establish the identity of the beneficiary at the time of the pay-out or at the time of the exercise by the beneficiary of its vested rights.[25]

When should due diligence measures be applied?

8.28 Generally, it is a requirement that verification of the identity of the customer and the beneficial owner take place before the establishment of a business relationship or the carrying out of the transaction.[26] However, the directive is mindful of the vagaries of every day commercial life in recognising that individual member states may allow verification of the identity of the customer and the beneficial owner to be completed during the establishment of a business relationship if necessary so as not to interrupt the normal conduct of business and where there is little risk of money laundering or terrorist financing. In such situations, those procedures must be completed as soon as practicable after initial contact.[27] It will be necessary to consult with the appropriate national laws in each case. Similarly mindful of commercial reality, the directive also provides for a derogation that may allow the opening of an account with a credit institution or financial institution, including accounts that permit transactions in transferable securities, provided that there are adequate safeguards in place to ensure that transactions are not carried out by the customer or on its behalf until full compliance with the customer due diligence requirements.[28] However, the above derogations should be considered in the light of the general requirement that where an obliged entity is unable to comply with the customer due diligence requirements it must not carry out a transaction through a bank account, establish a business relationship or carry out the transaction, and must terminate the business relationship and consider making a suspicious transaction report to the appropriate financial intelligence unit.[29]

What about existing customers?

8.29 The customer due diligence requirements extend in scope to cover not just all new customers but existing ones also. Obliged entities must apply the customer due diligence measures, at appropriate times, to existing customers on a risk-sensitive basis, including at times when the relevant circumstances of a customer change.[30] Clearly a rolling obligation is created in this regard.

What if the perceived risk level is low?

8.30 Where an obliged entity identifies areas of lower risk, they may be permitted to apply simplified customer due diligence measures.[31] However, prior to doing so, they must positively ascertain that the business relationship or the transaction presents a lower degree of risk,[32] whilst always ensuring sufficient monitoring of the transactions and business relationships to enable the detection of unusual or suspicious transactions.[33]

25 ibid, Art 13.6.
26 ibid, Art 14.1.
27 ibid, Art 14.2.
28 ibid, Art 14.3.
29 ibid, Art 14.4.
30 ibid, Art 14.5.
31 ibid, Art 15.1.
32 ibid, Art 15.3.
33 ibid, Art 15.3.

8.31 The following non-exhaustive list of factors and types of evidence of potentially lower risk should, at minimum, be considered.

CUSTOMER RISK FACTORS

8.32

(a) Public companies listed on a stock exchange and subject to disclosure requirements (either by stock exchange rules or through law or enforceable means), which impose requirements to ensure adequate transparency of beneficial ownership.

(b) Public administrations or enterprises.

(c) Customers that are resident in geographical areas of lower risk as set out in point (3).

PRODUCT, SERVICE, TRANSACTION OR DELIVERY CHANNEL RISK FACTORS

8.33

(a) Life insurance policies for which the premium is low.

(b) Insurance policies for pension schemes if there is no early surrender option and the policy cannot be used as collateral.

(c) A pension, superannuation or similar scheme that provides retirement benefits to employees, where contributions are made by way of deduction from wages, and the scheme rules do not permit the assignment of a member's interest under the scheme.

(d) Financial products or services that provide appropriately defined and limited services to certain types of customers, so as to increase access for financial inclusion purposes.

(e) Products where the risks of money laundering and terrorist financing are managed by other factors such as purse limits or transparency of ownership (eg, certain types of electronic money).

GEOGRAPHICAL RISK FACTORS

8.34

(a) Member states.

(b) Third countries having effective AML/CFT systems.

(c) Third countries identified by credible sources as having a low level of corruption or other criminal activity.

(d) Third countries which, on the basis of credible sources such as mutual evaluations, detailed assessment reports or published follow-up reports, have requirements to combat money laundering and terrorist financing consistent with the revised FATF Recommendations and effectively implement those requirements.

What if the perceived risk level is high?

8.35 When dealing with natural persons or legal entities established in the third countries identified by the European Commission as high-risk third countries,[34] as well

34 This list is periodically reviewed, and as of February 2019 comprised 23 countries.

as in other cases of higher risk, obliged entities must apply enhanced customer due diligence measures to manage and mitigate those risks appropriately.[35]

8.36 The general duty requires obliged entities to examine, as far as reasonably possible, the background and purpose of all complex and unusually large transactions, and all unusual patterns of transactions, which have no apparent economic or lawful purpose. In particular, obliged entities shall increase the degree and nature of monitoring of the business relationship, in order to determine whether those transactions or activities appear suspicious.[36]

8.37 The following is a non-exhaustive list of factors and types of evidence of potentially higher risk:

Customer risk factors:

(a) the business relationship is conducted in unusual circumstances;

(b) customers that are resident in geographical areas of higher risk as set out below;

(c) legal persons or arrangements that are personal asset-holding vehicles;

(d) companies that have nominee shareholders or shares in bearer form;

(e) businesses that are cash-intensive;

(f) the ownership structure of the company appears unusual or excessively complex given the nature of the company's business.

Product, service, transaction or delivery channel risk factors:

(a) private banking;

(b) products or transactions that might favour anonymity;

(c) non-face-to-face business relationships or transactions, without certain safeguards, such as electronic signatures;

(d) payment received from unknown or unassociated third parties;

(e) new products and new business practices, including new delivery mechanism, and the use of new or developing technologies for both new and pre-existing products.

Geographical risk factors:

(a) without prejudice to Article 9, countries identified by credible sources, such as mutual evaluations, detailed assessment reports or published follow-up reports, as not having effective AML/CFT systems;

(b) countries identified by credible sources as having significant levels of corruption or other criminal activity;

(c) countries subject to sanctions, embargos or similar measures issued by, for example, the Union or the United Nations;

35 Directive (EU) 2015/849 of the European Parliament and of the Council of 20 May 2015 on the prevention of the use of the financial system for the purposes of money laundering or terrorist financing, amending Regulation (EU) No 648/2012 of the European Parliament and of the Council, and repealing Directive 2005/60/EC of the European Parliament and of the Council and Commission Directive 2006/70/EC, Art 18.1.

36 ibid, Art 18.2.

(d) countries providing funding or support for terrorist activities, or that have designated terrorist organisations operating within their country.

High risk countries

8.38 Enhanced due diligence measures are required in relation to the following jurisdictions (EMEA countries in bold):

(1) **Afghanistan**

(2) American Samoa

(3) The Bahamas

(4) **Botswana**

(5) Democratic People's Republic of Korea

(6) **Ethiopia**

(7) **Ghana**

(8) Guam

(9) **Iran**

(10) **Iraq**

(11) **Libya**

(12) **Nigeria**

(13) Pakistan

(14) Panama

(15) Puerto Rico

(16) Samoa

(17) **Saudi Arabia**

(18) Sri Lanka

(19) **Syria**

(20) Trinidad and Tobago

(21) **Tunisia**

(22) US Virgin Islands

(23) **Yemen**

What about foreign subsidiaries in high risk countries?

8.39 It should be noted that enhanced customer due diligence measures need not be invoked automatically with respect to branches or majority-owned subsidiaries of obliged entities established in the Union which are located in high-risk third countries, where those branches or majority-owned subsidiaries fully comply with the group-wide policies and procedures.

Politically exposed persons

8.40 With respect to transactions or business relationships with politically exposed persons, there is a requirement, in addition to the customer due diligence measures, for obliged entities to have in place appropriate risk management systems, including risk-based procedures, to determine whether the customer or the beneficial owner of the customer is a politically exposed person. Obliged entities must apply the following measures in cases of business relationships with politically exposed persons:[37]

(i) obtain senior management approval for establishing or continuing business relationships with such persons;[38]

(ii) take adequate measures to establish the source of wealth and source of funds that are involved in business relationships or transactions with such persons;[39]

(iii) conduct enhanced, ongoing monitoring of those business relationships.[40]

The requirement to apply additional measures to politically exposed persons continues for a period of at least 12 months after they cease to be classed as such and additionally obliged entities must take into account the continuing risk posed by that person and to apply appropriate and risk-sensitive measures until such time as that person is deemed to pose no further risk specific to politically exposed persons.[41] It should be noted that the above provisions apply *mutatis mutandis* to family members or persons known to be close associates of politically exposed persons.[42]

Reporting requirements

8.41 Generally, obliged entities, and, where applicable, their directors and employees, are required to cooperate fully with authorities by informing the appropriate national authority, including by filing a report, on their own initiative, where the obliged entity knows, suspects or has reasonable grounds to suspect that funds, regardless of the amount involved, are the proceeds of criminal activity or are related to terrorist financing, and by promptly responding to requests by the national authority for additional information in such cases.[43]

Protected disclosure

8.42 Disclosure of information in good faith by an obliged entity or by an employee or director of such an obliged entity will not constitute a breach of any restriction on disclosure of information imposed by contract or by any legislative, regulatory or administrative provision, and will not involve the obliged entity or its directors or employees in liability of any kind even in circumstances where they were not precisely aware of the underlying criminal activity and regardless of whether illegal activity actually occurred.[44] Generally, vindicated by national whistleblowing provisions, the directive is mindful of the position of persons disclosing by stipulating that employees and representatives of the obliged entity, who report suspicions of money laundering or terrorist financing internally or to the appropriate authorities, are protected from being exposed to threats or hostile action, and in particular from adverse or discriminatory employment actions.[45] It is submitted that all matters pertaining to such disclosures are considered in the light of national provisions.

37 ibid, Art 20.
38 ibid, Art 20.b.i.
39 ibid, Art 20.b.ii.
40 ibid, Art 20.b.ii.
41 ibid, Art 22.
42 ibid, Art 23.
43 ibid, Art 33.1.
44 ibid, Art 37.
45 ibid, Art 38.

Internal procedures and training

8.43 How corporates respond to the regulatory burden imposed by the directive and its corresponding national implementing provisions is guided by the directive itself which requires obliged entities to implement group-wide policies and procedures, including data protection policies and policies and procedures for sharing information within the group for AML/CFT purposes. Those policies and procedures shall be implemented effectively at the level of branches and majority-owned subsidiaries in member states and third countries.[46] Further, obliged entities must take measures proportionate to their risks, nature and size so that their employees are aware of the provisions adopted pursuant to this directive, including relevant data protection requirements. Such measures must include participation of their employees in special ongoing training programmes to help them recognise operations which may be related to money laundering or terrorist financing and to instruct them as to how to proceed in such cases.[47]

Sanctions

8.44 Obliged entities may be held liable for breaches of their respective national provisions (which transpose the directive). Any resulting sanctions are required to be effective, proportionate and dissuasive. It is of course open to individual member states to impose additional sanctions.[48] Sanctions may be imposed on obliged entities for breaches concerning the following that are serious, repeated, systematic, or a combination thereof:[49]

- customer due diligence;[50]
- suspicious transaction reporting;
- record-keeping;
- internal controls.

Features of sanctions

8.45 The directive stipulates that at least the following measures can be applied to relevant breaches:[51]

(a) a public statement which identifies the natural or legal person and the nature of the breach;

(b) an order requiring the natural or legal person to cease the conduct and to desist from repetition of that conduct;

(c) where an obliged entity is subject to an authorisation, withdrawal or suspension of the authorisation;

(d) a temporary ban against any person discharging managerial responsibilities in an obliged entity, or any other natural person, held responsible for the breach, from exercising managerial functions in obliged entities;

46 ibid, Art 45.1.
47 ibid, Art 46.1.
48 ibid, Art 59.4.
49 ibid, Art 59.
50 ibid, Arts 10–24.
51 ibid, Art 59. 2.

(e) maximum administrative pecuniary sanctions of at least twice the amount of the benefit derived from the breach where that benefit can be determined, or at least EUR 1,000,000.

In the case of financial institutions

8.46 Critically, where the obliged entity concerned is a credit institution or financial institution, the sanctions may be linked to turnover of the institution and may be subject to:[52]

(a) in the case of a legal person, maximum administrative pecuniary sanctions of at least EUR 5,000,000 or 10% of the total annual turnover according to the latest available accounts approved by the management body;

(b) in the case of a natural person, maximum administrative pecuniary sanctions of at least EUR 5,000,000, or in the member states whose currency is not the Euro, the corresponding value in the national currency on 25 June 2015.

Fifth Directive

8.47 After a series of terrorist attacks in Europe in 2016, 'the Fifth Directive'[53] was adopted in 2018. This amending Fifth Directive must be transposed into law in all member countries by 10 January 2020. The new directive seeks to tighten and enhance the EU's rules on preventing money laundering and terrorist financing in a variety of ways. The focus appears to be on virtual currency and those facilitating opaque transactions and may be summarised as:[54]

- Extending the scope of the directive to cover:
  - as well as auditors, external accountants and tax advisers, any other person who offers tax consultancy services;
  - estate agents when acting as intermediaries in the letting of immovable property for which the monthly rent exceeds €10,000;
  - art dealers where the value of a transaction is €10,000 or more;
- Improving access to information on beneficial ownership improving transparency in the ownership of companies and trusts.
- Prohibiting banks from keeping anonymous safe-deposit boxes (in addition to anonymous accounts and passbooks that were already covered by Directive (EU) 2015/849).
- Addressing risks linked to prepaid cards and virtual currencies by:
  - lowering the identification threshold for prepaid cardholders from the current €250 to €150; and
  - enabling national authorities to obtain information allowing them to trace the identity of the owner of the virtual currency;
- Strengthened cooperation between national authorities allowing them to share more information.

52 ibid, Art 59.3.

53 (EU) 2018/843 which amends Directive (EU) 2015/849.

54 Preventing abuse of the financial system for money laundering and terrorism purposes; available at https://eur-lex.europa.eu/legal-content/EN/TXT/HTML/?uri=LEGISSUM:230804_1&from=EN.

National legislative measures

8.48 Whilst the Fourth Directive sets the framework for dealing with money laundering issues in the European Union it remains for the individual member states to transpose these legislative aims into national law. The transposition process can be generally seen as being faithful to the terms of the directive around the European Union, however a thorough exposition of each member state's law is beyond the scope of this work. That said, the following is a list of related and implementing legislation pertaining to the UK and Ireland that deals with issues of money laundering and counter terrorist financing.

United Kingdom

8.49

- The Money Laundering, Terrorist Financing and Transfer of Funds (Information on the Payer) Regulations 2017
- The Information about People with Significant Control (Amendment) Regulations 2017
- The Scottish Partnerships (Register of People with Significant Control) Regulations 2017
- Anti-money laundering and combatting terrorist financing regulations 2016 – Second supplement to the *Gibraltar Gazette* no 4375 of 2017
- Proceeds of Crime Act 2015 (Amendment) Regulations 2016
- Proceeds of Crime Act 2015 Supervisory Bodies (Powers etc) Regulations 2017
- Proceeds of Crime Act 2015 (Amendment) Regulations 2017
- National Coordinator for Anti-money Laundering and Combatting Terrorist Financing (Amendment) Regulations 2017
- Register of Ultimate Beneficial Owners Regulations 2017
- Proceeds of Crime Act 2015 Register of Ultimate Beneficial Owners Regulations 2017
- Interpretation and General Clauses Act Trustees Act (Amendment) Regulations 2017
- Proceeds of Crime Act 2015 Register of Ultimate Beneficial Owners (Amendment) Regulations 2017
- Gibraltar's 2018 National Risk Assessment: Money Laundering and Terrorist Financing. This risk assessment is required under the 4th money laundering directive (4MLD)

Ireland

8.50

- Central Bank Act 1942
- Criminal Law Act 1997
- Non-fatal Offences Against the Person Act 1997

- Criminal Justice (Terrorist Offences) Act 2005
- Criminal Justice (Money Laundering and Terrorist Financing) Act 2010
- Central Bank Reform Act 2010 revised
- Property Services (Regulation) Act 2011
- Central Bank (Supervision and Enforcement) Act 2013 revised
- Protected Disclosures Act 2014 revised
- Companies Act 2014 revised
- Betting (Amendment) Act 2015
- Workplace Relations Act 2015 revised
- Data Protection Act 2018
- Criminal Justice (Money Laundering and Terrorist Financing) (Amendment) Act 2018
- Criminal Justice (Money Laundering and Terrorist Financing) (Amendment) Act 2018 (Commencement) Order 2018
- Criminal Justice (Money Laundering and Terrorist Financing) Act 2010 (section 25); (Prescribed Class of Designated Person) Regulations 2018
- Central Bank Act 1997
- European Union (Anti-money Laundering: Beneficial Ownership of Trusts) Regulations 2019

9 Antitrust and anticompetitive practices

'It's imperative that our people – whether through our broad-based training or via their direct managers – understand the company's perspective on integrity and how that translates to day-to-day behaviours.'

Mr Richard Buchband

Senior Vice President, General Counsel and Secretary

Manpower Group

Introduction

9.1 Words such as proliferation and escalation might describe the path of antitrust law and competition regulation which is, arguably, now global with a steady increase in the number of countries enacting these laws precluding anticompetitive behaviour. In the previous decades we've also observed increased cooperation among the various agencies tasked with the enforcement of those provisions.[1]

9.2 It will come as no great surprise that the biggest violators of antitrust laws are often large business organisations that operate multi-nationally.[2]

9.3 The two largest and as a result the most influential systems of antitrust/competition regulation are the United States of America and the European Union. Although they are not the only major players in global antitrust enforcement, the authors believe they are the most influential. The relevant agencies from both the

1 Assistant Attorney General Charles A James, 'International Antitrust in the 21st Century: Cooperation and Convergence' (OECD Global Forum on Competition, 17 October 2001).

2 Nicholas Passaro, 'Exploring If US & EU Antitrust Law Differences Are Substantive or Superficial by Re-Trying US Cases in the EU' (*SSRN*, 12 September 2016) https://ssrn.com/abstract=2837822 or http://dx.doi.org/10.2139/ssrn.2837822.

United States of America and the European Union are known to cooperate and work together to accomplish their respective duties and the enforcement of the law.[3]

Overview of European law

9.4 European antitrust policy is developed from two central rules set out in the Treaty on the Functioning of the European Union:

- Article 101[4] of the Treaty prohibits agreements between two or more independent market competitors which restrict competition. Horizontal agreements and vertical agreements are prohibited. Only limited exceptions are provided for.
- Article 102[5] of the Treaty prohibits firms that hold a dominant position in a market to abuse that position.

The Commission is empowered by the Treaty to apply these rules and has a number of investigative powers (eg, inspection at business and non-business premises, written requests for information, etc). The Commission may also impose fines on undertakings which violate the EU antitrust rules. The main rules on procedures are set out in Council Regulation (EC) 1/2003.

---

3 ibid.

4 Article 101 (ex Article 81 TEC):

1. The following shall be prohibited as incompatible with the internal market: all agreements between undertakings, decisions by associations of undertakings and concerted practices which may affect trade between Member States and which have as their object or effect the prevention, restriction or distortion of competition within the internal market, and in particular those which:
   (a) directly or indirectly fix purchase or selling prices or any other trading conditions;
   (b) limit or control production, markets, technical development, or investment;
   (c) share markets or sources of supply;
   (d) apply dissimilar conditions to equivalent transactions with other trading parties, thereby placing them at a competitive disadvantage;
   (e) make the conclusion of contracts subject to acceptance by the other parties of supplementary obligations which, by their nature or according to commercial usage, have no connection with the subject of such contracts.
2. Any agreements or decisions prohibited pursuant to this Article shall be automatically void.
3. The provisions of paragraph 1 may, however, be declared inapplicable in the case of:
   – any agreement or category of agreements between undertakings,
   – any decision or category of decisions by associations of undertakings,
   – any concerted practice or category of concerted practices,

   which contributes to improving the production or distribution of goods or to promoting technical or economic progress, while allowing consumers a fair share of the resulting benefit, and which does not:
   (a) impose on the undertakings concerned restrictions which are not indispensable to the attainment of these objectives;
   (b) afford such undertakings the possibility of eliminating competition in respect of a substantial part of the products in question

5 Article 102 (ex Article 82 TEC):

Any abuse by one or more undertakings of a dominant position within the internal market or in a substantial part of it shall be prohibited as incompatible with the internal market in so far as it may affect trade between Member States.

Such abuse may, in particular, consist in:
(a) directly or indirectly imposing unfair purchase or selling prices or other unfair trading conditions;
(b) limiting production, markets or technical development to the prejudice of consumers;
(c) applying dissimilar conditions to equivalent transactions with other trading parties, thereby placing them at a competitive disadvantage;
(d) making the conclusion of contracts subject to acceptance by the other parties of supplementary obligations which, by their nature or according to commercial usage, have no connection with the subject of such contracts.

9.5 The European Commission and other National Authorities within the member states of the European Union are charged with the application and enforcement of Articles 101 and 102, to ensure that competition is not distorted or restricted in the European Union.

9.6 An enormous body of law in relation to antitrust matters has evolved over time in the EU, which means that elucidation of even the main features of the governing law is beyond the scope of this work. Instead the authors propose to set out the sources of the law and a few pointers in this regard so as to assist counsel in navigating towards cogent advice.[6]

The essential rules

9.7

- EU rules on competition apply directly in all EU member states.
- They are directly enforceable by both the European Commission and national competition authorities and courts.
- EU competition rules apply to 'undertakings', eg trade associations and other industry groupings.
- There are two broad types of prohibited behaviour:
  - Illegal contacts and agreements between companies which may be even be informal in nature. This may manifest as price fixing, sharing markets or customer allocation, production or output limitation, whether through bid rigging or otherwise. A typical example may be a distribution agreement between suppliers and re-sellers, which has the effect of maintaining prices at a certain level or dividing up a market unfairly. such agreements is provided by the Commission in specific guidelines.
  - Abuse of a dominant position. This may manifest as imposing unreasonably high or low prices creating discrimination between customers and distorted trading conditions on trading partners.
- All companies are subject to competition rules, with no differentiation according to their size. Being small is no excuse for not complying with the applicable EU or national competition rules.

Sample corporate policy

9.8 Many corporate entities with multi-jurisdictional operations bundle their competition policy aims in a hybrid document. It is important to ensure that all such attempts are sufficiently sophisticated in order to provide the best guidance to employees. A sample policy document is included in the appendices to this text.

Best practices

9.9 The European Commission have issued a comprehensive guide to best practice for the conduct of proceedings and complaints in relation to antitrust matters.[7]

6 Rules applicable to Antitrust enforcement – vol 1. See Council Regulation (EC) 1/2003.

7 Commission notice on best practices for the conduct of proceedings concerning Articles 101 and 102 TFEU Text with EEA relevance OJ C 308, 20.10.2011, pp 6–32.

9.9 *Antitrust and anticompetitive practices*

This is essential reading for any counsel who is anticipating or dealing with antitrust implications for their business. It provides guidance on a wide range of topics, including:

- Origin of cases
- Initial assessment and case allocation
- Opening of proceedings
- Languages
- Information requests
- Scope of request for information
- Self-incrimination
- Time limits
- Confidentiality
- Meetings and other contacts with the parties and third parties
- Power to take statements (interviews)
- Inspections
- Legal professional privilege
- Information exchange between competition authorities
- State of play meetings
- Format of the state of play meetings
- Timing of the state of play meetings
- Triangular meetings
- Meetings with the Commissioner or the Director-General
- Review of key submissions
- Possible outcomes of the investigation phase
- Right to be heard
- Statement of Objections
- Purpose and content of the Statement of Objections
- Possible imposition of remedies and arguments of the parties
- Possible imposition of fines and arguments of the parties
- Transparency
- Access to file
- Procedures for facilitating the exchange of confidential information between parties to the proceedings
- Written reply to the Statement of Objections
- Rights of complainants and interested third persons
- Oral hearing
- Supplementary Statement of Objections and letter of facts

- Possible outcomes of this phase
- Initiation of commitment discussions
- Preliminary assessment
- Submission of the commitments
- The 'market test' and subsequent discussions with the parties

Dawn raids

9.10 When carrying out its duty to investigate anticompetitive agreements or other violations of competition law the European Commission (and other regulatory authorities) has the undisputed authority to conduct surprise onsite inspections called 'Dawn Raids'. A Dawn Raid is just as risky for the target as it will be stressful for the target company's directors, managers and other employees.

9.11 There is a great danger, should employees be caught unaware or unprepared, of the target company (their employer) being fined, and fined substantially, (even if later found to be completely innocent at the conclusion of the inspection) if its employees are uncooperative or act inappropriately during the execution phase of an inspection.

9.12 As the term suggests these visits by the Commission are unannounced; occur, usually, early in the morning; and **do not** require a court issued warrant. The rules pertaining to the necessity of a warrant for inspections by national authorities differ depending on jurisdiction.

9.13 If inspectors from the European Commission arrive: (1) the Commission's officers must not be hindered or prevented from beginning their inspection; (2) the target company's legal department should be immediately notified by the target's reception and or security team; (3) the target company's legal department should, immediately, notify and instruct external counsel as well as request urgent immediate onsite assistance at the location or locations being inspected; and (4) one more time for good measure, the Commission's officers should not be hindered or prevented from conducting their inspection.

9.14 Suffice it to say the Commission's authority to: (1) search a company's premises; (2) review all paper files, electronic data storage files and media, email and IT network; (3) make and remove copies of paper files and/or electronic data (including confidential files and communications) is extensive; but not wholly unlimited.

9.15 Any passing 'heroic' instinct by an employee, a receptionist or a security guard which centres on an attempt to limit the scope of the inspection is fraught with risk and such a thought must be immediately abandoned. Only an executive officer of the target, who has the benefit of contemporaneous onsite advice and assistance from experienced specialist legal counsel should be allowed to order such action.

9.16 It is therefore wise to ensure that security staff, reception staff and key employees have at a minimum basic instructions and knowledge of what to do in the event of a Dawn Raid. If nothing else, they should be aware of the four rules above.

9.17 If you are the General Counsel of business with a substantial footprint in the European Union your business will likely have some form of competition or antitrust compliance training programme. We recommend that in addition to training a Dawn Raid checklist or dos and don'ts is delivered to all key employees, department heads and corporate officers as well as reception and security personnel for quick reference should the authorities come knocking.

The consequences of breaking EU competition law

9.18 The European Commission takes the enforcement of Articles 101 and 102 very seriously. Contravention of EU competition law can bring with it eyewatering fines.

9.19 Fines are ultimately limited to 10% of the overall annual turnover of the company. This 10% limit may be based on the turnover of the group to which the company belongs if the parent of that group exercised decisive influence over the operations of the subsidiary during the infringement period. There is also a limitation period of five years from the end of the infringement until the beginning of the Commission's investigation. A European Commission produced fact sheet on this subject is reproduced in the appendices hereto. It is succinct and does not require complete regurgitation here.

Cartel activity

9.20 If the dreaded day ever arises when you as General Counsel or a business leader learn (and confirm) that someone somewhere in your organisation has colluded with a third party or parties and that such collusion is in contravention of European Union competition law you have a very strategic choice to quickly consider.

9.21 Why the rush? Your quick and decisive action is necessary because the Commission actively encourages companies (that are involved in a cartel) to come forward with evidence to help the Commission detect cartels and build its case. The first company to provide sufficient evidence of a cartel, thereby enabling the Commission to pursue a case against the cartel, may receive full immunity from fines;[8] subsequent companies that cooperate can receive reductions of up to 50% on the fine that would otherwise be imposed.[9]

9.22 It may seem counterintuitive to many lawyers not to contest an allegation of infringement and for a company to come clean and turn itself in but let me remind you of the old proverb; that there is no honour among thieves. Given: (1) the quantum of the potential fines; (2) that only the first company to come forward and provide sufficient evidence of a said prohibited behaviour will receive clemency; and (3) your duty as a General Counsel to protect the company and the equity interests of its shareholders the choice, at least for me, and my recommendation to my CEO and main board of directors is clear, as is my choice of footwear, under these circumstances from that point forward it would be running shoes.

9.23 The reason for the above is because I've already been called upon to clean up this very mess. I once joined a company that had, a few months before I started, been

8 Leniency Notice (OJ C298, 8.12.2006, p 17).

9 As set out in the Commission's fact sheet, to benefit from the Leniency Notice, companies can approach the Commission directly or through a legal adviser. There are dedicated phone numbers where a company can seek assistance from a Commission official (tel: +32 2 298.41.90 or +32 2 298.41.91), and a dedicated fax number (fax: +32 2 299.45.85).

rather heavily fined for being part of a cartel. The company had been convicted because one of its co-conspirators turned itself in and instead of taking a cooperative approach with the commission the company challenged the allegations of anticompetitive behaviour at every turn. So I say again, put your running shoes on because there is no honour among thieves or members of a cartel operating anticompetitively in the European Union.

10 Communications compliance

'The single biggest problem in communication is the illusion that it has taken place.'

George Bernard Shaw

Introduction

10.1 Wait for it … email. This chapter could perhaps have found a home amongst the myriad issues contained in the chapter on human resources. However, it was felt that, given the frequency with which this question arises, it was deserving of a fiefdom of its own. Email is often derided and bemoaned, and the quote above retains its relevance, yet email remains one of, if not the, key corporate communication channel. While infinite legal liability might be created courtesy of its content, the manner in which the sender is identified and the collateral information accompanying that identification is something of a vexed question and not without the potential for controversy itself. Even in the digital age, the simple act of signing one's name is a powerful expression upon which significant reliance may be placed, so much so it is legislated for in many jurisdictions.

The requirement to provide company information in email

10.2 One of the most mundane but necessary questions Counsel receives often comes in the form of what information should be included at the foot of company email correspondence.[1] While presenting as benign in appearance, this question

1 Frequently referred to on a colloquial basis as a 'disclaimer' which is erroneous and has no connection to the legal disclaiming of a right or gift.

comes with latent complexity. Subtle differences exist as between the various EMEA jurisdictions. These divergences are driven by the interaction of a patchwork of national legislation of varying maturity and EU law. Any new employee typically asks what should appear at the foot of his or her email. Typically a template is copied from a colleague which has the unfortunate effect of perpetuating and spreading error. However, if starting *de novo*, a range of irritating questions present themselves:

- Is there a legal requirement to display any particular information about a company in its email?
- If so, which company should be referred to? Does one refer to a subsidiary or a group company, or both?
- Are the legal requirements met by simply including a hypertext link to certain company information?
- Are there any requirements of form that must be adhered to?
- What language should the information be presented in and should translations be provided?
- Are there any statutory requirements concerning other statements that should appear in the communication?

Confidentiality

10.3 It is commonplace for companies to issue notes at the foot of correspondence relating to confidentiality, privacy or even claims to privilege. Whilst rarely required as a mandatory inclusion, such statements are frequently of questionable value and their legal effectiveness is opaque at best. Local advice should be retained particularly in relation to claims of privilege relating to legal advice or litigation.

National requirements

10.4 This section will endeavour to set out an analysis of the national requirements of a selection of EMEA jurisdictions with examples set out thereafter. Certain general themes do emerge from the analysis. Typically, business email as a specific form has not been provided for specifically under national law regimes. Hence, requisite information for inclusion in email has not been proscribed in most cases. Similarly, the language any information should appear in has not been proscribed. Matters of form and formatting are typically provided for by means of adherence to nebulous standards of prominence, legibility and/or ability to mislead, rather than compliance with certain specific criteria. Commonly, consumer led legislative provisions will apply to the fairness and intelligibility of the communication.

Belgium[2]

10.5 The requirement under Belgian law is: (i) the company's registered name; (ii) the company's type, which should be legible and placed in direct proximity before or after the company name; (iii) the address of the company's registered office; (iv) the company's registered number; (v) the words 'registre des personnes morales'/'rec htspersonenregister' or 'RPM'/'RPR' followed by the commercial court where the

2 Belgian Companies Code, Arts 78, 79 and 80.

company is registered; and (vi) whether the company is in liquidation (if appropriate).[3] It should be noted that the above information should concern the entity that the communication is written on behalf of.

Czech Republic[4]

10.6 Under Czech law, where the electronic communication is intended to be used for a commercial purpose it should include, without ambiguity: (i) full company name (including the legal form of the company); (ii) the company's registered seat; (iii) which register the company has been registered and its register number); and (iv) the company's identification number.[5] Information concerning the company's registered capital is often included on a non-mandatory basis. Generally, where dealing with a consumer the language utilised to provide the above information should be the same as that which was used to conclude the contract.

Denmark

10.7 The main requirements are: (i) the company's registered name; (ii) the company's registration no (CVR no); and (iii) the address of the company's registered office. It should also be noted that:

- Limited Liability companies should state company type.
- Where share capital is stated, both subscribed and paid up amounts should be displayed.
- Foreign companies should state the details of any registers they are listed on in their domestic jurisdiction.

It should be noted that the above information should concern the entity that the communication is written on behalf of.

Finland[6]

10.8 Essential communications emanating from a limited liability company are: (i) the business identity code; (ii) the registered business name; (iii) domicile; (iv) address; and (v) any notice of possible liquidation.[7] As regards what information should be provided by an affiliate of a foreign company, it is required that the company display: (i) the business identity code; (ii) the entrepreneur's business name; (iii) legal form; (iv) domicile; (v) register into which the entrepreneur has been entered in his or her home country; (vi) registration number in that register; and (vii) any notice of possible liquidation.

France[8]

10.9 The central requirements are: (i) the company's name; (ii) the legal form of the company; (iii) the company's registration number; (iv) the company's registry location (preceded by 'RCS' if it is registered in France); (v) the address of the company's registered office; and (vi) whether the company is in the process

---

3 ibid.
4 Civil Code, ss 435, 187(2) and 3019 and Business Corporation Act, s 7.
5 ibid.
6 Business Information Act (244/2001), s 15.
7 ibid.
8 French Commercial Code, Art R. 123-237 & R. 123-238.

of insolvency proceedings. If the corporate body is a commercial company with its registered office overseas, the following information should be included: (i) the company's name; (ii) the legal form of the company; (iii) the address of the company's registered office; (iv) the registration number of the relevant country; and (v) whether the company is subject to insolvency proceedings where appropriate.

Germany[9]

10.10 Under German law the requirement is: (i) the full company name; (ii) the legal form of the company; (iii) the company's registered seat (eg, Munich / München); (iv) the register at which the company has been registered and its register number; (v) the names of all managing directors at the company; and (vi) if the articles of association provide for a company advisory board, the full names of its members.[10]

Greece[11]

10.11 All company documents, under Greek law (including emails and websites) must include, at least, the following: the Registry with which the company is registered; the company's registration number; the company's legal form (eg, listed, commercial, industrial, single shareholder, banking, sports etc); the registered office address; and whether the company is under liquidation.

Hungary[12]

10.12 Under Hungarian law, limited liability companies and companies limited by shares must indicate the following information in their business emails and on their website: the name of the competent Court of Registration keeping the company's files; the name and registered seat of the company; the company registration number of the company; and if necessary, information on any liquidation or voluntary liquidation.

Republic of Ireland[13]

10.13 The central requirement under Irish law is: (i) the registered name and legal form of the company; (ii) the place of registration of the company; (iii) the company's registered number; (iv) the address of the company's registered office; and (v) the forename (or initials) and surnames and any former forenames and surnames of the directors of the company and their nationality, if not Irish.

10.14 There are other requirements that only apply to certain companies:

- in the case of a Designated Activity Company or a Company Limited by Guarantee, the fact that that the company is one of these types of companies;
- in the case of a company being wound up, the fact that it is so; and
- any reference to the share capital of a company must refer to the paid-up share capital only.

---

9 German Limited Liability Company Act, s 35a.

10 The information above relates to a German limited liability company, the most common company form in Germany. There are other requirements that will only apply to certain other types of companies which should be considered by local counsel.

11 Codified Law 2190/1920, Art 7(c).

12 Act V of 2006 on company registration, ss 63(2), (4).

13 Companies Act 2014, s 151; Registration of Business Names Act 1963, s 4.

The above disclosure requirements apply to an Irish-registered company, irrespective of whether it is carrying on business under a trading name (ie, a name which is not its full corporate name).

Italy

10.15 Under Italian law[14] the required information is: (i) the full company name and form of the company (and if the company only has a sole shareholder this must be expressly stated); (ii) indication of the company exercising the direction and coordination (if applicable); (iii) the registered office of the company; (iv) the tax code, VAT number and Enterprises' Register number of the company, REA number; (v) the company's registered capital; and (vi) certified electronic email (PEC email address). All information should be provided in the Italian language.

Netherlands[15]

10.16 Under the law of the Netherlands, the core information required is: (i) the company's registered number; and (ii) the company's legal name. If the company is a 'besloten/naamloze vennootschap' under Dutch law (ie, a limited liability company/ public limited company), the company must include the following information in its business emails as well: (i) the address of the company's registered office; (ii) the company's legal form; and (iii) the company's registered name if the company's legal name deviates from its registered name.

Norway

10.17 Under Norwegian law, the core information required is: (i) the company's registered name; (ii) the company's registered number; and, if the company is registered in the Norwegian VAT registry, the letters 'MVA' behind its registered number. For limited liability companies, the company information must also contain: (i) the registry where the company is registered; (ii) its form of organisation (eg, 'AS' for limited liability companies and 'ASA' for public limited liability companies); (iii) the location of its head office; and (iv) information stating that the company is under liquidation or similar administration if this is the case.

Poland[16]

10.18 Under Polish law, the following must be included in all letters and commercial orders issued by a company in paper and electronic form: (i) the business name, seat and address of the company; (ii) the designation of the registration court with which the company's documentation is stored and the number under which the company is entered into the register; (iii) the tax identification number (NIP); and (iv) the amount of the initial and paid-up capital.

---

14 Italian Civil Code, Art 2250.

15 Dutch Trade Register Act ('Handelsregisterwet').

16 Commercial Companies Code (Kodeks spółek handlowych), ss 127, 206 and 374 (EU Directive 2003/58/EC). Also see Freedom of Economic Activity Act, s 21 (ustawa o swobodzie działalności gospodarczej).

Portugal[17]

10.19 Under Portuguese law, the core information required is: (i) the company's registered name; (ii) the legal form of the company; (iii) the address of the company's registered office; (iv) the registry location; (v) the company's registered number/tax payer number; and (vi) for private limited liability companies/joint stock companies:

- capital stock;
- paid-up capital stock; and
- the amount of equity capital as resulting from the last approved balance sheet, whenever it is equal or inferior to half of the capital stock.

If the company is in liquidation, this must be mentioned in all communications.

Romania[18]

10.20 Under Romanian company law, the following information is required in any document: (i) corporate name; (ii) legal form; (iii) registered office; (iv) registration number with the Trade Register Office; (v) sole registration code; (vi) share capital (in case of joint stock companies both the subscribed and paid share capital should be mentioned); (vii) management system, only in case of joint stock companies that implemented a two tier management system; and (viii) in case of branches of foreign entities, the trade register and registration number of the parent company.

Russia

10.21 There is no applicable Russian legislation which imposes requirements for specific company information to be included in a business email or other correspondence.

Spain

10.22 No specific requirements are present in Spanish law as the Directives 2003/58/EC and 2009/101/EC have not been specifically transposed in Spain. Companies may want to include information in any case for the sake of international continuity.

Sweden[19]

10.23 The core information required (for a limited company) is: (i) the full name of the company (as it is registered, including the word 'aktiebolag' (ie, limited company) provided that it is written out in the registered articles of association); (ii) the location in which the company's registered office is situated, that is, the municipality/county designated in the registered articles of association and in the company register; and (iii) the company's registration number. It should be noted that if the company has gone into liquidation/bankruptcy, such facts must also be stated.

17 Portuguese Commercial Companies Code (Decree-law No 262/86, of 2/9, as amended).

18 Companies law No 31/1990 and Electronic commerce law No 365/2002.

19 Swedish Companies Act (2005:551), ch 28, s 5.

Switzerland[20]

10.24 The legal requirements regarding the use of business names of foreign companies is exclusively governed in Switzerland by the law of the state governing the considered company.[21] It is usually accepted, however, that the use of business names in email correspondence in Switzerland cannot be misleading for the correspondent.

10.25 In general, in correspondence, or order forms and invoices and official communications, the business or other name entered in the commercial register must be given in full and un-amended. Shortened names, logos, trade names, brand names and similar may also be used. The business name must be clearly identifiable via email especially in correspondence leading to the formation of a contract, for example through e-commerce.

Turkey[22]

10.26 The Turkish Commercial Code sets out the company information required to be included in a business letter (which may include emails), as follows: (i) the company's (registered) title; (ii) the company's registered number; (iii) the registered website of the company (if the company is under an obligation to possess a website); and (iv) the address of the company's registered headquarters. If the company is incorporated as the Turkish branch of the foreign parent company, the headquarters of the foreign parent company as well as the address of the branch shall be disclosed in the branch's registered title, alongside with the expression 'branch'.

United Kingdom[23]

10.27 Under English law, the core information required is: (i) the company's registered name; (ii) the part of the UK in which the company is registered; (iii) the company's registered number; and (iv) the address of the company's registered office. There are other requirements that will only apply to certain companies – for example, CICs, investment companies, or companies that are exempt from the obligation to use the word 'limited' as part of their registered name.

20 Swiss Code of Obligations, s 954a and Federal Act on Private International Law, s 155 let d.
21 Federal Act on Private International Law, s 155 let d.
22 See Turkish Commercial Code.
23 Company, Limited Liability Partnership and Business (Names and Trading Disclosures) Regulations 2015 (basis: EU Directive 2003/58/EC).

11 Data protection in the EMEA

'Everyone has the right to the protection of personal data concerning him or her.'

Article 8(1) of the Charter of Fundamental Rights of the European Union

Introduction

11.1 The EU's new General Data Protection Regulation (hereafter 'GDPR') came into effect on 25 May 2018. Compliance with it impacted businesses and their legal budgets globally for at least two years running. I believe most of my colleagues and peers, suffered from GDPR fatigue along with a number of sleepless nights in contemplation of bringing our business into compliance with GDPR. If you work in either the legal or IT departments of a business in the EU, or linked to the EU, and you managed to missed out on the GDPR fire drill then I salute you and your ingenuity. If, however, your business ignored GDPR or is still struggling to comply with it, .. well, *bonne chance mon ami*!

11.2 Data Protection is enshrined in the most cherished of European law's governing documents that the protection of natural persons in relation to the processing of personal data is a fundamental right in that everyone has the right to the protection of personal data concerning him or her.[1] However, the European Union, whilst adopting laudable goals, recognises that a balance must be struck as the right to the protection of personal data is not an absolute right, it must be considered in relation to its function in society and be balanced against other fundamental rights,

1 Article 8(1) of the Charter of Fundamental Rights of the European Union (the 'Charter') and Article 16(1) of the Treaty on the Functioning of the European Union (TFEU).

in accordance with the principle of proportionality.[2] Arguably, one of the most far reaching, ambitious and important pieces of European law ever enacted, the GDPR[3] which became directly effective and binding upon member states as of 25 May 2018 seeks to harmonise the protection of fundamental rights and freedoms of natural persons in respect of processing activities and to ensure the free flow of personal data between member states. This was seen as a necessary reply to the 'substantial increase in cross-border flows of personal data'. It was also noted that increasingly, 'Member States are being called upon by Union law to cooperate and exchange personal data so as to be able to perform their duties or carry out tasks on behalf of an authority in another Member State', and that 'rapid technological developments and globalisation have brought new challenges for the protection of personal data'.[4]

11.3 As regards scope, GDPR's reach creates challenges for corporate counsel, not just in the European Union but also extra-jurisdictionally, in relation to any jurisdictions that might be sharing or receiving personal data with a member state. It should be noted at the outset that the intent of GDPR was not to apply to the processing of personal data by a natural person in the course of a purely personal or household activity and thus with no connection to a professional or commercial activity.[5]

11.4 GDPR establishes a number of key principles that must be observed and these principles together with salient points, will be illuminated in the coming pages.

General Data Protection Regulation

Scope

11.5 GDPR applies to the processing of personal data in the context of the activities of an establishment of a controller or a processor in the Union, regardless of whether the processing takes place in the Union or not.[6]

11.6 However, GDPR does remove from the scope of the text, the processing of personal data that occurs, *inter alia*:

- in the course of an activity which falls outside the scope of Union law;
- by a natural person in the course of a purely personal or household activity;
- by competent authorities for the purposes of the prevention, investigation, detection or prosecution of criminal offences or the execution of criminal penalties, including the safeguarding against and the prevention of threats to public security.[7]

2 Regulation (EU) 2016/679 of the European Parliament and of the Council of 27 April 2016 on the protection of natural persons with regard to the processing of personal data and on the free movement of such data, and repealing Directive 95/46/EC (General Data Protection Regulation) or hereafter 'GDPR' per Recital 4.

3 Regulation (EU) 2016/679 of the European Parliament and of the Council of 27 April 2016 on the protection of natural persons with regard to the processing of personal data and on the free movement of such data, and repealing Directive 95/46/EC (General Data Protection Regulation) or hereafter 'GDPR',

4 GDPR, Recital 5.

5 ibid, Recital 18.

6 ibid, Art 3.1.

7 ibid, Art 2.

Extra jurisdictional effect

11.7 GDPR does however apply to the processing of personal data of data subjects who are in the Union by a controller or processor not established in the Union, where the processing activities are related to:

(a) the offering of goods or services, irrespective of whether a payment of the data subject is required, to such data subjects in the Union; or

(b) the monitoring of their behaviour as far as their behaviour takes place within the Union.

Further, GDPR applies to the processing of personal data by a controller *not* established in the Union, but in a place where member state law applies by virtue of public international law.[8]

Definitions

11.8 Key to the appreciation of GDPR is an understanding of the often technical terms contained within and which will litter the following pages. Hence it is useful to set out some of the more useful definitions here at the outset.

Personal data[9]

11.9 Any information relating to an identified or identifiable natural person ('data subject'); an identifiable natural person is one who can be identified, directly or indirectly, in particular by reference to an identifier such as a name, identification number, location data, online identifier or to one or more factors specific to the physical, physiological, genetic, mental, economic, cultural or social identity of that natural person.

Processing[10]

11.10 Any operation or set of operations which is performed on personal data or on sets of personal data, whether or not by automated means, such as collection, recording, organisation, structuring, storage, adaptation or alteration, retrieval, consultation, use, disclosure by transmission, dissemination or otherwise making available, alignment or combination, restriction, erasure or destruction.

Profiling[11]

11.11 Any form of automated processing of personal data consisting of the use of personal data to evaluate certain personal aspects relating to a natural person, in particular to analyse or predict aspects concerning that natural person's performance at work, economic situation, health, personal preferences, interests, reliability, behaviour, location or movements.

Pseudonymisation[12]

11.12 The processing of personal data in such a manner that the personal data can no longer be attributed to a specific data subject without the use of additional

8 ibid, Art 3.3.
9 ibid, Art 4.
10 ibid, Art 4.
11 ibid, Art 4.
12 ibid, Art 4.

information, provided that such additional information is kept separately and is subject to technical and organisational measures to ensure that the personal data are not attributed to an identified or identifiable natural person.

Controller[13]

11.13 The natural or legal person, public authority, agency or other body which, alone or jointly with others, determines the purposes and means of the processing of personal data; where the purposes and means of such processing are determined by Union or member state law, the controller or the specific criteria for its nomination may be provided for by Union or member state law.

Processor[14]

11.14 A natural or legal person, public authority, agency or other body which processes personal data on behalf of the controller.

Recipient[15]

11.15 A natural or legal person, public authority, agency or another body, to which the personal data are disclosed, whether a third party or not. However, public authorities which may receive personal data in the framework of a particular inquiry in accordance with Union or member state law shall not be regarded as recipients; the processing of those data by those public authorities shall be in compliance with the applicable data protection rules according to the purposes of the processing.

Consent[16]

11.16 Consent of the data subject means any freely given, specific, informed and unambiguous indication of the data subject's wishes by which he or she, by a statement or by a clear affirmative action, signifies agreement to the processing of personal data relating to him or her.

Personal data breach[17]

11.17 A breach of security leading to the accidental or unlawful destruction, loss, alteration, unauthorised disclosure of, or access to, personal data transmitted, stored or otherwise processed.

Genetic data[18]

11.18 Personal data relating to the inherited or acquired genetic characteristics of a natural person which give unique information about the physiology or the health of that natural person and which result, in particular, from an analysis of a biological sample from the natural person in question.

---

13 ibid, Art 4.
14 ibid, Art 4.
15 ibid, Art 4.
16 ibid, Art 4.
17 ibid, Art 4.
18 ibid, Art 4.

Biometric data[19]

11.19 Personal data resulting from specific technical processing relating to the physical, physiological or behavioural characteristics of a natural person, which allow or confirm the unique identification of that natural person, such as facial images or dactyloscopic data.

Data concerning health[20]

11.20 Personal data related to the physical or mental health of a natural person, including the provision of health care services, which reveal information about his or her health status.

Binding corporate rules[21]

11.21 Personal data protection policies which are adhered to by a controller or processor established on the territory of a member state for transfers or a set of transfers of personal data to a controller or processor in one or more 'third' countries within a group of undertakings, or group of enterprises engaged in a joint economic activity.

Main establishment[22]

11.22 This means: (a) as regards a controller with establishments in more than one member state, the place of its central administration in the Union, unless the decisions on the purposes and means of the processing of personal data are taken in another establishment of the controller in the Union and the latter establishment has the power to have such decisions implemented, in which case the establishment having taken such decisions is to be considered to be the main establishment; (b) as regards a processor with establishments in more than one member state, the place of its central administration in the Union, or, if the processor has no central administration in the Union, the establishment of the processor in the Union where the main processing activities in the context of the activities of an establishment of the processor take place to the extent that the processor is subject to specific obligations under the GDPR.

Key principles

11.23 The GDPR is uncharacteristic in many regards. Happily, one such atypical departure for legislation is the clear and concise fashion in which GDPR establishes the fundamental principles to be applied when processing personal data. It is submitted that if no other sections of the legislation were retained, the following should be closely examined and considered most valuable in terms of general guidance.

1. *Lawfulness, fairness and transparency*[23]

   Personal data shall be processed lawfully, fairly and in a transparent manner in relation to the data subject.

19 ibid, Art 4.
20 ibid, Art 4.
21 ibid, Art 4.
22 ibid, Art 4.
23 ibid, Art 5.1(a).

2. *Purpose limitation*[24]

   Personal data shall be collected for specified, explicit and legitimate purposes and not further processed in a manner that is incompatible with those purposes; further processing for archiving purposes in the public interest, scientific or historical research purposes or statistical purposes shall, in accordance with Article 89(1), not be considered to be incompatible with the initial purposes.

3. *Data minimisation*[25]

   Personal data shall be adequate, relevant and limited to what is necessary in relation to the purposes for which they are processed.

4. *Accuracy*[26]

   Personal data shall be accurate and, where necessary, kept up to date; every reasonable step must be taken to ensure that personal data that are inaccurate, having regard to the purposes for which they are processed, are erased or rectified without delay.

5. *Storage limitation*[27]

   Personal data shall be kept in a form which permits identification of data subjects for no longer than is necessary for the purposes for which the personal data are processed; personal data may be stored for longer periods insofar as the personal data will be processed solely for archiving purposes in the public interest, scientific or historical research purposes or statistical purposes in accordance with Article 89(1) subject to implementation of the appropriate technical and organisational measures required by the GDPR in order to safeguard the rights and freedoms of the data subject ('storage limitation');

6. *Integrity and confidentiality*[28]

   Personal data shall be processed in a manner that ensures appropriate security of the personal data, including protection against unauthorised or unlawful processing and against accidental loss, destruction or damage, using appropriate technical or organisational measures.

7. *Accountability*[29]

   Article 5 sets out a further key idea. Namely, the controller shall be responsible for, and be able to demonstrate compliance with, the above six principles. This represents a significant and notable alteration to the burden of proof in processing personal data and shapes much of the corporate response to this issue.

What amounts to lawful 'processing'

11.24 The GDPR continues its benevolent approach to providing guidance to those required to advise upon such matters where it sets out the nature of what amounts to a legal basis for processing of personal data.

24 ibid, Art 5.1(b).
25 ibid, Art 5.1(c).
26 ibid, Art 5.1(d).
27 ibid, Art 5.1(e).
28 ibid, Art 5.1(f).
29 ibid, Art 5.2.

11.25 Processing shall be lawful only if and to the extent that at least one of the following applies:

(a) *Explicit consent*[30]

The data subject has given consent to the processing of his or her personal data for one or more specific purposes.

(b) *Necessary pursuant to contract*[31]

The processing is necessary for the performance of a contract to which the data subject is party or in order to take steps at the request of the data subject prior to entering into a contract.

(c) *Legal obligation*[32]

Processing is necessary for compliance with a legal obligation to which the controller is subject.

(d) *Vital interest*[33]

The processing is necessary in order to protect the vital interests of the data subject or of another natural person.

(e) *Public interest*[34]

The processing is necessary for the performance of a task carried out in the public interest or in the exercise of official authority vested in the controller.

(f) *Legitimate interest*[35]

The processing is necessary for the purposes of the legitimate interests pursued by the controller or by a third party, except where such interests are overridden by the interests or fundamental rights and freedoms of the data subject which require protection of personal data, in particular where the data subject is a child.

Point (f) above shall not apply to processing carried out by public authorities in the performance of their tasks. Point (c) and (e) above may be subject to significant divergence at a national level.

Purpose alteration

11.26 What may be a central consideration to corporate counsel is how the lawfulness of the processing of data is affected by post fact change in the purpose for which the data is being processed. Where the processing for a purpose other than that for which the personal data have been collected is not based on the data subject's consent, the controller shall, in order to ascertain whether processing for another purpose is compatible with the purpose for which the personal data are initially collected, take into account, *inter alia*: any link between the purposes for which the personal data have been collected and the purposes of the intended further processing; the context in which the personal data have been collected, in particular regarding the relationship between data subjects and the controller; the nature of the personal data, in particular whether special categories of personal data are processed, or whether personal data related to criminal convictions and offences are processed; the possible

30 ibid, Art 6.1(a).
31 ibid, Art 6.1(b).
32 ibid, Art 6.1(c).
33 ibid, Art 6.1(d).
34 ibid, Art 6.1(e).
35 ibid, Art 6.1(f).

consequences of the intended further processing for data subjects; the existence of appropriate safeguards, which may include encryption or pseudonymisation.[36]

Consent

11.27 Much of the corporate compliance burden in relation to data protection under GDPR can be traced to the following considerations in relation to consent. Where processing is based on consent, the controller shall be able to demonstrate that the data subject has consented to the processing of his or her personal data.[37] If the data subject's consent is given in the context of a written declaration which also concerns other matters, the request for consent shall be presented in a manner which is clearly distinguishable from the other matters, in an intelligible and easily accessible form, using clear and plain language. Any part of such a declaration which constitutes an infringement of the GDPR shall not be binding.[38] The data subject shall have the right to withdraw his or her consent at any time. The withdrawal of consent shall not affect the lawfulness of processing based on consent before its withdrawal. Prior to giving consent, the data subject shall be informed thereof. It shall be as easy to withdraw as to give consent.[39] When assessing whether consent is freely given, utmost account shall be taken of whether, *inter alia*, the performance of a contract, including the provision of a service, is conditional on consent to the processing of personal data that is not necessary for the performance of that contract.[40]

Special categories of data – prohibitions and derogations

11.28 As a general statement GDPR prohibits the processing of certain categories of data. Specifically, the processing of personal data revealing racial or ethnic origin, political opinions, religious or philosophical beliefs, or trade union membership, and the processing of genetic data, biometric data for the purpose of uniquely identifying a natural person, data concerning health or data concerning a natural person's sex life or sexual orientation are prohibited under GDPR. [41]

11.29 A series of derogations are available from the above general prohibition where one of the following applies:

Explicit consent

11.30 The data subject has given explicit consent to the processing of those personal data for one or more specified purposes, except where Union or member state law provide that the prohibition may not be lifted by the data subject.[42]

Employment and social security

11.31 The processing is necessary for the purposes of carrying out the obligations and exercising specific rights of the controller or of the data subject in the field of employment and social security and social protection law in so far as it is authorised by Union or member state law or a collective agreement pursuant to member state law

36 ibid, Art 6.4.
37 ibid, Art 7.1.
38 ibid, Art 7.2.
39 ibid, Art 7.3.
40 ibid, Art 7.4.
41 ibid, Art 9.1.
42 ibid, Art 9.2(a).

providing for appropriate safeguards for the fundamental rights and the interests of the data subject.[43]

Vital interests

11.32 The processing is necessary to protect the vital interests of the data subject or of another natural person where the data subject is physically or legally incapable of giving consent.[44]

Legitimate activity

11.33 The processing is carried out in the course of its legitimate activities with appropriate safeguards by a foundation, association or any other not-for-profit body with a political, philosophical, religious or trade union aim and on condition that the processing relates solely to the members or to former members of the body or to persons who have regular contact with it in connection with its purposes and that the personal data are not disclosed outside that body without the consent of the data subjects.[45]

Publically available

11.34 The processing relates to personal data which are manifestly made public by the data subject.[46]

Judicial process

11.35 The processing is necessary for the establishment, exercise or defence of legal claims or whenever courts are acting in their judicial capacity.[47]

Pubic interest

11.36 The processing is necessary for reasons of substantial public interest, on the basis of Union or member state law which shall be proportionate to the aim pursued, respect the essence of the right to data protection and provide for suitable and specific measures to safeguard the fundamental rights and the interests of the data subject.[48]

Health and wellbeing

11.37 The processing is necessary for the purposes of preventive or occupational medicine, for the assessment of the working capacity of the employee, medical diagnosis, the provision of health or social care or treatment or the management of health or social care systems and services on the basis of Union or member state law or pursuant to contract with a health professional.[49]

Public health

11.38 Processing is necessary for reasons of public interest in the area of public health, such as protecting against serious cross-border threats to health or ensuring

43 ibid, Art 9.2(b).
44 ibid, Art 9.2(c).
45 ibid, Art 9.2(d).
46 ibid, Art 9.2(e).
47 ibid, Art 9.2(f).
48 ibid, Art 9.2(g).
49 ibid, Art 9.2(h).

high standards of quality and safety of health care and of medicinal products or medical devices, on the basis of Union or member state law which provides for suitable and specific measures to safeguard the rights and freedoms of the data subject, in particular professional secrecy.[50]

Academic research

11.39 The processing is necessary for archiving purposes in the public interest, scientific or historical research purposes or statistical purposes based on Union or member state law which shall be proportionate to the aim pursued, respect the essence of the right to data protection and provide for suitable and specific measures to safeguard the fundamental rights and the interests of the data subject.[51]

Rights of the data subject

Information to be provided to data subjects when collecting information

11.40 Where personal data relating to a data subject are collected from the data subject, the controller shall, at the time when personal data are obtained, provide the data subject with all of the following information:[52]

- the identity and the contact details of the controller and, where applicable, of the controller's representative;
- the contact details of the data protection officer, where applicable;
- the purposes of the processing for which the personal data are intended as well as the legal basis for the processing;
- where the processing is based on legitimate interests, which interests are pursued by the controller or by a third party;
- the recipients or categories of recipients of the personal data, if any;
- where applicable, the fact that the controller intends to transfer personal data to a third country or international organisation and reference to the appropriate or suitable safeguards and the means by which to obtain a copy of them or where they have been made available.

11.41 Additionally, the controller must provide the data subject with the following further information necessary to ensure fair and transparent processing:[53]

- the period for which the personal data will be stored, or if that is not possible, the criteria used to determine that period;
- the existence of the right to request from the controller access to and rectification or erasure of personal data or restriction of processing concerning the data subject or to object to processing as well as the right to data portability;
- the existence of the right to withdraw consent at any time, without affecting the lawfulness of processing based on consent before its withdrawal;
- the right to lodge a complaint with a supervisory authority;

50 ibid, Art 9.2(i).
51 ibid, Art 9.2(j).
52 ibid, Art 13.1.
53 ibid, Art 13.2.

- whether the provision of personal data is a statutory or contractual requirement, or a requirement necessary to enter into a contract, as well as whether the data subject is obliged to provide the personal data and of the possible consequences of failure to provide such data;
- the existence of automated decision-making, including profiling, referred to and, at least in those cases, meaningful information about the logic involved, as well as the significance and the envisaged consequences of such processing for the data subject.

Right of access by data subject

11.42 As something of a corollary to the above rights, the data subject shall have the right to obtain from the controller confirmation as to whether or not personal data concerning him or her are being processed, and, where that is the case, access to the personal data and the following information:

- the purposes of the processing;
- the categories of personal data concerned;
- the recipients or categories of recipient to whom the personal data have been or will be disclosed, in particular recipients in third countries or international organisations;
- where possible, the envisaged period for which the personal data will be stored, or, if not possible, the criteria used to determine that period;
- the existence of the right to request from the controller rectification or erasure of personal data or restriction of processing of personal data concerning the data subject or to object to such processing;
- the right to lodge a complaint with a supervisory authority;
- where the personal data are not collected from the data subject, any available information as to their source;
- the existence of automated decision-making, including profiling, and, at least in those cases, meaningful information about the logic involved, as well as the significance and the envisaged consequences of such processing for the data subject.

Where transferred to a third country or to an international organisation, the data subject shall have the right to be informed of the appropriate safeguards pursuant to Article 46 relating to the transfer.[54] The controller shall provide a copy of the personal data undergoing processing. For any further copies requested by the data subject, the controller may charge a reasonable fee based on administrative costs. Where the data subject makes the request by electronic means, and unless otherwise requested by the data subject, the information shall be provided in a commonly used electronic form.[55]

Right of rectification

11.43 The data subject has the right to obtain from the controller without undue delay the rectification of inaccurate personal data concerning him or her. Taking into account the purposes of the processing, the data subject shall have the right to have

54 ibid, Art 15.2.
55 ibid, Art 15.3.

incomplete personal data completed, including by means of providing a supplementary statement.[56]

Right to erasure

11.44 The right to be forgotten achieved much notoriety in recent years owing to publicised litigation. Stated simply, the data subject has the right to obtain from the controller the erasure of personal data concerning him or her without undue delay and the controller has the obligation to erase personal data without undue delay where *inter alia* one of the following grounds applies:

(a) the personal data are no longer necessary in relation to the purposes for which they were collected or otherwise processed;

(b) the data subject withdraws consent on which the processing is based and where there is no other legal ground for the processing;

(c) the data subject objects to the processing and there are no overriding legitimate grounds for the processing, or the data subject objects to the processing;

(d) the personal data have been unlawfully processed;

(e) the personal data have to be erased for compliance with a legal obligation in Union or member state law to which the controller is subject.

There are exceptions and limitations placed on the above right. Namely, the above shall not apply to the extent that processing is necessary for exercising the right of freedom of expression and information; for compliance with a legal obligation; for the performance of a task carried out in the public interest; for reasons of public interest in the area of public health; for archiving purposes in the public interest, scientific or historical research purposes or statistical purposes in accordance with Article 89(1) in so far as the right referred to in paragraph 1 is likely to render impossible or seriously impair the achievement of the objectives of that processing; or for the establishment, exercise or defence of legal claims.[57]

11.45 GDPR specifically provides for a range of further rights, an in depth discussion of which is beyond the scope of this work, in particular in relation to automated individual decision-making, including profiling; the right to object; the right to data portability; and rights relating to notification, details of which are set out in Section 3 of GDPR.

Obligations

What is required of the controller?

11.46 The controller is required to implement appropriate technical and organisational measures to ensure and to be able to demonstrate that processing is performed in accordance with GDPR[58] including the implementation of appropriate data protection policies[59] and adherence to approved codes of conduct, all of which will be useful in demonstrating compliance.[60] Each controller and, where applicable,

---

56 ibid, Art 16.
57 ibid, Art 17.
58 ibid, Art 24.1.
59 ibid, Art 24.2.
60 ibid, Art 24.3.

the controller's representative, shall maintain a record of processing activities under its responsibility.[61]

What is required of the processor?

11.47 Where processing is to be carried out on behalf of a controller, the controller shall use only processors providing sufficient guarantees to implement appropriate technical and organisational measures in such a manner that processing will meet the requirements of the GDPR and ensure the protection of the rights of the data subject.[62] The processor must not engage another processor without prior specific or general written authorisation of the controller.[63]

Processing must be governed by contract

11.48 Processing must be governed by a contract or other legal act under Union or member state law, that is binding on the processor with regard to the controller and that sets out the subject-matter and duration of the processing, the nature and purpose of the processing, the type of personal data and categories of data subjects and the obligations and rights of the controller. That contract or other legal act shall stipulate, in particular, that the processor,[64] or where applicable, the processor's representative shall maintain a record of all categories of processing activities carried out on behalf of a controller, to include.[65]

(a) processes the personal data only on documented instructions from the controller, including with regard to transfers of personal data to a third country or an international organisation;

(b) ensures that persons authorised to process the personal data have committed themselves to confidentiality or are under an appropriate statutory obligation of confidentiality;

(c) takes all measures required for the purposes of security;

(d) respects the conditions set out above for engaging another processor;

(e) taking into account the nature of the processing, assists the controller by appropriate technical and organisational measures, insofar as this is possible, for the fulfilment of the controller's obligation to respond to requests for exercising the data subject's rights;

(f) assists the controller in ensuring compliance with the obligations pursuant to data security and data breaches taking into account the nature of processing and the information available to the processor;

(g) at the choice of the controller, deletes or returns all the personal data to the controller after the end of the provision of services relating to processing, and deletes existing copies unless Union or member state law requires storage of the personal data;

(h) makes available to the controller all information necessary to demonstrate compliance with these obligations and allows for and contributes to audits, including inspections, conducted by the controller or another auditor mandated by the controller.

61 ibid, Art 30.1.
62 ibid, Art 28.1.
63 ibid, Art 28.2.
64 ibid, Art 28.3 et seq.
65 ibid, Art 30.2.

Data breaches

11.49 In the case of a personal data breach, the controller shall *without undue delay* and, where feasible, not later than 72 hours after having become aware of it, notify the personal data breach to the supervisory authority competent unless the personal data breach is unlikely to result in a risk to the rights and freedoms of natural persons.[66]

11.50 Where the notification to the supervisory authority is not made within 72 hours, it shall be accompanied by reasons for the delay.[67] The processor shall notify the controller without undue delay after becoming aware of a personal data breach.[68]

11.51 The notification of a data breach should contain details regarding the following matters:[69]

The nature of the personal data

Including where possible, the categories and approximate number of data subjects concerned and the categories and approximate number of personal data records concerned;

Identify the Data Protection Officer

It should communicate the name and contact details of the data protection officer or other contact point where more information can be obtained;

Consequences

It should describe the likely consequences and implications of the personal data breach;

Response

It should describe the measures taken or proposed to be taken by the controller to address the personal data breach, including, where appropriate, measures to mitigate its possible adverse effects.

Where, and in so far as, it is not possible to provide the information at the same time, the information may be provided in phases without undue further delay. All breaches should be appropriately documented.[70]

11.52 When the personal data breach is likely to result in a high risk to the rights and freedoms of natural persons, the controller should communicate the personal data breach to the data subject without undue delay.[71] Plain language should be utilised.

Data Protection Officer

11.53 GDPR sets out circumstances in which it will be appropriate for a controller and/or processor to appoint a Data Protection Officer. This decision is one for specific

66 ibid, Art 33.
67 ibid, Art 33.1.
68 ibid, Art 33.2.
69 ibid, Art 33.3.
70 ibid, Art 33.4–5.
71 ibid, Art 34.1.

legal advice in each applicable jurisdiction.[72] In addition GDPR stipulates a range of governance issues which affect the role of Data Protection Officer and tasks which should be separately considered.[73]

Transfers of personal data outside of the European Union

11.54 As a starting point the European Union considers that any transfer of personal data to a third country or to an international organisation shall take place only if subject to the safeguards contained in GDPR. All provisions must be applied in order to ensure that the level of protection of natural persons is not undermined. How this might be achieved is considered below.

Generally, there are a number of pathways by which international transfers of data should proceed.

1. *Transfers on the basis of an adequacy decision*

   A transfer of personal data to a third country or an international organisation may take place where the Commission has decided that the third country (or organisation) in question ensures an adequate level of protection. Such a transfer does not require any specific authorisation.[74]

2. *Transfers subject to appropriate safeguards*

   A controller or processor may transfer personal data to a third country or an international organisation only if the controller or processor has provided appropriate safeguards, and on condition that enforceable data subject rights and effective legal remedies for data subjects are available. This may be achieved in a number of ways:[75]

   (a) a legally binding and enforceable instrument between public authorities or bodies;

   (b) binding corporate rules;

   (c) standard data protection clauses as adopted by the European Commission;[76]

   (d) standard data protection clauses adopted by a supervisory authority;[77]

   (e) an approved code of conduct together with binding and enforceable commitments of the controller or processor in the third country to apply the appropriate safeguards, including as regards data subjects' rights; or

   (f) an approved certification mechanism together with binding and enforceable commitments of the controller or processor in the third country to apply the appropriate safeguards, including as regards data subjects' rights.

The appropriate safeguards may be set out, in particular, by contractual clauses between the controller or processor and the controller, processor or the recipient of the personal data in the third country or international organisation.[78]

72 ibid, Art 37.
73 ibid, Arts 38–39.
74 ibid, Art 45.1.
75 ibid, Art 46.2.
76 In accordance with the examination procedure referred to in Art 93.2.
77 And approved by the Commission pursuant to the examination procedure referred to in Art 93.2.
78 ibid, Art 46.4.

12 Environmental, social and governance

> 'We have always supported our employees and fostered a culture of inclusion and respect – this includes the right to marry whomever they choose and to have that union legally recognized.'
>
> Deborah P Majoras
>
> Chief Legal Officer and Secretary
>
> Proctor and Gamble

Introduction

12.1 Hope. It is a powerful concept and one that is perhaps now necessary more than ever in relation to environmental questions. Hope now exists that environmental, social and governance, a phrase that now commonly travels under the acronym 'ESG' might describe how corporate entities will engage with considerations that effect their ethical impact on their stakeholders, employees and the wider community. It describes a growing awareness of the importance of a range of issues that typically are not reflected in the annual reports of a corporate entity but are increasingly important to how the entity does its business. Whilst perhaps born of a sense of outrage as to certain high level political events, such as the introduction of the apartheid regime in South Africa, this means viewing the corporate impact has come to encompass an enormous range of topics and concerns, some of which remain unenumerated and embryonic in nature. While commonly referring, in broad brush strokes, to issues of environmental sustainability, nuclear energy and other energy utilisation and generation, diversity, human rights, workers' rights, consumer protection and animal welfare, company management structure, employee relations, executive and employee compensation, it is clear that the list of concerns is non-exhaustive and continually evolving. Indeed, climate change is increasingly considered of central importance to discussions on this topic at a corporate level. The authors have set out below some of the more important and relevant information, as it pertains to the EMEA region, on this subject, which it is hoped will guide corporate counsel who are new to such concerns and their implications in the EMEA region.

Environment

Introduction

12.2 Set out below is a list of European and UK primary and secondary legislation in relation to environmental issues that impact upon corporate entities. Many of these instruments create onerous compliance obligation for corporate entities and counsel should remain aware of developments on such topics.

Topic	Relevant legislation
Environmental management	EMAS Regulation 2009 (Regulation (EC) No 1221/2009
	Commission Decision (EU) 2012/2285 of 6 December 2012
Environmental reporting	UK Companies Act 2006
	Large and Medium-sized Companies and Groups (Accounts and Reports) Regulations 2008, SI 2008/410
	Non-Financial Reporting Directive 2014
	Companies, Partnerships and Groups (Accounts and Non-Financial Reporting) Regulations 2016, SI 2016/1245
	Companies (Directors' Report) and Limited Liability Partnerships (Energy and Carbon Report) Regulations 2018, SI 2018/1155
Pollution prevention	Medium Combustion Plants Directive 2015
Environmental eco-systems	Directive 2011/92/EU of the European Parliament and of the Council of 13 December 2011 on the assessment of the effects of certain public and private projects on the environment (EIA Directive 2011)
	Directive 2014/52/EU of the European Parliament and of the Council of 16 April 2014 amending Directive 2011/92/EU on the assessment of the effects of certain public and private projects on the environment (EIA Directive 2014)
Climate change	EU Emissions Trading System (EU ETS)
	EU ETS Linking Directive 2004
	Directive 2004/101/EC of the European Parliament and of the Council of 27 October 2004 amending Directive 2003/87/EC establishing a scheme for greenhouse gas emission allowance trading within the Community, in respect of the Kyoto Protocol's project mechanisms

Topic	Relevant legislation
	EU ETS Amending Directive 2009
	Directive 2009/29/EC of the European Parliament and of the Council of 23 April 2009 amending Directive 2003/87/EC so as to improve and extend the greenhouse gas emission allowance trading scheme of the Community
	Aviation Emissions Directive 2008
	EU ETS Amending Directive 2009
	Phase IV EU ETS Directive 2018
Product stewardship[1]	Classification, Labelling and Packaging (CLP Regulation 2008) (EC/1272/2008)
	Batteries Directive 2006 (Regulation (EU) No 528/2012 of the European Parliament and of the Council of 22 May 2012 concerning the making available on the market and use of biocidal products).
	REACH Regulation 2006
	RoHS Directive 2011
	Directive (EU) 2017/2102 of the European Parliament and of the Council of 15 November 2017 amending Directive 2011/65/EU on the restriction of the use of certain hazardous substances in electrical and electronic equipment (OJ 2017 L 305/8) (RoHS Directive 2017)
Resource efficiency	Energy Efficiency Directive 2012
	Energy Efficiency Directive 2018

Social

Equality and employee relations

12.3 Every EU worker has certain minimum rights relating to health and safety at work, including in relation to general rights and obligations, workplaces, work equipment, specific risks and protections for vulnerable workers. Similarly there must be equal opportunities for women and men in relation to matters of treatment at work, pregnancy, maternity leave and parental leave. Every worker is entitled to protection against discrimination based on sex, race, religion, age, disability and sexual orientation. Every worker is also entitled to protection in relation to part-time work, fixed-term contracts, working hours, employment of young people, informing and consulting employees. The sum total of these rights represents a body of law that is far beyond the scope of this work. Further discussion is had in the chapter relating to human resources.

Whistleblowing

12.4 This topic is of particular relevance to corporate counsel as unlawful activities and abuse of law may occur in any organisation, whether private or public, big or small. They can take many forms, such as corruption or fraud, malpractice or

1 Please see chapter on product compliance for a broader discussion.

negligence. And if they are not addressed, they can sometimes result in serious harm to the public interest. People who work for an organisation or are in contact with it in their work related activities are often the first to know about such occurrences and are, therefore, in a privileged position to inform those who can address the problem. Whistleblowers, that is persons who report (within the organisation concerned or to an outside authority) or disclose (to the public) information on a wrongdoing obtained in a work-related context, help prevent damage and detect threat or harm to the public interest that may otherwise remain hidden. However, they are often discouraged from reporting their concerns for fear of retaliation. For these reasons, the importance of providing effective whistleblower protection for safeguarding the public interest is increasingly acknowledged both at European and international level. The whistleblower protection currently available across the EU is fragmented, hence the EU has drafted a proposal for a new directive on the protection of persons reporting on breaches of Union law which sets out a range of protections. Of significant relevance to corporate counsel is the proposed requirement that workers and their trade unions should be fully consulted on envisaged internal procedures for facilitating whistleblowing.[2]

National example

12.5 Fragmented protections are available at a national level around Europe. In particular a good example is that of the UK and its Public Interest Disclosure Act of 1998[3] which seeks to protect individuals who make certain disclosures of information in the public interest; to allow such individuals to bring action in respect of victimisation. Such disclosures may be defined as:

> '... any disclosure of information which, in the reasonable belief of the worker making the disclosure, tends to show one or more of the following:[4]
>
> (a) that a criminal offence has been committed, is being committed or is likely to be committed,
>
> (b) that a person has failed, is failing or is likely to fail to comply with any legal obligation to which he is subject,
>
> (c) that a miscarriage of justice has occurred, is occurring or is likely to occur,
>
> (d) that the health or safety of any individual has been, is being or is likely to be endangered,
>
> (e) that the environment has been, is being or is likely to be damaged, or
>
> (f) that information tending to show any matter falling within any one of the preceding paragraphs has been, is being or is likely to be deliberately concealed.'
>
> 'A worker has the right not to be subjected to any detriment by any act, or any deliberate failure to act, by his employer done on the ground that the worker has made a protected disclosure.'[5]

2 See Proposal for a Directive of the European Parliament and of the Council on the protection of persons reporting on breaches of Union law – Brussels, 23.4.2018 COM(2018) 218.
3 Which amends the Employment Rights Act 1996.
4 Public Interest Disclosure Act 1998, s 1.
5 ibid, s 2.

Health and safety at work

12.6 The welfare of people whilst at work has undergone a revolution in the EMEA region over many decades. While patchy and piecemeal attempts at safeguarding those at work typically occurred in conjunction with the ebb and flow of workers' rights on a political level, the EU sought, since its creation, to create a framework to harmonise and encourage efforts in this regard.

Legislative aims

12.7 A battery of legislation has been developed committed to the adoption of minimum requirements for encouraging improvements, especially in the working environment, to guarantee a better level of protection of the safety and health of workers,[6] encouraging improvements in conditions in this area and harmonising conditions while maintaining the improvements made.

12.8 Member states have a basic responsibility to encourage improvements in the safety and health of workers on their territory,[7] whereas taking measures to protect the health and safety of workers at work also helps, in certain cases, to preserve the health and possibly the safety of persons residing in those territories.

12.9 It was recognised that member states' legislative systems covering safety and health at the workplace differed widely and needed to be improved. Further, national provisions on the subject, which often include technical specifications and/or self-regulatory standards, typically result in different levels of safety and health protection and allow competition at the expense of safety and health.[8]

12.10 It has been historically considered axiomatic at an institutional level, that the incidence of accidents at work and occupational diseases were too high and that preventive measures must be introduced or improved without delay in order to safeguard the safety and health of workers and ensure a higher degree of protection.

12.11 The council directive of 1989 sought to ensure an improved degree of protection, it was noted therein that as a basic requirement workers and/or their representatives must be informed of the risks to their safety and health and of the measures required to reduce or eliminate these risks. Similarly, workers must also be in a position to contribute, by means of balanced participation in accordance with national laws and/or practices, to seeing that the necessary protective measures are taken.

Relevant legislative instruments

12.12 A full treatise on Health and Safety legislation in the EMEA region is most certainly beyond the scope of this work. However, it is considered by the authors beneficial to set out some preliminary information, relevant to corporate counsel at a European level, to allow for a wider discussion on the matter and to allow for issue identification. The implementation of such policy at a national level should, in specific cases, be referred to local counsel.

---

6 Council Directive 89/391/EEC of 12 June 1989 on the introduction of measures to encourage improvements in the safety and health of workers at work.

7 See preamble to Council Directive 89/391/EEC of 12 June 1989 on the introduction of measures to encourage improvements in the safety and health of workers at work.

8 ibid, as per directive recitals.

Framework Directive

12.13 Council Directive 89/391/EEC on the introduction of measures to encourage improvements in the safety and health of workers at work (Framework Directive) applies to all sectors of activity, both public and private, except for specific public service activities, such as the armed forces, the police or certain civil protection services. It is of fundamental importance as it is the basic safety and health legal act which lays down general principles concerning the prevention and protection of workers against occupational accidents and diseases. It contains principles concerning the prevention of risks, the protection of safety and health, the assessment of risks, the elimination of risks and accident factors, the informing, consultation and balanced participation and training of workers and their representatives.

Protection for temporary workers

12.14 Council Directive 91/383/EEC on the safety of temporary workers (Temporary Workers Directive) provides that a temporary worker must be informed beforehand of any risks he or sheshe faces in any activity he or she takes up. They must be informed of any special occupational qualifications or skills or special medical surveillance required, and if there are increased specific risks involved in the activity.[9]

Pregnant and breastfeeding workers

12.15 Council Directive 92/85/EEC sets out the minimum requirements to ensure the safety of pregnant workers and workers who have recently given birth or are breastfeeding. The Directive also includes provisions for physical movements and postures, mental and physical fatigue and other types of physical and mental stress. Neither may such workers be exposed to agents that might harm their health or that of their child.[10]

Protections for young people at work

12.16 Council Directive 94/33/EC provides for the protection of young people at work. Member states are required to take the necessary measures to prohibit work by children. The minimum working or employment age must not be lower than the minimum age at which compulsory full-time schooling, as imposed by national law, ends or 15 years in any event.[11] This directive shall apply to any person under 18 years of age having an employment contract or an employment relationship defined by the law in force. Exceptions can be adopted by member states for occasional work or short-term work, involving domestic service in a private household or work regarded as not being harmful, damaging or dangerous to young people in a family undertaking. The legislation defines 'young people' as people under the age of 18 and 'children' as young people under the age of 15 or who are still in full-time compulsory education in accordance with national legislation. Adolescents are young people between the ages of 15 and 18 who are no longer in full-time compulsory education in accordance with national legislation.

9 See also guidance provided by the European Agency for Safety and Health at Work.

10 'Pregnant and breastfeeding workers may under no circumstances be obliged to perform duties for which the assessment has revealed a risk of exposure to agents, which would jeopardize their safety or health', European Agency for Safety and Health at Work.

11 See also guidance provided by the European Agency for Safety and Health at Work.

Manual handling of loads

12.17 Council Directive 90/269/EEC sets outs employers' obligations in respect of manual handling of loads where there is a risk of injury. Employers shall take appropriate organisational measures, or shall use the appropriate means, in particular mechanical equipment, in order to avoid the need for the manual handling of loads by workers. Where the need for the manual handling of loads by workers cannot be avoided, the employer shall take the appropriate organisational measures, use the appropriate means or provide workers with such means in order to reduce the risk involved in the manual handling of such loads.[12] In particular, the guidance notes that wherever the need for manual handling of loads by workers cannot be avoided, the employer shall organise workstations in such a way as to make such handling as safe and healthy as possible and assess, in advance if possible, the health and safety conditions of the type of work involved, and in particular examine the characteristics of loads.

The use of work equipment by workers at work

12.18 Directive 2009/104/EC now governs this area. In particular, the employer is required under the directive to take every measure to ensure the safety of the work equipment made available to workers. During the selection of the work equipment the employer shall pay attention to the specific working conditions which exist at the workplace, especially in relation to safety and health of the workers. If risks cannot be fully eliminated during the operation of the work equipment, the employer shall take appropriate measures to minimise them. Furthermore it is a requirement that throughout its working life, the employer must keep the work equipment compliant by means of adequate maintenance. The employer shall ensure that the work equipment is installed correctly and is operating properly by inspection/testing of the work equipment (initial, after assembly, periodic and special) by competent persons. The results of inspections shall be recorded and kept.[13]

The use of personal protective equipment at the workplace

12.19 Council Directive 89/656/EEC sets out the employers' obligations as regards the provision and use of personal protective equipment. Personal protective equipment must be used when the risks cannot be avoided or sufficiently limited by technical means of collective protection or procedures of work organisation. All personal protective equipment must:[14]

- be appropriate for the risks involved, without itself leading to any increased risk;
- correspond to existing conditions at the workplace;
- take account of ergonomic requirements and the worker's state of health;
- fit the wearer correctly after any necessary adjustment.

---

12 Please see guidance provided by the European Agency for Safety and Health at Work and Annex 1 thereto.

13 See guidance provided by the European Agency for Safety and Health at Work.

14 See Annexes to legislation and guidance from the European Agency for Safety and Health at Work for specific advice relating to requirements in this regard.

Work with display screen equipment

12.20 Council Directive 90/270/EEC requires that employers are obliged to perform an analysis of workstations in order to evaluate the safety and health conditions to which they give rise for their workers, particularly as regards possible risks to eyesight, physical problems and problems of mental stress. They shall take appropriate measures to remedy the risks found taking account of the additional and/or combined effects of the risks so found. Workers shall also receive information on all aspects of safety and health relating to their workstation. Workers or their representatives shall be informed of any health and safety measure taken by the employer. Every worker must also receive training in use of the workstation before commencing this type of work and whenever the organisation of the workstation is substantially modified.

Requirements at temporary or mobile construction sites

12.21 Council Directive 92/57/EEC sets out that the project supervisor must nominate person(s) responsible for the coordination of health and safety at sites where several firms are present. Where a person responsible for coordination is appointed, the project supervisor or client remains responsible for safety and health. The person(s) responsible for coordination on the site shall ensure that employers and self-employed persons apply the general prevention principles, particularly in respect of the situations described, and that the health and safety plan is taken into account when necessary. They shall also organise cooperation between employers in matters of health and safety and check that the working procedures are being implemented correctly as well as ensure that no unauthorised persons enter the site.[15] The employers' obligations are, *inter alia*:

- To adhere to the minimum safety and health requirements applicable to work sites set out in Annex IV to the directive. The aspects covered include energy distribution systems, emergency routes and exits, ventilation, temperature, traffic routes and danger areas, sanitary installations, etc.
- To act on the comments of the health and safety coordinator.

Workers in surface and underground mineral-extracting industries

12.22 Council Directive 92/104/EEC requires that employers must take the following measures to safeguard the health and safety of workers by ensuring that:

- workplaces are designed, constructed, equipped, commissioned, operated and maintained to allow workers to perform the work assigned to them without endangering their own and others' health or safety;
- operation of workplaces takes place under the supervision of a person in charge;
- work involving a special risk is only carried out by competent staff in accordance with employers' instructions;
- all safety instructions are comprehensible to workers;
- appropriate first-aid facilities are available; and
- any relevant safety drills are performed regularly.

15 See guidance provided by the European Agency for Safety and Health at Work.

Requirements for work on board fishing vessels

12.23 Council Directive 93/103/EC requires that workers and their representatives must be informed of all measures to be taken regarding safety and health on board vessels and this information must be comprehensible to the workers concerned. Workers must be given suitable training on safety and health on board vessels and on accident prevention. The training must cover fire-fighting, the use of life-saving and survival equipment, the use of fishing gear and hauling equipment as well as the use of signs and hand signals. Moreover, any person likely to command a vessel must be given detailed training.[16]

Requirements for improved medical treatment on board vessels

12.24 The objective of Council Directive 92/29/EEC is to improve medical assistance at sea since a vessel represents a workplace involving a wide range of risks. Specific advice and guidance is available via the European Agency for Safety and Health at Work as to the medical equipment and supplies that must be provided on board vessels.

Protection of the health and safety of workers from the risks related to chemical agents

12.25 Council Directive 98/24/EC governs the protection of workers from the risks related to chemical agents at work. The employer must determine whether any hazardous chemical agents are present at the workplace and assess any risk to the safety and health arising from their presence. The employer must be in possession of an assessment of the risk and this assessment shall be kept up-to-date, particularly if there have been significant changes or if the results of health surveillance show it to be necessary. In the case of activities involving exposure to several hazardous chemical agents, the risks must be assessed on the basis of the risk presented by all such chemical agents in combination.

Protection of workers from the risks related to exposure to asbestos

12.26 A common fear for corporate counsel arises in this regard. Council Directive 2009/148/EC sets out the protection requirements of workers from the risks related to exposure to asbestos. This directive applies to activities in which workers are or may be exposed to dust arising from asbestos or materials containing asbestos in the course of their work. If any activity is likely to involve such risk of exposure, a risk assessment must be carried out including consultation with the workers. The risk assessment has to determine the nature and degree of the workers' exposure to dust arising from asbestos or materials containing asbestos and it must be revised if circumstances change significantly. If the exposure of the worker is sporadic and of low intensity with the exposure limit not exceeded, the activity need not to be notified, health assessment of workers and clinical surveillance are not obligatory and workers need not be registered.[17]

Protection from carcinogens or mutagens

12.27 Council Directive 2004/37/EC on the protection of workers from the risks related to exposure to carcinogens or mutagens sets out that the employer must

16 See guidance provided by the European Agency for Safety and Health at Work.

17 This directive was adopted and the previous directive 83/477/EEC and its amendments have been repealed.

assess and manage the risk of exposure to carcinogens or mutagens. This process shall be renewed regularly and data shall be supplied to the authorities upon request. Special attention should be paid to investigate and take account of all possible ways of exposure (including all skin-related possibilities), and to persons at particular risk. The directive requires that workers' exposure must be prevented. If replacement is not possible, the employer shall use a closed technological system. The employer shall reduce the use of carcinogens or mutagens by replacing them with a substance that is not dangerous or less dangerous. Where a closed system is not technically possible, the employer shall reduce exposure to the minimum.

Exposure of workers to noise

12.28 Noise-induced hearing loss claims are a frequent occurrence, though the frequency with which these cases arise may be said to be waning and typically arise on a historical basis given the broad adoption of improved practices. Council Directive 2003/10/EC sets out the requirements regarding the exposure of workers to the risks from noise at work. The employer shall assess and, if necessary, measure the levels of exposure to noise to which workers are exposed. This has to be done in accordance with the obligations laid down in the Framework Directive. Results of the risk assessment have to be recorded on a suitable medium and kept up to date on a regular basis. The risk assessment shall be updated on a regular basis, particularly if there have been significant changes which could render it out of date, or if the results of health surveillance show it to be necessary. When carrying out the risk assessment, the employer must give particular attention to level, type and duration of exposure, exposure limit/action values, health effects spreading from particular sensitivity of the worker, interactions with other risks (ototoxic substances, vibrations), the exposure to noise beyond normal working hours under his responsibility, and noise caused by warning signals at work. The risks arising from exposure to noise must be eliminated or reduced to a minimum.

Protection of workers from exposure to biological agents

12.29 Council Directive 2000/54/EC sets out the protections for workers from risks related to exposure to biological agents at work. Employers should avoid using a harmful biological agent by replacing it with one which is not dangerous or less dangerous to workers' health, if possible. Workers' risk of exposure to biological agents should be reduced where possible to protect their health and safety. Where the results of the risk assessment reveal a risk to workers' health or safety, employers shall, when requested, make available to the competent authority appropriate information. Employers must ensure hygiene and individual protection by prohibiting eating or drinking in working areas, providing protective clothing, providing appropriate toilet and washing facilities, and maintaining protective equipment properly. Further, workers and their representatives must receive appropriate training involving working with biological agents and be provided with written instructions and display notices of the procedure to be followed in case of a serious accident.

Working time

12.30 Council Directive 2003/88/EC, referred to as the 'Working Time' Directive is of particular practical importance to corporate counsel. It is a wide-ranging directive designed to ensure that every worker is entitled to a minimum daily rest period of 11 consecutive hours per 24-hour period. Moreover, they shall take the measures necessary to ensure that, per each seven-day period, every worker is entitled to a minimum uninterrupted rest period of 24 hours (plus the 11 hours' daily rest if possible). In addition the directive requires that every worker is entitled to a rest break if the working day is longer than six hours. Details including duration and the terms on which it is granted, shall be laid down in collective agreements, agreements between the two sides of industry or by national legislation. Further, the average weekly working time must not exceed 48 hours and every worker is entitled to paid annual leave of at least four weeks. This minimum period of paid annual leave cannot be replaced by an allowance except where the employment relationship is terminated.[18]

Human rights

12.31 The Convention for the Protection of Human Rights and Fundamental Freedoms, also referred to as the European Convention on Human Rights, came into force in 1953. It was the first instrument to give effect to certain of the rights stated in the Universal Declaration of Human Rights and make them binding. Since its adoption, the Convention has been amended a number of times and supplemented with many rights in addition to those set forth in the original text.[19] The European Convention on Human Rights was implemented almost universally in the EU and in the UK by the Human Rights Act 1998.[20]

12.32 The European Convention on Human Rights and its implementing legislation across Europe finds frequent utilisation in a corporate context, most notably in employment disputes. This will be considered further in this text in the context of human resources[21] and data protection.[22]

Brexit implications

12.33 There has been a degree of commentary as to the future of the European Convention on Human Rights in the UK given the Brexit process, however at the time of writing there is no clarity on this matter.

Timely payment of suppliers

12.34 The EU directive on combating late payments in commercial transactions[23] and the directive on combating late payments in commercial transactions (recast)[24] require member states to make provision for the payment of interest in relation to certain contracts which has been largely implemented in member states.

Interest on the late payment of certain debts in the UK

12.35 By way of example, in the UK suppliers can claim statutory interest where a buyer hasn't paid an undisputed and valid invoice within 30 days (or any earlier payment date agreed in the contract). Interest is not paid automatically and this act

18 Significant guidance is available from the European Agency for Safety and Health at Work.
19 See European Court of Human Rights website – www.echr.coe.int.
20 See also the Charter of Fundamental Rights of the EU (EU Charter).
21 See ch 5.
22 See ch 11.
23 2000/35/EC.
24 2011/7/EU.

applies to contracts for the supply of goods or services where the purchaser and the supplier are each acting in the course of a business, other than an excepted contract.[25]

Governance

Bribery and corruption

12.36 The UK Bribery Act 2010[26] came into force on 8 April 2010 and it is one of a small number of key anti-bribery and anti-corruption measures and creates various offences, one of which can be committed by commercial organisations which fail to prevent persons associated with them from committing bribery on their behalf. It is a full defence for an organisation to prove that despite a particular case of bribery it nevertheless had adequate procedures in place to prevent persons associated with it from bribing.

Jurisdiction

12.37 Perhaps the key feature of the Act that gives the provision the transcendent relevance is that UK courts will have jurisdiction not only over offences that occur in the UK but also over offences outside the UK where the person committing them has a close connection with the UK by virtue of being a British national or ordinarily resident in the UK, a body incorporated in the UK or a Scottish partnership. What amounts to a close connection is provided for by the Act and corporate counsel should take careful note of the potential for application of these provisions in all scenarios involving bribery.

A close connection with the UK

12.38 A person has a close connection with the UK if, and only if, the person was one of the following at the time the acts or omissions concerned were done or made:

- a British citizen;
- a British overseas territories citizen;
- a British national (overseas);
- a British overseas citizen;
- a person who under the British Nationality Act 1981 was a British subject;
- a British protected person within the meaning of that Act;
- an individual ordinarily resident in the UK;
- a body incorporated under the law of any part of the UK;
- a Scottish partnership.

Irrelevance of locus of the offence

12.39 An offence is committed irrespective of whether the acts or omissions which form part of the offence take place in the UK or elsewhere.

25 Late Payment of Commercial Debts (interest) Act 1998, s 2 as amended by The Late Payment of Commercial Debts Regulations 2002.
26 This Act is separately considered at ch 15.

Corporate governance and directors

12.40 While the duties of directors, particularly those serving within common law jurisdictions, are often times onerous and contained in disparate pieces of legislation and guidance, it is helpful for corporate counsel to appreciate, at a high level, a sense of governance issues that will impact upon directors. While a thorough exposition of these duties and obligations is beyond the scope of this work, a selection of key issues are set out below from a UK perspective given the preponderance of large multi-national commercial entities who have primary listings in the UK, hence its utility as an analogue to commence consideration of wider EMEA matters.

Companies Act duties

12.41 A useful starting point for the consideration of directors' duties is Part 15 of the UK Companies Act 2006.[27] Once again, directors' duties alone could fill many volumes, what follows is a selection of pertinent matters for corporate counsel and is in no way exhaustive.

12.42 The Act proscribes a range of duties for directors of companies of varying sizes and types, particularly in relation to accounting and corporate governance matters for example:

- Duty to keep accounting records (section 386)
- Where and for how long records to be kept (section 388)
- Accounts to give true and fair view (section 393)
- Duty to prepare individual accounts (section 394)
- Duty to prepare group accounts (section 399)
- The provision of Information about related undertakings (section 409)
- The provision of Information about off-balance sheet arrangements (section 410A)
- The Provision of Information about employee numbers and costs (section 411).
- The provision of Information about directors' benefits: remuneration (section 412)
- Duty to prepare a strategic report (section 414A)
- Duty to prepare directors' report (section 415)
- Duty to prepare remuneration report (section 421)

Of particular interest to corporate counsel may be the duty, as part of the strategic report, for the company to make what is referred to as a 'non-financial information statement'[28] The Act provided guidance as to what this statement must contain,[29] which warrants inclusion hereafter.

12.43 The statement must contain information, to the extent necessary for an understanding of the company's development, performance and position and the impact of its activity, relating to, as a minimum:[30]

---

27 As amended by Companies (Miscellaneous Reporting) Regulations 2018 (Miscellaneous Reporting) Regulations, SI 2018/860.
28 Companies Act 2006, s 414CA.
29 ibid, s 414CB.
30 ibid, s 414CB(1).

- environmental matters (including the impact of the company's business on the environment);
- the company's employees;
- social matters;
- respect for human rights; and
- anti-corruption and anti-bribery matters.

Further, the Act requires that the information must include:[31]

- a brief description of the company's business model;
- a description of the policies pursued by the company in relation to the matters mentioned in subsection (1)(a) to (e) and any due diligence processes implemented by the company in pursuance of those policies;
- a description of the outcome of those policies;
- a description of the principal risks relating to the matters mentioned in above arising in connection with the company's operations and, where relevant and proportionate:
  - a description of its business relationships, products and services which are likely to cause adverse impacts in those areas of risk; and
  - a description of how it manages the principal risks.
- a description of the non-financial key performance indicators relevant to the company's business.

If the company does not pursue policies in relation to one or more of the matters mentioned in subsection above the statement must provide a clear and reasoned explanation for the company's not doing so.[32]

UK Corporate Governance Code

12.44 Published in 2018,[33] the UK Corporate Governance Code seeks to enhance the governance structures between companies, shareholders and stakeholders. The Code notes at the outset that:

> 'Companies do not exist in isolation. Successful and sustainable businesses underpin our economy and society by providing employment and creating prosperity. To succeed in the long-term, directors and the companies they lead need to build and maintain successful relationships with a wide range of stakeholders. These relationships will be successful and enduring if they are based on respect, trust and mutual benefit. Accordingly, a company's culture should promote integrity and openness, value diversity and be responsive to the views of shareholders and wider stakeholders.'[34]

31 ibid, s 414CB(2).

32 ibid, s 414CB(4).

33 As applicable to accounting periods beginning on or after 1 January 2019. For accounting periods prior to this date please see 'UK Corporate Governance Code 2016' available at https://www.frc.org.uk/directors/corporate-governance-and-stewardship/uk-corporate-governance-code

34 The UK Corporate Governance Code, p 1.

12.45 The Code goes on to set out the basis underpinning its rationale:

> 'At the heart of this Code is an updated set of Principles that emphasise the value of good corporate governance to long-term sustainable success. By applying the Principles, following the more detailed Provisions and using the associated guidance, companies can demonstrate throughout their reporting how the governance of the company contributes to its long term sustainable success and achieves wider objectives.'[35]

12.46 The Code applies to all companies with a premium listing, whether incorporated in the UK or elsewhere, and comprises five key principles which it suggests that applicable companies will comply with or explain:

1. Board Leadership and Company Purpose

   The Code opines that a successful company is led by an effective and entrepreneurial board, whose role is to promote the long-term sustainable success of the company, generating value for shareholders and contributing to wider society.[36] The board should establish the company's purpose, values and strategy, and satisfy itself that these and its culture are aligned. It further requires that all directors must act with integrity, lead by example and promote the desired culture.[37] Further, it is incumbent on the board to ensure that the necessary resources are in place for the company to meet its objectives and measure performance against them. The board should also establish a framework of prudent and effective controls, which enable risk to be assessed and managed.[38] In order for the company to meet its responsibilities to shareholders and stakeholders, the Code requires that the board should ensure effective engagement with, and encourage participation from, these parties.[39] It further requires that the board should ensure that workforce policies and practices are consistent with the company's values and support its long-term sustainable success whilst allowing and enabling the workforce should be able to raise any matters of concern.[40]

2. Division of Responsibilities

   The Code helpfully sets out guidance on the nature and scope of key individuals' roles and responsibilities. The chair leads the board and is responsible for its overall effectiveness in directing the company. The chair should demonstrate objective judgement throughout their tenure and promote a culture of openness and debate. In addition, the chair facilitates constructive board relations and the effective contribution of all non-executive directors, and ensures that directors receive accurate, timely and clear information.[41] It notes that the board should include an appropriate combination of executive and non-executive (and, in particular, independent non-executive) directors, such that no one individual or small group of individuals dominates the board's decision-making. There should be a clear division of responsibilities between the leadership of the board and the executive leadership of the company's business.[42] It requires that non-executive directors should have sufficient time to meet their board responsibilities and that

35 ibid, p 1.
36 ibid, p 1, para 1(A).
37 ibid, p 1, para 1(B).
38 ibid, p 1, para 1(C).
39 ibid, p 1, para 1(D).
40 ibid, p 1, para 1(E).
41 ibid, p 1, para 2(F).
42 ibid, p 1, para 2(G).

they should provide constructive challenge, strategic guidance, offer specialist advice and hold management to account.[43] The board, supported by the company secretary, is required to ensure that it has the policies, processes, information, time and resources it needs in order to function effectively and efficiently.[44]

3. Composition, Success and Evaluation

   The Code provides guidance of an operational nature also. It requires that appointments to the board should be subject to a formal, rigorous and transparent procedure, and that an effective succession plan should be maintained for board and senior management. It calls for both appointments and succession plans to be based on merit and objective criteria and, within this context, should promote diversity of gender, social and ethnic backgrounds, cognitive and personal strengths.[45] The board and its committees should have a combination of skills, experience and knowledge. The code notes that consideration should be given to the length of service of the board as a whole and membership regularly refreshed[46] and that annual evaluation of the board should consider its composition, diversity and how effectively members work together to achieve objectives. Individual evaluation should demonstrate whether each director continues to contribute effectively.

4. Audit, Risk and Internal Control

   The Code suggests that the board should establish formal and transparent policies and procedures to ensure the independence and effectiveness of internal and external audit functions and satisfy itself on the integrity of financial and narrative statements.[47] The board should present a fair, balanced and understandable assessment of the company's position and prospects. The board should establish procedures to manage risk, oversee the internal control framework, and determine the nature and extent of the principal risks the company is willing to take in order to achieve its long-term strategic objectives.[48]

5. Remuneration

   The Code also sets out that remuneration policies and practices should be designed to support strategy and promote long-term sustainable success. Executive remuneration should be aligned to company purpose and values, and be clearly linked to the successful delivery of the company's long-term strategy.[49] A formal and transparent procedure for developing policy on executive remuneration and determining director and senior management remuneration should be established. No director should be involved in deciding their own remuneration outcome.[50] Directors should exercise independent judgement and discretion when authorising remuneration outcomes, taking account of company and individual performance, and wider circumstances.[51]

43 ibid, p 1, para 2(H).
44 ibid, p 1, para 2(I).
45 ibid, p 1, para 3(J).
46 ibid, p 1, para 3(K).
47 ibid, p 1, para 4(M).
48 ibid, p 1, para 4(O).
49 ibid, p 1, para 5(P).
50 ibid, p 1, para 5(Q).
51 ibid, p 1, para 5(R).

Economic sanctions

12.47 Economic sanctions may be loosely defined as the withdrawal of customary trade and financial relations for foreign and security policy purposes. They may be comprehensive, prohibiting commercial activity with regard to an entire country, like the long-standing US embargo of Cuba, or they may be targeted, blocking transactions of and with particular businesses, groups, or individuals.

12.48 Corporate counsel must be aware of the broad strokes of such sanctions including advisers of multi-national companies who trade across a wide range of jurisdictions. Sanctions screening is a commonplace element of customer and third party due diligence in any such trading entity. Counsel should be aware of the sources of these sanctions from a legislative perspective, some of which are set out below with a particular emphasis on the UK legislative framework which refers to a wide range of international sources.

12.49 A precedent corporate policy in relation to third party due diligence is set out in the annexes to this text.

The UN Security Council sanctions committee list

12.50 The Security Council has established 30 sanctions regimes, in Southern Rhodesia, South Africa, the former Yugoslavia, Haiti, Iraq, Angola, Rwanda, Sierra Leone, Somalia and Eritrea, Eritrea and Ethiopia, Liberia, DRC, Côte d'Ivoire, Sudan, Lebanon, DPRK, Iran, Libya, Guinea-Bissau, CAR, Yemen, South Sudan and Mali, as well as against ISIL (Da'esh) and Al-Qaida and the Taliban. These measures have ranged from comprehensive economic and trade sanctions to more targeted measures such as arms embargoes, travel bans, and financial or commodity restrictions. There are 14 ongoing sanctions regimes which focus on supporting political settlement of conflicts, nuclear non-proliferation, and counter-terrorism. Each regime is administered by a sanctions committee chaired by a non-permanent member of the Security Council.[52]

The EU sanctions list

12.51 The Council of the European Union have developed a useful research tool referred to as the EU Sanction Map (www.sanctionsmap.eu/) which provides information on sanctions that are agreed by the EU member states and are adopted by the EU Council. It also covers sanctions regimes that are imposed by the UN and implemented by the EU Council.

HM Treasury's consolidated list of targets (UK)

12.52 Her Majesty's Treasury makes available a list that provides information to help you decide whether you are dealing with someone who is subject to sanctions. It lists:

- Full name.
- Any known aliases.
- Honorary, professional or religious titles.
- Date of birth.

52 Further details are available at www.un.org/securitycouncil/sanctions/information.

- Place of birth.
- Nationality.
- Passport details.
- National identification numbers (eg, ID cards, Social Security Numbers, etc).
- Address.
- Any additional information that may be useful (eg, nicknames, details of family, etc).
- Title of the financial sanctions regime under which the designated person is listed.
- The date when the designated person was added to the list by HM Treasury.
- When the information regarding the designated person/entity was last updated by HM Treasury.
- A unique ID reference number relating to the designated person/entity.

A similar list is produced by the US Office of Foreign Assets Control but is considered superfluous to the discussion in an EMEA context.

UK legal framework for sanctions

12.53 The below selection of relevant EMEA legislation is country specific and is a useful touchstone for existing UK led sanctions and should be considered in the due diligence process.

Yemen	(European Union Financial Sanctions) Regulations 2014, SI 2014/3349
Syria	(European Union Financial Sanctions) (Amendment) Regulations 2013, SI 2013/877
Lebanon	(United Nations Sanctions) (Overseas Territories) (Amendment) Order 2007, SI 2007/2131
Democratic Republic of the Congo	(United Nations Sanctions) (Overseas Territories) Order 2015, SI 2015/1382
Iraq	(Sanctions) (Overseas Territories) Order 2015, SI 2015/1383
Russia	Export Control (Russia, Crimea and Sevastopol Sanctions) (Amendment) Order 2014, SI 2014/2932

13 Product compliance and related issues

Introduction

13.1 What is required in order to give effect to the goals of the European Union, with regard to the operation of the single market and creating and maintaining the free flow of goods within the EU and beyond, is almost overwhelming. A multitude of legislative efforts have been made in order to harmonise aspects of product safety and compliance and to ensure that only compliant products are placed on the market within the EU. While a rich and wide-ranging story, the legislative genesis of much of these efforts is beyond the scope of this work. However, it is proposed to set out the key considerations corporate counsel should be aware of. Although what follows is not a comprehensive treatise, the salient features should become apparent.

The free movement of goods and the law

13.2 The principle of mutual recognition, central to many of the EU's initiatives, was set out in the *locus classicus* – the 'Cassis de Dijon' case[1] which provides the key elements for mutual recognition which have been described as:

- Products lawfully manufactured or marketed in one member state should in principle move freely throughout the Union where such products meet equivalent levels of protection to those imposed by the member state of destination.
- In the absence of Union harmonisation legislation, member states are free to legislate on their territory subject to the Treaty rules on free movement of goods (Articles 34–36 TFEU).
- Barriers to free movement which result from differences in national legislation may only be accepted if national measures:

1 Judgment of the Court of Justice of 20 February 1979 – *Rewe-Zentral AG v Bundesmonopolverwaltung für Branntwein*, Case 120/78. European Court reports 1979, p 649.

- are necessary to satisfy mandatory requirements (such as health, safety, consumer protection and environmental protection);
- serve a legitimate purpose which justifies overriding the principle of free movement of goods; and
- can be justified with regard to the legitimate purpose and are proportionate with the aims.

13.3 A broad range of legislative measures have been developed since the *Cassis* case with the aim of providing for a new model legislative framework which has considerably changed the balance of EU legislative provisions from being fundamentally oriented at setting product related requirements to be met when products are placed on the market to an equal emphasis on enforcement aspects during the whole lifecycle of products.[2] This rationale for the new legislative framework has been described as:[3]

> 'The evolution of EU legislative techniques in this area has been progressive, tackling issues one after another, although sometimes in parallel, culminating in the adoption of the New Legislative Framework: essential or other legal requirements, product standards, standards and rules for the competence of conformity assessment bodies as well as for accreditation, standards for quality management, conformity assessment procedures, CE marking, accreditation policy, and lately market surveillance policy including the control of products from third countries. The New Legislative Framework now constitutes a complete system bringing together all the different elements that need to be dealt with in product safety legislation in a coherent, comprehensive legislative instrument that can be used across the board in all industrial sectors, and even beyond (environmental and health policies also have recourse to a number of these elements), whenever EU legislation is required.'

Key features of the General Product Safety Directive

13.4 As one of the central planks of the legislative framework, some of the more important aspects of the General Product Safety Directive (GPSD)[4] are set out below:

- Legal or administrative action may take place against any person in the supply or distribution chain who can be considered responsible for a non-compliant product.
- The Directive on product liability covers all movables and electricity, as well as raw materials and components of final products.
- Producers are obliged to place on the market only products which are safe.
- It establishes the Rapid Alert System which is used for dangerous non-food products (RAPEX, Rapid Alert System) between member states and the Commission.

---

2 Commission Notice on the implementation of EU products rules 2013 (2013/C 272/01), para 1.2.1.
3 ibid, para 1.2.3.
4 Directive 2001/95/EC of the European Parliament and of the Council of 3 December 2001 on general product safety.

General principle of product liability legislation

13.5 Some of the more important aspects of the product liability framework are also set out below as presented in the Commission Notice on the implementation of EU products rules 2013 (2013/C 272/01) – 'The Blue Guide':[5]

- Legal or administrative action may take place against any person in the supply or distribution chain who can be considered responsible for a non-compliant product.
- It applies only to defective products which do not provide the safety that a person is entitled to expect. The fact that a product is not fit for the use expected is not enough.
- Liability, the responsibility to pay for damages, is placed on the producer.
- A producer is either a manufacturer of a finished product or a component part of a finished product, producer of any raw material, or any person who presents himself as a manufacturer (for example by affixing a trademark).
- Importers placing products on the Union market from third countries are all considered to be producers under the Directive on product liability.
- If the producer cannot be identified, each supplier of the product becomes liable, unless he informs the injured person within a reasonable time of the identity of the producer, or of the person who supplied him with the product.
- When several persons are liable for the same damage, they are all jointly and severally liable.

Generally, the producer is not automatically liable for damage caused by the product. The injured person, whether or not he is the buyer or user of the defective product, must claim his rights to obtain compensation. The victims will be paid only if they prove that they have suffered damage, the product was defective, and this product caused the damage. If the injured person contributes to the damage, the producer's liability may be reduced or even eliminated. However, the victims do not need to prove that the producer was negligent because the Directive on product liability is based on the principle of no-fault liability. Thus, the producer will not be exonerated even if he proves he was not negligent, if an act or omission of a third person contributes to the damage caused, if he has applied standards, or if his product has been tested.

General defences

13.6 The producer will not have to pay, if he proves:[6]

- he did not place the product on the market (eg, the product was stolen);
- the product was not defective when he placed it on the market (thus he proves that the defect was caused subsequently);
- the product was not manufactured to be sold or distributed for economic purpose;
- the defect was caused due to compliance with mandatory regulations issued by the public authorities (which excludes national, European and international standards);
- the state of scientific and technical knowledge at the time when the product was put on the market could not as such enable the existence of the defect to be

5 Commission Notice on the implementation of EU products rules 2013 (2013/C 272/01), para 1.4.
6 ibid, para 1.4.

discovered (the development risks defence), or where he is a subcontractor, that the defect was due either to the design of the finished product or to defective instructions given to him by the producer of the finished product.

Limitations

13.7 It should be noted that 10 years after the product is placed on the market, the producer ceases to be liable, and the victim must file an action within three years of the damage, the defect and the identity of the producer being known.[7]

Related legislation

13.8 Set out below is a list of the relevant pieces of European legislation that in part make up the framework.

- The restriction of the use of certain hazardous substances in electrical and electronic equipment (Directive 2011/65/EU)
- Appliances burning gaseous fuels (Directive 2009/142/EC)
- Ecodesign requirements for energy-related products (Directive 2009/125/EC)
- Simple pressure vessels (Directive 2009/105/EC and Directive 2014/29/EU)
- Toys' safety (Directive 2009/48/EC)
- Electrical equipment designed for use within certain voltage limits (Directive 2006/95/EC and Directive 2014/35/EU)
- Machinery (Directive 2006/42/EC)
- Electromagnetic compatibility (Directive 2004/108/EC and Directive 2014/30/EU)
- Measuring instruments (Directive 2004/22/EC and Directive 2014/32/EU)
- Non-automatic weighing instruments (Directive 2009/23/EC and Directive 2014/31/EU)
- Cableway installations designed to carry persons (Directive 2000/9/EC)
- Radio equipment and telecommunications terminal equipment (Directive 1999/5/EC and Directive 2014/53/EU)
- Active implantable medical devices (Directive 90/385/EEC)
- Medical devices (Directive 93/42/EEC)
- In vitro diagnostic medical devices (Directive 98/79/EC)
- Pressure equipment (Directive 97/23/EC and Directive 2014/68/EU)
- Transportable Pressure equipment (Directive 2010/35/EU)
- Aerosol Dispensers (Directive 75/324/EEC as amended)
- Lifts (Directive 95/13/EC and 2014/33/EU)
- Recreational craft (Directive 94/25/EC and Directive 2013/53/EU)

7 ibid, para 1.4.

- Equipment and protective systems intended for use in potentially explosive atmospheres (Directive 94/9/EC and Directive 2014/34/EU)
- Explosives for civil uses (Directive 93/15/EEC and Directive 2014/28/EU)
- Pyrotechnics (Directive 2013/29/EU)
- Regulation on the Labelling of Tyres (Regulation (EC) No 1222/2009)
- Personal protective equipment (Directive 89/686/EEC)
- Marine equipment (Directive 96/98/EC and Directive 2014/90/EU)
- Noise emission in the environment by equipment for use outdoors (Directive 2000/14/EC)
- Emissions from non-road mobile machinery (Directive 97/68/EC as amended)
- Energy labelling (Directive 2010/30/EU)

When does European legislation apply

Application of legislation

13.9 Relevant legislation applies when a product is *placed on the market* and to any subsequent operation which constitutes making it available until it reaches the end-user.[8] The legislation applies to all forms of selling and product offered in a catalogue or by means of electronic commerce has to comply with harmonisation legislation when the catalogue or website directs its offer to the market within the European Union and includes an ordering and shipping system.[9]

13.10 The Union harmonisation legislation applies to newly manufactured products but also to used and second-hand products imported from a third country when they enter the Union market for the first time. The legislation similarly applies to finished products.[10]

Making a product available on the market

13.11 A product is made available on the market when it is supplied for distribution, consumption or use on the market within the European Union in the course of a commercial activity, whether in return for payment or free of charge.[11] It should be noted that the concept of 'making available' refers to each individual product.[12]

Placing on the market

13.12 A product is placed on the market when it is made available for the first time on the Union market. Products made available on the market must comply with the applicable Union harmonisation legislation at the moment of placing on the market. It should also be noted that the act of placing a product on the market is for a manufacturer or an importer, that is the manufacturer and the importer are the only economic operators who place products on the market.

8 ibid, para 2.1.
9 ibid, para 2.1.
10 ibid, para 2.1.
11 ibid, para 2.2.
12 ibid, para 2.2.

Products from outside the EU

13.13 Irrespective of their origin, products must be compliant with the applicable Union harmonisation legislation if they are made available on the Union market. Before they can reach the end-user in the EU, products coming from countries outside the EU must be entered for the procedure of release for free circulation and be checked by authorities responsible for border controls.[13]

Putting into service

13.14 The moment of putting into service is relevant for some Union harmonisation legislation and it has been defined as taking place at the moment of first use within the European Union by the end user for the purposes for which it was intended.[14]

Intended use

13.15 It is a general principle which appears to adopt a risk-based approach, that manufacturers must match a level of protection corresponding to the use they prescribe to the product under the conditions of use which can be reasonably foreseen.[15]

Geographical application

13.16 Union harmonisation legislation applies to the member states of the EU and to certain European territories to the extent necessary to give effect to the arrangements set out in the Accession Treaty of the relevant member states.[16] The Agreement on the European Economic Area is established between the European Union and Iceland, Liechtenstein and Norway. The Agreement extends the internal market to these three EFTA states — commonly known as EEA EFTA states. The Customs Union Agreement between the EU and Turkey aims to ensure the free movement of products between the EU and Turkey, by eliminating import controls at the EU-Turkey border on such products.[17]

Manufacturers, importers, representatives, distributors

13.17 While a thorough exposition on the rights and obligations of each species of actor under the legislative framework for product compliance is beyond the scope of this work, it is nevertheless useful to set out some key definitions in that regard.

Manufacturers

13.18 The manufacturer is defined as any natural or legal person who manufactures a product or has a product designed or manufactured, and places it on the market under his own name or trademark.[18]

---

13 ibid, para 2.4.
14 ibid, para 2.5.
15 ibid, para 2.7.
16 ibid, para 2.8.
17 ibid, para 2.8.
18 ibid, para 3.1.

13.19 It should be noted that:[19]

- the manufacturer is responsible for the conformity assessment of the product and is subject to a series of obligations including traceability requirements;
- when placing a product on a market in the European Union, the responsibilities of a manufacturer are the same whether the manufacturer is established outside the European Union or in a member state;
- the manufacturer must cooperate with the competent national authorities in charge of market surveillance in case of a product presenting a risk or being non-compliant.

Authorised representative

13.20 Irrespectively of whether the entity is established in the EU or not, the manufacturer may appoint an authorised representative in the Union to act on their behalf in carrying out specific tasks.[20] It should also be noted that the guidance provided by the European Union states that:[21]

- The delegation of tasks from the manufacturer to the authorised representative must be explicit and set out in writing, in particular to define the contents and limits of the representative's tasks.
- The tasks that may be delegated to the authorised representative according to the Union harmonisation legislation are of an administrative nature. Thus, the manufacturer may neither delegate the measures necessary to ensure that the manufacturing process assures compliance of the products nor the drawing up of technical documentation, unless otherwise provided for.
- Further, an authorised representative cannot modify the product on his own initiative in order to bring it into line with the applicable Union harmonisation legislation.

Importer

13.21 The importer is a natural or legal person established in the Union who places a product from a third country on the EU market.[22] The obligations of the importer are said to build on the obligations of the manufacturer. Guidance suggests that the importer needs neither a mandate from the manufacturer, nor a preferential relationship with the manufacturer like the authorised representative. However, the importer must ensure, in order to fulfil their responsibilities, that a contact with the manufacturer can be established.[23]

Distributors

13.22 The distributor is similarly defined as a natural or a legal person in the supply chain, other than the manufacturer or the importer, who makes a product available on the market.[24] The guidance in relation to distributors' duties suggests that:[25]

19 ibid, para 3.1.
20 ibid, para 3.2.
21 ibid, para 3.2.
22 ibid, para 3.3.
23 eg, to make the technical documentation available to the requesting authority. Commission Notice on the implementation of EU products rules 2013 (2013/C 272/01), para 3.3.
24 Commission Notice on the implementation of EU products rules 2013 (2013/C 272/01), para 3.4.
25 ibid, para 3.4.

> '[A] ... Distributor must act with due care in relation to the applicable requirements. They have to know, for instance, which products must bear the CE marking, what information is to accompany the product (for example the EU declaration of conformity), what are the language requirements for labelling, user instructions or other accompanying documents, and what is a clear indication of the product being non-compliant. Distributors have an obligation to demonstrate to the national market surveillance authority that they have acted with due care and ensure that the manufacturer, or his authorised representative, or the person who provided him with the product has taken the measures required by the applicable Union harmonisation legislation as listed in the obligations for distributors.'

Product requirements

Essential requirements

13.23 The concept of 'essential requirements' is referred to in the Commission Notice (2013/C 272/01). A large part of Union harmonisation legislation limits legislative harmonisation to a number of essential requirements that are of public interest and essential requirements define the results to be attained, or the hazards to be dealt with, but do not specify the technical solutions for doing so.[26] Further, it can be of assistance to think of essential requirements as:[27]

> '... designed to provide and ensure a high level of protection. They either arise from certain hazards associated with the product (for example physical and mechanical resistance, flammability, chemical, electrical or biological properties, hygiene, radioactivity, accuracy), or refer to the product or its performance (for example provisions regarding materials, design, construction, manufacturing process, instructions drawn up by the manufacturer), or lay down the principal protection objective (for example by means of an illustrative list). Often they are a combination of these.'

13.24 Fundamental to the understanding of essential requirements is that they seek to define the results to be attained, or the hazards to be dealt with, but do not specify the technical solutions for doing so.[28] The precise technical solution may be provided by a standard or by other technical specifications or be developed in accordance with general engineering or scientific knowledge laid down in engineering and scientific literature at the discretion of the manufacturer. This flexibility allows manufacturers to choose the way to meet the requirements.

13.25 The application of harmonised standards and the presumption of conformity it may give rise to are issues that are beyond the scope of this work but considered in great detail in the guidance set out hereinafter as issued by the European Commission.[29]

---

26 ibid, para 4.1.1.
27 ibid, para 4.1.1.
28 ibid, para 4.1.1.
29 ibid, para 4.1.2.

Traceability requirements

13.26 Primarily, traceability allows for:[30]

- Tracing the history of the product and support efforts aimed at market surveillance.
- Authorities to find the liable economic operators and obtain evidence of the product compliance.

The traceability requirements include labelling the product and identifying the economic operators in the distribution chain. Specifically, the reference provisions of Decision No 768/2008/EC reflected in Union harmonisation legislation require:[31]

(1) Manufacturers must indicate the following three elements:

  (a) their name;

  (b) registered trade name or registered trade mark; and

  (c) the address at which they can be contacted, on the product or, where that is not possible, on its packaging or in a document accompanying the product. The address must indicate a single point at which the manufacturer can be contacted.

(2) Importers must similarly indicate three elements: their name, registered trade name or registered trade mark and the address at which they can be contacted, on the product or, where that is not possible, on its packaging or in a document accompanying the product;

(3) Manufacturers to ensure that their products bear a type, batch, serial or model number or other element allowing their identification, or, where the size or nature of the product does not allow it, that the required information is provided on the packaging or in a document accompanying the product; and

(4) Economic operators to identify any economic operator who has supplied them with a product and any economic operator to whom they have supplied a product.

Technical documentation

13.27 The manufacturer must draw up technical documentation intended to provide information on the design, manufacture and operation of the product and containing information to demonstrate the conformity of the product to the applicable requirements.[32]

13.28 The contents of the technical documentation are laid down, in each Union harmonisation act, in accordance with the products concerned.[33] The documentation must include a description of the product and of its intended use and cover the design, manufacture and operation of the product. As to the details included in the documentation, this depends on the nature of the product and on what is considered as necessary, from the technical point of view, for demonstrating the conformity of the product to the essential requirements.[34]

30 ibid, para 4.2.
31 ibid, para 4.2.2.
32 ibid, para 4.3.
33 ibid, para 4.3.
34 Annex II to Decision No 768/2008/EC sets out useful guidance on what should be included by way of content. See Commission Notice on the implementation of EU products rules 2013 (2013/C 272/01), para 4.3.

Declarations of conformity

13.29 The key aspects of declarations of conformity are set out in the Commission Notice[35] and related legislation. Generally, the manufacturer or the authorised representative established within the Union must draw up and sign an EU declaration of conformity as part of the conformity assessment procedure provided for in the Union harmonisation legislation.[36]

13.30 The EU declaration of conformity must contain all relevant information to identify the Union harmonisation legislation according to which it is issued, as well as:[37]

- the manufacturer;
- the authorised representative;
- the notified body if applicable;
- the product; and
- where appropriate a reference to harmonised standards or other technical specifications.

Single declaration

13.31 It is also notable that a single declaration of conformity is required whenever a product is covered by several pieces of legislation requiring such a declaration.[38]

Specific requirements

13.32 The model declaration of Decision No 768/2008/EC[39] contains the following requirements as interpreted by the guidance contained in the Commission Notice:[40]

(1) A number identifying the product. This number does not need to be unique to each product. It could refer to a product, batch, type or a serial number. This is left to the discretion of the manufacturer.

(2) The name and address of the manufacturer or the authorised representative issuing the declaration.

(3) A statement that the declaration is issued under the sole responsibility of the manufacturer.

(4) The identification of the product allowing traceability. This is basically any relevant information supplementary to point (1) describing the product and allowing for its traceability. It may where relevant for the identification of the product contain an image, but unless specified as a requirement in the Union harmonisation legislation this is left to the discretion of the manufacturer.

35 Commission Notice on the implementation of EU products rules 2013 (2013/C 272/01), para 4.4.
36 ibid, para 4.4.
37 ibid, para 4.4.
38 ibid, para 4.4.
39 ibid, Annex III.
40 ibid, para 4.4.

(5) All relevant Union harmonisation legislation complied with; the referenced standards or other technical specifications (such as national technical standards and specifications) in a precise, complete and clearly defined way; this implies that the version and/or date of the relevant standard is specified,

(6) The name and identification number of the notified body when it has been involved in the conformity assessment procedure and the reference to the relevant certificate, if applicable.

(7) All supplementary information that may be required (eg, grade, category), if applicable.

(8) The date of issue of the declaration; signature and title or an equivalent marking of authorised person; this could be any date after the completion of the conformity assessment.

Marking requirements – the CE mark

13.33 The key aspects of the CE mark may be summarised as follows:[41]

- The CE marking indicates the conformity of the product with the Union legislation applying to the product and providing for CE marking.[42]
- The CE marking is affixed on products that will be placed on the EEA and Turkish market, whether they are manufactured in the EEA, in Turkey or in another country. [43]
- Regulation (EC) No 765/2008 lays down the general principles governing the CE marking while Decision No 768/2008/EC provides for rules governing its affixing. [44]
- Sectoral Union harmonisation texts providing for CE marking are based on Regulation (EC) No 765/2008 and Decision No 768/2008/EC.[45]
- The CE marking is affixed by the manufacturer (established inside or outside the Union), or by his authorised representative established within the Union.[46]
- By affixing the CE marking the manufacturer declares it his sole responsibility that the product conforms to all applicable Union legislative requirements, and that the appropriate conformity assessment procedures have been successfully completed.[47]
- The CE marking must take the prescribed form. If the CE marking is reduced or enlarged the proportions must be respected.[48]

Conformity assessments

13.34 The technical aspects associated with assessments of conformity, that is the process carried out by the manufacturer of demonstrating whether specified

41 ibid, para 4.5.
42 ibid, para 4.5.1.1.
43 ibid, para 4.5.1.1.
44 ibid, para 4.5.1.2.
45 ibid, para 4.5.1.2.
46 ibid, para 4.5.1.3.
47 ibid, para 4.5.1.3.
48 ibid, para 4.5.1.4.

requirements relating to a product have been fulfilled,[49] are beyond the scope of this work. However, details are set out in the guidance contained in the Commission Notice[50] and the associated legislation, pertaining to the modular structure of the conformity assessment; the actors in conformity assessments; an overview of procedures; the rationale for selecting a certain module; and the assessment bodies etc.

Useful references

Further guidance

13.35 A multitude of guidance papers have been produced in relation to a wide variety of subject matters. Mostly produced by the European Union, they are an invaluable aid to counsel on technical matters and a selection of them are set out below.

Guidance subject matter	Address
Guidance documents from the Expert Group on Toy Safety	http://ec.europa.eu/growth/sectors/toys/safety/guidance/index_en.htm
Measuring instruments and non-automatic weighing instruments	http://ec.europa.eu/growth/single-market/goods/building-blocks/legal-metrology/measuring-instruments/guidance-standards/index_en.htm
Chemicals	http://echa.europa.eu/support/guidance
Low Voltage Directive	http://ec.europa.eu/growth/sectors/electrical-engineering/lvd-directive/index_en.htm
Electromagnetic Compatibility (EMC)	http://ec.europa.eu/growth/sectors/electrical-engineering/emc-directive/index_en.htm
Radio and telecommunications terminal equipment (R&TTE) Guidance	http://ec.europa.eu/growth/sectors/electrical-engineering/rtte-directive/index_en.htm
Medical Devices	http://ec.europa.eu/growth/sectors/medical-devices/guidance/index_en.htm
Construction Products Regulation (CPR)	http://ec.europa.eu/growth/sectors/construction/product-regulation/faq/index_en.htm
Automotive industry	http://ec.europa.eu/growth/sectors/automotive/index_en.htm
RoHS 2	http://ec.europa.eu/environment/waste/rohs_eee/events_rohs3_en.htm
Pressure Equipment Directive (PED)	http://ec.europa.eu/growth/sectors/pressure-gas/pressure-equipment/guidelines/index_en.htm

49 ibid, para 5.1.1.
50 ibid, para 5 et seq.

Guidance subject matter	Address
Machinery	http://ec.europa.eu/growth/sectors/mechanical-engineering/machinery/index_en.htm
Cableways	http://ec.europa.eu/growth/sectors/mechanical-engineering/cableways/index_en.htm
Lifts	http://ec.europa.eu/growth/sectors/mechanical-engineering/lifts/index_en.htm
Personal Protective Equipment	http://ec.europa.eu/growth/sectors/mechanical-engineering/personal-protective-equipment/index_en.htm
Noise emission in the environment by equipment for use outdoors	http://ec.europa.eu/growth/sectors/mechanical-engineering/noise-emissions/index_en.htm
Potentially Explosive Atmospheres	http://ec.europa.eu/growth/sectors/mechanical-engineering/atex/index_en.htm
Healthcare industries	http://ec.europa.eu/growth/sectors/healthcare/index_en.htm
General Product Safety	http://ec.europa.eu/consumers/safety/prod_legis/index_en.htm
RAPEX Rapid Alert System Guidelines	http://ec.europa.eu/consumers/consumers_safety/safety_products/rapex/index_en.htm
European standards	http://ec.europa.eu/growth/single-market/european-standards/policy/framework/index_en.htm
Standardisation	http://ec.europa.eu/growth/single-market/european-standards/vademecum/index_en.htm

Official websites

13.36 A range of useful official websites exist which deal with, amongst others, the European single market for goods,[51] the internal market for products,[52] European standards[53] and the rapid alert system for non-food products posing a serious risk.[54] These are worthy of consultation.

51 http://ec.europa.eu/growth/single-market/goods/index_en.htm.

52 ibid.

53 http://ec.europa.eu/growth/single-market/european-standards/index_en.htm.

54 http://ec.europa.eu/consumers/consumers_safety/safety_products/rapex/index_en.htm.

List of important EU legislation and decisions

13.37

Subject matter	Full title	Number
Accreditation and market surveillance	Regulation (EC) No 765/2008 of the European Parliament and of the Council of 9 July 2008 setting out the requirements for accreditation and market surveillance relating to the marketing of products and repealing Regulation (EEC) No 339/93	765/2008
	Decision No 768/2008/EC of the European Parliament and of the Council of 9 July 2008 on a common framework for the marketing of products	768/2008/EC
National technical rules	Regulation (EC) No 764/2008 of the European Parliament and of the Council of 9 July 2008 laying down procedures relating to the application of certain national technical rules to products lawfully marketed in another Member State and repealing Decision No 3052/95/EC	764/2008
Approximation of the laws	Council Directive 85/374/EEC of 25 July 1985 on the approximation of the laws, regulations and administrative provisions of the Member States concerning liability for defective products	85/374/EEC (1999/34/EC)
General Product Safety	Directive 2001/95/EC of the European Parliament and of the Council of 3 December 2001 on General Product Safety	2001/95/EC
Standardisation	Regulation (EU) No 1025/2012 of the European Parliament and of the Council of 25 October 2012 on European standardisation	1025/2012
Electrical equipment	Council Directive of 19 February 1973 on the harmonisation of the laws of Member States relating to electrical equipment designed for use within certain voltage limits	73/23/EEC 93/68/EEC 2006/95/EC
Electrical equipment	Directive 2014/35/EU of the European Parliament and of the Council of 26 February 2014 on the harmonisation of the laws of the Member States relating to the making available on the market of electrical equipment designed for use within certain voltage limits (recast)	2014/35/EU
Safety of toys	Directive 2009/48/EC of the European Parliament and of the Council of 18 June 2009 on the safety of toys	2009/48/EC

Subject matter	Full title	Number
Electromagnetic compatibility	Council Directive 89/336/EEC of 3 May 1989 on the approximation of the laws of the Member States relating to electromagnetic compatibility	89/336/EEC 92/31/EEC 93/68/EEC 2004/108/EC (98/13/EC)
Electromagnetic compatibility	Directive 2014/30/EU of the European Parliament and of the Council of 26 February 2014 on the harmonisation of the laws of the Member States relating to electromagnetic compatibility (recast)	2014/30/EU
Machinery	Directive of the European Parliament and of the Council of 22 June 1998 on the approximation of the laws of the Member States relating to machinery	98/37/EC 98/79/EC
Personal protective equipment	Council Directive of 21 December 1989 on the approximation of the laws of the Member States relating to personal protective equipment	89/686/EEC 93/68/EEC 93/95/EEC 96/58/EC
Non-automatic weighing instruments	Directive 2009/23/EC of the European Parliament and of the Council of 23 April 2009 on non-automatic weighing instruments	90/384/EEC 93/68/EEC 2009/23/EC
Non-automatic weighing instruments	Directive 2014/31/EU of the European Parliament and of the Council of 26 February 2014 on the harmonisation of the laws of the Member States relating to the making available on the market of non-automatic weighing instruments (recast)	2014/31/EU
Measuring instruments	Directive 2004/22/EC of the European Parliament and of the Council of 31 March 2004 on measuring instruments	2004/22/EC
Measuring instruments	Directive 2014/32/EU of the European Parliament and of the Council of 26 February 2014 on the harmonisation of the laws of the Member States relating to the making available on the market of measuring instruments (recast)	2014/32/EU
Medical devices	Council Directive 93/42/EEC of 14 June 1993 concerning medical devices	93/42/EEC 98/79/EC 2000/70/EC 2001/104/EC 2007/97/EC
Active implantable medical devices	Council Directive of 20 June 1990 on the approximation of the laws of the Member States relating to active implantable medical devices	90/385/EEC 93/42/EEC 93/68/EEC

Subject matter	Full title	Number
In vitro diagnostic medical devices	Directive 98/79/EC of the European Parliament and of the Council of 27 October 1998 on in vitro diagnostic medical devices	98/79/EC
Appliances burning gaseous fuels	Council Directive 90/396/EEC of 29 June 1990 on the approximation of the laws of the Member States relating to appliances burning gaseous fuels	90/396/EEC 93/68/EEC 09/142/EC
Explosives for civil uses	Council Directive of 5 April 1993 on the harmonisation of the provisions relating to the placing on the market and supervision of explosives for civil uses	93/15/EEC
Explosives for civil uses	Directive 2014/28/EU of the European Parliament and of the Council of 26 February 2014 on the harmonisation of the laws of the Member States relating to the making available on the market and supervision of explosives for civil uses (recast)	2014/28/EU
Pyrotechnic articles	Directive 2007/23/EC of the European Parliament and of the Council of 23 May 2007 on the placing on the market of pyrotechnic articles	2007/23/EC
Pyrotechnic articles	Directive 2013/29/EU of the European Parliament and of the Council of 12 June 2013 on the harmonisation of the laws of the Member States relating to the making available on the market of pyrotechnic articles (recast)	2013/29/EU
Potentially explosive atmospheres	Directive 94/9/EC of the European Parliament and the Council of 23 March 1994 on the approximation of the laws of the Member States concerning equipment and protective systems intended for use in potentially explosive atmospheres	94/9/EC
Potentially explosive atmospheres	Directive 2014/34/EU of the European Parliament and of the Council of 26 February 2014 on the harmonisation of the laws of the Member States relating to equipment and protective systems intended for use in potentially explosive atmospheres (recast)	2014/34/EU
Recreational craft	Directive 94/25/EC of the European Parliament and of the Council of 13 June 1994 on the approximation of the laws, regulations and administrative provisions of the Member States relating to recreational craft	94/25/EC 03/44/EC

Subject matter	Full title	Number
Recreational craft and personal watercraft	Directive 2013/53/EU of the European Parliament and of the Council of 20 November 2013 on recreational craft and personal watercraft and repealing Directive 94/25/EC	2013/53/EU
Lifts	European Parliament and Council Directive 95/13/EC of 29 June 1995 on the approximation of the laws of the Member States relating to lifts	95/13/EC
Lifts	Directive 2014/33/EU of the European Parliament and of the Council of 26 February 2014 on the harmonisation of the laws of the Member States relating to lifts and safety components for lifts (recast)	2014/33/EU
Cableway installations designed to carry persons	Directive 2000/9/EC of the European Parliament and of the Council of 20 March 2000 relating to cableway installations designed to carry persons	2000/9/EC
Pressure equipment	Directive 97/23/EC of the European Parliament and of the Council of 29 May 1997 on the approximation of the laws of the Member States concerning pressure equipment	97/23/EC
Pressure equipment	Directive 2014/68/EU of the European Parliament and of the Council of 15 May 2014 on the harmonisation of the laws of the Member States relating to the making available on the market of pressure equipment (recast)	2014/68/EU
Simple pressure vessels	Directive 2009/105/EC of the European Parliament and of the Council of 13 September 2009 relating to simple pressure vessels	2009/105/EC
Simple pressure vessels	Directive 2014/29/EU of the European Parliament and of the Council of 26 February 2014 on the harmonisation of the laws of the Member States relating to the making available on the market of simple pressure vessels (recast)	2014/29/EU
Transportable pressure equipment	Directive 2010/35/EU of the European Parliament and of the Council of 13 June 2010 on transportable pressure equipment	2010/35/EC
Aerosol dispensers	Council Directive of 20 May 1975 on the approximation of the laws of the Member States relating to aerosol dispensers	75/324/EEC 94/1/EC 2008/47/EC

Subject matter	**Full title**	**Number**
Radio equipment and telecommunications terminal equipment	Directive 99/5/EC of the European Parliament and of the Council relating to radio equipment and telecommunications terminal equipment and the mutual recognition of their conformity	99/5/EC
Radio equipment	Directive 2014/53/EU of the European Parliament and of the Council of 13 April 2014 on the harmonisation of the laws of the Member States relating to the making available on the market of radio equipment and repealing Directive 1999/5/EC	2014/53/EU
Energy-related products	Directive 2009/125/EC of the European Parliament and of the Council of 21 October 2009 establishing a framework for the setting of ecodesign requirements for energy-related products	2009/125/EC
Non-road mobile machinery	Directive 97/68/EC of the European Parliament and of the Council on the approximation of the laws of the Member States relating to measures against the emission of gaseous and particulate pollutants from internal combustion engines to be installed in non-road mobile machinery	97/68/EC 2002/88/EC 2004/26/EC 2006/105/EC 2010/26/EU 2011/88/EU 2012/46/EU
Noise emission	Directive 2000/14/EC of the European Parliament and of the Council of 8 May 2000 on the approximation of the laws of the Member States relating to the noise emission in the environment by equipment for use outdoors	2000/14/EC 2005/88/EC 219/2009
Hazardous substances in electrical and electronic equipment (RoHS)	Directive 2011/65/EU of the European Parliament and of the Council of 8 June 2011 on the restriction of the use of certain hazardous substances in electrical and electronic equipment (RoHS)	2011/65/EU
Waste electrical and electronic equipment (WEEE)	Directive 2012/19/EU of the European Parliament and of the Council of 4 July 2012 on waste electrical and electronic equipment (WEEE)	2012/19/EU
Marine equipment	Council Directive 96/98/EC of 20 December 1996 on marine equipment	96/98/EC
Marine equipment	Directive 2014/90/EU of the European Parliament and of the Council of 23 July 2014 on marine equipment and repealing Council Directive 96/98/EC	2014/90/EU

Subject matter	**Full title**	**Number**
The rail system	Council Directive 2008/57/EC of 17 June 2008 on the interoperability of the rail system within the Community	2008/57/EC 2009/131/EC 2011/18/EU 2013/9/EU
Packaging and packaging waste	European Parliament and Council Directive 94/62/EC of 20 December 1994 on packaging and packaging waste	94/62/EC 2004/12/EC 2005/20/EC
European Air Traffic Management	Regulation (EC) No 552/2004 of the European Parliament and of the Council of 10 March 2004 on the interoperability of the European Air Traffic Management network	552/2004 1070/2009
Energy-related products	Directive 2010/30/EU of the European Parliament and of the Council of 19 May 2010 on the indication by labelling and standard product information of the consumption of energy and other resources by energy-related products	2010/30/EU
Fuel efficiency – tyres	Regulation (EC) No 1222/2009 of the European Parliament and of the Council of 25 November 2009 on the labelling of tyres with respect to fuel efficiency and other essential parameters	1222/2009

14 Transparency and fairness in supply chains

'It's imperative that our people – whether through our broad-based training or via their direct managers – understand the company's perspective on integrity and how that translates to day-to-day behaviours.'

Mr Richard Buchband

Senior Vice President, General Counsel and Secretary

Manpower Group

Introduction

14.1 We, the authors, believe that General Counsel have the ability to impact the ethical direction of the organisation on a daily basis. US counsel will of course be familiar with a range of transparency measures that govern their interactions with partners up and down the supply chain. The UK has been at the forefront of implementing measures to protect the most vulnerable amongst society in this regard. Similarly, a sense of fair play must permeate the supply chains that corporate actors operate within and antitrust provisions have their counterpart in the EU in the form of competition law. The equitable function of markets and supply chains is at the core of the European project and central to the implementation of a single market for goods and services. Taken together, these two issues might be thought of as transparency and fairness in supply chains and are worthy of consideration in detail, not least because infractions of these legal frameworks can lead to an enormity of financial and reputational/ethical peril.

Transparency in supply chains

14.2 The European Union and many member states have recognised trafficking in human beings is a serious crime, often committed within the framework of organised crime.[1] It has been referred to in various European instruments as a gross violation of fundamental rights and explicitly prohibited by the Charter of Fundamental Rights of the European Union. Preventing and combating trafficking in human beings is considered a priority for the European Union and the member states.

14.3 To that end, the European Union concluded Directive 2011/36/EU of 5 April 2011 on preventing and combating trafficking in human beings and protecting its victims. Whilst this directive required member states to provide for specific offences related to trafficking, the directive did not substantively deal with the issue of transparency in supply chains.

14.4 The UK, as part of its implementing legislation, transposing the European directive, made specific provision in its Modern Slavery Act 2015 in relation to the responsibility of corporate actors to ensuring that human trafficking and related offences do not occur within their own supply chains.

Modern slavery

14.5 The Modern Slavery Act 2015 comprehensively defined the issue:[2]

> 'Modern slavery is a brutal form of organised crime in which people are treated as commodities and exploited for criminal gain. The true extent of modern slavery in the United Kingdom, and indeed globally, is unknown. Modern slavery, in particular human trafficking, is an international problem and victims may have entered the United Kingdom legally, on forged documentation or clandestinely, or they may be British citizens living in the United Kingdom. Modern slavery takes a number of forms, including sexual exploitation, forced labour and domestic servitude, and victims come from all walks of life. Victims are often unwilling to come forward to law enforcement or public protection agencies, not seeing themselves as victims, or fearing further reprisals from their abusers. In particular, there may be particular social and cultural barriers to men identifying themselves as victims. Victims may also not always be recognised as victims of modern slavery by those who come into contact with them.'

Corporate obligations

14.6 Whilst a full analysis of the offences created by the Act, the sanctions that are applicable and the implications of the Act are beyond the scope of this work, the Act is of key importance to corporate counsel insofar as it related to the obligations of corporate actors as contained within section 54. The section itself is rather lengthy but nevertheless merits full consideration and reproduction here:[3]

---

1 Directive 2011/36/EU of the European Parliament and of the Council of 5 April 2011 on preventing and combating trafficking in human beings and protecting its victims, and replacing Council Framework Decision 2002/629/JHA.

2 Explanatory notes to the Modern Slavery Act 2015.

3 Modern Slavery Act 2015, s 54.

'54. (1) A commercial organisation within subsection (2) must prepare a slavery and human trafficking statement for each financial year of the organisation.

(2) A commercial organisation is within this subsection if it—

(a) supplies goods or services, and

(b) has a total turnover of not less than an amount prescribed by regulations made by the Secretary of State.

(3) For the purposes of subsection (2)(b), an organisation's total turnover is to be determined in accordance with regulations made by the Secretary of State.

(4) A slavery and human trafficking statement for a financial year is—

(a) a statement of the steps the organisation has taken during the financial year to ensure that slavery and human trafficking is not taking place—

(i) in any of its supply chains, and

(ii) in any part of its own business, or

(b) a statement that the organisation has taken no such steps.

(5) An organisation's slavery and human trafficking statement may include information about—

(a) the organisation's structure, its business and its supply chains;

(b) its policies in relation to slavery and human trafficking;

(c) its due diligence processes in relation to slavery and human trafficking in its business and supply chains;

(d) the parts of its business and supply chains where there is a risk of slavery and human trafficking taking place, and the steps it has taken to assess and manage that risk;

(e) its effectiveness in ensuring that slavery and human trafficking is not taking place in its business or supply chains, measured against such performance indicators as it considers appropriate;

(f) the training about slavery and human trafficking available to its staff.

(6) A slavery and human trafficking statement—

(a) if the organisation is a body corporate other than a limited liability partnership, must be approved by the board of directors (or equivalent management body) and signed by a director (or equivalent);

(b) if the organisation is a limited liability partnership, must be approved by the members and signed by a designated member;

(c) if the organisation is a limited partnership registered under the Limited Partnerships Act 1907, must be signed by a general partner;

(d) if the organisation is any other kind of partnership, must be signed by a partner.

(7) If the organisation has a website, it must—

(a) publish the slavery and human trafficking statement on that website, and

(b) include a link to the slavery and human trafficking statement in a prominent place on that website's homepage.

(8) If the organisation does not have a website, it must provide a copy of the slavery and human trafficking statement to anyone who makes a written request for one, and must do so before the end of the period of 30 days beginning with the day on which the request is received.

(9) The Secretary of State—

(a) may issue guidance about the duties imposed on commercial organisations by this section;

(b) must publish any such guidance in a way the Secretary of State considers appropriate.

(10) The guidance may in particular include further provision about the kind of information which may be included in a slavery and human trafficking statement.

(11) The duties imposed on commercial organisations by this section are enforceable by the Secretary of State bringing civil proceedings in the High Court for an injunction or, in Scotland, for specific performance of a statutory duty under section 45 of the Court of Session Act 1988.

(12) For the purposes of this section—

"commercial organisation" means—

(a) a body corporate (wherever incorporated) which carries on a business, or part of a business, in any part of the United Kingdom, or

(b) a partnership (wherever formed) which carries on a business, or part of a business, in any part of the United Kingdom,

and for this purpose "business" includes a trade or profession;

"partnership" means—

(a) a partnership within the Partnership Act 1890,

(b) a limited partnership registered under the Limited Partnerships Act 1907, or

(c) a firm, or an entity of a similar character, formed under the law of a country outside the United Kingdom;

"slavery and human trafficking" means—

(a) conduct which constitutes an offence under any of the following—

(i) section 1, 2 or 4 of this Act,

(ii) section 1, 2 or 4 of the Human Trafficking and Exploitation (Criminal Justice and Support for Victims) Act (Northern Ireland) 2015 (c. 2 (N.I.)) (equivalent offences in Northern Ireland),

(iii) section 22 of the Criminal Justice (Scotland) Act 2003 (asp 7) (traffic in prostitution etc),

(iv) section 4 of the Asylum and Immigration (Treatment of Claimants, etc.) Act 2004 (trafficking for exploitation),

(v) section 47 of the Criminal Justice and Licensing (Scotland) Act 2014 (asp 13) (slavery, servitude and forced or compulsory labour), or

(b) conduct which would constitute an offence in a part of the United Kingdom under any of those provisions if the conduct took place in that part of the United Kingdom.'

Analysis of section 54 obligations

To whom does it apply?

14.7 The basic requirement is that every commercial organisation of a certain size must prepare a slavery and human trafficking statement for each financial year of the organisation.[4] The section applies to commercial organisations that supply goods or services, and have a total annual turnover of not less than £36m.

14.8 Total turnover is calculated as: (a) the turnover of that organisation, and (b) the turnover of any of its subsidiary undertakings (including those operating wholly outside the UK).[5]

Geographic application

14.9 In terms of geographic reach, the guidance produced by the UK government and subsection 12 of section 54 define commercial organisations and partnerships in broad terms. The section will apply to a body corporate (wherever incorporated) which carries on a business, or part of a business, in any part of the United Kingdom.[6] It would appear that even a *de minimis* presence in the UK will attract the obligations of the section, where the financial criteria have been exceeded.

What should be included in the statement?

14.10 A statement should include the steps the organisation has taken during the financial year to ensure that slavery and human trafficking is not taking place: (i) in any of its supply chains, and (ii) in any part of its own business, or an explicit statement of the fact that the organisation has taken no such steps.[7]

14.11 The Act explicitly outlines six categories of information that should be supplied. The guidance to the legislation suggests that this provision does not require businesses to take any steps in these areas, but it provides a clear indication as to what a business could include. The government expects many businesses would choose to cover these areas, and this in turn would make statements easier to assess and compare.[8] The suggested information provided should be:

(a) the organisation's structure, its business and its supply chains;

(b) its policies in relation to slavery and human trafficking;

(c) its due diligence processes in relation to slavery and human trafficking in its business and supply chains;

---

4 Modern Slavery Act 2015, s 54(1).

5 See Guidance to Modern Slavery Act, 2015 – a Practical Guide, available at https://assets.publishing.service.gov.uk/government/uploads/system/uploads/attachment_data/file/649906/Transparency_in_Supply_Chains_A_Practical_Guide_2017.pdf.

6 Modern Slavery Act 2015, s 54(12).

7 Modern Slavery Act 2015, s 54(4).

8 See Explanatory notes to the Modern Slavery Act 2015, s 54.

(d) the parts of its business and supply chains where there is a risk of slavery and human trafficking taking place, and the steps it has taken to assess and manage that risk;

(e) its effectiveness in ensuring that slavery and human trafficking is not taking place in its business or supply chains, measured against such performance indicators as it considers appropriate;

(f) the training about slavery and human trafficking available to its staff.

Corporate governance in relation to the statement

14.12 The Act requires that any statement in relation to the following kinds of corporate entities be approved and signed by the following persons:[9]

Corporate entity	Approved/signed by
A body corporate other than a limited liability partnership	It must be approved by the board of directors (or equivalent management body) and signed by a director (or equivalent)
A limited liability partnership	It must be approved by the members and signed by a designated member
A limited partnership registered under the Limited Partnerships Act 1907	It must be signed by a general partner
If the organisation is any other kind of partnership	It must be signed by a partner

Publication of the statement – electronic

14.13 Where a relevant organisation has a website it publishes the slavery and human trafficking statement on that website, and includes a link to the slavery and human trafficking statement in a prominent place on that website's homepage. Anecdotally, the Home Office in the UK would appear to favour a link to the statement appearing on the front page of a website in terms of satisfying the prominence criteria.[10]

Publication of the statement – non-electronic

14.14 If the organisation does not have a website, it must provide a copy of the slavery and human trafficking statement to anyone who makes a written request for one, and must do so before the end of the period of 30 days beginning with the day on which the request is received.[11]

Sample statement

14.15 For US firms with even a *de mimimis* presence in the UK it is frequently the case that a statement in relation to the California Transparency in Supply Chains Act and the UK Modern Slavery Act will be required. It would appear permissible to satisfy both obligations by means of a joint statement, and a sample statement is set out in the Appendices hereto.

9 Modern Slavery Act 2015, s 54(6).
10 Modern Slavery Act 2015, s 54(7)
11 Modern Slavery Act 2015, s 54(8).

FURTHER GUIDANCE

14.16 As required by the section, the Secretary of State in the UK with responsibility for implementation of the Modern Slavery Act has issued a comprehensive guidance note entitled 'Transparency in Supply Chains etc. – A practical guide' and it is available on the uk.gov web portal.

Non-disclosure agreements

Recent developments

14.17 Following on from a number of high-profile cases, there has been an increased level of legislative scrutiny, particularly in the UK, regarding the use of confidentiality clauses, typically deployed in non-disclosure type agreements. In 2019, the UK government issued a proposal to alter how such clauses are deployed and used and set upon a course of consultation with stakeholders as to how to shape a legislative response to the mis-use of confidentiality clauses. The intention of the government was set out in a paper of March 2019:[12]

> 'The Government is committed to upholding and upgrading workers' rights, having placed good work and good jobs at the centre of the modern Industrial Strategy. As part of our commitment to this upgrade, we are now consulting to ensure that harassment or discrimination of any sort cannot be tolerated in the workplace. The purpose of this consultation is to seek evidence and views of the use of confidentiality clauses in the employment context, and to propose further regulation to tackle their misuse.'

14.18 Noting the legitimate deployment of confidentiality clauses in a corporate context as:

> '... having a right and proper place in the employment context. They can be used primarily in two ways: as part of employment contracts, to protect trade secrets for example, and as part of settlement agreements, for example to allow both sides of an employment dispute to move on with a clean break.'

14.19 It went on to comment however, that:

> '... there is evidence that despite these protections some employers have used confidentiality clauses to suggest victims of harassment cannot make any disclosures and intimidate them into silence when they have faced harassment or discrimination. For example, a confidentiality clause might be all encompassing, to make a worker believe that they cannot discuss anything that occurs in the workplace with anybody, despite case law establishing that this is not necessarily the case. A confidentiality clause might suggest to the worker that they do not have rights, such as whistleblowing or taking a matter to a tribunal that in fact cannot be abrogated. Or they could be unreasonably expansive and insist that a worker not discuss the issue under consideration with people such as the police, a doctor, or a therapist.'

12 Confidentiality Clauses – Consultation on measures to prevent misuse in situations of workplace harassment or discrimination, available at gov.uk.

14.20 Hence, the UK government is now exploring whether there should be more limitations on confidentiality clauses in the employment context, to make it easier for workers and their advisers to understand when they are permitted in law to make a disclosure to the police or other people despite the existence of a confidentiality clause. Similarly it will explore how to ensure workers are clear about the rights they maintain when they sign a confidentiality clause or start work for a new employer and also how to enforce any new regulations on confidentiality clauses.[13]

Conclusion

14.21 Whilst concrete legislative measures are, perhaps, some distance off, it would be submitted that corporate counsel be mindful of how such UK measures (which may adopt a broad extra-jurisdictional reach) may impact their utilisation of non-disclosure agreements in the future.

Antitrust and anticompetitive practices

Overview of European law

14.22 European antitrust policy is developed from two central rules set out in the Treaty on the Functioning of the European Union:

- Article 141[14] of the Treaty prohibits agreements between two or more independent market competitors which restrict competition. Horizontal agreements and vertical agreements are prohibited. Only limited exceptions are provided for.

---

13 See Confidentiality Clauses – Consultation on measures to prevent misuse in situations of workplace harassment or discrimination, available at gov.uk.

14 Article 141 (ex Article 81 TEC):

1. The following shall be prohibited as incompatible with the internal market: all agreements between undertakings, decisions by associations of undertakings and concerted practices which may affect trade between Member States and which have as their object or effect the prevention, restriction or distortion of competition within the internal market, and in particular those which:
   (a) directly or indirectly fix purchase or selling prices or any other trading conditions;
   (b) limit or control production, markets, technical development, or investment;
   (c) share markets or sources of supply;
   (d) apply dissimilar conditions to equivalent transactions with other trading parties, thereby placing them at a competitive disadvantage;
   (e) make the conclusion of contracts subject to acceptance by the other parties of supplementary obligations which, by their nature or according to commercial usage, have no connection with the subject of such contracts.
2. Any agreements or decisions prohibited pursuant to this Article shall be automatically void.
3. The provisions of paragraph 1 may, however, be declared inapplicable in the case of:
   – any agreement or category of agreements between undertakings,
   – any decision or category of decisions by associations of undertakings,
   – any concerted practice or category of concerted practices,

   which contributes to improving the production or distribution of goods or to promoting technical or economic progress, while allowing consumers a fair share of the resulting benefit, and which does not:
   (a) impose on the undertakings concerned restrictions which are not indispensable to the attainment of these objectives;
   (b) afford such undertakings the possibility of eliminating competition in respect of a substantial part of the products in question

- Article 142[15] of the Treaty prohibits firms that hold a dominant position in a market to abuse that position.

The Commission is empowered by the Treaty to apply these rules and has a number of investigative powers (eg, inspection at business and non-business premises, written requests for information, etc). The Commission may also impose fines on undertakings which violate the EU antitrust rules. The main rules on procedures are set out in Council Regulation (EC) 1/2003.

14.23 National Competition Authorities are charged to apply Articles 141 and 142 of the Treaty fully, to ensure that competition is not distorted or restricted.

14.24 The enormous body of law in relation to antitrust matters in the EU means that elucidation of even the main features of the governing law is beyond the scope of this work. Instead it is proposed to set out the sources of the law in this regard so as to assist counsel in navigating towards cogent advice.[16]

The essential rules

14.25

- EU rules on competition apply directly in all EU member states.
- They are directly enforceable by both the European Commission and national competition authorities and courts.
- EU competition rules apply to 'undertakings', eg trade associations and other industry groupings.
- There are two broad types of prohibited behaviour:
  - Illegal contacts and agreements between companies which may be even be informal in nature. This may manifest as price fixing, sharing markets or customer allocation, production or output limitation, whether through bid rigging or otherwise. A typical example may be a distribution agreement between suppliers and re-sellers, which has the effect of maintaining prices at a certain level or dividing up a market unfairly. such agreements is provided by the Commission in specific guidelines.
  - Abuse of a dominant position. This may manifest as imposing unreasonably high or low prices creating discrimination between customers and distorted trading conditions on trading partners.

---

15 Article 142 (ex Article 82 TEC):
Any abuse by one or more undertakings of a dominant position within the internal market or in a substantial part of it shall be prohibited as incompatible with the internal market in so far as it may affect trade between Member States.
Such abuse may, in particular, consist in:
(a) directly or indirectly imposing unfair purchase or selling prices or other unfair trading conditions;
(b) limiting production, markets or technical development to the prejudice of consumers;
(c) applying dissimilar conditions to equivalent transactions with other trading parties, thereby placing them at a competitive disadvantage;
(d) making the conclusion of contracts subject to acceptance by the other parties of supplementary obligations which, by their nature or according to commercial usage, have no connection with the subject of such contracts.

16 Rules applicable to Antitrust enforcement – vol 1, available at https://ec.europa.eu/competition/antitrust/legislation/handbook_vol_1_en.pdf.

- All companies are subject to competition rules, with no differentiation according to their size. Being small is no excuse for not complying with the applicable EU or national competition rules.

Sample corporate policy

14.26 Many corporate entities with multi-jurisdictional operations bundle their competition policy aims in a hybrid document. It is important to ensure that all such attempts are sufficiently sophisticated in order to provide the best guidance to employees. A sample policy document is included in the appendices to this text.

Best practices

14.27 The European Commission have issued a comprehensive guide to best practice for the conduct of proceedings and complaints in relation to antitrust matters.[17] This is essential reading for any counsel who is anticipating or dealing with antitrust implications for their business. It provides guidance on a wide range of topics, including:

- Origin of cases
- Initial assessment and case allocation
- Opening of proceedings
- Languages
- Information requests
- Scope of request for information
- Self-incrimination
- Time limits
- Confidentiality
- Meetings and other contacts with the parties and third parties
- Power to take statements (interviews)
- Inspections
- Legal professional privilege
- Information exchange between competition authorities
- State of play meetings
- Format of the state of play meetings
- Timing of the state of play meetings
- Triangular meetings
- Meetings with the Commissioner or the Director-General
- Review of key submissions
- Possible outcomes of the investigation phase

17 Commission notice on best practices for the conduct of proceedings concerning Articles 101 and 102 TFEU Text with EEA relevance OJ C 308, 20.10.2011, pp 6–32.

- Right to be heard
- Statement of Objections
- Purpose and content of the Statement of Objections
- Possible imposition of remedies and arguments of the parties
- Possible imposition of fines and arguments of the parties
- Transparency
- Access to file
- Procedures for facilitating the exchange of confidential information between parties to the proceedings
- Written reply to the Statement of Objections
- Rights of complainants and interested third persons
- Oral hearing
- Supplementary Statement of Objections and letter of facts
- Possible outcomes of this phase
- Initiation of commitment discussions
- Preliminary assessment
- Submission of the commitments
- The 'market test' and subsequent discussions with the parties

PART 4

REGARDING GEO-POLITICAL UPHEAVAL AND THE BUSINESS

15 Geo-political considerations for corporate counsel – Brexit

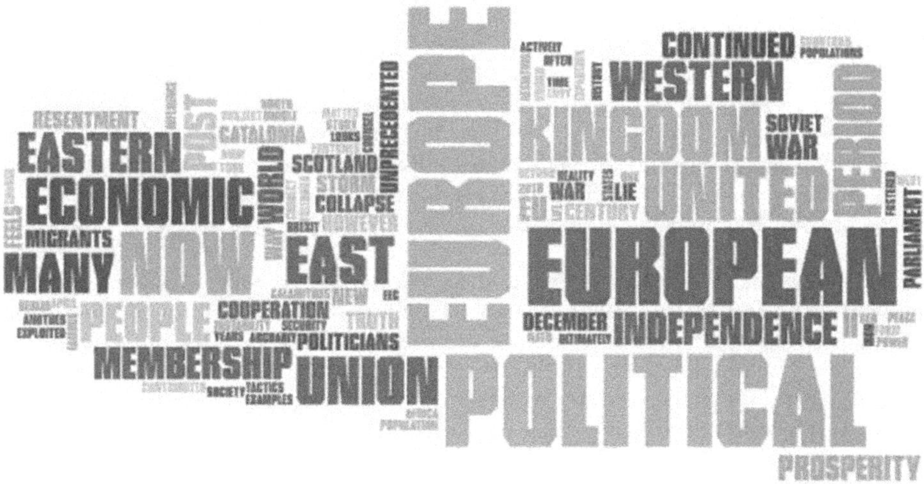

'There are endless unknowns, and no forecast of a century can be either complete or utterly correct.'

George Friedman

The Next 100 Years: A Forecast for the 21st Century

Introduction

15.1 Think of the calamitous periods of social upheaval, political instability and war Europe endured through the 18th and 19th centuries, and well beyond into the 20th century. However, thanks to the post World War II Marshal Plan (April 1948–December 1951); the security and cooperation fostered by the creation of NATO (April 1949 and ongoing); the economic security and cooperation first fostered by the European Coal and Steel Community (1951 and continued by its successor institutions the EEC and the European Union) the second half of the 20th century was largely, arguably, a period of relative stability, decolonisation, economic growth, peace and prosperity for Western Europe.

15.2 All of Europe, however, did not share equally in this post-war political and economic rebirth or its resulting peace and prosperity. For the people of Eastern Europe, the horrors of World War II were followed by a 45-year ordeal of political subjugation and economic stagnation. This period of deprivation was foretold, by Winston Churchill, as early as March 1946 in his famous Iron Curtain speech:

> 'From Stettin in the Baltic to Trieste in the Adriatic, an iron curtain has descended across the Continent. Behind that line lie all the capitals of the

ancient states of Central and Eastern Europe. Warsaw, Berlin, Prague, Vienna, Budapest, Belgrade, Bucharest and Sofia, all these famous cities and the populations around them lie in the Soviet sphere and are all subject in one form or another, not only to Soviet influence but to a very high and in many cases increasing measure of control from Moscow.'

15.3 This unfortunate state of affairs in the East continued unabated until the collapse of the Berlin Wall in November 1989 and then ultimately ended with collapse of the Soviet Union on 26 December 1991. Then and only then did the fortunes of Eastern Europe begin to change. The reunification of Germany occurred in 1990, the eastern expansion of membership in NATO followed at pace and the membership of the European Union ballooned Eastward at an unprecedented rate from 2004.

15.4 To the uninitiated, or the unaware, this looks a promising story with a very positive narrative post 1990. The reality on the ground, as of the date of publication, in the United Kingdom and other places in Western Europe is however far from rosy.

15.5 The reality is that the generation of young adults who lived through and remember the 1930s and 1940s is now all but gone. The lessons of the period are all but forgotten and the history of the period 1930 to 1980 is but a footnote, marginalised by a public education system that is arguably too politically correct and intimidated by the subject matter to teach the harsh truths, prejudices and political tactics that precipitated World War II, enabled the Holocaust and ultimately lead Europe to its calamitous climax in 1945. Western Europe was reborn in 1946 but the East was imprisoned. Its people were subjected to 45 years of continued repression and depravation.

15.6 With the fall of the Iron Curtin, the collapse of the Eastern European Stalinist police states and the resulting expansion of the European Union to the East, many millions of individuals took advantage of their new found EU rights and especially its enshrined freedom of movement. These people moved West away from the then collapsed Eastern economies to find new lives and work in Western Europe. Their wages flooded back East in support their families and heavily contributed, along with the flood of aid from the EU, to fund economic miracles in their Eastern homelands.

15.7 In parallel existed the still incessant instability and strife in the Middle East; wars in Iraq and Afghanistan; political insurrection and regime change in the Middle East and North Africa; and a civil war in Syria, all of which contributed to the epic rise of religious fundamentalism and the radical Islamic terror group known is ISIS. These factors resulted in an unprecedented flow (post World War II) of political refugees and economic migrants from the middle East and North Africa, many of whom were and are bound for the promise of a better life in Western Europe.

15.8 Migration benefited many a European economy but migrants were and are often quite unfairly distrusted. Furthermore, many are resented by portions of the local population who, for whatever reasons are, and have been, unable to achieve the same degree of success and prosperity in their home countries as many migrants quickly enjoyed. Fear, envy and resentment, as history teaches, is a powerful intoxicant when exploited and unfortunately is and has been actively exploited for some time by those in Western European society who would exploit if not ferment distrust, bigotry and ideological/theological supremacy to gain political influence and power. Potential examples abound: the English National Front; the UK Independence Party; Marine Le Pen's National Rally in France; Italy's Five Star Movement; Austria's Freedom Party and so forth.

15.9 The stabilising influences that the European Union and its forbearers brought to Europe through economic prosperity and cross-border cooperation are being actively undermined and subverted by the tactics of these groups. The optimism that membership in the European Union once brought to countries such as the United Kingdom, (which at the time of its entrance into membership of the EEC was widely known as the sick man of Europe), has been consigned to oblivion just like its 1980s contemporary, the hit British TV show *Auf Wiedersehen, Pet.*

15.10 Those wishing to raise their own fortunes and power by harnessing fear, envy and resentment have of late grown bolder. In the United Kingdom they are elected to the EU Parliament and even the mother of Parliaments. The population is daily inundated by a now commonplace thundering dishonesty from those now occupying the land's highest political office. These nationalists are emboldened all the more by the lack of leadership and ethical void that now occupies the once Hallowed Halls of the Presidency of Britain's once most special ally.

15.11 We now hear talk of a period of post-truth period politics in the West. I'll go one further, we seem to be in a period where not only have fact and truth been discarded by our political leaders (not to mention their bewitched followers), this is compounded by the total absence of anything resembling conscience or shame by these dastardly demigods.

15.12 When almost on a daily basis there are new articles in the mainstream press tabulating the number of lies told by the various politicians on any given day since his election[1] or an esteemed Queen's Counsel feels obliged to stand in open court to challenge the legitimacy and legality of the actions of a United Kingdom prime minister while in so doing feels it is necessary and appropriate to accuse said prime minister 'of having a record characterised by incontinent mendacity' as in-house counsel and business leaders, no matter our citizenship or allegiance, we must no longer choose to ignore these unpalatable political machinations but recognise them for what they are, actual threats to our businesses, their hard won codes of conduct and business practice and, even more fundamentally, a danger to the foundation of the way of life those lads died protecting, on the landing grounds of Utah, Sword, Omaha, Gold, Juno and the beaches of Iwo Jima.[2]

15.13 For more than two years now a violent thundering political storm (born out of the use of misinformation and playing off of a segment of the populations' fears and resentment) has been raging. It has divided the United Kingdom's politicians and the people of the United Kingdom. That storm is about when, if and how or not the United Kingdom will end its membership in the European Union. It feels as if all civility in society is draining away; that people and politicians alike believe any statement becomes fact, and every lie becomes truth, if simply repeated loudly and often. The very union, the continued existence of this Kingdom in its current form are as a result, at risk. The people of Scotland who wish ardently to remain in the EU are now seeking to have another binding referendum, for the independence of Scotland, which now looks more likely than not, as a result.

15.14 Brexit is not the only geo-political storm raging in Europe. In 2018 The European Commission took an unprecedented step and launched legal action against the Polish government over changes to the way judges are appointed in that

1 *New York Times* (30 April 2019) 'Late Night Congratulates Trump on His 10,000th Lie'.

2 Auslan Cramb 'Scottish court is told that Boris Johnson "approved shutdown of Parliament in mid-August"' *The Telegraph* (3 September 2019).

country accusing it of undermining the independence of its courts. In addition, the governments of Romania, Hungary and Turkey have also been called out formally for undermining the rule of law and the independence of their respective Judiciary.[3]

15.15 The Parliament of Catalonia, in Barcelona, unilaterally issued a declaration of independence from Spain on 27 October 2017 in favour of creating a Catalan Republic. In response the Spanish government in Madrid dissolved the Parliament of Catalonia, imposed direct rule and called a snap regional election for 21 December 2017. The parties supporting independence again won by a majority.[4] That story is a long way from being concluded.

15.16 Beyond Catalonia are other now ominous and (hitherto never before) credible separatist movements in Scotland (UK); Flanders, Wallonia (Belgium); the Veneto (Italy) and Basque Country (Spain and France) that all merit watchful attention. The present United Kingdom and Catalonian experiences are very good examples how difficult, expensive, destabilising and damaging political strife can be to countries and the businesses that operate in them.

15.17 I leave you with a question. Should we be worried by this post-truth, post-shame period in which, it is now beyond question, Europe (as well as the United States of America) are in the grips of a resurgence of nationalism? If your business needs certainty and the rule of law to prosper; if it desires competent independent courts to which to refer disputes; if it worries that politicians are being blatantly and knowingly mendacious, their supporters blindly accepting their obvious odious obfuscation and equally accepting of their vitriol the answer, at least for me, is clear. Perhaps more often as I continue to observe this carnival of depravity with a historian's eye I ask myself, have we been here before? My inner reply, terrifies.

15.18 What follows is as an objective look at Brexit as we could muster when trying to cut through the obfuscation. It is accompanied by our best wet finger in the wind guide, at as at the date of publishing, to the issues likely in the event of Brexit.

15.19 At a special meeting of the European Council on 25 November 2018 an Agreement on the withdrawal of the United Kingdom of Great Britain and Northern Ireland from the European Union was endorsed by the leaders of both sides. Political difficulty has ensued in the United Kingdom as regards ratifying and approving this agreement, which remains in abeyance. However, in terms of understanding the Brexit process and its attendant implications for corporate counsel, it is perhaps useful to commence by setting out some background information together with key features of the proposed solution.[5]

Article 50

15.20 On 29 March 2017 the United Kingdom, following the outcome of a referendum held resulting in its decision to leave the European Union, notified its intention to withdraw from the European Union in accordance with Article 50 of the Treaty on European Union.

---

3 Council of Europe, Commission for Human Rights, 'The Independence of Judges and the Judiciary under threat' 3 September 2019.

4 'Separatist parties in Spain's Catalonia win majority in election' (CNN, 22 December 2017).

5 As of the time of writing, the Withdrawal Agreement remains unapproved by the Parliament of the United Kingdom and therefore has not yet been ratified by the other 27 member states of the European Union.

The 'Divorce Agreement'

15.21 In the intervening period both sides sought to set out the arrangements for the withdrawal of the United Kingdom from the Union taking account of the framework for their future relationship, by concluding what became known as the Withdrawal Agreement, or more colloquially as the 'Divorce Agreement' to ensure an orderly withdrawal of the United Kingdom from the European Union.[6]

15.22 Critically, pursuant to Article 50, and subject to the arrangements laid down in the withdrawal agreement, the law of the Union in its entirety ceases to apply to the United Kingdom from the date of entry into force of the Withdrawal Agreement.

15.23 During the negotiations on the Withdrawal Agreement it was recognised that it was necessary to provide reciprocal protection for European Union citizens and for United Kingdom nationals, as well as their respective family members, where they have exercised free movement rights before a date set in the Withdrawal Agreement, and to ensure that their rights under the Withdrawal Agreement are enforceable and based on the principle of non-discrimination; recognising also that rights deriving from periods of social security insurance should be protected.

15.24 In general, both sides were adamant that it was necessary to ensure an orderly withdrawal through various separation provisions whilst aiming to prevent disruption and to provide legal certainty to citizens and economic operators as well as to judicial and administrative authorities in the European Union and in the United Kingdom, while not excluding the possibility of relevant separation provisions being superseded by the anticipated agreement(s) on the future relationship.

The implementation period

15.25 It was also considered that it was in the interests of both the Union and the United Kingdom to determine a transition or implementation period during which European Union law, including international agreements, should be applicable to and in the United Kingdom, and, as a general rule, with the same effect as regards the member states, in order to avoid disruption in the period during which the agreement(s) on the future relationship will be negotiated.

15.26 It was noted and proposed by both sides that even if European Union law will be applicable to and in the United Kingdom during the transition period, the specificities of the United Kingdom as a state having withdrawn from the Union mean that it will be important for the United Kingdom to be able to take steps to prepare and establish new international arrangements of its own, including in areas of European Union exclusive competence, provided such agreements do not enter into force or apply during that period, unless so authorised by the Union.

The impasse

15.27 The European Union were adamant that, for an orderly withdrawal of the United Kingdom from the European Union, it was also necessary to establish, in separate protocols to the Withdrawal Agreement, durable arrangements addressing the

6 Agreement on the withdrawal of the United Kingdom of Great Britain and Northern Ireland from the European Union and the European Atomic Energy Community, as endorsed by leaders at a special meeting of the European Council on 25 November 2018

very specific situations relating to Ireland/Northern Ireland and matters of, inter alia, customs and product compliance that would be impacted by the decision to leave the European Union.

15.28 At the time of writing, both the Withdrawal Agreement (which has since been amended) and the political declaration on the future relationship between the United Kingdom and European Union remain to be ratified.

Legislative impacts

15.29 Given the current lack of clarity regarding the ratification and implementation of the Withdrawal Agreement, it is difficult to draw definitive conclusions as to the impact of the Brexit process for corporate counsel. However, such implications may be derived for an assessment of the United Kingdom domestic legislation that is planned to be brought forth in order to give effect to Brexit process. In order to provide corporate counsel with optimum assistance in this regard, the authors have set out hereafter a (non-exhaustive) selection of issues that will, almost certainly, be impacted by any conclusion of the Brexit process.

Topic	**Legislation**
Governing legislation	European Union (Withdrawal) Act 2018
Anti-money laundering	Sanctions and Anti-Money Laundering Act 2018
Transport	Haulage Permits and Trailer Registration Act 2018
Nuclear	Nuclear Safeguards Act 2018
Taxation	Taxation (Cross-border Trade) Act 2018
Trade	Trade Bill 2017–19
Agriculture	Agriculture Bill 2017–19
Fisheries	Fisheries Bill 2017–19
Immigration	Immigration and Social Security Co-ordination (EU Withdrawal) Bill 2017–19
Healthcare	Healthcare (International Arrangements) Bill 2017–19
Financial services	Financial Services (Implementation of Legislation) Bill [HL] 2017–19
Environment	Environmental Principles and Governance Bill 2017–19
Animal welfare	Animal Welfare (Sentencing and Recognition of Sentience) Bill
Business operations	The EU Export Credits Legislation (Revocation) (EU Exit) (No 2) Regulations 2019
Environment	The Food and Feed Hygiene and Safety (Amendment) (Northern Ireland) (EU Exit) Regulations 2019
Environment	The Regulated Products (Amendment) (Northern Ireland) (EU Exit) Regulations 2019
Environment	The REACH etc. (Amendment etc.) (EU Exit) (No 2) Regulations 2019
Business operations	The Greenhouse Gas Emissions Trading Scheme (Amendment) (EU Exit) (No 2) Regulations 2019

Topic	Legislation
Business operations	The Competitiveness of Enterprises and Small and Medium-Sized Enterprises (Revocation) (EU Exit) Regulations 2019
Environment	The Quick-frozen foodstuffs (Amendment) (EU Exit) Regulations 2019
Environment	The Animal Health, Plant Health, Seeds and Seed Potatoes (Amendment) (EU Exit) Regulations 2019
Transport	International Road Passenger Transport (Amendment) (Northern Ireland) (EU Exit) Regulations 2019
Intellectual property	The Customs (Enforcement of Intellectual Property Rights) (Amendment) (EU Exit) Regulations 2019
Data protection	The Data Protection, Privacy and Electronic Communications (Amendments etc) (EU Exit) (No 2) Regulations 2019
E-Commerce	The Electronic Communications (Amendment etc) (EU Exit) Regulations 2019
Sanctions	The Sanctions (Amendment) (EU Exit) (No 2) Regulations 2019
Environment	The Environmental Impact Assessment (Amendment) (Northern Ireland) (EU Exit) (No 2) Regulations 2019
Environment	The Waste (Miscellaneous Amendments) (Northern Ireland) (EU Exit) Regulations 2019
Environment	The Environmental Protection (Amendment) (Northern Ireland) (EU Exit) Regulations 2019
Environment	The Waste (Miscellaneous Amendments) (EU Exit) (No 2) Regulations 2019
Transport	The Common Rules for Access to the International Market for Coach and Bus Services (Amendment etc) (EU Exit) Regulations 2019
Health	The Nutrition (Amendment) (Northern Ireland) (EU Exit) Regulations 2019
Environment	The Animal Health and Welfare (Amendment) (Northern Ireland) (EU Exit) Regulations 2018
Environment	The Environmental Impact Assessment (Amendment) (Northern Ireland) (EU Exit) Regulations 2018
Business operations	The Investment Exchanges, Clearing Houses and Central Securities Depositories (Amendment) (EU Exit) Regulations 2018
E-Commerce	The Electronic Commerce (Amendment etc.) (EU Exit) Regulations 2019
E-Commerce	The Export Control (Amendment) (EU Exit) Regulations 2019
Contracts	The Law Applicable to Contractual Obligations and Non-Contractual Obligations (Amendment etc) (EU Exit) Regulations 2018

Topic	Legislation
Environment	The International Waste Shipments (Amendment) (EU Exit) Regulations 2018
Environment	The Renewables Obligation (Amendment) (EU Exit) Regulations 2018
Business operations	The EU Export Credits Legislation (Revocation) (EU Exit) Regulations 2018
Sanctions	The Sanctions (Amendment) (EU Exit) Regulations 2018
Environment	The Air Quality (Miscellaneous Amendment and Revocation of Retained Direct EU Legislation) (EU Exit) Regulations 2018
Business operations	The Provision of Services (Amendment) (EU Exit) Regulations 2018
Trusts	The Electronic Identification and Trust Services for Electronic Transactions (Amendment etc) (EU Exit) Regulations 2018
Business operations	The Health and Safety (Amendment) (Northern Ireland) (EU Exit) Regulations 2018
Enforcement Orders	The European Enforcement Order, European Order for Payment and European Small Claims Procedure (Amendment etc) (EU Exit) Regulations 2018
Corporate governance	The Companies, Limited Liability Partnerships and Partnerships (Amendment etc) (EU Exit) Regulations 2019
Employment law	The Employment Rights (Amendment) (EU Exit) Regulations 2019
Employment law	The Employment Rights (Amendment) (Northern Ireland) (EU Exit) Regulations 2018
Corporate Governance	The European Public Limited-Liability Company (Amendment etc) (EU Exit) Regulations 2018
Consumer protection	Consumer Protection (Amendment etc) (EU Exit) Regulations 2018
Intellectual property	The Intellectual Property (Copyright and Related Rights) (Amendment) (EU Exit) Regulations 2019
Business operations	The Weighing and Measuring Equipment and Meters (Amendment of Secondary Legislation) (EU Exit) Regulations 2018
Litigation	The Service of Documents and Taking of Evidence in Civil and Commercial Matters (Revocation and Saving Provisions) (EU Exit) Regulations 2018
Transport	The Heavy Goods Vehicles (Charging for the Use of Certain Infrastructure on the Trans-European Road Network) (Amendment) (EU Exit) Regulations 2018
Consumer credit	The Consumer Credit (Amendment) (EU Exit) Regulations 2018

Topic	**Legislation**
Consumer protection	The Consumer Protection (Enforcement) (Amendment etc) (EU Exit) Regulations 2018
Health and safety	The Health and Safety (Amendment) (EU Exit) Regulations 2018
Freedom of information	The Freedom of Information Act 2000 (Amendment) (EU Exit) Regulations 2018

Aspects of Brexit legislation

The EU Export Credits Legislation (Revocation) (EU Exit) (No 2) Regulations 2019

15.30 These Regulations revoke and replace the EU Export Credits Legislation (Revocation) (EU Exit) Regulations 2019, which contained an error in the scope of EU direct legislation which that instrument purportedly revoked. Also, it revokes certain direct EU legislation as soon as it forms part of domestic law when the United Kingdom leaves the EU, because at that time that legislation will have no practical application in relation to the United Kingdom or any part of it or be redundant or substantially redundant.

The Food and Feed Hygiene and Safety (Amendment) (Northern Ireland) (EU Exit) Regulations 2019

15.31 The purpose of this measure is to ensure Northern Ireland legislation relating to food and feed hygiene and safety listed below continues to operate effectively after the United Kingdom leaves the EU. In particular with respect to:

- The General Food Regulations (Northern Ireland) 2004
- The Food Hygiene Regulations (Northern Ireland) 2006
- The Quick-frozen Foodstuffs (No 2) Regulations (Northern Ireland) 2007
- The Meat (Official Controls Charges) Regulations (Northern Ireland) 2009
- The Official Feed and Food Controls Regulations (Northern Ireland) 2009
- The Plastic Kitchenware (Conditions on Imports from China) Regulations (Northern Ireland) 2011
- The Animal Feed (Composition, Marketing and Use) Regulations (Northern Ireland) 2016

The Regulated Products (Amendment) (Northern Ireland) (EU Exit) Regulations 2019

15.32 The purpose of this measure is to ensure Northern Ireland legislation relating to regulated products listed below continues to operate effectively after the United Kingdom leaves the European Union. Specifically in relation to such measures as the Genetically Modified Food Regulations (Northern Ireland) 2004, the Materials and Articles in Contact with Food Regulations (Northern Ireland) 2012, the Food Additives, Flavourings, Enzymes and Extraction Solvents Regulations (Northern Ireland) 2013 and The Novel Foods Regulations (Northern Ireland) 2017.

The REACH etc (Amendment etc) (EU Exit) (No 2) Regulations 2019

15.33 Under the EU REACH Regulation, downstream users of chemical substances within the EEA do not have to register the substances they use. This includes United Kingdom companies who are currently sourcing substances from suppliers in the rest of the EEA. However, these United Kingdom companies will become importers into the United Kingdom market after Brexit, which means they will have the duty to register the substances. The REACH measure provides transitional support to these companies through an interim notification system for imports instead of requiring them to undertake a full registration immediately after EU Exit.

The Greenhouse Gas Emissions Trading Scheme (Amendment) (EU Exit) (No 2) Regulations 2019

15.34 In the event that the United Kingdom withdraws from the EU without a deal the United Kingdom would not have an agreement in place to continue participating in the EU Emissions Trading System (EU ETS), which would create inoperability in existing legislation. The Greenhouse Gas Emissions Trading Scheme (Amendment) (EU Exit) Regulations 2019 revoked certain provisions that will cease to apply on exit day and amended others to address those inoperability issues.

The Customs (Enforcement of Intellectual Property Rights) (Amendment) (EU Exit) Regulations 2019

15.35 This instrument will ensure that United Kingdom legislation is in place after exit day enabling HM Revenue and Customs (HMRC) to continue to be able to enforce intellectual property rights at the United Kingdom border in the event that the United Kingdom leaves the EU without a withdrawal agreement.

The Data Protection, Privacy and Electronic Communications (Amendments etc) (EU Exit) (No 2) Regulations 2019

15.36 The General Data Protection Regulation (GDPR) applies directly across all EU member states, including the United Kingdom, until Exit Day. It regulates the processing of personal data by data controllers and processors with an establishment in the EU; and by those outside the EU which are processing data about individuals who are in the EU for the purposes of providing them with goods and services or monitoring their behaviour. The instrument amends the transitional provisions of the main Regulations to provide that transfers of personal data from the United Kingdom in reliance on Privacy Shield can only take place after 29 March 2019 in a no deal scenario, if the certified Privacy Shield company has a privacy policy which includes a commitment to comply with the Privacy Shield Principles in relation to personal data transferred from the United Kingdom. This maintains consistency with arrangements prior to the United Kingdom's withdrawal from the EU.

The Sanctions (Amendment) (EU Exit) (No 2) Regulations 2019

15.37 The Sanctions (Amendment) (EU Exit) (No 2) Regulations 2019 amend provisions deriving from European Union (EU) legislation which have been retained in domestic law under the European Union (Withdrawal) Act (2018). The instrument ensures that aspects of the financial sanctions regimes in relation to Afghanistan, Burundi, the Central African Republic, Egypt, the Republic of Guinea, Iraq, Lebanon and Syria (in relation to the 14 February 2005 terrorist bombing in Beirut), the Republic of Maldives, Mali, Somalia, Sudan, Tunisia, Ukraine and Yemen, will continue to be implemented after the United Kingdom (UK) leaves the EU.

The Environmental Impact Assessment (Amendment) (Northern Ireland) (EU Exit) (No 2) Regulations 2019

15.38 This instrument amends our existing implementation of Directive 2001/42/EC of the European Parliament and of the Council of 27 January 2001 ('the SEA Directive') on the assessment of certain plans and programmes on the environment. The principal regulations being amended are: The Environmental Assessment of Plans and Programmes Regulations (Northern Ireland) 2004; The Environmental Impact Assessment (Forestry) Regulations (Northern Ireland) 2006; The Environmental Impact Assessment (Agriculture) Regulations (Northern Ireland 2007; and The Water Resources (Environmental Impact Assessment) Regulations (Northern Ireland) 2017.

The Law Applicable to Contractual Obligations and Non-Contractual Obligations (Amendment etc) (EU Exit) Regulations 2018

15.39 The purpose of this measure is to ensure that the European Union rules that determine the law applicable to contractual and non-contractual obligations continue to operate effectively in domestic law after the United Kingdom's exit from the EU. Those EU rules are contained, in particular, in Regulation (EC) No 593/2008 on the law applicable to contractual obligations ('Rome I') and Regulation (EC) No 864/2007 on the law applicable to non-contractual obligations ('Rome II').

15.40 Rome I establishes the rules applicable to EU member states (except Denmark) that determine which country's laws apply to contractual obligations raising cross-border issues. Rome I replaced the rules in the 1980 Rome Convention on the law applicable to contractual obligations, with effect from 17 December 2009, although the 1980 Rome Convention continues to apply to certain contracts entered into before Rome I entered into force. Rome II establishes the rules applicable to EU member states (except Denmark) that determine the law applicable to non-contractual obligations raising cross-border issues.

15.41 Upon the United Kingdom's exit from the EU, Rome I and Rome II, and the domestic legislation that gave effect to these EU Regulations, will be retained under the European Union (Withdrawal) Act 2018 (the 'Withdrawal Act') but will contain deficiencies that need correcting in order for the rules on applicable law to continue to work effectively as United Kingdom domestic law after exit day. The United Kingdom will also cease to participate in the 1980 Rome Convention, meaning the Convention's rules will no longer apply to the United Kingdom as a matter of international law. Amendments are needed to the Contracts (Applicable Law) Act 1990, which incorporated the 1980 Rome Convention into domestic law, in order to preserve the substantive rules of the Convention so that they will continue to apply to existing contracts entered into between 1 April 1991 (the date on which the Rome Convention came into force) and 16 December 2009 (after which Rome 1 replaced the Convention in the relevant EU member states).

15.42 As a result of these Regulations, from exit day, the substantive rules in Rome I, Rome II and the 1980 Rome Convention will continue to apply (as amended) as domestic law in all parts of the United Kingdom to determine the law applicable to contractual and non-contractual obligations.

The Provision of Services (Amendment) (EU Exit) Regulations 2018

15.43 The EU Services Directive (2006/123/EC) aims to develop the single market in services by breaking down barriers to cross-border trade within the European Union (EU). Specifically, the directive aims to simplify administrative procedures and remove obstacles for services activities; enhance mutual trust between member states through effective administrative cooperation; and improve the quality of service providers and strengthen consumer rights in the single market. The Regulations prevent competent authorities (meaning bodies with a supervisory or regulatory role, including local authorities, national regulators and professional bodies) from imposing discriminatory, disproportionate or unnecessary requirements on EEA businesses who seek to provide services on either a permanent or temporary basis in the United Kingdom. The amended Regulations will continue to benefit United Kingdom businesses by placing obligations on United Kingdom competent authorities and the way they regulate access to, or exercise of, the services in the scope of the Regulations.

The European Enforcement Order, European Order for Payment and European Small Claims Procedure (Amendment etc) (EU Exit) Regulations 2018

15.44 EU Regulations established procedures for the national courts of EU member states (other than Denmark, which does not apply the measures) to deal with cross-border civil and commercial claims, providing standard, simplified procedures for obtaining and/or enforcing orders or judgments in certain types of claims. Specifically: The European Enforcement Order (EEO) procedure is a simplified way of enforcing judgments from uncontested debt claims (ie, claims where the debtor has admitted liability or not responded to the claim or not appeared at court having initially responded) across different EU member states. The European Orders for Payment (EOP) procedure is a simplified procedure for pursuing uncontested EU cross-border monetary claims. The European Small Claims Procedure (ESCP) is a simplified procedure for making cross-border claims with a value of up to €5,000, which is designed for claimants to be able to use without needing to instruct lawyers.

15.45 The European Enforcement Order, the European Order for Payment and European Small Claims Procedure (Amendment etc) (EU Exit) Regulations 2018 revoke the retained EEO, EOP and ESCP Regulations and variously revoke and amend related EU amending measures and domestic legislation (other than the relevant court rules which will be the subject of separate SIs). EEOs, EOPs and ESCP judgments issued by EU member state courts will no longer be recognised or enforceable in the United Kingdom.

15.46 United Kingdom courts will be unable to certify judgments as EEOs, issue EOPs or ESCP judgments. It will still be possible to make claims which would have been capable, pre-exit, of being pursued in the United Kingdom under the EOP or ESCP Regulations, but these will need to be made in the appropriate court as ordinary civil claims, and recognition and enforcement of judgments and orders will need to be sought in the courts of the state where enforcement is intended to take place, in accordance with relevant national laws.

The Companies, Limited Liability Partnerships and Partnerships (Amendment etc) (EU Exit) Regulations 2019

15.47 The amendments cover various processes, functions and requirements as they apply to United Kingdom and EEA businesses, including filing requirements with the Companies Registrar (Companies House). There are also a small number of amendments to address the special treatment given in the legislation to EEA businesses or businesses with listing on or access to the EEA regulated markets, as these provisions will no longer be appropriate once the United Kingdom leaves the European Union.

The Employment Rights (Amendment) (EU Exit) Regulations 2019

15.48 This instrument makes amendments to employment law to reflect the withdrawal of the United Kingdom from the European Union (EU) in the event that there is no deal with the EU. The amendments ensure the legislation is clear by removing or amending language that is no longer appropriate once the United Kingdom has exited the EU. Such a broad range of topics are amended by this measure that it is beyond the scope of this work.

Consumer Protection (Amendment etc) (EU Exit) Regulations 2018

15.49 As the United Kingdom will no longer be a member of the EU single market, it will no longer be appropriate for the practices on an importer into the EEA to trigger a right to redress under United Kingdom law. The references to EEA states in the language requirements are being changed so that these requirements continue to operate as they do before exit day. As the United Kingdom will no longer be a member of the EU single market, it will no longer be appropriate for the practices on an importer into the EEA to trigger a right to redress under United Kingdom law. The references to EEA states in the language requirements are being changed so that these requirements continue to operate as they do before exit day.

The Intellectual Property (Copyright and Related Rights) (Amendment) (EU Exit) Regulations 2019

15.50 This instrument amends the Copyright, Designs and Patents Act 1988 (CDPA), and associated regulations, to correct deficiencies in, and failures of, retained EU law to operate effectively as a result of the United Kingdom leaving the European Union. This instrument will ensure retained EU law contains appropriate references to the 'European Union', 'member state', etc, which does not presuppose the United Kingdom's membership of the EU. Additionally, the instrument aims to give continued effect to cross-border mechanisms and their underlying policies wherever possible. Where this is not possible (eg, because the policy concerns a reciprocal obligation operating between EU member states), the mechanism is given unilateral effect within the United Kingdom. Where it would not be appropriate to give unilateral effect (as it would create adverse consequences for United Kingdom businesses if preserved in a one-sided way), the mechanism is brought to an end.

The Service of Documents and Taking of Evidence in Civil and Commercial Matters (Revocation and Saving Provisions) (EU Exit) Regulations 2018

15.51 As the EU Service and Evidence Regulations that apply to the EU member states will not extend to the United Kingdom, and as this instrument revokes the retained Regulations and related instruments, the United Kingdom will no longer transmit documents for service in EU member states under the Service Regulation, and will no longer comply with requests made by EU member states under that Regulation to serve documents on parties in the United Kingdom.

15.52 In relation to the taking of evidence, the United Kingdom will no longer issue requests under the Evidence Regulations for evidence to be taken from parties in EU member states. Neither will the United Kingdom execute or consent to requests made by EU member states under the Evidence Regulation to take evidence from parties in the United Kingdom.

15.53 The United Kingdom, like most EU member states, is a contracting state to two Hague Conventions relevant to service and evidence: the Convention of 15 November 1965 on the Service Abroad of Judicial and Extrajudicial Documents in Civil or Commercial Matters (the Hague Service Convention); and the Convention of 18 March 1970 on the Taking of Evidence Abroad in Civil or Commercial Matters (the Hague Evidence Convention). Post EU Exit, requests for service of judicial and non-judicial documents and for taking of evidence in cross-border civil and commercial matters involving the United Kingdom and states that are party to the Hague Conventions (contracting states) will be conducted under the two Hague Conventions.

The future relationship between the United Kingdom and the EU

What will the future look like?

15.54 In general terms both the European Union and the United Kingdom expressed mutual determination to work together to safeguard the rules-based international order of trade, the rule of law and promotion of democracy, and high standards of free and fair trade and workers' rights, consumer and environmental protection, and cooperation against internal and external threats to their values and interests.[7] Accordingly it was envisaged that there would be a broad, deep and flexible partnership across trade and economic cooperation, law enforcement and criminal justice, foreign policy, security and defence and wider areas of cooperation. In general terms it may be useful to set out a direction of travel on certain issues that will be of relevance to corporate counsel.

Core values

15.55 Both parties agree that the future relationship should be underpinned by shared values such as the respect for and safeguarding of human rights and fundamental freedoms, democratic principles, the rule of law and support for non-proliferation.

Data protection

15.56 Particular significance was attached to the area of data protection. The parties deemed that in view of the importance of data flows and exchanges across the future relationship, the parties are committed to ensuring a high level of personal data protection to facilitate such flows between them.

15.57 It was noted by the parties that the European Union's data protection rules provide for a framework allowing the European Commission to recognise a third country's data protection standards as providing an adequate level of protection, thereby facilitating transfers of personal data to that third country. It was envisaged that the European Commission will assess with respect to the United Kingdom as soon as

7 Political Declaration setting out the Framework for the Future Relationship Between the European Union and the United Kingdom – 25 November 2018.

possible after the United Kingdom's withdrawal, endeavouring to adopt decisions by the end of 2020, if the applicable conditions are met. The European Union recognised that the United Kingdom intends to establish its own international transfer regime, and will in the same timeframe take steps to ensure the comparable facilitation of transfers of personal data to the European Union, if the applicable conditions are met. It was further noted that the future relationship will not affect the parties' autonomy over their respective personal data protection rules.

The future of trade in goods between the parties

15.58 The political declaration envisages a future where the parties have a trading relationship on goods that is as close as possible, with a view to facilitating the ease of legitimate trade.[8] It was proposed that these arrangements will take account of the fact that following the United Kingdom's withdrawal from the European Union, the parties will form separate markets and distinct legal orders. There was specific concern in relation to the movement of goods, in particular, it was noted that the moving of goods across borders can pose risks to the integrity and proper functioning of these markets, which are managed through customs procedures and checks. However, with a view to facilitating the movement of goods across borders, the parties envisage comprehensive arrangements that will create a free trade area, combining deep regulatory and customs cooperation, underpinned by provisions ensuring a level playing field for open and fair competition.

15.59 Both parties, perhaps quixotically, intend that this economic partnership should ensure that there are no tariffs, fees, charges or quantitative restrictions across all sectors, with ambitious customs arrangements that build and improve on the single customs territory provided for in the Withdrawal Agreement which obviates the need for checks on rules of origin.

15.60 Whilst seeking to preserve regulatory autonomy, it is the intent of the parties to put in place provisions to promote regulatory approaches that are transparent, efficient, promote avoidance of unnecessary barriers to trade in goods and are compatible to the extent possible.

Technological solutions

15.61 It was also noted that the parties will seek to put in place ambitious customs arrangements, in pursuit of their overall objectives. In doing so, the parties envisage making use of all available facilitative arrangements and technologies, in full respect of their legal orders and ensuring that customs authorities are able to protect the parties' respective financial interests and enforce public policies.

15.62 To this end, they intend to consider mutual recognition of trusted traders' programmes, administrative cooperation in customs matters and mutual assistance, including for the recovery of claims related to taxes and duties, and through the exchange of information to combat customs fraud and other illegal activity. Such facilitative arrangements and technologies will also be considered in developing any alternative arrangements for ensuring the absence of a hard border on the island of Ireland on a permanent footing.

---

8 ibid.

Customs checks and controls

15.63 Of particular interest to corporate counsel will be the implications for customs checks and controls, given the central importance of the same to the corporate entities trade. The parties envisaged that the extent of the United Kingdom's commitments on customs and regulatory cooperation, including with regard to alignment of rules, would be taken into account in the application of related checks and controls, considering this as a factor in reducing risk.

15.64 Much of the above might be described as a wish to be as ambitious as possible in respect of customs provisions, while respecting the integrity of their respective markets and legal orders.

Services

15.65 The intention of both parties appears to be to conclude ambitious, comprehensive and balanced arrangements on trade in services and investment in services and non-services sectors, respecting each party's right to regulate. It is envisaged that these arrangements would cover all modes of supply and provide for the absence of substantially all discrimination in the covered sectors, with exceptions and limitations as appropriate. The arrangements will therefore almost certainly impact, at a minimum:

- professional and business services;
- telecommunications services;
- courier and postal services;
- distribution services;
- environmental services;
- financial services;
- transport services; and
- other services of mutual interest.

Of particular note was the parties' determination to ensure that the arrangements should allow for the temporary entry and stay of natural persons for business purposes in defined areas.

15.66 With regard to financial services, and perhaps mindful of the importance of the City of London, it is expected that both parties will have equivalence frameworks in place that allow them to declare a third country's regulatory and supervisory regimes equivalent for relevant purposes. It was suggested that the parties should start assessing equivalence with respect to each other under these frameworks as soon as possible after the United Kingdom's withdrawal from the European Union.

Intellectual property

15.67 It is intended that both parties will in due course provide for the protection and enforcement of intellectual property rights to stimulate innovation, creativity and economic activity, going beyond the standards of the WTO Agreement on Trade-Related Aspects of Intellectual Property Rights and the World Intellectual Property Organisation Conventions where relevant. This is in order to preserve the parties' current high levels of protection, inter alia, of certain rights under copyright law, such as the sui generis right on databases and the artists' resale right. It was noted that the parties should maintain the freedom to establish their own regimes for the exhaustion of intellectual property rights and that they should establish a mechanism for cooperation and exchange of information on intellectual property issues of mutual interest, such as respective approaches and processes regarding trademarks, designs and patents.

Miscellaneous matters

15.68 If further proof was ever required that geo-political events and their intersection with legal developments are of essential reading to counsel in all manner of enterprises, then it is present in abundance in the judgment of the UK Supreme Court in *R v The Prime Minister.*[9] In an extraordinary and unanimous ruling of the Court (comprised of 11 Justices) the court held that advice given by the Prime Minister to the Queen of England was unlawful:

> 'The logical approach … is to start at the beginning, with the advice that led to it [suspension of parliament]. That advice was unlawful. It was outside the powers of the Prime Minister to give it. This means that it was null and of no effect.'

15.69 Whilst this ruling could be considered in a narrow context of constitutional interpretation, its real value for readers of this text is its confirmation that the ordinary humdrum of mercantile endeavour with which we are largely engaged with on a daily basis, can, on occasion, be directly impacted upon by the ruling of a court on a matter of great constitutional technicality. Hence, surveillance of such geo-political and legal interfaces are of singular importance to corporate counsel in providing strategic advice.

9 *R (on the application of Miller) (Appellant) v The Prime Minister (Respondent) Cherry and others (Respondents) v Advocate General for Scotland (Appellant) (Scotland) On appeals from* [2019] EWHC 2381 (QB) and [2019] CSIH 49.

PART 5

REGARDING THE FUTURE OF THE BUSINESS

16 Future challenges and opportunities

'We are committed to help students build their futures'

Mr Jonathan Graham

EVP, General Counsel & Secretary

Amgen

Introduction

16.1 We have seen unparalleled legal innovation in the 20th century. The century opened to a rather sleepy, legally stagnate regime of laws, largely English in origin. War, political upheaval, existential threats and an emergence of the importance of personal rights intervened to upend the legal order. No longer does the law emanate from the two dimensional world of national legislatures and courts but rather legal actors all now inhabit multi-dimensional frameworks that have additional dimensions in the form of intergovernmental and supranational cooperation, international law, and an ever expanding rules and rights-based approach to international cooperation.

16.2 In seeking to cast one's gaze further afield to identify the issues that will have a bearing on legal thought as the 21st century continues, the authors have selected two topics to provide a brief sense of how the respective issues might emerge and how, from a legal perspective, they might be approached with key issues highlighted.

Space law

16.3

> 'I've been thinking about laws on Mars. There's an international treaty saying that no country can lay claim to anything that's not on Earth. By another treaty if you're not in any country's territory, maritime law applies. So Mars is international waters … Nobody explicitly gave me permission to do this, and they can't until I'm on board the Ares IV. So I'm going to be taking a craft over in international waters without permission, which by definition … makes me a pirate. Mark Watney: Space Pirate.'[1]

Whilst not seeking to address the merits of the protagonist's legal opinion on the question of jurisdictional disputes in space, Ridley Scott's production of Andy Weir's novel does draw a most interesting legal parallel between the early days of maritime commerce and the emergence of space as the next great frontier for mercantile interests and how a growing body of extra-terrestrial jurisprudence will become ever more relevant.

16.4 Indeed, the transition from space being the sole preserve of government agencies to one where private individuals and corporations are capable of financing and executing viable and profitable commercial projects has not gone unnoticed, notwithstanding the high degree of international oversight that is set out in the treaties. Goldman Sachs have identified significant potential in relation to launch capability, communications and exploration[2] while going on to suggest that 'investment interest has helped reduce launch costs and spur innovation across related industries, opening up a new chapter in the history of the space economy'.

16.5 Underpinning such commercial grasping for the stars will undoubtedly be a need for a clear understanding of the framework of space-related legislation on a global basis. A point not lost on the authors of a recent paper who considered the vast (and lucrative) opportunity of mining near-Earth asteroids from a legal/commercial perspective and noted the regulatory uncertainty attached to such endeavours.[3] The authors highlight the complexities related to proprietary claims to space-based resources and how property rights are central to the development of these resources. Commentary has suggested that future ventures will be underpinned by solutions drawn along parallels to existing terrestrial models.[4] Echoes of a maritime and colonial past abound!

16.6 The term 'space law' has been defined as:

> '… the rules, principles and standards of international law appearing in the five international treaties and five sets of principles governing outer space which have been developed under the auspices of the United Nations.'[5]

1 *The Martian* (20th Century Fox, 2015).
2 Noah Poponak, 'Space: The Next Investment Frontier' (Goldman Sachs, 3 May 2017) available at. https://www.goldmansachs.com/insights/podcasts/episodes/05-22-2017-noah-poponak.html.
3 Scot W Anderson, Korey Christensen and Julia LaManna, 'The development of natural resources in outer space' (2018) *Journal of Energy & Natural Resources Law*; DOI: 10.1080/02646811.2018.1507343.
4 Henry R Hertzfeld and Frans G von der Dunk, 'Bringing Space Law into the Commercial World: Property Rights Without Sovereignty' (2005) 6 *Chi J Int'l L* 81, 81–82.
5 United Nations Office for Outer Space Affairs, available at http://www.unoosa.org/oosa/en/ourwork/index.html.

What follows is a brief precis of the key documents and their essential purposes to assist with the commencement of discussions on this emerging issue for counsel.

What are the key documents?

16.7 Key documents underpinning the legal framework in space are:

- The 'Outer Space Treaty' – The Treaty on Principles Governing the Activities of States in the Exploration and Use of Outer Space, Including the Moon and Other Celestial Bodies, 27 January 1967, 18 UST 2410, 610 UNTS 205.
- The 'Moon Agreement' – Agreement Governing the Activities of States on the Moon and Other Celestial Bodies, 18 December 1979, 1363 UNTS 3.
- The 'Liability Convention' – Convention on International Liability for Damage Caused by Space Objects, 29 March 1972, 24 UST 2389, 961 UNTS 187.
- The 'Rescue Agreement' – Agreement on the Rescue of Astronauts, the Return of Astronauts and the Return of Objects Launched into Outer Space, 22 April 1968, 19 UST 7570, 672 UNTS 119.
- The 'Registration Convention' – Convention on Registration of Objects Launched into Outer Space, 14 January 1975, 28 UST 695, 1023 UNTS.

The Outer Space Treaty

What were the aims?

16.8 Concluded in the late 1960s and in the midst of the height of the space race, the parties to the Outer Space Treaty were inspired by the great prospects opening up before mankind as a result of man's entry into outer space, whilst recognising the common interest of all mankind in the progress of the exploration and use of outer space for peaceful purposes. The parties were clearly mindful of the potential inherent in such activities and noted that the exploration and use of outer space should be carried on for the benefit of all peoples irrespective of the degree of their economic or scientific development. Legal implications were to the fore from the outset as the parties noted their express desire to contribute to broad international cooperation in the scientific *as well as* the legal aspects of the exploration and use of outer space for peaceful purposes. It was the hope and belief of those nations that such cooperation would contribute to the development of mutual understanding and to the strengthening of friendly relations between states and peoples.[6]

Based upon the tenets of international law

16.9 Primarily, the exploration and use of outer space, including the Moon and other celestial bodies, shall be carried out for the benefit and in the interests of all countries, irrespective of their degree of economic or scientific development, and shall be the province of all mankind.[7] The treaty rejected nationalist or imperialistic notions in that it mandated that outer space, including the Moon and other celestial bodies, shall be free for exploration and use by all states without discrimination of any kind, on a basis of equality and in accordance with international law, and there shall

---

6 Preamble to The Treaty on Principles Governing the Activities of States in the Exploration and Use of Outer Space, Including the Moon and Other Celestial Bodies, 27 January 1967, 18 UST 2410, 610 UNTS 205.

7 ibid, Art 1.

be free access to all areas of celestial bodies.[8] Indeed, the treaty explicitly excluded sovereignty as a basis for exploration of space by means of use or occupation, or by any other means[9] declaring international law as key to 'maintaining international peace and security and promoting international co-operation and understanding'.[10] It was further set out that states who are parties to the Treaty shall bear international responsibility for national activities in outer space, including the Moon and other celestial bodies, whether such activities are carried on by governmental agencies or by non-governmental entities, and for assuring that national activities are carried out in conformity with the provisions set forth in the present Treaty.[11]

Potential liability

16.10 With regard to the question of liability for damage it was noted that each state party to the Treaty that launches or procures the launching of an object into outer space, including the Moon and other celestial bodies, and each state party from whose territory or facility an object is launched, is internationally liable for damage to another state party to the Treaty or to its natural or juridical persons by such object or its component parts on the Earth, in air or in outer space, including the Moon and other celestial bodies.[12]

Jurisdiction

16.11 A state party to the treaty on whose registry an object launched into outer space is carried shall retain jurisdiction and control over such object, and over any personnel thereof, while in outer space or on a celestial body. Ownership of objects launched into outer space, including objects landed or constructed on a celestial body, and of their component parts, is not affected by their presence in outer space or on a celestial body or by their return to the Earth.[13]

Responsible behaviour required

16.12 If a state party to the Treaty has reason to believe that an activity or experiment planned by it or its nationals in outer space, including the Moon and other celestial bodies, would cause potentially harmful interference with activities of other states parties in the peaceful exploration and use of outer space, including the Moon and other celestial bodies, it shall undertake appropriate international consultations before proceeding with any such activity or experiment.[14] Additionally, it was deemed necessary to explicitly state that parties should operate in a transparent way. Article 11 required that In order to promote international co-operation in the peaceful exploration and use of outer space, states parties to the Treaty conducting activities in outer space, including the Moon and other celestial bodies, agree to inform the Secretary-General of the United Nations as well as the public and the international scientific community, to the greatest extent feasible and practicable, of the nature, conduct, location and results of such activities. On receiving the said information, the Secretary-General of the United Nations should be prepared to disseminate it immediately and effectively.[15] It was further noted that all stations, installations,

8 ibid, Art 1.
9 ibid, Art 2
10 ibid, Art 3.
11 ibid, Art 6.
12 ibid, Art 7.
13 ibid, Art 8.
14 ibid, Art 9.
15 ibid, Art 11.

equipment and space vehicles on the Moon and other celestial bodies shall be open to representatives of other states parties to the Treaty on a basis of reciprocity.[16]

Parties to the Treaty and ratification

16.13 The UN maintains a Treaty status noting all parties and dates of ratification and this may be found at www.unoosa.org/documents/pdf/spacelaw/treatystatus/AC105_C2_2018_CRP03E.pdf.

The Moon Agreement

What were the aims?

16.14 Noting the achievements of states in the exploration and use of the Moon and other celestial bodies, and mindful that the Moon, as a natural satellite of the Earth, has an important role to play in the exploration of outer space, the states sought to set out certain key matters explicitly in relation to the Moon. The states were determined to promote on the basis of equality the further development of co-operation among states in the exploration and use of the Moon and other celestial bodies, whilst desiring to prevent the Moon from becoming an area of international conflict. The parties were mindful of the benefits which may be derived from the exploitation of the natural resources of the Moon and other celestial bodies even though the viability of exploitation of such resources was a way off. Nonetheless the parties understood the need to define and develop the provisions of international instruments in relation to the Moon and other celestial bodies, in order to further progress in the exploration and use of outer space.[17]

Extra-territorial reach

16.15 The eponymous agreement did however reach beyond our nearest neighbour, as the provisions of the Agreement relating to the Moon also apply to other celestial bodies within the solar system, other than the Earth, except in so far as specific legal norms enter into force with respect to any of these celestial bodies.[18]

The province of all mankind

16.16 Echoing the terms of the Outer Space Treaty, the Moon Agreement explicitly stated that the exploration and use of the Moon be the province of all mankind and be carried out for the benefit and in the interests of all countries, irrespective of their degree of economic or scientific development. Due regard shall be paid to the interests of present and future generations as well as to the need to promote higher standards of living and conditions of economic and social progress and development in accordance with the Charter of the United Nations.[19] Similar notification requirements as those present in the Outer Space Treaty were contained, and expanded upon in the Agreement.[20] Somewhat presciently, questions as to environmental integrity presented themselves to the contracting parties, placing environmental considerations to the fore. The Agreement required that parties be obliged to take measures to prevent the disruption of the existing balance of the environment whether by introducing adverse changes in that environment, by its harmful contamination through the introduction

16 ibid, Art 12.
17 ibid.
18 ibid, Art 1.
19 ibid, Art 4.
20 ibid, Art 5.

of extra-environmental matter or otherwise. States parties shall also take measures to avoid harmfully affecting the environment of the Earth through the introduction of extra-terrestrial matter or otherwise.[21]

Exclusion of claims of sovereignty

16.17 The Moon and its natural resources were established to be, unambiguously, the common heritage of mankind and not subject to national appropriation by any claim of sovereignty, by means of use or occupation, or by any other means.[22] The Agreement also contained an express prohibition on property rights pertaining to the Moon, as neither the surface nor the subsurface of the Moon, nor any part thereof or natural resources in place, shall become the property of any state, international intergovernmental or non-governmental organisation, national organisation or non-governmental entity or of any natural person.[23]

A basis in international law

16.18 The primacy of international law was restated with the Agreement noting parties have the right to exploration and use of the Moon without discrimination of any kind, on a basis of equality and in accordance with international law.[24]

A regime to allow for exploitation

16.19 Parties to the Agreement committed to establishing an international regime, including appropriate procedures, to govern the exploitation of the natural resources of the Moon noting that such exploitation is imminently feasible.[25] However, the parties were keen to point out that an equitable sharing by all states parties in the benefits derived from those resources, whereby the interests and needs of the developing countries, as well as the efforts of those countries which have contributed either directly or indirectly to the exploration of the Moon, shall be given special consideration.[26]

Jurisdiction

16.20 The parties committed to retain jurisdiction and control over their personnel, vehicles, equipment, facilities, stations and installations on the Moon. The ownership of space vehicles, equipment, facilities, stations and installations should not be affected by their presence on the Moon.[27]

Responsible behaviour required

16.21 Parties to this Agreement are required to bear international responsibility for national activities on the Moon, whether such activities are carried on by governmental agencies or by non-governmental entities. They must also ensure that national activities are carried out in conformity with the provisions set forth in the Agreement. Parties are similarly required to ensure that non-governmental entities

21 ibid, Art 7.
22 ibid, Art 11.
23 ibid, Art 11.3
24 ibid, Art 11.4.
25 ibid, Art 11.5
26 ibid, Art 11.7
27 ibid, Art 12.

under their jurisdiction shall engage in activities on the Moon only under the authority and continuing supervision of the appropriate state party.[28]

Parties to the Treaty and ratification

16.22 The UN maintains a treaty status noting all parties and dates of ratification and may be found at: www.unoosa.org/documents/pdf/spacelaw/treatystatus/AC105_C2_2018_CRP03E.pdf.

The Liability Convention

16.23 A concept always close to the hearts of legal professionals, the question of liability is not constrained by gravity and has similarly slipped the surly bonds of earth. It is of such importance that it merits its own Convention! It is worthwhile considering some of its provisions:

What were the aims?

16.24 Once again the central aim was clear and unambiguous. The parties recognised the need to create effective international rules and procedures concerning liability for damage caused by space objects and to ensure, in particular, the prompt payment under the terms of this Convention of a full and equitable measure of compensation to victims of such damage.[29] The parties noted that damage in this case would extend to that suffered by individual and natural persons.[30]

Absolute liability

16.25 The key statement is set out in Article 2 wherein it states that 'A launching State shall be absolutely liable to pay compensation for damage caused by its space object on the surface of the Earth or to aircraft flight.'[31] A launching state in this regard being simply a state from whose territory or facility a space object is launched.[32]

Fault-based liability

16.26 In the event of damage being caused elsewhere than on the surface of the Earth to a space object of one launching state or to persons or property on board such a space object by a space object of another launching state, the latter will be liable only if the damage is due to its fault or the fault of persons for whom it is responsible.[33] In the event of damage being caused elsewhere than on the surface of the Earth to a space object of one launching state or to persons or property on board such a space object by a space object of another launching state, and of damage thereby being caused to a third state or to its natural or juridical persons, the first two states shall be jointly and severally liable to the third state, to the extent indicated by the following:[34]

(a) If the damage has been caused to the third state on the surface of the Earth or to aircraft in flight, their liability to the third state shall be absolute;

28 ibid, Art 14.
29 Convention on International Liability for Damage Caused by Space Objects, 29 March 1972, 24 UST 2389, 961 UNTS 187.
30 ibid, Art 1.
31 ibid, Art 2.
32 ibid, Art 2.
33 ibid, Art 2.
34 ibid, Art 2.

(b) If the damage has been caused to a space object of the third state or to persons or property on board that space object elsewhere than on the surface of the Earth, their liability to the third state shall be based on the fault of either of the first two states or on the fault of persons for whom either is responsible.

Joint and several liability

16.27 Whenever two or more states jointly launch a space object, they shall be jointly and severally liable for any damage caused.[35] A launching state which has paid compensation for damage shall have the right to present a claim for indemnification to other participants in the joint launching. The participants in a joint launching may conclude agreements regarding the apportioning among themselves of the financial obligation in respect of which they are jointly and severally liable. Such agreements shall be without prejudice to the right of a state sustaining damage to seek the entire compensation due under this Convention from any or all of the launching states which are jointly and severally liable. Accordingly, a state from whose territory or facility a space object is launched shall be regarded as a participant in a joint launching.[36]

Exoneration from liability

16.28 Full exoneration from absolute liability shall be granted to the extent that a launching state establishes that the damage has resulted either wholly or partially from gross negligence or from an act or omission done with intent to cause damage on the part of a claimant state or of natural or juridical persons it represents.[37] However, no exoneration whatever shall be granted in cases where the damage has resulted from activities conducted by a launching state which are not in conformity with international law including, in particular, the Charter of the United Nations and the Treaty on Principles Governing the Activities of States in the Exploration and Use of Outer Space, including the Moon and Other Celestial Bodies.[38]

Generally

16.29 The above are a general statement of principles and further exposition is beyond the scope of this work. However, as space opens up to commercial endeavour, the apportionment of liability will be a key consideration in contracts governing such interactions given the cost matrix involved.

Parties to the Treaty and Ratification

16.30 The UN maintains a treaty status noting all parties and dates of ratification and may be found at: www.unoosa.org/documents/pdf/spacelaw/treatystatus/AC105_C2_2018_CRP03E.pdf.

The Rescue Agreement

16.31 As the name would suggest, this agreement sought to give certainty and protection to personnel and property involved.

35 ibid, Art 5.
36 ibid, Art 5.3.
37 ibid, Art 6.1.
38 ibid, Art 6.2.

Recovery from a contracting state

16.32 Generally, if, owing to accident, distress, emergency or unintended landing, the personnel of a spacecraft land in territory under the jurisdiction of a contracting party, it shall immediately take all possible steps to rescue them and render them all necessary assistance.[39]

Recovery from the high seas

16.33 If information is received or it is discovered that the personnel of a spacecraft have alighted on the high seas or in any other place not under the jurisdiction of any state, those contracting parties which are in a position to do so shall, if necessary, extend assistance in search and rescue operations for such personnel to assure their speedy rescue.[40]

Retention of title

16.34 Upon request of the launching authority, objects launched into outer space or their component parts found beyond the territorial limits of the launching authority shall be returned to or held at the disposal of representatives of the launching authority.[41]

Generally

16.35 Whilst conceived in a time when the protection of proprietary information and technology was a political imperative, these general principles retain value in a future where the protection of intellectual property will almost certainly be a strategic advantage.

Parties to the Treaty and Ratification

16.36 The UN maintains a Treaty status noting all parties and dates of ratification and this may be found at www.unoosa.org/documents/pdf/spacelaw/treatystatus/AC105_C2_2018_CRP03E.pdf.

The Registration Convention

16.37 Desiring that a central register of objects launched into outer space be established and maintained, on a mandatory basis, this Convention requires that when a space object is launched into Earth orbit or beyond, the launching state shall register the space object by means of an entry in an appropriate registry. Little more needs to be said in this regard for the purposes of this work. Further information can be found within the document.[42]

Governing principles

16.38 The UN have similarly adopted a range of principles set out across five UN declarations.

---

39 Agreement on the Rescue of Astronauts, the Return of Astronauts and the Return of Objects Launched into Outer Space, 22 April 1968, 19 UST 7570, 672 UNTS 119 – The Rescue Treaty, Art 2.

40 ibid, Art 3.

41 ibid, Art 5.

42 See https://treaties.un.org/doc/Treaties/1976/09/19760915%2003-08%20AM/Ch_XXIV_01p.pdf.

Declaration of legal principles[43]

16.39 Certain principles govern the activities of States in the Exploration and Uses of Outer Space including:

- The exploration and use of outer space shall be carried on for the benefit and in the interests of all mankind.
- Outer space and celestial bodies are free for exploration and use by all states on a basis of equality and in accordance with international law.
- Outer space and celestial bodies are not subject to national appropriation by claim of sovereignty, by means of use or occupation, or by any other means.
- The activities of states in the exploration and use of outer space shall be carried on in accordance with international law, including the Charter of the United Nations, in the interest of maintaining international peace and security and promoting international cooperation and understanding.
- States bear international responsibility for national activities in outer space, whether carried on by governmental agencies or by non-governmental entities, and for assuring that national activities are carried on in conformity with the principles set forth in the present Declaration. The activities of non-governmental entities in outer space shall require authorisation and continuing supervision by the State concerned. When activities are carried on in outer space by an international organisation, responsibility for compliance with the principles set forth in this Declaration shall be borne by the international organisation and by the states participating in it.
- In the exploration and use of outer space, states shall be guided by the principle of cooperation and mutual assistance and shall conduct all their activities in outer space with due regard for the corresponding interests of other states. If a state has reason to believe that an outer space activity or experiment planned by it or its nationals would cause potentially harmful interference with activities of other states in the peaceful exploration and use of outer space, it shall undertake appropriate international consultations before proceeding with any such activity or experiment. A state which has reason to believe that an outer space activity or experiment planned by another state would cause potentially harmful interference with activities in the peaceful exploration and use of outer space may request consultation concerning the activity or experiment.
- The state on whose registry an object launched into outer space is carried shall retain jurisdiction and control over such object, and any personnel thereon, while in outer space. Ownership of objects launched into outer space, and of their component parts, is not affected by their passage through outer space or by their return to the Earth. Such objects or component parts found beyond the limits of the state of registry shall be returned to that state, which shall furnish identifying data upon request prior to return.
- Each state which launches or procures the launching of an object into outer space, and each state from whose territory or facility an object is launched, is internationally liable for damage to a foreign state or to its natural or juridical persons by such object or its component parts on the Earth, in air space, or in outer space.
- States shall regard astronauts as envoys of mankind in outer space, and shall render to them all possible assistance in the event of accident, distress, or emergency

43 General Assembly resolution 1962 (XVIII) of 13 December 1963.

landing on the territory of a foreign state or on the high seas. Astronauts who make such a landing shall be safely and promptly returned to the state of registry of their space vehicle.

Broadcasting principles[44]

CERTAIN PRINCIPLES GOVERNING THE USE BY STATES OF ARTIFICIAL EARTH SATELLITES FOR INTERNATIONAL DIRECT TELEVISION BROADCASTING

16.40 It was clear to the parties that the establishment of principles for international direct television broadcasting will contribute to the strengthening of international cooperation in this field and further the purposes and principles of the Charter of the United Nations. The General principles are as follows:

- Activities in the field of international direct television broadcasting by satellite should be carried out in a manner compatible with the sovereign rights of states, including the principle of non-intervention, as well as with the right of everyone to seek, receive and impart information and ideas.
- Such activities should promote the free dissemination and mutual exchange of information and knowledge in cultural and scientific fields, assist in educational, social and economic development, particularly in the developing countries, enhance the quality of life of all peoples and provide recreation with due respect to the political and cultural integrity of states.
- Activities in the field of international direct television broadcasting by satellite should be conducted in accordance with international law.
- Every state has an equal right to conduct activities in the field of international direct television broadcasting by satellite and to authorise such activities by persons and entities under its jurisdiction. All states and peoples are entitled to and should enjoy the benefits from such activities. Access to the technology in this field should be available to all states without discrimination on terms mutually agreed by all concerned.
- Activities in the field of international direct television broadcasting by satellite should be based upon and encourage international cooperation. Such cooperation should be the subject of appropriate arrangements. Special consideration should be given to the needs of the developing countries in the use of international direct television broadcasting by satellite for the purpose of accelerating their national development.
- Any international dispute that may arise from activities covered by these principles should be settled through established procedures for the peaceful settlement of disputes agreed upon by the parties to the dispute.
- States should bear international responsibility for activities in the field of international direct television broadcasting by satellite carried out by them or under their jurisdiction.

44 General Assembly resolution 37/92 of 10 December 1982.

Remote sensing principles[45]

Governing the sensing of the earth from outer space

16.41 The parties believed a detailed consideration of the legal implications of remote sensing of the Earth from space was critical, a prescient thought when personal data has become commoditised and benefits from asymmetric protections globally. The following general principles were set out:

- The term 'primary data' means those raw data that are acquired by remote sensors borne by a space object and that are transmitted or delivered to the ground from space by telemetry in the form of electromagnetic signals, by photographic film, magnetic tape or any other means.
- Remote sensing activities shall be carried out for the benefit and in the interests of all countries, irrespective of their degree of economic, social or scientific and technological development, and taking into particular consideration the needs of the developing countries.
- Remote sensing activities shall be conducted in accordance with international law.
- These activities shall be conducted on the basis of respect for the principle of full and permanent sovereignty of all states and peoples over their own wealth and natural resources, with due regard to the rights and interests, in accordance with international law, of other states and entities under their jurisdiction. Such activities shall not be conducted in a manner detrimental to the legitimate rights and interests of the sensed state.
- States carrying out remote sensing activities shall promote international cooperation in these activities. To this end, they shall make available to other states opportunities for participation therein. Such participation shall be based in each case on equitable and mutually acceptable terms.
- In order to maximise the availability of benefits from remote sensing activities, states are encouraged, through agreements or other arrangements, to provide for the establishment and operation of data collecting and storage stations and processing and interpretation facilities, in particular within the framework of regional agreements or arrangements wherever feasible.
- States participating in remote sensing activities shall make available technical assistance to other interested states on mutually agreed terms.
- Remote sensing shall promote the protection of the Earth's natural environment. To this end, states participating in remote sensing activities that have identified information in their possession that is capable of averting any phenomenon harmful to the Earth's natural environment shall disclose such information to states concerned.
- As soon as the primary data and the processed data concerning the territory under its jurisdiction are produced, the sensed state shall have access to them on a non-discriminatory basis and on reasonable cost terms. The sensed state shall also have access to the available analysed information concerning the territory under its jurisdiction in the possession of any state participating in remote sensing activities on the same basis and terms, taking particularly into account the needs and interests of the developing countries.

45 General Assembly resolution 41/65 of 3 December 1986.

Nuclear power sources principles[46]

16.42 Governing the Use of Nuclear Power Sources in Outer Space. It was recognised that for some missions in outer space nuclear power sources are particularly suited or even essential owing to their compactness, long life and other attributes. However, it was equally recognised that there was a need, in this respect, for a set of principles containing goals and guidelines to ensure the safe use of nuclear power sources in outer space. Briefly:

- Activities involving the use of nuclear power sources in outer space shall be carried out in accordance with international law.
- In order to minimise the quantity of radioactive material in space and the risks involved, the use of nuclear power sources in outer space shall be restricted to those space missions which cannot be operated by non-nuclear energy sources in a reasonable way.
- States launching space objects with nuclear power sources on board shall endeavour to protect individuals, populations and the biosphere against radiological hazards. The design and use of space objects with nuclear power sources on board shall ensure, with a high degree of confidence, that the hazards, in foreseeable operational or accidental circumstances, are kept below acceptable levels.
- The reliability of systems important for safety shall be ensured, inter alia, by redundancy, physical separation, functional isolation and adequate independence of their components.

Benefits Declaration[47]

16.43 Setting out the International Cooperation in the Exploration and Use of Outer Space for the benefit and in the interest of all states, taking into particular account the needs of developing countries. Briefly:

- International cooperation in the exploration and use of outer space for peaceful purposes shall be conducted in accordance with the provisions of international law.
- It shall be carried out for the benefit and in the interest of all states, irrespective of their degree of economic, social or scientific and technological development, and shall be the province of all mankind. Particular account should be taken of the needs of developing countries.
- States are free to determine all aspects of their participation in international cooperation in the exploration and use of outer space on an equitable and mutually acceptable basis. Contractual terms in such cooperative ventures should be fair and reasonable and they should be in full compliance with the legitimate rights and interests of the parties concerned as, for example, with intellectual property rights.
- All states, particularly those with relevant space capabilities and with programmes for the exploration and use of outer space, should contribute to promoting and fostering international cooperation on an equitable and mutually acceptable basis. In this context, particular attention should be given to the benefit for and the interests of developing countries and countries with incipient space programmes

46 General Assembly resolution 47/68 of 14 December 1992.

47 General Assembly resolution 51/122 of 13 December 1996.

stemming from such international cooperation conducted with countries with more advanced space capabilities.

- International cooperation should be conducted in the modes that are considered most effective and appropriate by the countries concerned, including, inter alia, governmental and non-governmental; commercial and non-commercial; global, multilateral, regional or bilateral; and international cooperation among countries in all levels of development.

National law

16.44 A growing body of laws are developing globally on a state level and set out below are the EMEA jurisdictions that have significant legislative measures in place.

Country	Law	Link
Austria	Austrian Federal Law on the Authorisation of Space Activities and the Establishment of a National Space Registry (Austrian Outer Space Act, adopted by the National Council on 6 December 2011, entered into force on 28 December 2011)	www.unoosa.org/documents/pdf/spacelaw/national/austria/austrian-outer-space-actE.pdf
	Regulation of the Federal Minister for Transport, Innovation and Technology in Implementation of the Federal Law on the Authorisation of Space Activities and the Establishment of a National Space Registry (Outer Space Regulation BGBl. II No 36/2015)	www.unoosa.org/documents/pdf/spacelaw/national/austria/Austrian_Outer_Space_Regulation_German_original_BGBLA_2015_II_36E-unofficial-translation.pdf
Belgium	Law of 17 September 2005 on the Activities of Launching, Flight Operation or Guidance of Space Objects	www.belspo.be/belspo/space/doc/beLaw/Loi_en.pdf
Finland	Act on Space Activities (63/2018)	http://finlex.fi/en/laki/kaannokset/2018/en20180063.pdf
	Decree of the Ministry of Economic Affairs and Employment on Space Activities (74/2018)	http://finlex.fi/en/laki/kaannokset/2018/en20180074.pdf
France	Decree 62-153, Regulations Relating to the CNES	www.legifrance.gouv.fr/affichTexte.do?cidTexte=JORFTEXT000000299367&categorieLien=cid
	Law No 61-1382, 20 December 1961 Statute of the Centre National d'Etudes Spatiales (CNES)	www.legifrance.gouv.fr/affichTexte.do;jsessionid=CA3F95A6A00137FDA02C410E1EDAE268.tpdjo11v_2?cidTexte=JORFTEXT000000512451&dateTexte=19611220

Country	Law	Link
	Decree 89-508 & Decree 90-1102, concerning the Space Committee	www.legifrance.gouv.fr/affichTexte.do;jsessionid=79784140F80990AD5C3B4FEECB19033B.tpdjo12v_1?cidTexte=JORFTEXT000021533568&categorieLien=id
Germany	Law governing the transfer of responsibilities for space activities	www.unoosa.org/oosa/en/ourwork/spacelaw/nationalspacelaw/germany/raueg_1998G.html
	Act to give Protection against the Security Risk to the Federal Republic of Germany by the Dissemination of High-Grade Earth Remote Sensing Data	www.unoosa.org/documents/doc/spacelaw/national/germany-satdsigGE.doc
	Law governing the transfer of administrative functions in the sector of outer space activities	www.unoosa.org/documents/pdf/spacelaw/national/Germany_RAUeG_EN.pdf
	Satellite Data Security Act – Terminology	www.unoosa.org/documents/pdf/spacelaw/national/Germany_SatDSiG_Terminology.pdf
	Satellite Data Security Act	www.unoosa.org/documents/pdf/spacelaw/national/Germany_SatDSiG_CN.pdf
Kazakhstan	Law of the Republic of Kazakhstan on Space Activities (No.528-IV of 6 January 2012)	www.unoosa.org/documents/pdf/spacelaw/national/kazakhstan/528-IV_2012-01-06E.pdf
Netherlands	Rules Concerning Space Activities and the Establishment of a Registry of Space Objects (Space Activities Act)	www.unoosa.org/oosa/en/ourwork/spacelaw/nationalspacelaw/netherlands/space_activities_actE.html
	Decree of 13 November 2007, containing rules with regard to a registry of information concerning space objects (Space Objects Registry Decree)	www.unoosa.org/documents/doc/spacelaw/national/netherlands/decree-2007-11-13E.doc
	Order of the Minister of Economic Affairs dated 7 February 2008, No WJZ 7119929, containing rules governing licence applications for the performance of space activities and the registration of space objects	www.unoosa.org/documents/doc/spacelaw/national/netherlands/order-wjz7119929_2008_02_07E.doc

Country	Law	Link
	Form for registration of space objects (Annex 1 by article 4 of the 'Regeling aanvraag vergunning ruimtevaartactiviteiten en registratie')	www.unoosa.org/documents/doc/spacelaw/national/netherlands/soregistrationform2010E.doc
	Order of the Minister of Economic Affairs dated 16 April 2010, No WJZ/10020347, containing amendments to rules governing licence applications for the performance of space activities and the registration of space objects	www.unoosa.org/documents/doc/spacelaw/national/netherlands/wjz10020347_2010-04-16E.doc
	Decree of 19 January 2015 expanding the scope of the Space Activities Act to include the control of unguided satellites (Unguided Satellites Decree)	www.unoosa.org/documents/pdf/spacelaw/national/Netherlands_BZ116174A.pdf
	Order by the Minister of Economic Affairs of 26 June 2015, No WJZ/15055654, amending the Space Activities Licence Application and Registration Order, in connection with changes to the application form	www.unoosa.org/documents/pdf/spacelaw/national/Netherlands_BZ116174B.pdf
Norway	No 38, 13 June 1969, Act on Launching Objects from Norwegian Territory into Outer Space	www.unoosa.org/oosa/en/ourwork/spacelaw/nationalspacelaw/norway/act_38_1969E.html
Russian Federation	Decree 5663-1 About Space Activity	www.unoosa.org/oosa/en/ourwork/spacelaw/nationalspacelaw/russian_federation/decree_5663-1_E.html
	Presidential Edict No 185, About structure of management of space activity in Russian Federation (25 February 1992)	www.unoosa.org/oosa/en/ourwork/spacelaw/nationalspacelaw/russian_federation/edict_1992E.html
	Russian Presidential Edict No 2005: 'On the Organization of the Further Utilization of the Baikonur Cosmodrome in the Interests of the Russian Federation's Space Activity'	www.unoosa.org/oosa/en/ourwork/spacelaw/nationalspacelaw/russian_federation/edict_2005_1994E.html
	Russian Presidential Edict No 104 – Statute on Licensing Space Operations	www.unoosa.org/oosa/en/ourwork/spacelaw/nationalspacelaw/russian_federation/decree_104_1996E.html

Country	Law	Link
	Decree No 422, 'On Measures to Fulfil the Russian Federal Space Program and International Space Agreements'	www.unoosa.org/oosa/en/ourwork/spacelaw/nationalspacelaw/russian_federation/decree_422_1996E.html
	Resolution No 468, Regulations of the Russian Space Agency	www.unoosa.org/oosa/en/ourwork/spacelaw/nationalspacelaw/russian_federation/resolution_468_1995E.html
	Agreement between the Government of the Russian Federation and the Cabinet of Ministers of Ukraine on Technology Safeguards Associated with Cooperation in the Field of the Exploration and Use of Outer Space for Peaceful Purposes and in the Development and Operation of Space Rocket and Rocket Equipment	www.unoosa.org/documents/pdf/spacelaw/national/RF-ukraine-techsafeguardsE.pdf
South Africa	Statutes of the Republic of South Africa – Trade and Industry No 84 of 1993, Space Affairs Act, 1993	www.unoosa.org/oosa/en/ourwork/spacelaw/nationalspacelaw/south_africa/space_affairs_act_1993E.html
	Space Affairs Amendment Act1995	www.unoosa.org/oosa/en/ourwork/spacelaw/nationalspacelaw/south_africa/space_affairs_amendment_act_1995E.html
	No 36 of 2008: South African National Space Agency Act, 2008.	www.unoosa.org/documents/pdf/spacelaw/national/safrica/Act36-2008.pdf
	No 21 of 2007: Astronomy Geographic Advantage Act, 2007	www.unoosa.org/documents/pdf/spacelaw/national/safrica/Act21-2007E.pdf
	National Space Policy, 2008	www.unoosa.org/documents/pdf/spacelaw/national/safrica/nat-policyE.pdf
Spain	ROYAL DECREE 278/1995, dated 24 February 1995, establishing in the Kingdom of Spain of the Registry foreseen in the Convention adopted by the United Nations General Assembly on 2 November 1974	www.unoosa.org/oosa/en/ourwork/spacelaw/nationalspacelaw/spain/royal_decree_278_1995E.html

Country	Law	Link
Sweden	Act on Space Activities (1982:963)	www.unoosa.org/oosa/en/ourwork/spacelaw/nationalspacelaw/sweden/act_on_space_activities_1982E.html
	Decree on Space Activities (1982:1069)	www.unoosa.org/oosa/en/ourwork/spacelaw/nationalspacelaw/sweden/decree_on_space_activities_1982E.html
United Kingdom	Outer Space Act 1986	www.legislation.gov.uk/ukpga/1986/38/introduction

Luxembourg and proprietary rights in space

16.45 Luxembourg is one of the countries at the forefront of creating a regulatory regime favourable to establishing a commercial presence in space with the stated aim of reinforcing Luxembourg's role 'as a European hub for the exploration and use of space resources'.[48] Deputy Prime Minister, Minister of the Economy, Étienne Schneider said in 2017:

> 'Luxembourg is the first adopter in Europe of a legal and regulatory framework recognizing that space resources are capable of being owned by private companies. The Grand Duchy thus reinforces its position as a European hub for the exploration and use of space resources. The legal framework is part of the expertise ecosystem and the business-friendly, innovation-nurturing environment that Luxembourg is offering to space industry companies. By adopting almost unanimously the respective draft law, the Luxembourg Parliament confirmed the strong political cross-party and national commitment to the SpaceResources.lu initiative.'

The Grand Duchy has now created a framework that gives commercial entities rights in relation to resources that they extract in space.[49]

What is the outlook for the future?

16.46 It is clear that the private pursuit and utilisation of space-based resources is in its infancy. It is inevitable that as this commercial bridgehead into space expands so too will a plethora of support services develop and supply chains coalesce in tandem. As the traversing of seas and the exploitation of the resources of 'New World' of the 16th and 17th centuries necessitated a new legal underpinning for mercantile expansion, so too will space, the final frontier, require such similar underpinnings. While terrestrial models will undoubtedly inform, innovation and creativity will be required by global legislators.

48 'Luxembourg Is the First European Nation to Offer a Legal Framework for Space Resources Utilization' (Press Release, Luxembourg Ministry of the Economy, 13 July 2017).

49 Enacted 1 August 2017.

Climate change and the law

16.47

> 'There's one issue that will define the contours of this century more dramatically than any other, and that is the urgent and growing threat of a changing climate.'[50]

Introduction

16.48 A wide and growing body of legislation is emerging across EMEA that has at its core a desire to address climate change concerns. What follows is a brief discussion on a small number of EU legislative measures that are of particular relevance to corporate governance. It is submitted that the regulatory burden for corporate actors will inevitably expand in coming years in addition to the risks associated with climate change related litigation that companies and corporate counsel may face. Whilst this discussion is somewhat grounded in the abstract, a case study is set out in relation to what is required from a corporate governance perspective in the UK which may serve as a useful and informative analogue.

Renewable Energy Directive

16.49 The Renewable Energy Directive establishes an overall policy for the production and promotion of energy from renewable sources in the EU. It requires the EU to fulfil at least 20% of its total energy needs with renewables by 2020 – to be achieved through the attainment of individual national targets. All EU countries must also ensure that at least 10% of their transport fuels come from renewable sources by 2020.[51]

16.50 The Directive specifies national renewable energy targets for each country, taking into account its starting point and overall potential for renewables. These targets range from a low of 10% in Malta to a high of 49% in Sweden.[52]

Energy Efficiency Directive

16.51 The 2012 Energy Efficiency Directive establishes a set of binding measures to help the EU reach its 20% energy efficiency target by 2020. Under the Directive, all EU countries are required to use energy more efficiently at all stages of the energy chain, from production to final consumption.[53]

16.52 On 30 November 2016 the Commission proposed an update to the Energy Efficiency Directive, including a new 30% energy efficiency target for 2030, and measures to update the Directive to make sure the new target is met.[54]

---

50 President of the United States, Barack Obama's address to the United Nations, 23 September 2014.
51 https://ec.europa.eu/energy/en/topics/renewable-energy/renewable-energy-directive.
52 ibid.
53 https://ec.europa.eu/energy/en/topics/energy-efficiency/energy-efficiency-directive.
54 ibid.

Energy audits

16.53 An 'energy audit' means a systematic procedure with the purpose of obtaining adequate knowledge of the energy consumption profile of a building or group of buildings, an industrial or commercial operation or installation or a private or public service, identifying and quantifying cost-effective energy saving opportunities, and reporting the findings.[55]

16.54 Under Article 8(4) of the EED, the member states must ensure that large enterprises ('that are not SMEs') carry out regular energy audits. Article 8(4) does not exclude any sector (for example Emissions Trading Systems – ETS – sectors or Integrated Pollution Prevention and Control – IPPC – licence holders). To be able to ensure that large enterprises fulfil the obligations established in Article 8(4), member states have to identify the enterprises that fall under this obligation. Member states must follow the definition of the category of 'small and medium-sized enterprises' or 'SMEs'.[56] According to this definition, SMEs are 'enterprises' as defined,[57] the category of micro, small and medium-sized enterprises is made up of enterprises which employ fewer than 250 persons and which have an annual turnover not exceeding EUR 50 million, and/or an annual balance sheet total not exceeding EUR 43 million. This harmonised definition allows consistent requirements for companies operating in different EU member states.[58] It follows from the definition that the number of employees is the main criterion for determining whether an enterprise is an SME. The headcount is accompanied by a financial criterion, either turnover or balance sheet total. A SME does not need to satisfy both financial criteria.[59]

16.55 As recently as 2019, there was confirmation from the European Union that these efforts have been largely successful:

> 'The EU is on track to meet its 2020 renewable target, with eleven Member States already above their national targets. And as Europe heads to become the world's first major economy to go climate neutral by 2050, we will need to step up our efforts. In a climate-neutral Europe, power generation should be fully decarbonised by 2050, more than 80% of the EU's electricity will be produced by renewable energy sources. To get there, the momentum created by renewables for competitiveness, growth and jobs in Europe must continue.'[60]

It is clear that climate goals will form part of the ordering of the economic and social fabric of Europe in the decades ahead. Without doubt, these goals will translate, not only into an increasing regulatory burden for corporate actors, but will form a strategic pillar for any company doing business in the Union in the years to come.

---

55 Commission Staff Working Document: Guidance note on Directive 2012/27/EU on energy efficiency Commission Guidance /* SWD/2013/0447 final */.

56 See Art 2(26) of the Directive.

57 See Title I of the Annex to Commission Recommendation 2003/361/EC of 6 May 2003.

58 Commission Guidance note referred to above, clause 20.

59 ibid, Clause 22.

60 EU Climate Action and Energy Commissioner Miguel Arias Cañete, available at https://ec.europa.eu/info/news/europe-leads-global-clean-energy-transition-latest-eurostat-data-confirms-2019-feb-12_en.

Implementation

16.56 The transposition of the Directive into national law has been patchy and not entirely uniform. However, the European Union has produced guidance in relation to the implementation of the general principles surrounding the 'Energy Audit' which will assist companies in determining how such audits should proceed.[61]

Case study – UK

16.57 One of the key pieces of legislation in the UK that seeks to implement the various European directives on energy efficiency is what's known as the 'Energy Regulations'.[62] This regime may be seen as a useful analogue for how many of the European Union member states have implemented the directives, however caution should always be used in presupposing national legislative measures.

16.58 The Energy Regulations require that companies to whom the Regulations apply will need to prepare a Group Directors' Report that includes disclosures about energy usage and efficiency.

Explanation of the Regulation's requirements

16.59 The Energy Regulations amend certain provisions in the 'existing regulations'[63] which are a subset of the Companies Act 2006 with respect to the information about energy usage/performance that needs to be disclosed in the Directors' Report/Group Directors' Report:

- For quoted companies:[64] The Energy Regulations develop Part 7 of Schedule 7 of the existing Regulations.
- For unquoted companies: The Energy Regulations=s add a new Part ('Part 7A') to Schedule 7 of the existing Regulations requiring disclosure about greenhouse gas emissions, energy consumption and energy efficiency action.

The Energy Regulations also amend certain provisions in The Limited Liability Partnerships (Accounts and Audit) (Application of Companies Act 2006) Regulations 2008, which should be noted but go beyond the scope of this work.

What do you need to do?

16.60 In summary, Part 7 of the Energy Regulations requires that the Directors' Report must disclose the following information in relation to the reporting period:

- quantity of emissions in tonnes of $CO2$;
- quantity of energy consumed in kWh;
- measures taken in the period to increase energy efficiency.

61 See https://ec.europa.eu/energy/sites/ener/files/final_report_-_development_of_guidelines_and_recommendations_on_the_impl.pdf.

62 The Companies (Directors' Report) and Limited Liability Partnerships (Energy and Carbon Report) Regulations 2018, SI 2018/1155.

63 The Large and Medium-sized Companies and Groups (Accounts and Reports) Regulations 2008, SI 2008/410.

64 Companies Act 2006, s 385 defines a 'quoted company' as one whose equity shares have been admitted to an official list under the Financial Services and Markets Act 2000.

Are there exemptions?

16.61 These are set out in subsections 20A–20E of Part 7A. Some of the more relevant exemptions are as follows:

- A subsidiary (S) need not comply if its parent (P) prepares group accounts that include S, and P's Group Directors' Report complies with Part 7/7A.
- A company that meets the definition of 'medium-sized'[65] (ie, turnover of less that £36m; balance sheet total of £18m, employees numbering less than 250) for the current and previous reporting year need not comply.

When do we need to do it?

16.62 The Energy Regulations will come into force in the UK on 1 April 2019 and shall apply to financial years beginning after 31 March 2019.

Conclusions

16.63 Such reordering of strategic considerations as are inevitable by the growth of climate change related legislation will assuredly give rise to a range of collateral concerns for corporate counsel over and above simple regulatory concerns. It has been stated that claims for failing to mitigate impacts of climate change under public and private nuisance, negligence, failure to warn, trespass and unjust enrichment laws will emerge in greater number as will claims for failing to adapt to the impacts of climate change. Company directors and trustees who have duties to act in the best interests of their company or members, must adapt their business strategies to take into account the risks of climate change. [66] Interestingly, the author suggests that claims will also arise for failure to disclose climate-related risks to shareholders. It is submitted that this opinion has significant merit and the placing of climate considerations at the centre of corporate governance concerns appears inevitable.

65 Companies Act 2006, s 465.

66 The legal perspective: Climate change's influence on future business ventures – keynote address at the European Refining and Technology Conference, on 28 November 2018 by Alice Garton.

PART 6

REGARDING ANY OTHER BUSINESS

17 Primer in trusts

Introduction

17.1 Become familiar with a most peculiar creature, I was once told. Trusts are one of the great curiosities of the legal world. Sometimes mercurial and illusive, they frequently appear in corporate life, oftentimes with associated complexity and opacity. Whilst once a vehicle of choice for many transaction and ownership structures in the common law world, the use of trusts is coming under increasing regulatory scrutiny across the EMEA region in the wake of a number of financial scandals. Trusts appear to enjoy varying levels of institutional *distrust* across Europe in particular and regulatory surveillance of such devices shall inexorably increase.[1] Whilst historically considered of dubious character in the civil law jurisdiction, trusts nevertheless retain relevance across the EMEA region and their use attracts a range of treatments. This chapter will set out basic common principles relating to trusts, and the role and duties of their trustees – the genesis of which can be traced to the UK being the spiritual home of this peculiar creature of the law. It should be said that what follows is not a specific analysis of trust law in any particular jurisdiction but rather a synthesis of general principles and common themes.

What is a trust?

17.2 Numerous academic commentators and members of the judiciary have attempted to define the term 'trust' with varying degrees of success. The most concise definition is suggested by Keeton and Sheridan in *The Law of Trusts*:[2]

> 'A trust is the relationship which arises whenever a person (called the trustee) is compelled in equity to hold property, whether real or personal, and whether by legal or equitable title, for the benefit of some persons (of

---

1 *Financial Times*, 27 February 2017.

2 12th edn (Southampton, Barry Rose Law Publishers Ltd, 1993) 3.

whom he may be one and who are termed beneficiaries) or for some object permitted by law, in such a way that the real benefit accrues, not to the trustee, but to the beneficiaries or other objects of the trust.'

How are trusts different to other concepts?

17.3 It is important that trusts be distinguished from other legal concepts that resemble trusts. The reason for such segregation is threefold: first, to compare the different legal consequences of a trust and the related legal concepts; secondly, to identify the circumstances in which one concept must exist to the exclusion of the other; and thirdly, to identify the circumstances in which a trust may co-exist with any related concept.

What is bailment?

17.4 This is a common law relationship that allows for the delivery of goods upon a condition that they be returned when the purpose of the bailment has been carried out, for example if you take your car into a garage for a service. There are a number of distinctions between a trust and a bailment:

- Bailment derives from common law; trusts are creatures of equity.
- Bailment only applies to personal chattels; trusts apply to any type of property.
- A bailor can vary or enforce a bailment; a settlor cannot without a reserved power to do so.
- A bailor cannot dispose of title; a settlor may transfer the title of goods.

What is agency?

17.5 There are a number of similarities between the relationship of trustee and beneficiary and principal and agent, in that both trustees and agents have fiduciary obligations and are forbidden from acting for their own benefit. Agency can be distinguished from a trust on a variety of levels:

- The trust relationship is proprietary in nature, agency is personal.
- Agency is usually terminated by death, a trust is not.
- There must exist some form of agreement between principal and agent; this is not required between a trustee and beneficiary.
- An agent can expose his principal to liability, unlike a trustee.
- A trustee must only carry out the terms of the trust and is not bound to follow a beneficiary's instructions; an agent must adhere to their principal's wishes.
- Unlike a trustee, an agent does not have title to goods in their possession.

How are contracts different?

17.6 Contracts and trusts are fundamentally different concepts. A trust is an equitable proprietary relationship, which can arise independently of agreement; a contract can be described as a personal obligation resulting from agreement between the parties.

- Generally a contract cannot be enforced by a third party; however, a beneficiary is always entitled to enforce a trust even though he is not a party to the agreement that created the trust.
- Generally, a beneficiary under a trust can enforce it in the absence of any consideration given. On the other hand, a contract is only enforceable if supported by consideration.

What powers does a trust convey?

17.7 A power is an authority which is vested in a particular person that allows him to deal with or dispose of property that he does not have ownership of. While trusts are of an imperative nature, powers are discretionary. Powers may be legal but trusts are always equitable.

What about wills and intestacy?

17.8 A personal representative realises and distributes the assets of an estate. The relationship between a personal representative and a beneficiary under a will is similar to the relationship that exists between trustee and beneficiary. Both personal representatives and trustees are subject to fiduciary duties in the performance of their functions.

What kind of trusts are there?

17.9 It is possible to classify trusts in a number of ways; for example, by virtue of their objects (beneficiaries) or how they were created. There is no universal agreement as to the proper classification of trusts; however, the following categorisations reflect the conventional understanding:

What is an express trust?

17.10 This is created by an express declaration of the testator or settlor either by an instrument *inter vivos* (during the life of a person) or by will. All express trusts must observe certain formalities and contain a number of essential elements, which are known as 'the three certainties'.

What is a constructive trust?

17.11 A constructive trust is a type of trust that is imposed by the court and comes into being irrespective of the subjective intentions of the parties involved. The historical basis for this type of trust was to prevent fraud, but more recently it has been utilised whenever justice and good conscience require it.

What is a resulting trust?

17.12 The resulting trust, or implied trust as it is sometimes known, arises from the presumed but unexpressed intention of the testator or settlor. Resulting trusts are divided into two categories:

- Automatic resulting trusts – where an express trust fails for some reason, the property will result back to the settlor or estate.
- Presumed intention resulting trust – occurs as a result of an inference drawn by the court having regard to the donor's intentions.

What are simple and special trusts?

17.13 This classification of trusts differentiates between the nature of the duties that are imposed upon the trustees. A simple or bare trust does not impose any duties on the trustees even though property is vested in the trustees. Under a special trust, a trustee is obligated to carry out duties imposed on him by the testator or settlor and therefore to take a more active role in the administration of the trust.

What are discretionary and fixed trusts?

17.14 A discretionary trust empowers the trustee with a degree of discretion in deciding which beneficiaries should be entitled to the trust property. In a fixed trust each of the beneficiaries has a fixed entitlement to a specified share in the trust property.

What are protective trusts?

17.15 The essence of this type of trust is to prevent beneficiaries from disposing of any or all of the beneficial interest as long as the trust is in existence.

What are purpose trusts?

17.16 These trusts are for the benefit of purposes rather than for beneficiaries and as a general rule are invalid. Private purpose trusts are sometimes termed 'trusts of imperfect obligation' because the trustees are not strictly obliged to carry out the terms of the trust.

What formalities are required to create a trust?

17.17 Generally, the law has always erred on the side of formality, equity has generally taken a more informal approach and this applies to the creation of trusts. However, statute has intervened in certain circumstances, such as where an express trust is created in respect of land which, in some jurisdictions, requires a note or memorandum in writing.

What are the essential elements of a trust?

17.18 Aside from complying with the formalities outlined above, it is not necessary to utilise a precise formula in the creation of a valid express trust. However, certain elements, which have come to be known as 'the three certainties', must be present for a valid express trust to exist. These are:

(i) certainty of intention;

(ii) certainty of subject matter; and

(iii) certainty of objects.

Certainty of intention

17.19 There exists no formula of words to demonstrate intention to create a trust, not even the word 'trust' is required. With regard to certainty of intention, a distinction is drawn between imperative and precatory words. Imperative words place a trust obligation on the donee, precatory words do not. Precatory words are words merely of hope and desire, for example, 'in hope that'.

Certainty of subject matter

17.20 It is imperative that the property which is the subject matter of the trust and the beneficial interest of each beneficiary in that property be of sufficient certainty. Of course, it is an altogether different matter when the trustees are given discretion in this regard.

Certainty of objects

17.21 It is important that the objects or beneficiaries of a trust be identified with sufficient clarity as to enable the trustees and, if necessary, the court, to properly administer the trust, having regard to the settlor's intentions. Generally, in order to be valid, a trust must be one which the court can ultimately control and execute.

Fixed trusts

17.22 In order for a fixed trust to be valid, all beneficiaries must be clearly identified in the trust instrument. This requirement gives rise to the 'complete list test', otherwise known as the class ascertainable rule. This test requires the trustees to be in a position to compile a complete list of all the beneficiaries.

Discretionary trusts

17.23 A discretionary trust obligates trustees to distribute trust property to the beneficiaries, but they have discretion in the selection of beneficiaries.

17.24 It is important to note that the test is whether it can be said with certainty of any potential claimant that he is or is not a member of the class.

Administrative unworkability

17.25 It has been suggested that a trust may fail for uncertainty where the class of beneficiaries is so hopelessly wide as to not form anything like a class.[3]

Conceptual and evidential uncertainty

17.26 This denotes that a trust may fail in circumstances where the description used to define a class of beneficiaries is conceptually uncertain. It requires that a mechanism exist whereby it is possible to say with certainty whether any party is or is not a member of a class under the trust.

---

3 *McPhail v Doulton* [1971] AC 424. United Kingdom Decision.

How are trusts constituted?

17.27 Completely constituted trusts are those in which the trust property is vested in the trustees for the benefit of the beneficiaries; a trust remains incompletely constituted until the property is vested. A completely constituted trust is binding on the settlor and unless an express power exists to do so, cannot be revoked. It is important at this stage to note that while a completely constituted trust will be enforced even at the suit of a volunteer, the courts will not enforce an incompletely constituted trust. A beneficiary can be described as a volunteer if he has not provided valuable consideration as understood at common law.

Equity will not assist a volunteer to perfect an imperfect gift

Is a transfer of trust property required?

17.28 For a trust to be completely constituted there has to be an effective transfer of property rather than a mere intention to transfer the property and in order to ensure that a trust is completely constituted, the settlor must have done everything in his power to effect the transfer.

What about where the trust is declared by the settlor?

17.29 It is possible for a settlor to declare himself to be a trustee of his own property for the benefit of third parties. However, the court will usually require an irrevocable declaration of trusts to be made, which is a manifestation of the settlor's intentions.

Resulting trusts

What are the characteristics of resulting trusts?

17.30 A resulting trust is a type of implied trust that arises automatically by operation of the law. It is applied in situations in which the transferee is required by equity to hold property on trust for the transferor. In effect, the resulting trust arises to plug a gap in the beneficial ownership of property when the intention of the owner is unclear.

Can resulting trusts occur automatically?

17.31 An automatically resulting trust is one that arises when property is transferred to another on trust but some of the beneficial interest is not disposed of. It is characterised as a default mechanism that historically was viewed as having nothing to do with the intention of the parties. Such a trust will automatically arise in the following circumstances:

What happens when a trust fails?

17.32 In the situation where an express trust fails entirely for whatever reason, a resulting trust will arise for the purpose of holding trust property in favour of the settlor or his estate.

Failure to exhaust beneficial interest

17.33 There exists a possibility that circumstances will occur which have the effect of preventing the complete disposal of the beneficial interest under the trust.

What is a Quistclose trust?

17.34 A useful summary of the circumstances that give rise to a Quistclose trust was given by Lord Millett in *Twinsectra Ltd v Yardley*:[4]

> 'Such arrangements are commonly described as creating a Quistclose trust … When the money is advanced, the lender acquires a right, enforceable in equity, to see that it is applied for the stated purpose, or more accurately to prevent its application for any other purpose. This prevents the borrower from obtaining any beneficial interest in the money, at least while the designated purpose is still capable of being carried out.'

17.35 In *Barclays Bank Ltd v Quistclose Investments Ltd*,[5] a company, R, arranged to borrow monies from a lender 'on condition that it is used to pay the forthcoming dividend' that was due. The bank confirmed that the money 'will only be used for the purpose of paying the dividend'. The House of Lords ruled that in such circumstances, a trust was created of which the bank had notice and upon the failure to pay the dividend, the monies were repayable to the lender.

17.36 Evans-Lombe J commented in *Copper v PRG Powerhouse Ltd*,[6] that whether or not money has been paid subject to a purpose trust is a question of fact. He stated that '[i]f a purpose trust is be established, it is necessary for the payer to show that the arrangement pursuant to which the payment was made defined the purpose for which it was made in such a way that it was understood by the recipient that it was not at his free disposal'.

What is a presumed resulting trust?

17.37 A presumed resulting trust, or purchase money trust as it is also known, arises where property is transferred to a third party who gives no consideration and an inference arises that the third party holds the property on trust for the grantor.

How to rebut the presumption of a resulting trust

17.38 The presumption of resulting trust may be rebutted in the following circumstances:

Where there is illegality or fraud

17.39 *Symes v Hughes*[7] is authority for the proposition that a resulting trust will not arise in circumstances where the trust was created for an illegal purpose. In *Ayerst v Jenkins*,[8] Lord Selborne refused to grant the relief sought on the basis that the presumption of a resulting trust could be rebutted by evidence of the plaintiff's own illegality unless the result would be 'to effectuate an unlawful object or to defeat a legal prohibition or to protect a fraud'.

---

4 [2002] 2 AC 164 at 184.
5 [1970] AC 567.
6 [2008] EWHC 498 (Ch).
7 (1870) LR 9 Eq 475.
8 (1873) LR 16 Eq 275.

17.40 In the important decision of the House of Lords in *Tinsley v Milligan*,[9] Lord Browne-Wilkinson stated that illegality can render a proprietary interest unenforceable in certain circumstances, but only where it is necessary for the claimant to rely on the illegality in order to prove that an interest exists.

17.41 In *Lowson v Coombes*,[10] the Court of Appeal held that the claimant was entitled to a beneficial interest in the trust, in circumstances where the trust had been created for an illegal purpose, but it was not necessary to rely on the illegality in order to establish his claim.

Where there is intention to benefit the transferee

17.42 Where evidence can establish that it was the transferor's intention to benefit the transferee, no resulting trust will arise. This principle is best illustrated by the case of *Standing v Bowring*,[11] where the Court of Appeal held that where there is ample evidence to demonstrate that the transferor, at the time of the transaction, intended to benefit the transferee, no resulting trust will arise.

17.43 In the recent decision from the British Columbia Court of Appeal in *Romaine Estate v Romaine*,[12] Levine J.A. stated that 'all of the evidence of the donor's intention, written or oral, at the time a transfer that is claimed to be a gift was made, is admissible to determine whether the transfer was a gift'.

Constructive trusts

What are the characteristics of a constructive trust?

17.44 A constructive trust arises by the operation of law, and not as a result of either the express or implied intention of the parties to the trust. It is a trust that operates in equity to prevent a person from deriving profit from fraudulent conduct or by taking an unfair benefit of a fiduciary position.

17.45 A UK decision by Edmund Davies LJ in *Carl Zeiss Stiftung v Herbert Smith & Co (No 2)*[13] was of the view that:

> '... a constructive trust is a trust which is imposed by equity in order to satisfy the demands of justice and good conscience without reference to any express or presumed intention of the parties.'

17.46 However, he qualified this definition by stating that:

> 'English law provides no clear and all-embracing definition of a constructive trust. Its boundaries have been left perhaps deliberately vague, so as not to restrict the court by technicalities in deciding what the justice of a particular case may demand.'

9 [1994] 1 AC 340.
10 [1999] Ch 373.
11 (1886) 31 Ch D 282.
12 (2001) 205 DLR (4th) 320 at 335.
13 [1969] 2 Ch 276 at 300.

17.47 Constructive trusts have often been seen as trusts that arise when fairness demands it. However, it is important to note that it was held by the court in *Lonrho Plc v Fayed (No 2)*[14] that the imposition of such trusts 'must be based on principle; there must be some relationship between the relief granted and the circumstances which gave rise to it'.

What is a new model constructive trust?

17.48 The new model constructive trust was instituted by Lord Denning in the House of Lords decision in *Hussey v Palmer*,[15] where he stated that equity would impose a constructive trust 'whenever justice and good conscience requires it'. Such trusts have been subsequently recognised in a number of jurisdictions.[16]

Is the trust void and/or voidable?

17.49 A perfectly valid private trust may not be upheld in circumstances where it is held to be contrary to public policy, or in fact illegal. Trusts that are contrary to public policy or illegal are generally void *ab initio*, in that they are deemed to have never come into effect. On the other hand, trusts that are merely voidable will remain in force until such time as their validity is undermined.

17.50 It is important to distinguish between conditions precedent and conditions subsequent as it more often than not relates to the condition of validity of a trust. A condition precedent will prevent a trust from coming into existence until a specified condition is satisfied. A condition subsequent does not prevent the trust from coming into force, but may render it liable to divestment if a specified act occurs.

17.51 It is noteworthy that where real property is held on trust subject to a condition precedent, the trust will fail in its entirety if the condition is held to be void. Unlike a void trust, a trust that is voidable remains in being until a court sets it aside. Trust may be voidable in a number of ways, including fraud, misrepresentation, mistake, undue influence and duress. We are concerned with the statutory intervention which has proscribed for certain trusts to be set aside.

How are trusts administered?

What does the office of trustee entail?

17.52 The following concerns the nature of trustee's duties, powers and liabilities. The office of trustee is said to be burdensome in nature and in the performance of his office, a trustee must act wholly in the interest of the trust. Generally, the trustee stands to gain nothing from the trust, unless an express provision exists in the trust authorising remuneration. He is under an obligation to act with the highest standards of integrity and can be subjected to personal liability if that standard is not met. Generally, there is no minimum number of trustees required, except where statute requires otherwise. For practical reasons it is typically preferable to appoint at least two. Furthermore, there is generally no upper limit on the number of trustees.

14 [1992] 1 WLR 1 at 9.
15 [1972] 1 WLR 1286 at 1290.
16 Irish decision of Barr J in *Kelly v Cahill* [2001] 1 IR 56 at 62.

How are trustees appointed?

17.53 The appointment of trustees may occur in a number of ways:

- A settlor may appoint a trustee when the trust is being created.
- The power to appoint a trustee may be contained within the trust instrument.
- By statutory authority.

How are trustees removed?

17.54 Trustees can be removed in a number of ways:

- Where there is express provision in the trust instrument.
- Where full valid consent of all of the beneficiaries, who are of full age, is obtained.
- Where a court of competent jurisdiction removes trustees where they act incompetently or dishonestly.

Can a trustee retire?

17.55 A person cannot be compelled to take up the office of trustee; however, if the appointment is accepted or not disclaimed within a reasonable period of time, the circumstances in which a trustee may retire are limited and are as follows:

- A trustee may retire on foot of an express provision in the trust instrument providing for it.
- Where there is agreement between all of the beneficiaries.

What are the duties of trustees?

17.56 Upon appointment, trustees must ensure that they become acquainted with the terms of the trust and check the status of the trust property, that is, has the trust fund been invested in accordance with the provision of the trust instrument? Kekewich J in *Hallows v Lloyd*[17] stated that:

> 'This raises the important question, what are the duties of persons becoming new trustees of a settlement? … I think that when persons are asked to become new trustees, they are bound to enquire of what the property consists that is proposed to be handed over to them, and what are the trusts. They ought also to look into the trust documents and papers to ascertain what notices appear among them of encumbrances and other matters affecting the trust.'

17.57 The duties of a trustee are extremely onerous and have to be carried out with the utmost diligence. If it is found that a trustee has failed to act in a responsible and reasonable manner, then they may be held personally liable for breach of trust. Paramount to the trustee's functions is the fiduciary duty that is imposed by equity. This duty places the trustee under a strict obligation to carry out the function of the

17 (1888) 39 Ch D 686.

trust with the utmost good faith. There are a number of specific duties that a trustee must consider in carrying out the office of trustee, as follows.

Are there restrictions on investment?

17.58 Unless the trust instrument contains an express investment clause, the duty to invest will be typically regulated by legislation and will usually prescribe permitted investment vehicles, for example sate securities, securities of semi-state bodies, securities of financial institutions or other companies which are listed on a recognised stock exchange.

17.59 In *Re Harari's Settlement Trusts*,[18] Jenkins J was of the opinion that trustees can invest trust property 'in or upon such investments as to them may seem fit'. It seems therefore, that trustees have the authority to invest in whatever manner they wish, providing they honestly believe that such investment is desirable.

17.60 It is important to note that even when a trustee stays within the authorised list of investment, either under the trust instrument itself or by statute, he must exercise the utmost prudence.

17.61 The standard of care and prudence that is expected of a trustee was considered by Lindley LJ in *Learoyd v Whiteley*,[19] where he held that in addition to acting in a reasonable manner as would be expected from the prudent man investing on his own behalf, the trustee was obligated to take account of those for whom he was morally bound to provide.

17.62 A more flexible approach to the standard of care was adopted in the case of *Bartlett v Barclays Bank Trust Ltd*,[20] where Brightman J stated:

> 'The cases establish that it is the duty of a trustee to conduct the business of the trust with the same care as an ordinary prudent man of business would extend towards his own affairs … That does not mean that the trustee is bound to avoid all risk and in effect act as insurer of the trust fund.'

17.63 Hoffmann J in *Nestle v National Westminster Bank Plc*[21] admitted that 'trustees must act fairly in making investment decisions …'.

17.64 It should be noted that trustees may pursue an ethical investment policy provided that such investments were not financially disadvantageous to the beneficiaries. The question of ethical investment is most relevant to trusts that are charitable in nature. In *Harries v Church Commissioners*,[22] Nicholls VC understood that the law will not require a trustee to make an investment that would bring the charity into disrepute; however, an element of prudence must be maintained so as not to make moral statements at the expense of the beneficiaries.

---

18 [1949] 1 All ER 430.
19 (1886) 33 Ch D 347.
20 [1980] Ch 515 at 531.
21 [1993] 1 WLR 1260.
22 [1993] 2 All ER 300.

May a trustee make a profit?

17.65 It is a well-established principle that a trustee may not profit from his position unless provision is expressly made for same in the trust instrument. This principle is to prevent the trustee from making any secret profit from the trust or any financial benefit that is not authorised by the trust instrument.

17.66 Subject to narrow exception a trustee is prohibited from purchasing any property belonging to the trust, as he would effectively be vendor and purchaser. 'Self-dealing' as it is commonly known is voidable at the instance of any beneficiary, however fair and reasonable the transaction.

Must a trustee keep accounts and provide information?

17.67 Trustees are under an obligation to keep accurate accounts of the trust property, with the beneficiaries having a right to inspect such accounts.

Is there a duty on trustees to distribute property?

17.68 Trustees are under an obligation to properly distribute the trust property as per the trust instrument. The identity of all beneficiaries must be ascertained prior to distribution as any beneficiary who receives no money or is underpaid as a result of the failure of the trustee to identify them has a right of action against that trustee. Usually, an application to court for directions can be made where trustees are in any doubt in relation to the claims of beneficiaries and they will be protected from liability if they follow the court's direction.

17.69 In circumstances where it is unknown whether a beneficiary is alive, or his whereabouts are unknown, the court can typically authorise distribution after a certain period of time. This procedure is commonly known as a 'Benjamin Order' and can be granted after a period of seven years has elapsed after the last contact with the beneficiary.[23]

Can a trustee delegate authority?

17.70 The principle of non-delegation prevents trustees from transferring their duties under the trust to third parties. The office of trustee is one which cannot be delegated to another as it is personal to the person who was appointed under the trust. That said, the trust instrument may specifically provide for delegation. It was stated by Lord Langdale MR in *Turner v Corney*,[24] that 'trustees who take on themselves the management of property for the benefit of others have no right to shift their duty on other persons'.

17.71 It is of course possible for a trustee to delegate certain functions to professional advisers, such as solicitors and accountants. However, such delegation is on the proviso that the trustee exercises a reasonable degree of supervision over the third party.

23 *In Re Benjamin* [1902] 1 Ch 723.
24 (1841) 5 Beav 515 at 517.

What are the powers of trustees?

17.72 Trustees may exercise such powers as are bestowed upon them by the trust instrument or by legislation. A power can be distinguished from duty, in that it is discretionary and not compulsory.

May a trustee sell property?

17.73 Trustees have no inherent power to sell trust property. The power must come from:

- the trust instrument;
- statute; or
- court order.

What about maintenance and advancement?

17.74 Trusts commonly make provision for the maintenance of infants through the income generated by trust property. The trustee's power to do this may arise from the trust instrument or statute. Advancement, on the other hand, relates to the possibility of the trustees permitting part of the trust capital to be paid or used for the benefit of a beneficiary prior to his interest becoming vested.

What other powers does a trustee have?

17.75 Typical powers are as follows:

- Power to renew leases.
- Power to issue receipts.
- Power to compound liabilities.
- Power to delegate.
- Power to apply to court to resolve disputes.

What liability do trustees face?

17.76 A trustee is both liable for his acts of omission and acts of commission. In circumstances where a trustee fails to exercise the required degree of supervision of the trust, he may be liable to make good the losses that the trust has suffered, once the beneficiaries can establish breach of trust. Further, a trustee may be called to account for any profit that he has made as a result of the breach.

17.77 Generally, trustees are only liable for their own breaches and not those of co-trustees. However, a failure to intervene to prevent known breaches of the trustee by co-trustees may attract liability.

17.78 Where an authorised investment is improperly disposed of, the measure of the trustee's liability will be the costs of repurchase of the investment at the current market rate.

17.79 It should be noted that where a trustee has committed a breach of trust, it is a defence if the said breach was instigated by, participated in or consented to by the beneficiaries (see *Re Pauling's Settlement Trusts*[25]).

International recognition of trusts

17.80 Considering that the trust, as developed in courts of equity in common law jurisdictions and adopted with some modifications in other jurisdictions, is a unique legal institution, and desiring to establish common provisions on the law applicable to trusts and to deal with the most important issues concerning the recognition of trusts, 17 countries concluded a Convention to this effect in 1985.

17.81 The current contracting nations are:

- Australia
- Canada
- People's Republic of China
- Cyprus
- France
- Italy
- Liechtenstein
- Malta
- Monaco
- Netherlands
- Panama
- San Marino
- Switzerland
- United Kingdom
- United States of America

17.82 The Convention specifies the law applicable to trusts and governs their recognition and defined 'trust' as referring to the legal relationships created – *inter vivos* or on death – by a person, the settlor, when assets have been placed under the control of a trustee for the benefit of a beneficiary or for a specified purpose.[26]

What are the recognised characteristics of a trust under the Convention?

17.83 Pursuant to the Convention, a trust has the following characteristics:

(a) the assets constitute a separate fund and are not a part of the trustee's own estate;

(b) title to the trust assets stands in the name of the trustee or in the name of another person on behalf of the trustee;

25 [1962] 1 WLR 86.
26 Convention on the Law Applicable to Trusts and on their Recognition, Art 2.

(c) the trustee has the power and the duty, in respect of which he is accountable, to manage, employ or dispose of the assets in accordance with the terms of the trust and the special duties imposed upon him by law.

17.84 Notably, the Convention recognises that the reservation by the settlor of certain rights and powers, and the fact that the trustee may himself have rights as a beneficiary, are not necessarily inconsistent with the existence of a trust.[27]

Exceptions

17.85 The Convention applies only to trusts created voluntarily and evidenced in writing.[28] Also, the Convention does not apply to preliminary issues relating to the validity of wills or of other acts by virtue of which assets are transferred to the trustee.[29] The Convention also specifically states that it does not apply to the extent that the applicable law in a jurisdiction does not provide for trusts or the category of trusts involved.[30]

17.86 Specifically, no state shall be bound to recognise a trust the significant elements of which, except for the choice of the applicable law, the place of administration and the habitual residence of the trustee, are more closely connected with states which do not have the institution of the trust or the category of trust involved.[31]

17.87 However, the Convention shall not prevent the application of rules of law more favourable to the recognition of trusts.[32]

What law will govern the trust?

17.88 Under the Convention, a trust shall be governed by the law chosen by the settlor. The choice must be express or be implied in the terms of the instrument creating or the writing evidencing the trust, interpreted, if necessary, in the light of the circumstances of the case. Where the law chosen does not provide for trusts or the category of trust involved, the choice shall not be effective and the governing law shall be determined by reference to Article 7 of the Convention. Where no applicable law has been chosen, a trust shall be governed by the law with which it is most closely connected. In ascertaining the law with which a trust is most closely connected reference shall be made in particular to:[33]

(a) the place of administration of the trust designated by the settlor;

(b) the situs of the assets of the trust;

(c) the place of residence or business of the trustee;

(d) the objects of the trust and the places where they are to be fulfilled.

27 The Convention, Art 2.
28 ibid, Art 3.
29 ibid, Art 4.
30 ibid, Art 5.
31 ibid, Art 13.
32 ibid, Art 14.
33 ibid, Art 7.

What aspects of the trust shall be governed?

17.89 The law specified by the settlor or by default, the Convention, shall govern the validity of the trust, its construction, its effects, and the administration of the trust. In particular that law shall govern:[34]

(a) the appointment, resignation and removal of trustees, the capacity to act as a trustee, and the devolution of the office of trustee;

(b) the rights and duties of trustees among themselves;

(c) the right of trustees to delegate in whole or in part the discharge of their duties or the exercise of their powers;

(d) the power of trustees to administer or to dispose of trust assets, to create security interests in the trust assets, or to acquire new assets;

(e) the powers of investment of trustees;

(f) restrictions upon the duration of the trust, and upon the power to accumulate the income of the trust;

(g) the relationships between the trustees and the beneficiaries including the personal liability of the trustees to the beneficiaries;

(h) the variation or termination of the trust;

(i) the distribution of the trust assets;

(j) the duty of trustees to account for their administration.

17.90 In applying this aspect of the Convention, it should be noted that severability is contemplated, particularly in matters of administration, which may be governed by a different law.[35] The law applicable to the validity of the trust shall determine whether that law or the law governing a severable aspect of the trust may be replaced by another law.[36]

What does recognition imply?

17.91 A trust created in accordance with the law specified by either by the settlor or by the Convention, shall be recognised as a trust. Such recognition shall imply, as a minimum, that the trust property constitutes a separate fund, that the trustee may sue and be sued in his capacity as trustee, and that he may appear or act in this capacity before a notary or any person acting in an official capacity. Insofar as the law applicable to the trust requires or provides, such recognition shall imply, in particular:[37]

(a) that personal creditors of the trustee shall have no recourse against the trust assets;

(b) that the trust assets shall not form part of the trustee's estate upon his insolvency or bankruptcy;

(c) that the trust assets shall not form part of the matrimonial property of the trustee or his spouse nor part of the trustee's estate upon his death;

(d) that the trust assets may be recovered when the trustee, in breach of trust, has mingled trust assets with his own property or has alienated trust assets. However,

34 ibid, Art 8.
35 ibid, Art 9.
36 ibid, Art 10.
37 ibid, Art 11.

the rights and obligations of any third party holder of the assets shall remain subject to the law determined by the choice of law rules of the forum.

Conflicts of law

17.92 The Convention does not prevent the application of provisions of the law designated by the conflict rules of the forum, in so far as those provisions cannot be derogated from by voluntary act, relating in particular to the following matters:[38]

(a) the protection of minors and incapable parties;

(b) the personal and proprietary effects of marriage;

(c) succession rights, testate and intestate, especially the indefeasible shares of spouses and relatives;

(d) the transfer of title to property and security interests in property;

(e) the protection of creditors in matters of insolvency;

(f) the protection, in other respects, of third parties acting in good faith.

If recognition of a trust is prevented by application of the preceding paragraph, the court shall try to give effect to the objects of the trust by other means.[39]

17.93 The Convention does not prevent the application of those provisions of the law of the forum which must be applied even to international situations, irrespective of rules of conflict of laws. If another state has a sufficiently close connection with a case then, in exceptional circumstances, effect may also be given to rules of that state which have the same character as mentioned in the preceding paragraph.[40]

Where there are a number of territorial units in a state

17.94 For the purpose of identifying the law applicable under the Convention, where a state comprises several territorial units each of which has its own rules of law in respect of trusts, any reference to the law of that state is to be construed as referring to the law in force in the territorial unit in question.[41] Further, a state within which different territorial units have their own rules of law in respect of trusts is not bound to apply the Convention to conflicts solely between the laws of such units.[42]

Trust registration

17.95 Typically, you will need the following information in order to register a trust, irrespective of location, albeit some regional variation will apply. To register a trust you'll need, in addition to the name of the trust:

- the trust address and telephone number;
- the date the trust was established;
- the country where the trust is resident;

38 ibid, Art 15.

39 It should be noted that Art 17 of the Convention may be disregarded when their application would be manifestly incompatible with public policy (ordre public).

40 The Convention, Art 16.

41 ibid, Art 23.

42 ibid, Art 24.

- details of the trust assets including addresses and values.

You'll also need to provide information about all:

- trustees;
- settlors;
- beneficiaries or class of beneficiaries, where they can be determined;
- protectors (if any) and any other person exercising control over the trust.

The information needed about each person or organisation occupying that role includes:

- name;
- date of birth;
- National Insurance number if they're UK resident, unless a minor;
- an address and passport or ID number for non UK residents, if there is no National Insurance number;
- Unique Tax Reference (UTR) (if an organisation).

Appendix A

EU controller to non EU/ EEA processor – standard clauses

The standard contractual clauses set out in the Appendix are considered as offering adequate safeguards with respect to the protection of the privacy and fundamental rights and freedoms of individuals and as regards the exercise of the corresponding rights as required by Article 26(2) of Directive 95/46/EC. (GDPR).[1]

STANDARD CONTRACTUAL CLAUSES (PROCESSORS)

For the purposes of Article 26(2) of Directive 95/46/EC for the transfer of personal data to processors established in third countries which do not ensure an adequate level of data protection

Name of the data exporting organisation: …

Address:

Tel. …; fax …; e-mail: …

Other information needed to identify the organisation

(the data exporter)

And

Name of the data importing organisation: …

Address: …

Tel. …; fax …; e-mail: …

Other information needed to identify the organisation:

(the data importer)

each a 'party'; together 'the parties',

HAVE AGREED on the following Contractual Clauses (the Clauses) in order to adduce adequate safeguards with respect to the protection of privacy and fundamental rights and freedoms of individuals for the transfer by the data exporter to the data importer of the personal data specified in Appendix 1.

1 Commission Decision of 5 February 2010 on standard contractual clauses for the transfer of personal data to processors established in third countries under Directive 95/46/EC of the European Parliament and of the Council (notified under document C(2010) 593) (Text with EEA relevance) (2010/87/EU).

Clause 1

Definitions

For the purposes of the Clauses:

(a) 'personal data', 'special categories of data', 'process/processing', 'controller', 'processor', 'data subject' and 'supervisory authority' shall have the same meaning as in Directive 95/46/EC of the European Parliament and of the Council of 24 October 1995 on the protection of individuals with regard to the processing of personal data and on the free movement of such data (1);

(b) 'the data exporter' means the controller who transfers the personal data;

(c) 'the data importer' means the processor who agrees to receive from the data exporter personal data intended for processing on his behalf after the transfer in accordance with his instructions and the terms of the Clauses and who is not subject to a third country's system ensuring adequate protection within the meaning of Article 25(1) of Directive 95/46/EC;

(d) 'the sub-processor' means any processor engaged by the data importer or by any other sub-processor of the data importer who agrees to receive from the data importer or from any other sub-processor of the data importer personal data exclusively intended for processing activities to be carried out on behalf of the data exporter after the transfer in accordance with his instructions, the terms of the Clauses and the terms of the written subcontract;

(e) 'the applicable data protection law' means the legislation protecting the fundamental rights and freedoms of individuals and, in particular, their right to privacy with respect to the processing of personal data applicable to a data controller in the Member State in which the data exporter is established;

(f) 'technical and organisational security measures' means those measures aimed at protecting personal data against accidental or unlawful destruction or accidental loss, alteration, unauthorised disclosure or access, in particular where the processing involves the transmission of data over a network, and against all other unlawful forms of processing.

Clause 2

Details of the transfer

The details of the transfer and in particular the special categories of personal data where applicable are specified in Appendix 1 which forms an integral part of the Clauses.

Clause 3

Third-party beneficiary clause

(1) The data subject can enforce against the data exporter this Clause, Clause 4(b) to (i), Clause 5(a) to (e), and (g) to (j), Clause 6(1) and (2), Clause 7, Clause 8(2), and Clauses 9 to 12 as third-party beneficiary.

(2) The data subject can enforce against the data importer this Clause, Clause 5(a) to (e) and (g), Clause 6, Clause 7, Clause 8(2), and Clauses 9 to 12, in cases where the data exporter has factually disappeared or has ceased to exist in law unless any successor entity has assumed the entire legal obligations of the data exporter by contract or by operation of law, as a result of which it takes on the rights and

obligations of the data exporter, in which case the data subject can enforce them against such entity.

(3) The data subject can enforce against the sub-processor this Clause, Clause 5(a) to (e) and (g), Clause 6, Clause 7, Clause 8(2), and Clauses 9 to 12, in cases where both the data exporter and the data importer have factually disappeared or ceased to exist in law or have become insolvent, unless any successor entity has assumed the entire legal obligations of the data exporter by contract or by operation of law as a result of which it takes on the rights and obligations of the data exporter, in which case the data subject can enforce them against such entity. Such third-party liability of the sub-processor shall be limited to its own processing operations under the Clauses.

(4) The parties do not object to a data subject being represented by an association or other body if the data subject so expressly wishes and if permitted by national law.

Clause 4

Obligations of the data exporter

The data exporter agrees and warrants:

(a) that the processing, including the transfer itself, of the personal data has been and will continue to be carried out in accordance with the relevant provisions of the applicable data protection law (and, where applicable, has been notified to the relevant authorities of the Member State where the data exporter is established) and does not violate the relevant provisions of that State;

(b) that it has instructed and throughout the duration of the personal data-processing services will instruct the data importer to process the personal data transferred only on the data exporter's behalf and in accordance with the applicable data protection law and the Clauses;

(c) that the data importer will provide sufficient guarantees in respect of the technical and organisational security measures specified in Appendix 2 to this contract;

(d) that after assessment of the requirements of the applicable data protection law, the security measures are appropriate to protect personal data against accidental or unlawful destruction or accidental loss, alteration, unauthorised disclosure or access, in particular where the processing involves the transmission of data over a network, and against all other unlawful forms of processing, and that these measures ensure a level of security appropriate to the risks presented by the processing and the nature of the data to be protected having regard to the state of the art and the cost of their implementation;

(e) that it will ensure compliance with the security measures;

(f) that, if the transfer involves special categories of data, the data subject has been informed or will be informed before, or as soon as possible after, the transfer that its data could be transmitted to a third country not providing adequate protection within the meaning of Directive 95/46/EC;

(g) to forward any notification received from the data importer or any sub-processor pursuant to Clause 5(b) and Clause 8(3) to the data protection supervisory authority if the data exporter decides to continue the transfer or to lift the suspension;

(h) to make available to the data subjects upon request a copy of the Clauses, with the exception of Appendix 2, and a summary description of the security measures, as well as a copy of any contract for sub-processing services which has to be made in accordance with the Clauses, unless the Clauses or the contract contain commercial information, in which case it may remove such commercial information;

(i) that, in the event of sub-processing, the processing activity is carried out in accordance with Clause 11 by a sub-processor providing at least the same level of protection for the personal data and the rights of data subject as the data importer under the Clauses; and

(j) that it will ensure compliance with Clause 4(a) to (i).

Clause 5

Obligations of the data importer (2)

The data importer agrees and warrants:

(a) to process the personal data only on behalf of the data exporter and in compliance with its instructions and the Clauses; if it cannot provide such compliance for whatever reasons, it agrees to inform promptly the data exporter of its inability to comply, in which case the data exporter is entitled to suspend the transfer of data and/or terminate the contract;

(b) that it has no reason to believe that the legislation applicable to it prevents it from fulfilling the instructions received from the data exporter and its obligations under the contract and that in the event of a change in this legislation which is likely to have a substantial adverse effect on the warranties and obligations provided by the Clauses, it will promptly notify the change to the data exporter as soon as it is aware, in which case the data exporter is entitled to suspend the transfer of data and/or terminate the contract;

(c) that it has implemented the technical and organisational security measures specified in Appendix 2 before processing the personal data transferred;

(d) that it will promptly notify the data exporter about:

  (i) any legally binding request for disclosure of the personal data by a law enforcement authority unless otherwise prohibited, such as a prohibition under criminal law to preserve the confidentiality of a law enforcement investigation;

  (ii) any accidental or unauthorised access; and

  (iii) any request received directly from the data subjects without responding to that request, unless it has been otherwise authorised to do so;

(e) to deal promptly and properly with all inquiries from the data exporter relating to its processing of the personal data subject to the transfer and to abide by the advice of the supervisory authority with regard to the processing of the data transferred;

(f) at the request of the data exporter to submit its data-processing facilities for audit of the processing activities covered by the Clauses which shall be carried out by the data exporter or an inspection body composed of independent members and in possession of the required professional qualifications bound by a duty of confidentiality, selected by the data exporter, where applicable, in agreement with the supervisory authority;

(g) to make available to the data subject upon request a copy of the Clauses, or any existing contract for sub-processing, unless the Clauses or contract contain commercial information, in which case it may remove such commercial information, with the exception of Appendix 2 which shall be replaced by a summary description of the security measures in those cases where the data subject is unable to obtain a copy from the data exporter;

(h) that, in the event of sub-processing, it has previously informed the data exporter and obtained its prior written consent;

(i) that the processing services by the sub-processor will be carried out in accordance with Clause 11;

(j) to send promptly a copy of any sub-processor agreement it concludes under the Clauses to the data exporter.

Clause 6

Liability

(1) The parties agree that any data subject, who has suffered damage as a result of any breach of the obligations referred to in Clause 3 or in Clause 11 by any party or sub-processor is entitled to receive compensation from the data exporter for the damage suffered.

(2) If a data subject is not able to bring a claim for compensation in accordance with paragraph 1 against the data exporter, arising out of a breach by the data importer or his sub-processor of any of their obligations referred to in Clause 3 or in Clause 11, because the data exporter has factually disappeared or ceased to exist in law or has become insolvent, the data importer agrees that the data subject may issue a claim against the data importer as if it were the data exporter, unless any successor entity has assumed the entire legal obligations of the data exporter by contract of by operation of law, in which case the data subject can enforce its rights against such entity.

The data importer may not rely on a breach by a sub-processor of its obligations in order to avoid its own liabilities.

(3) If a data subject is not able to bring a claim against the data exporter or the data importer referred to in paragraphs 1 and 2, arising out of a breach by the sub-processor of any of their obligations referred to in Clause 3 or in Clause 11 because both the data exporter and the data importer have factually disappeared or ceased to exist in law or have become insolvent, the sub-processor agrees that the data subject may issue a claim against the data sub-processor with regard to its own processing operations under the Clauses as if it were the data exporter or the data importer, unless any successor entity has assumed the entire legal obligations of the data exporter or data importer by contract or by operation of law, in which case the data subject can enforce its rights against such entity. The liability of the sub-processor shall be limited to its own processing operations under the Clauses.

Clause 7

Mediation and jurisdiction

(1) The data importer agrees that if the data subject invokes against it third-party beneficiary rights and/or claims compensation for damages under the Clauses, the data importer will accept the decision of the data subject:

   (a) to refer the dispute to mediation, by an independent person or, where applicable, by the supervisory authority;

(b) to refer the dispute to the courts in the Member State in which the data exporter is established.

(2) The parties agree that the choice made by the data subject will not prejudice its substantive or procedural rights to seek remedies in accordance with other provisions of national or international law.

Clause 8

Cooperation with supervisory authorities

(1) The data exporter agrees to deposit a copy of this contract with the supervisory authority if it so requests or if such deposit is required under the applicable data protection law.

(2) The parties agree that the supervisory authority has the right to conduct an audit of the data importer, and of any sub-processor, which has the same scope and is subject to the same conditions as would apply to an audit of the data exporter under the applicable data protection law.

(3) The data importer shall promptly inform the data exporter about the existence of legislation applicable to it or any sub-processor preventing the conduct of an audit of the data importer, or any sub-processor, pursuant to paragraph 2. In such a case the data exporter shall be entitled to take the measures foreseen in Clause 5(b).

Clause 9

Governing law

The Clauses shall be governed by the law of the Member State in which the data exporter is established, namely …

Clause 10

Variation of the contract

The parties undertake not to vary or modify the Clauses. This does not preclude the parties from adding clauses on business related issues where required as long as they do not contradict the Clause.

Clause 11

Sub-processing

(1) The data importer shall not subcontract any of its processing operations performed on behalf of the data exporter under the Clauses without the prior written consent of the data exporter. Where the data importer subcontracts its obligations under the Clauses, with the consent of the data exporter, it shall do so only by way of a written agreement with the sub-processor which imposes the same obligations on the sub-processor as are imposed on the data importer under the Clauses (3). Where the sub-processor fails to fulfil its data protection obligations under such written agreement the data importer shall remain fully liable to the data exporter for the performance of the sub-processor's obligations under such agreement.

(2) The prior written contract between the data importer and the sub-processor shall also provide for a third-party beneficiary clause as laid down in Clause 3 for cases

where the data subject is not able to bring the claim for compensation referred to in paragraph 1 of Clause 6 against the data exporter or the data importer because they have factually disappeared or have ceased to exist in law or have become insolvent and no successor entity has assumed the entire legal obligations of the data exporter or data importer by contract or by operation of law. Such third-party liability of the sub-processor shall be limited to its own processing operations under the Clauses.

(3) The provisions relating to data protection aspects for sub-processing of the contract referred to in paragraph 1 shall be governed by the law of the Member State in which the data exporter is established, namely …

(4) The data exporter shall keep a list of sub-processing agreements concluded under the Clauses and notified by the data importer pursuant to Clause 5(j), which shall be updated at least once a year. The list shall be available to the data exporter's data protection supervisory authority.

Clause 12

Obligation after the termination of personal data-processing services

(1) The parties agree that on the termination of the provision of data-processing services, the data importer and the sub-processor shall, at the choice of the data exporter, return all the personal data transferred and the copies thereof to the data exporter or shall destroy all the personal data and certify to the data exporter that it has done so, unless legislation imposed upon the data importer prevents it from returning or destroying all or part of the personal data transferred. In that case, the data importer warrants that it will guarantee the confidentiality of the personal data transferred and will not actively process the personal data transferred anymore.

(2) The data importer and the sub-processor warrant that upon request of the data exporter and/or of the supervisory authority, it will submit its data-processing facilities for an audit of the measures referred to in paragraph 1.

On behalf of the data exporter:

Name (written out in full): …

Position: …

Address: …

Other information necessary in order for the contract to be binding (if any):

Signature …

On behalf of the data importer:

Name (written out in full): …

Position:

Address: …

Other information necessary in order for the contract to be binding (if any):

Signature …

(1) Parties may reproduce definitions and meanings contained in Directive 95/46/EC within this Clause if they considered it better for the contract to stand alone.

(2) Mandatory requirements of the national legislation applicable to the data importer which do not go beyond what is necessary in a democratic society on the basis of one of the interests listed in Article 13(1) of Directive 95/46/EC, that is, if they constitute a necessary measure to safeguard national security, defence, public security, the prevention, investigation, detection and prosecution of criminal offences or of breaches of ethics for the regulated professions, an important economic or financial interest of the State or the protection of the data subject or the rights and freedoms of others, are not in contradiction with the standard contractual clauses. Some examples of such mandatory requirements which do not go beyond what is necessary in a democratic society are, inter alia, internationally recognised sanctions, tax-reporting requirements or anti-money-laundering reporting requirements.

(3) This requirement may be satisfied by the sub-processor co-signing the contract entered into between the data exporter and the data importer under this Decision.

Appendix 1 to the Standard Contractual Clauses

This Appendix forms part of the Clauses and must be completed and signed by the parties

Data exporter

The data exporter is (please specify briefly your activities relevant to the transfer):

…

…

…

Data importer

The data importer is (please specify briefly activities relevant to the transfer):

…

…

Data subjects

The personal data transferred concern the following categories of data subjects (please specify):

…

…

…

Categories of data

The personal data transferred concern the following categories of data (please specify):

…

…

…

Special categories of data (if appropriate)

The personal data transferred concern the following special categories of data (please specify):

…

…

…

Processing operations

The personal data transferred will be subject to the following basic processing activities (please specify):

…

…

…

DATA EXPORTER

Name: …

Authorised Signature …

DATA IMPORTER

Name: …

Authorised Signature …

Appendix 2 to the Standard Contractual Clauses

This Appendix forms part of the Clauses and must be completed and signed by the parties.

Description of the technical and organisational security measures implemented by the data importer in accordance with Clauses 4(d) and 5(c) (or document/legislation attached):

…

…

…

…

ILLUSTRATIVE INDEMNIFICATION CLAUSE (OPTIONAL)

Liability

The parties agree that if one party is held liable for a violation of the clauses committed by the other party, the latter will, to the extent to which it is liable, indemnify the first party for any cost, charge, damages, expenses or loss it has incurred.

Indemnification is contingent upon:

(a) the data exporter promptly notifying the data importer of a claim; and

(b) the data importer being given the possibility to cooperate with the data exporter in the defence and settlement of the claim (1).

(1) Paragraph on liabilities is optional.

Appendix B

EU controller to non EU/ EEA controller – standard clauses

The standard contractual clauses set out in the Appendix are considered as offering adequate safeguards with respect to the protection of the privacy and fundamental rights and freedoms of individuals and as regards the exercise of the corresponding rights as required by Article 26(2) of Directive 95/46/EC. (GDPR).[1]

Standard contractual clauses for the transfer of personal data from the Community to third countries (controller to controller transfers)

Data transfer agreement

Between

_ (name)

_ (address and country of establishment)

hereinafter 'data exporter')

and

_ (name)

_ (address and country of establishment)

hereinafter 'data importer'

each a 'party'; together 'the parties'.

Clause 1

Definitions

For the purposes of the clauses:

(a) 'personal data', 'special categories of data/sensitive data', 'process/processing', 'controller', 'processor', 'data subject' and 'supervisory authority/authority' shall have the same meaning as in Directive 95/46/EC of 24 October 1995 (whereby 'the authority' shall mean the competent data protection authority in the territory in which the data exporter is established);

(b) 'the data exporter' shall mean the controller who transfers the personal data;

1 Commission Decision of 5 February 2010 on standard contractual clauses for the transfer of personal data to processors established in third countries under Directive 95/46/EC of the European Parliament and of the Council (notified under document C(2010) 593) (Text with EEA relevance) (2010/87/EU).

(c) 'the data importer' shall mean the controller who agrees to receive from the data exporter personal data for further processing in accordance with the terms of these clauses and who is not subject to a third country's system ensuring adequate protection;

(d) 'clauses' shall mean these contractual clauses, which are a free-standing document that does not incorporate commercial business terms established by the parties under separate commercial arrangements.

The details of the transfer (as well as the personal data covered) are specified in Annex B, which forms an integral part of the clauses.

Clause 2

Obligations of the data exporter

The data exporter warrants and undertakes that:

(a) The personal data have been collected, processed and transferred in accordance with the laws applicable to the data exporter.

(b) It has used reasonable efforts to determine that the data importer is able to satisfy its legal obligations under these clauses.

(c) It will provide the data importer, when so requested, with copies of relevant data protection laws or references to them (where relevant, and not including legal advice) of the country in which the data exporter is established.

(d) It will respond to enquiries from data subjects and the authority concerning processing of the personal data by the data importer, unless the parties have agreed that the data importer will so respond, in which case the data exporter will still respond to the extent reasonably possible and with the information reasonably available to it if the data importer is unwilling or unable to respond. Responses will be made within a reasonable time.

(e) It will make available, upon request, a copy of the clauses to data subjects who are third party beneficiaries under clause III, unless the clauses contain confidential information, in which case it may remove such information. Where information is removed, the data exporter shall inform data subjects in writing of the reason for removal and of their right to draw the removal to the attention of the authority. However, the data exporter shall abide by a decision of the authority regarding access to the full text of the clauses by data subjects, as long as data subjects have agreed to respect the confidentiality of the confidential information removed. The data exporter shall also provide a copy of the clauses to the authority where required.

Clause 3

Obligations of the data importer

The data importer warrants and undertakes that:

(a) It will have in place appropriate technical and organisational measures to protect the personal data against accidental or unlawful destruction or accidental loss, alteration, unauthorised disclosure or access, and which provide a level of security appropriate to the risk represented by the processing and the nature of the data to be protected.

(b) It will have in place procedures so that any third party it authorises to have access to the personal data, including processors, will respect and maintain the confidentiality and security of the personal data. Any person acting under the authority of the data importer, including a data processor, shall be obligated to process the personal data only on instructions from the data importer. This provision does not apply to persons authorised or required by law or regulation to have access to the personal data.

(c) It has no reason to believe, at the time of entering into these clauses, in the existence of any local laws that would have a substantial adverse effect on the guarantees provided for under these clauses, and it will inform the data exporter (which will pass such notification on to the authority where required) if it becomes aware of any such laws.

(d) It will process the personal data for purposes described in Annex B, and has the legal authority to give the warranties and fulfil the undertakings set out in these clauses.

(e) It will identify to the data exporter a contact point within its organisation authorised to respond to enquiries concerning processing of the personal data, and will cooperate in good faith with the data exporter, the data subject and the authority concerning all such enquiries within a reasonable time. In case of legal dissolution of the data exporter, or if the parties have so agreed, the data importer will assume responsibility for compliance with the provisions of clause I(e).

(f) At the request of the data exporter, it will provide the data exporter with evidence of financial resources sufficient to fulfil its responsibilities under clause III (which may include insurance coverage).

(g) Upon reasonable request of the data exporter, it will submit its data processing facilities, data files and documentation needed for processing to reviewing, auditing and/or certifying by the data exporter (or any independent or impartial inspection agents or auditors, selected by the data exporter and not reasonably objected to by the data importer) to ascertain compliance with the warranties and undertakings in these clauses, with reasonable notice and during regular business hours. The request will be subject to any necessary consent or approval from a regulatory or supervisory authority within the country of the data importer, which consent or approval the data importer will attempt to obtain in a timely fashion.

(h) It will process the personal data, at its option, in accordance with:

(i) the data protection laws of the country in which the data exporter is established, or

(ii) the relevant provisions (1) of any Commission decision pursuant to Article 25(6) of Directive 95/46/EC, where the data importer complies with the relevant provisions of such an authorisation or decision and is based in a country to which such an authorisation or decision pertains, but is not covered by such authorisation or decision for the purposes of the transfer(s) of the personal data (2), or

(iii) the data processing principles set forth in Annex A.

Data importer to indicate which option it selects:

Initials of data importer:_;

(i) It will not disclose or transfer the personal data to a third party data controller located outside the European Economic Area (EEA) unless it notifies the data exporter about the transfer and

(i) the third party data controller processes the personal data in accordance with a Commission decision finding that a third country provides adequate protection, or

(ii) the third party data controller becomes a signatory to these clauses or another data transfer agreement approved by a competent authority in the EU, or

(iii) data subjects have been given the opportunity to object, after having been informed of the purposes of the transfer, the categories of recipients and the fact that the countries to which data is exported may have different data protection standards, or

(iv) with regard to onward transfers of sensitive data, data subjects have given their unambiguous consent to the onward transfer

Clause 4

Liability and third party rights

(a) Each party shall be liable to the other parties for damages it causes by any breach of these clauses. Liability as between the parties is limited to actual damage suffered. Punitive damages (i.e. damages intended to punish a party for its outrageous conduct) are specifically excluded. Each party shall be liable to data subjects for damages it causes by any breach of third party rights under these clauses. This does not affect the liability of the data exporter under its data protection law.

(b) The parties agree that a data subject shall have the right to enforce as a third party beneficiary this clause and clauses I(b), I(d), I(e), II(a), II(c), II(d), II(e), II(h), II(i), III(a), V, VI(d) and VII against the data importer or the data exporter, for their respective breach of their contractual obligations, with regard to his personal data, and accept jurisdiction for this purpose in the data exporter's country of establishment. In cases involving allegations of breach by the data importer, the data subject must first request the data exporter to take appropriate action to enforce his rights against the data importer; if the data exporter does not take such action within a reasonable period (which under normal circumstances would be one month), the data subject may then enforce his rights against the data importer directly. A data subject is entitled to proceed directly against a data exporter that has failed to use reasonable efforts to determine that the data importer is able to satisfy its legal obligations under these clauses (the data exporter shall have the burden to prove that it took reasonable efforts).

Clause 5

Law applicable to the clauses

These clauses shall be governed by the law of the country in which the data exporter is established, with the exception of the laws and regulations relating to processing of the personal data by the data importer under clause II(h), which shall apply only if so selected by the data importer under that clause.

Clause 6

Resolution of disputes with data subjects or the authority

(a) In the event of a dispute or claim brought by a data subject or the authority concerning the processing of the personal data against either or both of the parties, the parties will inform each other about any such disputes or claims, and will cooperate with a view to settling them amicably in a timely fashion.

(b) The parties agree to respond to any generally available non-binding mediation procedure initiated by a data subject or by the authority. If they do participate in the proceedings, the parties may elect to do so remotely (such as by telephone or other electronic means). The parties also agree to consider participating in any other arbitration, mediation or other dispute resolution proceedings developed for data protection disputes.

(c) Each party shall abide by a decision of a competent court of the data exporter's country of establishment or of the authority which is final and against which no further appeal is possible.

Clause 7

Termination

(a) In the event that the data importer is in breach of its obligations under these clauses, then the data exporter may temporarily suspend the transfer of personal data to the data importer until the breach is repaired or the contract is terminated.

(b) In the event that:

(i) the transfer of personal data to the data importer has been temporarily suspended by the data exporter for longer than one month pursuant to paragraph (a);

(ii) compliance by the data importer with these clauses would put it in breach of its legal or regulatory obligations in the country of import;

(iii) the data importer is in substantial or persistent breach of any warranties or undertakings given by it under these clauses;

(iv) a final decision against which no further appeal is possible of a competent court of the data exporter's country of establishment or of the authority rules that there has been a breach of the clauses by the data importer or the data exporter; or

(v) a petition is presented for the administration or winding up of the data importer, whether in its personal or business capacity, which petition is not dismissed within the applicable period for such dismissal under applicable law; a winding up order is made; a receiver is appointed over any of its assets; a trustee in bankruptcy is appointed, if the data importer is an individual; a company voluntary arrangement is commenced by it; or any equivalent event in any jurisdiction occurs

then the data exporter, without prejudice to any other rights which it may have against the data importer, shall be entitled to terminate these clauses, in which case the authority shall be informed where required. In cases covered by (i), (ii), or (iv) above the data importer may also terminate these clauses.

(c) Either party may terminate these clauses if (i) any Commission positive adequacy decision under Article 25(6) of Directive 95/46/EC (or any superseding text) is issued in relation to the country (or a sector thereof) to which the data is transferred and processed by the data importer, or (ii) Directive 95/46/EC (or any superseding text) becomes directly applicable in such country.

(d) The parties agree that the termination of these clauses at any time, in any circumstances and for whatever reason (except for termination under clause VI(c)) does not exempt them from the obligations and/or conditions under the clauses as regards the processing of the personal data transferred.

Clause 8

Variation of these clauses

The parties may not modify these clauses except to update any information in Annex B, in which case they will inform the authority where required. This does not preclude the parties from adding additional commercial clauses where required.

Clause 9

Description of the transfer

The details of the transfer and of the personal data are specified in Annex B. The parties agree that Annex B may contain confidential business information which they will not disclose to third parties, except as required by law or in response to a competent regulatory or government agency, or as required under clause I(e). The parties may execute additional annexes to cover additional transfers, which will be submitted to the authority where required. Annex B may, in the alternative, be drafted to cover multiple transfers.

Dated: _

_

_

FOR DATA IMPORTER

FOR DATA EXPORTER

…

…

…

…

…

…

Appendix 1

DATA PROCESSING PRINCIPLES

1. Purpose limitation: Personal data may be processed and subsequently used or further communicated only for purposes described in Appendix 2 or subsequently authorised by the data subject.

2. Data quality and proportionality: Personal data must be accurate and, where necessary, kept up to date. The personal data must be adequate, relevant and not excessive in relation to the purposes for which they are transferred and further processed.

3. Transparency: Data subjects must be provided with information necessary to ensure fair processing (such as information about the purposes of processing and about the transfer), unless such information has already been given by the data exporter.

4. Security and confidentiality: Technical and organisational security measures must be taken by the data controller that are appropriate to the risks, such as against accidental or unlawful destruction or accidental loss, alteration, unauthorised disclosure or access, presented by the processing. Any person acting under the authority of the data controller, including a processor, must not process the data except on instructions from the data controller.

5. Rights of access, rectification, deletion and objection: As provided in Article 12 of Directive 95/46/EC, data subjects must, whether directly or via a third party, be provided with the personal information about them that an organisation holds, except for requests which are manifestly abusive, based on unreasonable intervals or their number or repetitive or systematic nature, or for which access need not be granted under the law of the country of the data exporter. Provided that the authority has given its prior approval, access need also not be granted when doing so would be likely to seriously harm the interests of the data importer or other organisations dealing with the data importer and such interests are not overridden by the interests for fundamental rights and freedoms of the data subject. The sources of the personal data need not be identified when this is not possible by reasonable efforts, or where the rights of persons other than the individual would be violated. Data subjects must be able to have the personal information about them rectified, amended, or deleted where it is inaccurate or processed against these principles. If there are compelling grounds to doubt the legitimacy of the request, the organisation may require further justifications before proceeding to rectification, amendment or deletion. Notification of any rectification, amendment or deletion to third parties to whom the data have been disclosed need not be made when this involves a disproportionate effort. A data subject must also be able to object to the processing of the personal data relating to him if there are compelling legitimate grounds relating to his particular situation. The burden of proof for any refusal rests on the data importer, and the data subject may always challenge a refusal before the authority.

6. Sensitive data: The data importer shall take such additional measures (e.g. relating to security) as are necessary to protect such sensitive data in accordance with its obligations under clause II.

7. Data used for marketing purposes: Where data are processed for the purposes of direct marketing, effective procedures should exist allowing the data subject at any time to 'opt-out' from having his data used for such purposes.

8. Automated decisions: For purposes hereof 'automated decision' shall mean a decision by the data exporter or the data importer which produces legal effects concerning a data subject or significantly affects a data subject and which is based solely on automated processing of personal data intended to evaluate certain personal aspects relating to him, such as his performance at work, creditworthiness, reliability, conduct, etc. The data importer shall not make any automated decisions concerning data subjects, except when:

   (a)

      (i) such decisions are made by the data importer in entering into or performing a contract with the data subject, and

      (ii) (the data subject is given an opportunity to discuss the results of a relevant automated decision with a representative of the parties making such decision or otherwise to make representations to that parties.

   or

   (b) where otherwise provided by the law of the data exporter.

Appendix 2

DESCRIPTION OF THE TRANSFER

(To be completed by the parties)

Data Subjects...

Purpose of the Transfer ...

Categories of Data...

Recipients...

Sensitive Data...

Data Protection registration information of the data exporter...

Additional useful information...

Contact Point for data protection enquiries...

A. Data Importer

B. Data Exporter

ILLUSTRATIVE COMMERCIAL CLAUSES (OPTIONAL)

Indemnification between the data exporter and data importer:

> 'The parties will indemnify each other and hold each other harmless from any cost, charge, damages, expense or loss which they cause each other as a result of their breach of any of the provisions of these clauses. Indemnification hereunder is contingent upon (a) the party(ies) to be indemnified (the 'indemnified party(ies)') promptly notifying the other party(ies) (the 'indemnifying party(ies)') of a claim, (b) the indemnifying party(ies) having sole control of the defence and settlement of any such claim, and (c) the indemnified party(ies) providing reasonable cooperation and assistance to the indemnifying party(ies) in defence of such claim.'.

Dispute resolution between the data exporter and data importer (the parties may of course substitute any other alternative dispute resolution or jurisdictional clause):

> 'In the event of a dispute between the data importer and the data exporter concerning any alleged breach of any provision of these clauses, such dispute shall be finally settled under the rules of arbitration of the International Chamber of Commerce by one or more arbitrators appointed in accordance with the said rules. The place of arbitration shall be [ ]. The number of arbitrators shall be [ ].'

Allocation of costs:

> 'Each party shall perform its obligations under these clauses at its own cost.'

Extra termination clause:

> 'In the event of termination of these clauses, the data importer must return all personal data and all copies of the personal data subject to these clauses to the data exporter forthwith or, at the data exporter's choice, will destroy all copies of the same and certify to the data exporter that it has done so, unless the data importer is prevented by its national law or local regulator from destroying or returning all or part of such data, in which event the data will be kept confidential and will not be actively processed for any purpose. The data importer agrees that, if so requested by the data exporter, it will allow the data exporter, or an inspection agent selected by the data exporter and not reasonably objected to by the data importer, access to its establishment to verify that this has been done, with reasonable notice and during business hours.'

(1) 'Relevant provisions' means those provisions of any authorisation or decision except for the enforcement provisions of any authorisation or decision (which shall be governed by these clauses).

(2) However, the provisions of Appendix 1.5 concerning rights of access, rectification, deletion and objection must be applied when this option is chosen and take precedence over any comparable provisions of the Commission Decision selected.

Appendix C

EU controller to non EU/ EEA controller – standard clauses

(Note – this set is no longer available for new users but continues to have effect in relation to arrangements put in place prior to 15 May 2010.)

Commission Decision 2002/16/EC, dated 27 December 2001 – in which the Commission approved model clauses for transfers from data controllers in the EEA to data processors outside the EEA.

Appendix D

Specimen CCTV policy – EMEA

EMEA Closed-Circuit Television (CCTV) Guidelines

The purpose of these Guidelines is to ensure the operation of Closed-Circuit Television ('CCTV') systems in an efficient and secure manner, and consistently with [___company___] privacy obligations. These Guidelines explicitly incorporate guidance from relevant data protection authorities, including the UK Information Commissioner's Office (ICO) CCTV Code of Practice[1] and the French Commission nationale de l'informatique et des libertés (CNIL) La vidéosurveillance-vidéoprotection au travail.[2]

Overview

The use of CCTV serves many important purposes. Among other things, CCTV helps to prevent theft, deter illegal behaviour, guard the physical safety of individuals, and protect [___company___] facilities and assets. However, CCTV also poses a risk to individuals' privacy rights, and in some cases, can constitute an unjustified violation of those rights. These Guidelines are meant to outline standard considerations that [___company___] to pursue its legitimate interests in the use of CCTV while also protecting the privacy rights of individuals who may be monitored by CCTV systems.

Placement and purpose

CCTV systems should be placed in locations consistent with their intended purposes, such as exterior areas of a building, entrances, reception areas, parking lots, production areas and other areas where security is particularly important or at risk. CCTV should not be placed in restrooms, changing areas, or areas used for trade unions or works councils. It is also important to follow local laws that may limit where CCTV can be used, such as prohibitions on having CCTV in canteens or smoking rooms. CCTV should also not be used to monitor employee productivity or attendance. CCTV on exterior areas should not focus on any residential property or public sidewalks.

Access limitations

Access to CCTV systems should be limited to the extent possible. CCTV monitors and recording systems should be in a secure, locked location. The number of employees that can access CCTV recordings locally or remotely should also be limited

1 https://ico.org.uk/media/1542/cctv-code-of-practice.pdf.
2 www.cnil.fr/sites/default/files/atoms/files/_videosurveillance_au_travail.pdf.

to the extent possible. All employees involved in handling CCTV recordings should be skilled and trained in data protection requirements.

If a third party (eg, a security company) will be monitoring the CCTV system on [___company___] behalf, a data processing agreement is needed with the third party. Contact [___company___] for the appropriate agreement.

If an individual requests access to the CCTV system or a recording from a particular period of time, the validity of the request should be verified before sharing the data. Contact local HR for assistance handling such requests, as they must be handled within 28 days of receipt. However, nothing in this section is intended to limit or interfere with responding to lawful requests by law enforcement.

Security

Ensure ALL default passwords are changed to a strong/complex password. Passwords must be a minimum of 8 characters long, have at least 1 uppercase letter, 1 lowercase letter, 1 number and 1 special character.

Video streams between cameras and the recording system should be encrypted to prevent improper access to images. URLs should be secure and start with 'https'. Remote connections to access the CCTV system should be similarly encrypted and connection should be via VPN or a stand-alone network.

Notice requirements

Easily-visible signs should be posted in areas subject to CCTV monitoring. The signs should provide individuals with notice of:

(1) the existence of CCTV in the area;

(2) the name of the data controller for the CCTV system;

(3) the legal basis for the system (ie, legitimate interests of the employer in securing its premises);

(4) the retention period for the images;

(5) the possibility of submitting a complaint to the relevant data protection authority; and

(6) the process of requesting access to video recordings of the individual.

For security reasons, the signs do not need to indicate the detailed location or orientation of cameras, as that information could substantially undermine the effectiveness of the CCTV system.

In addition, employee privacy notices should identify the use of CCTV as a type of data processing done by [___company___], and should further indicate the areas in which CCTV is used. If new areas are added to the coverage of the CCTV system, the privacy notices should be updated accordingly. The GDPR Lead or the Legal and Compliance Department should be contacted at [___company___] to update privacy notices and determine whether the update constitutes a material change.

Retention requirements

CCTV recordings should be deleted when no longer needed, in accordance with the applicable [___company___] retention policy and schedule, a copy of which can be located on the [___company___] site. In general, this period should not exceed 30 days and in some cases may be significantly shorter.

Data inventory and data protection impact assessment

The use of CCTV and any changes to a CCTV system need to be recorded in the [___company___] GDPR Article 30 Data Inventory located here. The [___company___] GDPR Lead will then undertake a data protection impact assessment to ensure that our use of CCTV incorporates privacy by design and does not pose a high-risk to the rights and freedoms of individuals – consistent with these Guidelines.

Appendix E

Specimen AML policy – EMEA

[___company___], including its affiliates, (collectively, '[___company___]' or the 'Company') is committed to conducting business ethically, honestly, and in accordance with all applicable laws. This includes taking risk-based steps to prevent money laundering and terrorist financing in connection with our business.

Background

Money laundering is a process criminals and others use to move funds gained from illegal activity through legitimate businesses to make the funds also appear legitimate.

Generally, money laundering occurs in three stages. Money first enters the financial system at the 'placement' stage, where the money generated from criminal activities is deposited into an account at a bank. At the 'layering' stage, the funds are transferred to other accounts or banks to further separate the money from its criminal origin. At the 'integration' stage, the funds are reintroduced into the economy and used to purchase legitimate assets or businesses, or possibly to fund other criminal activities.

Terrorist financing is carried out in a very similar manner to money laundering, but the source of the funds may or may not include illegal activities. Instead, in terrorist financing, the source of money that is ultimately used to fund or benefit terrorist activities is hidden using the steps mentioned above.

Individuals or companies engaging in money laundering or terrorist financing can take advantage of [___company___] legitimate business to assist with layering – for example, by purchasing goods from us and then cancelling the order and having the funds sent to a different account. They can also use our company at the integration stage to purchase goods from us using money from illegal sources and then reselling those goods for a profit.

For [___company___], involvement in money laundering or terrorist financing can result in lasting damage to our brands and our reputation, as well as a breakdown in consumer and shareholder confidence. Violations of anti-money laundering or counter terrorist financing laws can result in millions of dollars in fines and penalties, plus jail time for participants.

Policy

[___company___], including its employees, officers, directors, and third party agents and business partners acting on behalf of or for the benefit of the Company, do not knowingly engage in money laundering or terrorist financing and take steps to prevent those activities in connection with our business.

Compliance with this Policy as well as applicable US, EU, and other international anti-money laundering and counter terrorist financing laws is mandatory. Failure to do so may result in disciplinary action up to and including termination of employment or termination of your business relationship with [___company___].

As set forth in the Code of Conduct [___company___] has a strict non-retaliation policy to protect anyone making a good faith report of suspected misconduct, including suspected money laundering. Similarly, various countries have laws specifically protecting those who report suspected instances of money laundering.

Purpose

This policy provides guidance on [___company___] 'Know Your Customer' requirements (see below), customer screening requirements, as well as how to identify and report red flags of potential money laundering or terrorist financing. Its purpose is to ensure all [___company___] employees, officers, directors, and third party agents and business partners who work on [___company___] behalf globally understand and comply with applicable laws as well as [___company___] requirements. To the extent feasible, it applies to all customers, including anyone making payments on behalf of customers.

Know your customer requirements

A critical part of [___company___] anti-money laundering and counter terrorist financing compliance is ensuring that we know the individuals and companies with which we do business. The process of verifying the identity of customers is commonly called 'Know Your Customer' or 'KYC.' [___company___] KYC requirements are designed to provide guidance on how we can reasonably verify customers' identities before beginning business with them.

For each region, the individuals in Annex 2 (the 'Finance Owners') are responsible for developing KYC procedures to verify the identity of customers, including at a minimum, collection of the following:

- Name,
- Address,
- Industry, and
- Identification number, such as a taxpayer ID number or VAT number.

If another company is making a payment on a customer's behalf, we require the same information as we do for the customer. Depending on the circumstances, such payment arrangements could also be a red flag for money laundering.

High-risk KYC requirements

Some customers pose a higher money laundering or terrorist financing risk because of where they do business or the nature of their business. Customers will be deemed high-risk if they operate in one of the countries in Annex 1 to this policy.

For high-risk customers, we must take additional steps in order to be reasonably confident that we are not engaging in money laundering or terrorist financing ('High-Risk KYC Procedures'). For each region, the Finance Owners are responsible for developing High-Risk KYC Procedures, including steps such as:

- Identifying all beneficial owners of the customer and any parent companies;
- Identifying whether any beneficial owners of the customer or any parent companies are senior political figures, often called politically exposed persons or 'PEPs';

- Collecting bank references;
- Requiring explanations regarding the purpose and structure of transaction; and
- Requiring explanations regarding the purpose and structure of customer's business.

Refusal to Cooperate or Providing Intentionally Misleading Information

If a customer refuses to provide the information identified above or appears to have provided information that is intentionally misleading, report it to any of the resources in the Questions and Reporting section of this Policy to obtain clearance before proceeding with the transaction. For new or existing customers, refusal to provide information or providing intentionally misleading information may result in [___ company___] refusal to begin or continue business with the customer.

Customer screenings

Once a customer's identity has been verified, we must ensure that the customer is not subject to any trade sanctions or terrorist organization designations and that it is not known for engaging in illegal activities. For each region, the Finance Owners are responsible for developing procedures to implement screening to satisfy this Policy as well as [___company___] Trade Sanctions Policy.

Red flags

In the course of doing business, you may encounter certain circumstances that indicate a customer is potentially engaging in money laundering or terrorist financing. These are called 'red flags' and include instances when a:

- Company with no apparent relationship to the customer makes a payment on the customer's behalf;
- Customer frequently changes the bank account or company used to pay for purchases;
- Customer is engaging in business inconsistent with its background;
- Customer has very little or no business, revenues, or assets;
- Customer or payer is based in or transacts business through a financial secrecy haven, such as the British Virgin Islands, Cyprus, or the Seychelles;
- Customer refuses to or is reluctant to provide complete information about the nature and purpose of its business, such as the names of its owners, officers, and business location;
- Customer appears to only be acting as an agent for an undisclosed third party and refuses to identify the third party;
- Customer requests exemptions from reporting or record keeping requirements or tries to structure purchases and business to avoid those requirements;
- Customer makes large purchases in cash;
- Customer makes unusually large or small purchases in even amounts; or
- Customer pays for a purchase using one account or payment method then immediately requests a refund to a different account or payment method.

If you become aware of any of these red flags, immediately report them to one of the resources in the Questions and Reporting section of this Policy.

Suspicious activity reports

Please be aware that, if [___company___] suspects that it has been involved in money laundering or terrorist financing, it may be required to or may elect to file a Suspicious Activity Report ('SAR') with the relevant regulatory body. As required by relevant laws, the filing of a SAR or any investigation into money laundering must be kept strictly confidential to prevent 'tipping off' entities that may be engaged in money laundering or terrorist financing.

Questions and reporting

If you have any questions about this Policy, please contact the Legal and Compliance Department ([___company___]).

If you believe this Policy may have been violated, you should immediately report the issue to your manager, the [___company___] Legal and Compliance Department (), Human Resources Department, or confidential reporting system that can be accessed at any time by phone or the internet. Reports to [___company___] can be made anonymously, where permitted by local law.

As set forth in the Code of Conduct, [___company___] has a strict non-retaliation policy to protect anyone making a good faith report of suspected misconduct, including suspected violations of money laundering or counter terrorist financing laws.

Annex 1

Country

1. Afghanistan
2. Algeria
3. Angola
4. Armenia
5. Azerbaijan
6. Bahamas
7. Bangladesh
8. Belize
9. Belarus
10. Benin
11. Bolivia
12. Bosnia and Herzegovina
13. Burkina Faso
14. Burundi
15. British Virgin Islands
16. Cameroon
17. Comoros 18. Côte d'Ivoire (Ivory Coast)

19. Cayman Islands
20. Central African Republic
21. Chad
22. Colombia
23. Cyprus
24. Democratic Republic of the Congo
25. Djibouti
26. Guyana
27. Egypt
28. Equatorial Guinea
29. Eritrea
30. Estonia
31. Ethiopia
32. Gabon
33. Gambia
34. Georgia
35. Guinea
36. Guinea Bissau
37. Haiti
38. Kazakhstan
39. Kyrgyzstan
40. India
41. Indonesia
42. Iraq
43. Isle of Man
44. Israel
45. Jersey
46. Kenya
47. Lao PDR
48. Latvia
49. Lebanon
50. Lesotho
51. Liberia
52. Libya
53. Lithuania
54. Madagascar
55. Mali

56. Moldova
57. Mozambique
58. Myanmar (Burma)
59. Nepal
60. Niger
61. Nigeria
62. Pakistan
63. Palestinian Territory
64. Panama
65. Philippines
66. Republic of the Congo
67. Russia
68. Rwanda
69. Sao Tome and Principe
70. Saudi Arabia
71. Senegal
72. Seychelles
73. Sierra Leone
74. Somalia
75. Sri Lanka
76. South Sudan
77. Sudan
78. Tajikistan
79. Tanzania
80. Togo
81. Trinidad and Tobago
82. Tunisia
83. Turkey
84. Turkmenistan
85. Uganda
86. Ukraine
87. Uzbekistan
88. Vanuatu
89. Venezuela
90. Yemen
91. Zambia
92. Zimbabwe

Appendix F

Specimen third party due diligence policy – sanctions screening policy – EMEA

Third party due diligence procedures for new engagements and new contracts

Business Unit:

Before hiring for the first time or signing a new contract with any of the third party types listed below, the business is required to submit a Third Party Due Diligence Request on the Global Compliance SharePoint site so that the third party can be risk ranked and evaluated by Global Compliance. The SharePoint site is located at:

https://

Third Party Types that Require Due Diligence:

- Accountants
- Brokers
- Consultants that interact with our customers or the government on our behalf
- Contractors and Subcontractors that interact with our customers or the government on our behalf
- Customs Agents/Brokers
- Distributors
- Freight Forwarders
- Gestores (those who accompany our staff to meet with the government)
- Law Firms
- Logistics Service Providers
- Purchasing Agents
- Sales Agents
- Sales Representatives
- Service Providers that interact with our customers or the government on our behalf
- Sourcing Agents
- Suppliers that interact with our customers or the government on our behalf

- Tax Agents
- Third parties that obtain licenses or permits on our behalf

Note that only third party intermediaries, third parties that can interact with the government or customers on our behalf, must undergo due diligence. Other types of third parties, such as raw material suppliers that do not interact with our customers or the government on our behalf as well as customer types not listed above are not subject to this procedure. The scope of covered third parties is subject to change to reflect changes in risk over time.

Risk ranking will be calculated automatically on the SharePoint site by considering:

- Whether the third party will be interacting with government officials to perform the work (0 or 4 points).
- Whether the company was recommended by a government official/entity (0 or 6 points).
- The Corruption Perceptions Index score of the country in which the third party is based and the country(s) where services are being provided: (1, 2, or 3 points).
- The value of contract: (1, 2, or 3 points).

An overall score of 2–3 will be classified as Low Risk: The SharePoint site will route the request to Global Compliance for low-level screening.

An overall score of 4–5 will be classified as Medium Risk: Additional information will be requested on SharePoint. Once complete, the SharePoint site will route the request to Global Compliance for medium-level screening.

An overall score of 6 and above will be classified as High Risk: Additional information will be requested on SharePoint. Once complete, the SharePoint site will route the request to Global Compliance for high-level screening.

Global Compliance: Based on the risk ranking of the third party submitted by the business, Global Compliance will complete the following due diligence activities:

Low Risk (2–3):

- Check company or individual names against global watch lists including:
  - Sanctions lists.
  - Denied persons or party lists.
  - Politically Exposed Person (PEP) list.

Medium Risk (4–5):

- All low-risk due diligence activities.
- Adverse media searches in English and local language to screen for fraud, terrorism, organised crime, money laundering risks, and other financial crimes.

High Risk (6 and above):

- All medium-risk activities.
- Possible additional activities:
  - In-country investigation: confirmation the third party is operating business at provided address, tour of facility, reference checks, employee interviews, assess other businesses/subject matter experts to understand reputation of third party.

- Enhanced due diligence audits by third party.
- Review relevant third party controls.

For any red flags identified, global compliance will research the issues, develop a plan to reduce the risk, and/or work with the business to review the risks of the third party and collectively determine the appropriate path forward. Red flags must be resolved or the risk mitigated before proceeding with the relationship.

Examples of possible ways to reduce risk with third parties include:

- Contract provisions.
- Completing audits to further access the risks.
- Requiring the third party to complete a certification.
- Requiring the third party to develop and implement policies and/or training.

If a third party is listed on any applicable trade sanctions or restricted person list, they will not be approved for any [___company___] business.

Managing risk on an on-going basis

All active third parties will have additional, automated daily screening to detect any changes in their risk.

Additional requirements for enhanced due diligence may be implemented to manage the highest risks on a case-by-case basis, as determined by Global Compliance.

Third party due diligence procedures for existing third parties

For existing third parties, due diligence assessments will be completed using a risk-based approach.

(1) Global Compliance has completed a risk assessment survey at the [___company___] locations in the highest risk countries – defined as those countries with a score of less than 50 in the Transparency International Corruption Perceptions Index.

(2) Those third parties relationships with elevated risk identified in the assessments will go through the due diligence process first.

(3) Subsequent phases of due diligence will be multi-year and rolled out starting with the highest risk countries of [___company___] operation and moving towards lowest risk locations. The same scope of covered third parties listed above will be used for existing third parties.

(4) The scope of covered third parties, country risks, and relationship risks will be reviewed and updated as needed.

Appendix G

Specimen modern slavery/ transparency in supply chains statement

California Transparency in Supply Chains Act and UK Modern Slavery Act Statement

This Statement relates to the fiscal year ended December 31, 2017 ('fiscal 2017') and describes the activities of [___company___] and its consolidated subsidiaries ('[___company___], 'we', 'us' and 'our') to address slavery and human trafficking in our business and supply chains. Not all of the entities in our consolidated group are subject to the California Transparency in Supply Chains Act and the UK Modern Slavery Act. We have prepared this Statement on a consolidated basis for the entire [___company___] group because we have common policies and compliance programs relating to slavery and anti-human trafficking across our business.

This Statement was posted on June 30, 2018 and does not reflect changes to our compliance policies, practices or procedures that may have occurred after such date.

Overview

Business and supply chain overview

We are one of the world's largest designers, marketers and manufacturers of recognized consumer and end-user demanded brands used in businesses, schools and homes. We manufacture some of our products and some are third-party sourced. For fiscal 2017, we manufactured approximately half of our products locally where we operate, and sourced the remainder. We have manufacturing facilities in …

Sourcing primarily comes from China, but we also source from other North American, South American, Far Eastern and European countries. We maintain distribution centers in Australia, Brazil, Belgium, Canada, Czech Republic, England, France, Germany, Italy, Netherlands, New Zealand, Poland, Sweden, and the United States. We also have other smaller offices in China, England, Germany, Japan, Poland, Taiwan and the United States. For additional information concerning our manufacturing facilities and distribution centers, see our Annual Report on Form 10-K for fiscal 2017 that we filed with the U.S. Securities and Exchange Commission and any subsequent filings that we make. These filings are available on our website at: ….

Due to our internal hiring procedures, labor policies and the locations of most of our employees, [___company___] believes that the risks of slavery and human trafficking in our own workforce are remote. In addition, these risks are further mitigated since [___company___] does not use migrant labor. We have less influence over the labor practices of our sourced product vendors and their supply chains. Accordingly, we have established the compliance procedures discussed in this Statement primarily to mitigate the risk of slavery and human trafficking in our supply chains for third-party sourced products.

On February 1, 2017, we acquired [___company___] is a leading European manufacturer and marketer of office and consumer products. It takes products to market under the [___company___] in In our last Statement, we noted that we were in the process of integrating [___company___] policies and procedures relating to slavery and human trafficking with those of the rest of our business. That integration has been completed and selected aspects of that integration are discussed in this Statement. The [___company___] acquisition did not change our risk profile relating to slavery and human trafficking. In addition to having no known slavery and human trafficking controversies, prior to the acquisition, [___company___] had policies and procedures in place to address these issues.

Selected policies

[___company___] Code of Business Conduct and Ethics

[___company___] observes high ethical standards in the conduct of its business. The company respects internationally accepted legal principles and strives to obey the laws of those countries in which it does business. A detailed compilation of the company's commitment to ethical behavior is published in its Code of Business Conduct and Ethics, which is available to all stakeholders on our website at ....

Our Corporate Responsibility Principles provide, among other things, that [___ company___] employ a diverse workforce; compensate all employees fairly, consistent with local standards and practices; nurture an inclusive, collaborative work environment; and will not knowingly conduct business with third parties which employ children or other workers under conditions that would be abusive or exploitative.

Supplier Code of Conduct

As indicated in our Supplier Code of Conduct, which has been approved by senior leadership, [___company___] is committed to ensuring that workers are treated with respect and dignity and we seek relationships with suppliers that are committed to manufacturing under fair and safe labor conditions. The Supplier Code of Conduct is publicly available on our website at ....

In addition, it is distributed to employees as part of training, as well as to new suppliers in 15 languages including English. In 2017, the Supplier Code of Conduct was distributed to [___company___] suppliers as part of that business's integration into our slavery and human trafficking compliance program.

Among other things, the Supplier Code of Conduct provides that:

- Suppliers shall not use forced labor, whether in the form of prison labor, indentured labor, bonded labor, or otherwise.
- Suppliers shall not employ people younger than 15, under the minimum legal age or the minimum age for completing compulsory education in the country of manufacture, whichever is higher.
- Suppliers shall treat every employee with respect and dignity, and shall not subject any employee to physical, sexual, psychological, or verbal harassment or abuse.
- Suppliers shall pay employees at least the minimum wage required by local law, or the prevailing industry wage if no minimum wage law applies, and shall provide legally mandated benefits.

- Suppliers shall not require workers to work more than the maximum hours of daily and weekly labor set by local laws and workers should be granted at least one day off in every seven-day period, if required by local law.

The Supplier Code of Conduct indicates that the supplier is responsible for ensuring compliance by itself and any sub-contractor(s) and factories.

Verification of product supply chains to address and evaluate risks of slavery and human trafficking

[___company___] seeks to identify and evaluate the potential risks for slavery and human trafficking in its supply chains through reviewing the supplier's geographic location and the nature of its manufacturing activities for us. As discussed below, we also conduct factory assessments of new suppliers, as well as annual audits.

As a source of market intelligence to help identify risk [___company___] participates in various trade organization groups that are focused on this issue and utilizes industry benchmarking data and information published by the U.S. government to help identify potentially high risk areas.

Audit of suppliers

[___company___] Supplier Code of Conduct provides that, to ensure compliance with the Code, we have the right to monitor factories through audits by third parties and visits by ACCO Brands personnel. In addition, our forms of purchase order terms and conditions and manufacturing agreement provide for inspection rights to audit compliance with the Code of Conduct.

To become an [___company___] supplier, a supplier must undergo a factory assessment that reviews quality, social and security practices and standards. Our internal personnel conduct these assessments. Slavery and human trafficking risk are reviewed as part of the assessment.

In addition, we use a third-party service provider, which is a well-known international firm that specializes in supply chain audits, to conduct annual social responsibility audits of suppliers.

These audits include a slavery and human trafficking assessment. As part of our ongoing focus on mitigating supply chain risk, we are in the process of reviewing our supplier data collection process and reporting across a number of different areas, including slavery and human trafficking, with a view to determining whether to enhance our policies and/or procedures.

Factories that make finished products and/or branded components that identify [___company___] or any of its subsidiaries, a licensor or a customer are audited. In addition, all factories that make blank finished goods and [___company___] licensed products are audited. Other third party factories in designated low risk countries also are audited if determined to be appropriate by [___company___] compliance staff based on the perceived risk.

Audits include reviews of documents, interviews with workers and site visits of production facilities and worker housing. We conduct unannounced, semi-announced and announced audits, depending upon the risk profile of the supplier. Our audit program also includes unannounced audits to the extent a supplier is required to correct a violation to our Supplier Code of Conduct or local law. The frequency of audits is based on the perceived risk of the supplier and other relevant factors.

Our audit process includes a Corrective Action Plan ('CAP') on a specified time frame if deficiencies in an audit category are identified. The failure to complete requested corrective actions may result in termination of the supplier relationship.

Certifications and contractual terms and conditions

[___company___] requires suppliers that undergo audits to certify compliance with the Supplier Code of Conduct.

If we determine that a particular factory does not comply with our Supplier Code of Conduct, we typically strive to work with the supplier to develop and implement an appropriate CAP.

However, depending upon the circumstances, [___company___] may elect to end its relationship with a supplier at any time for failing to adhere to our Code.

In addition, our forms of purchase order terms and conditions and manufacturing agreement require that suppliers comply with our Supplier Code of Conduct and that they require their subcontractors and suppliers who manufacture products or components for us or who provide services for us abide by the Supplier Code of Conduct and any other codes, policies and procedures to which our direct supplier has agreed to comply.

Internal accountability standards and procedures

Relevant new employees are provided with a copy of the [___company___] Code of Business Conduct & Ethics and Supplier Code of Conduct. These materials also are included in our online employee intranet that all employees have access to. In addition, employees periodically undergo compliance and ethics training, including with respect to the Supplier Code of Conduct and our Corporate Responsibility Principles. Failure of employees to abide by the requirements of the [___company___] Code of Business Conduct & Ethics and our Corporate Responsibility Principles can result in corrective action up to and including termination of employment.

[___company___] has an independent compliance function that is headed by the Vice President, Associate General Counsel – Global Compliance and Litigation and Vice President, Global Compliance Operations to ensure that the Codes are supported. We also use specialist outside counsel to assist us with certain aspects of our slavery and human trafficking compliance.

Each factory's performance in relevant audit categories is reported to the compliance team, which works with the sourcing departments and suppliers to implement any CAPs and, together with the sourcing departments, monitors the implementation and effectiveness of the CAPs.

[___company___] maintains a supplier audit database that stores information on the results of supplier audits and any CAPs.

[___company___] has a hotline and confidential web form for employees, suppliers and other interested parties to report violations of its policies, including the provisions of the Supplier Code of Conduct that address slavery and human trafficking. Contact information for these mechanisms is on our website at www.

Training

[___company___] provides training to relevant employees and management on a local level who have direct responsibility for supply chain management. Our training includes, but is not limited to, training regarding slavery and human trafficking and mitigating the risk of the supply chain being impacted by the same. [___company___] also provides periodic training updates and refresher training to these personnel. In 2017, relevant [___company___] employees were trained on these issues. We periodically provide supplier training on slavery and human trafficking. In September 2018, [___company___] will host another Supplier Compliance Training Summit in Asia.

This follows on a similar summit that we held in 2016.

Solely for purposes of compliance with the UK Modern Slavery Act, this Statement has been approved by the Board of Directors of [___company___] and signed by a director of that entity.

A signed copy of this Statement is available upon request by contacting us at …

Appendix H

Specimen competition policy – EMEA

[___company___] Fair Competition Policy

[___company___], including its affiliates (collectively, [___company___]' or the 'Company'), is committed to conducting business ethically, honestly, and in accordance with all applicable laws. This includes complying with laws on fair competition.

Background

Fair competition refers to doing business and competing in a way that does not unjustifiably harm consumers. Fair competition laws have many different names around the world, including antitrust law in the United States, competition law in the EU and Australia, anti-monopoly law in China, and economic competition law in Latin America. Fair competition laws vary dramatically from region to region – conduct that is permissible in some countries or states may be strictly prohibited in others. All of these laws are, however, designed to protect competition for the ultimate benefit of consumers, as unlawful reductions in competition can lead to increased prices, reduced outputs, lower quality, and reduced innovation.

Fair competition laws not only prohibit certain agreements among competitors, but may also prohibit certain agreements between a company and its upstream suppliers or downstream distributors. Fair competition laws may also apply to a company's own independent conduct, particularly if it has a large share of the relevant market.

Policy

[___company___], including its employees, officers, directors, and third-party agents and business partners acting on behalf of or for the benefit of the Company, does not engage in illegal or unethical competitive practices. Compliance with this Policy as well as applicable U.S. state and federal, EU, and other fair competition laws is mandatory. Failure to do so may result in disciplinary action up to and including termination of employment or termination of your business relationship with [___company___].

Purpose

This Policy sets forth a general framework for ensuring fair competition [___ company___] Due to the variations in fair competition laws across the world, you should contact the in-house [___company___] Counsel who supports your region or another member of the Legal and Compliance Department at … with any specific questions.

Activities potentially raising fair competition concerns

Although the fair competition laws vary from region to region, certain practices are commonly regulated across the globe. The following activities are prohibited in all regions:

- Exchange of Confidential Information – Sharing our confidential information, such as pricing or sales plans, with competitors.
- Price Fixing – Agreeing with competitors to fix, raise, lower, maintain, or otherwise affect pricing or other terms of sale, including program dollars, marketing allowances, freight allowances, payment terms or material costs. In general, you should never discuss pricing with competitors.
- Boycotting – Agreeing with competitors to not do business with a certain supplier, distributor, or vendor.
- 'No-Poach' Agreements – Agreeing with competitors not to solicit or hire one another's employees.
- Bid Rigging – Colluding with competitors to affect the outcome of a bidding process.

Certain other activities may be acceptable in some circumstances. Before engaging in any of the following activities, you must contact the in-house [___company___] Counsel who supports your region or another member of the Legal and Compliance Department at … to ensure you are complying with all applicable laws:

- Dividing Markets – Agreeing with competitors to divide markets, such as divisions by geography, customer type, or product type.
- Exclusive Dealing – Entering into an agreement with a supplier, distributor, customer, or other vendor to only do business with us or to not carry competitors' products.
- Tying and Bundling – Requiring customers to purchase unrelated products together as a bundle.
- Predatory Pricing – Lowering prices below or equal to cost.
- Price Discrimination – Charging different customers different prices for the same goods.
- Retail Price Maintenance (RPM) Programs – Requiring resellers to sell products at a set price or above a minimum price.
- Minimum Advertised Price (MAP) Programs – Setting minimum prices above which retailers must advertise our product.
- Most Favored Nation Plus Arrangements – Requiring that we receive better pricing than any other company from a vendor or supplier.

It is important to note that an 'agreement' for purposes of fair competition laws does not need to be formal or written. An agreement can be inferred from the circumstances. For example, if competitors meet for a meal or at a trade show and then some or all subsequently raise their prices on competing products, an agreement could be inferred from the facts.

Remember too that, in addition to our products, our customers or dealers may also sell products of our direct competitors or their own private label products that compete with our products. Under these circumstances, our customers or dealers may be themselves our competitors for purposes of fair competition laws and may have to be treated as competitors as described in this Policy. In particular, you should not suggest pricing or promotions for any product not sold by [___company___] to the customer.

Any situation in which competitors are present together, such as at industry events or dealer meetings, heightens fair competition risks. If you are responsible for organizing an event where competitors will be present together, you should prepare a clear agenda of activities and consult with the in-house [___company___] Legal Counsel who supports your region or another member of the Legal and Compliance Department at … for guidance in advance of the event.

If you are present for any meeting where competitors' confidential information is being discussed or competitors are engaging in any of the behaviors listed above, you should immediately voice your disagreement with the discussion (called a 'noisy withdrawal'), then leave the conversation and contact the in-house [___company___] Legal Counsel who supports your region or another member of the Legal and Compliance Department at …

Receipt of competitors' confidential information

In seeking competitor information, you should use legitimate sources and never attempt to acquire such information unfairly or illegally. If you receive an email or other document containing a competitor's confidential information by accident, you should immediately contact the in-house [___company___] Legal Counsel who supports your region or another member of the Legal and Compliance Department at [___company___] for guidance. You may share the email with in-house [___company___] Legal Counsel but should not circulate it further.

Responsible communication

To ensure that our actions are not misconstrued, it is important to be careful when communicating internally or externally about topics such as pricing, the business rationale for certain actions, or our market position. You should focus on how a certain decision would benefit [___company___] or consumers, not how it would harm competitors. For instance, never say or write:

- About having a 'dominant' position in a market, or 'controlling' or 'owning' a market, etc.
- That certain of our actions will negatively impact competitors such as 'weaken competitors' or 'knock competitors out of the market' or 'kill our competition,' etc.
- Innuendos about agreements with competitors such as 'reaching an understanding' or having 'a meeting of the minds' or 'on the same page with so and so,' etc.
- Opinions that certain actions will ensure less competition

Dawn raids and requests for information

Various fair competition laws give the government the right to enter our premises unannounced to collect evidence of potential legal violations. These investigations are called 'dawn raids.' [___company___] complies and will comply with all legal government investigations and inspections. If you are ever involved in a dawn raid or receive a request for information from the government while at [___company___], you should:

- Immediately contact the in-house [___company___] Legal Counsel who supports your region or another member of the Legal and Compliance Department at …
- Request that the government wait for legal counsel, but do not refuse access to our premises or documents
- Cooperate with the government and instruct other employees to do the same
- Never delete or conceal any documents or emails that may be relevant to the investigation

Questions and reporting

If you have any questions about this Policy, please contact the in-house [___company___] Legal Counsel who supports your region or another member of the Legal and Compliance Department at …

If you believe this Policy may have been violated, you should immediately report the issue to your manager, another manager you trust, the [___company___] Legal and Compliance Department,the Human Resources Department,. a confidential reporting system that can be accessed at any time by phone or the internet. can be made anonymously, where permitted by local law.

As set forth in the Code of Conduct, [___company___] has a strict non-retaliation policy to protect anyone making a good faith report of suspected misconduct, including suspected fair competition violations.

Appendix I

EU Preparedness Statements on Brexit*

On 29 March 2017, the United Kingdom notified the European Council of its intention to leave the European Union. On 11 April 2019, the European Council (Article 50) decided, in agreement with the United Kingdom, to extend further the two-year period provided for by Article 50(3) of the Treaty on European Union, until 31 October 2019. In the event that the Withdrawal Agreement is not approved by the House of Commons by 31 October 2019, all Union primary and secondary law will cease to apply to the United Kingdom from 1 November 2019, 00:00h (CET) ('the withdrawal date'). The United Kingdom will then become a third country.

Please also note that:

In the event that the United Kingdom has not held elections to the European Parliament in accordance with applicable Union law and has not ratified the Withdrawal Agreement by 22 May 2019, the Decision referred to above shall cease to apply on 31 May 2019, and the withdrawal will therefore take place on 1 June 2019; and

Should the United Kingdom ratify the Withdrawal Agreement at any stage before 31 October 2019, the withdrawal will take place on the first day of the month following the completion of the ratification procedures.

These notices, which aim at preparing citizens and stakeholders for the withdrawal of the United Kingdom, set out the consequences in a range of policy areas.

In addition, EU decentralised agencies have published information in relation to the UK's withdrawal from the EU, for example the Community Plant Variety Office, the European Chemicals Agency, the European Medicines Agency and the European Union Intellectual Property Office. Furthermore, the three European Supervisory Authorities (the European Banking Authority, the European Securities and Markets Authority and the European Insurance and Occupational Pensions Authority) and the Single Supervisory Mechanism have issued opinions and guidance.

On 19 March 2018, the negotiators of the European Commission and the United Kingdom presented the progress made in the negotiation of a draft agreement on the withdrawal of the United Kingdom from the European Union. On 23 March 2018, the European Council (Art. 50) welcomed the agreement reached on parts of the legal text and called for intensified efforts to make progress on the remaining withdrawal issues. The European Council (Art 50) further stated that nothing was agreed until everything is agreed. This means that a transition period until 31 December 2020 may be agreed, but this is not certain at this stage. The European Council (Art 50) therefore called on the Commission, the High Representative of the Union for Foreign Affairs and Security Policy and the Member States to continue the work on preparedness at all levels for the consequences of the United Kingdom's withdrawal, taking into account all possible outcomes. The notices of the Commission services published on this website respond to this request. They set out the consequences of the withdrawal of the United Kingdom from the European Union without a formal, ratified agreement between the United Kingdom and the European Union.

★Source – https://ec.europa.eu/info/brexit-preparedness/brexit-notices-explanation_en.

Appendix J

Types of undertakings to which the accounting directive applies

Types of undertaking to which the directive applies

—

Belgium:

la société anonyme/de naamloze vennootschap, la société en commandite par actions/de commanditaire vennootschap op aandelen, la société privée à responsabilité limitée/de besloten vennootschap met beperkte aansprakelijkheid, la société coopérative à responsabilité limitée/de coöperatieve vennootschap met beperkte aansprakelijkheid;

—

Bulgaria:

акционерно дружество, дружество с ограничена отговорност, командитно дружество с акции;

—

the Czech Republic:

společnost s ručením omezeným, akciová společnost;

—

Denmark:

aktieselskaber, kommanditaktieselskaber, anpartsselskaber;

—

Germany:

die Aktiengesellschaft, die Kommanditgesellschaft auf Aktien, die Gesellschaft mit beschränkter Haftung;

—

Estonia:

aktsiaselts, osaühing;

—

Ireland:

public companies limited by shares or by guarantee, private companies limited by shares or by guarantee;

—

Greece:

η ανώνυμη εταιρία, η εταιρία περιορισμένης ευθύνης, η ετερόρρυθμη κατά μετοχές εταιρία;

—

Spain:

la sociedad anónima, la sociedad comanditaria por acciones, la sociedad de responsabilidad limitada;

—

France:

la société anonyme, la société en commandite par actions, la société à responsabilité limitée, la société par actions simplifiée;

—

Italy:

la società per azioni, la società in accomandita per azioni, la società a responsabilità limitata;

—

Cyprus:

Δημόσιες εταιρείες περιορισμένης ευθύνης με μετοχές ή με εγγύηση, ιδιωτικές εταιρείες περιορισμένης ευθύνης με μετοχές ή με εγγύηση;

—

Latvia:

akciju sabiedrība, sabiedrība ar ierobežotu atbildību;

—

Lithuania:

akcinės bendrovės, uždarosios akcinės bendrovės;

—

Luxembourg:

la société anonyme, la société en commandite par actions, la société à responsabilité limitée;

—

Hungary:

részvénytársaság, korlátolt felelősségű társaság;

—

Malta:

kumpanija pubblika – public limited liability company, kumpannija privata – private limited liability company,

soċjeta in akkomandita bil-kapital maqsum f'azzjonijiet – partnership en commandite with the capital divided into shares;

—

the Netherlands:

de naamloze vennootschap, de besloten vennootschap met beperkte aansprakelijkheid;

—

Austria:

die Aktiengesellschaft, die Gesellschaft mit beschränkter Haftung;

—

Poland:

spółka akcyjna, spółka z ograniczoną odpowiedzialnością, spółka komandytowo-akcyjna;

—

Portugal:

a sociedade anónima, de responsabilidade limitada, a sociedade em comandita por ações, a sociedade por quotas de responsabilidade limitada;

—

Romania:

societate pe acţiuni, societate cu răspundere limitată, societate în comandită pe acţiuni.

—

Slovenia:

delniška družba, družba z omejeno odgovornostjo, komanditna delniška družba;

—

Slovakia:

akciová spoločnosť, spoločnosť s ručením obmedzeným;

—

Finland:

yksityinen osakeyhtiö/privat aktiebolag, julkinen osakeyhtiö/publikt aktiebolag;

—

Sweden:

aktiebolag;

—

the United Kingdom:

Public companies limited by shares or by guarantee, private companies limited by shares or by guarantee

TYPES OF UNDERTAKINGS where all of the direct or indirect members of the undertaking having otherwise unlimited liability in fact have limited liability by reason of those members being undertakings which are

—

Belgium

la société en nom collectif/de vennootschap onder firma, la société en commandite simple/de gewone commanditaire vennootschap, la société coopérative à responsabilité illimitée/de coöperatieve vennootschap met onbeperkte aansprakelijkheid;

—

Bulgaria:

събирателно дружество, командитно дружество;

—

the Czech Republic:

veřejná obchodní společnost, komanditní společnost;

—

Denmark:

interessentskaber, kommanditselskaber;

—

Germany:

die offene Handelsgesellschaft, die Kommanditgesellschaft;

—

Estonia:

täisühing, usaldusühing;

—

Ireland:

partnerships, limited partnerships, unlimited companies;

—

Greece:

η ομόρρυθμος εταιρία, η ετερόρρυθμος εταιρία;

—

Spain:

sociedad colectiva, sociedad en comandita simple;

—

France:

la société en nom collectif, la société en commandite simple;

—

Italy:

la società in nome collettivo, la società in accomandita semplice;

—

Cyprus:

Ομόρρυθμες και ετερόρρυθμες εταιρείες (συνεταιρισμοί);

—

Latvia:

pilnsabiedrība, komandītsabiedrība;

—

Lithuania:

tikrosios ūkinės bendrijos, komanditinės ūkinės bendrijos;

—

Luxembourg:

la société en nom collectif, la société en commandite simple;

—

Hungary:

közkereseti társaság, betéti társaság, közös vállalat, egyesülés, egyéni cég;

—

Malta:

soċjeta f'isem kollettiv jew soċjeta in akkomandita, bil-kapital li mhux maqsum f'azzjonijiet meta s-soċji kollha li għandhom responsabbilita' llimitata huma soċjetajiet in akkomandita bil-kapital maqsum f'azzjonijiet — partnership en nom collectif or partnership en commandite with capital that is not divided into shares, when all the partners with unlimited liability are partnership en commandite with the capital divided into shares;

—

the Netherlands:

de vennootschap onder firma, de commanditaire vennootschap;

—

Austria:

die offene Gesellschaft, die Kommanditgesellschaft;

—

Poland:

spółka jawna, spółka komandytowa;

—

Portugal:

sociedade em nome colectivo, sociedade em comandita simples;

—

Romania:

societate în nume colectiv, societate în comandită simplă;

—

Slovenia:

družba z neomejeno odgovornostjo, komanditna družba;

—

Slovakia:

verejná obchodná spoločnosť, komanditná spoločnosť;

—

Finland:

avoin yhtiö/ öppet bolag, kommandiittiyhtiö/kommanditbolag;

—

Sweden:

handelsbolag, kommanditbolag;

—

the United Kingdom:

partnerships, limited partnerships, unlimited companies.

Index

[*All references are to paragraph numbers*]